Classifications are central to archaeology. Yet the theoretical literature on the subject – in both archaeology and the philosophy of science – bears very little relationship to what actually occurs in practice. This problem has long interested William Adams, a field archaeologist, and Ernest Adams, a philosopher of science, who describe their book as an ethnography of archaeological classification. It is a study of the various ways in which field archaeologists set about making and using classifications to meet a variety of practical needs.

The authors first discuss how humans form concepts. They then describe and analyze in detail a specific example of an archaeological classification, and go on to consider what theoretical generalizations can be derived from the study of actual in-use classifications. In a concluding section they review and critique existing theoretical literature on the subject of classification, showing how little relationship it bears to the realities of practice. Throughout the book, they stress the importance of having a clearly defined purpose and practical procedures when developing and applying classifications.

This book will be of interest not only to archaeologists and anthropologists, but also to philosophers of science, linguists, cognitive psychologists, biologists, and to scholars in all other fields in which classification plays a significant role.

Archaeological typology and practical reality

THE FAR SIDE

By GARY LARSON

"So what's this? I asked for a *hammer!* A hammer!
This is a crescent wrench! ... Well, maybe it's
a hammer. ... Damn these stone tools."

Frontispiece Archaeological typology in a nutshell. THE FAR SIDE, copyright 1986,
Universal Press Syndicate. Reprinted with permission. All rights reserved.

Archaeological typology and practical reality

A DIALECTICAL APPROACH TO ARTIFACT CLASSIFICATION AND SORTING

William Y. Adams
University of Kentucky
and
Ernest W. Adams
University of California at Berkeley

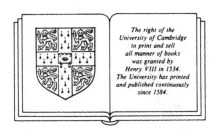

The right of the
University of Cambridge
to print and sell
all manner of books
was granted by
Henry VIII in 1534.
The University has printed
and published continuously
since 1584.

CAMBRIDGE UNIVERSITY PRESS
Cambridge
New York   Port Chester   Melbourne   Sydney

Published by the Press Syndicate of the University of Cambridge
The Pitt Building, Trumpington Street, Cambridge, CB2 1RP
40 West 20th Street, New York, NY 10011, USA
10 Stamford Road, Oakleigh, Melbourne 3166, Australia

First published 1991

Printed in Great Britain by The University Press, Cambridge

British Library cataloguing in publication data

Adams, William Y. (William Yewdale)(*1927–*
Archaeological typology and practical reality: a
dialectical approach to artifact classification and
sorting.
1. Archaeology. Classification
I. Title II. Adams, Ernest W.
930.1012

Library of Congress cataloguing in publication data

Adams, William Yewdale, 1927–
Archaeological typology and practical reality: a dialectical
approach to artifact classification and sorting / William Y. Adams
and Ernest W. Adams.
      p.   cm.
Includes bibliographical references and index.
ISBN 0 521 39334 5
1. Archaeology – Classification. 2. Antiquities – Classification.
3. Typology (Linguistics) I. Adams, Ernest W. (Ernest Wilcox),
1926– . II. Title.
CC72.7.A33 1991
930.1'012 – dc 20   90–41556 CIP

ISBN 0 521 39334 5 hardback

To Lucy W. Adams
Our Mother

If I were permitted to focus upon just a single issue and treat it as the focal point of the complex and tricky business of archaeological theory and its developmental course, I should single out the concept and operation of classification. I think the methodological development of archaeology in the twentieth century centers on the rethinking of classificatory problems.

K. C. Chang (1967: 4)

You have to understand that I don't consider myself to be a theoretician. My primary interest is to explain something out there that impinges upon me, and I would sell my soul to the devil if I thought it would help.

Eric Wolf (quoted in J. Friedman 1987: 114)

CONTENTS

List of figures	*page*	xiii
List of tables		xiv
The archaeologist's preface		xv
The philosopher's preface		xxii
PART I Introductory		1
1 Beginning points		3
2 Introductory theses		18
PART II The nature of types and typologies		27
3 Dimensions and elements of "typehood"		29
4 Perceptual and conceptual foundations		39
5 The dialectics of type formulation		50
6 The nature of types		63
7 The structure of typologies		76
8 A synthetic definition of typology and type		91
PART III Typology in action: the Medieval Nubian Pottery Typology		97
9 Origin and development of the Nubian Typology		99
10 Basic features of the Nubian Typology		110
11 The uses of the Nubian Typology		128
12 Philosophical implications		143
PART IV Pragmatics of archaeological typology		155
13 The starting point: purpose		157
14 The determinants of types: variables and attributes		169
15 The making of types: formulation, designation and description		182
16 The use of types: typing and sorting		194
17 The ordering of types: taxonomy and seriation		202
18 Variation and variability in archaeological classifications		214
19 The bottom line: practicality		233

20 Principles of practical typology 239
21 Information-theoretic formulations 244
PART V Classification, explanation, and theory 263
22 The Typological Debate 265
23 Issues and non-issues in the Typological Debate 278
24 Conceptual problems 296
25 The use and abuse of theory 305
26 Paradigms and progress 314
Appendices 327
A Glossary of definitions 329
B Specimen pottery ware description: Terminal
Christian Decorated White Ware 373
C Estimated dates for pottery wares found in Nubia 377
D Examples of pottery ware distribution data from
Qasr Ibrim 383

References 388
Index 412

FIGURES

1 The Medieval Nubian Pottery Typology:
  specimen page of vessel form illustrations   *page* 112
2 The Medieval Nubian Pottery Typology:
  specimen page of style illustrations   113
3 The Medieval Nubian Pottery Typology:
  classification of decorative motifs   114
4 The Medieval Nubian Pottery Typology:
  simplified chronology of ware groups   125
5 Specimen Nubian sherd tally sheet – side 1   132
6 Specimen Nubian sherd tally sheet – side 2   133
7 Specimen Nubian sherd index cluster card   134
8 Specimen Nubian pottery catalogue card   141
9 An example of a dendrogram   207
10 Examples of "battleship curves"   211
11 Examples of Nubian pottery ware illustrations   373

TABLES

1 The essential elements of "typehood"   *page* 31
2 Defining properties of sensory images, concepts,
   words, categories, classes, and types   48
3 Properties of lexicons, classifications, and typologies   49
4 Defining variables in Nubian pottery families, ware
   groups, and wares   107
5 Outline classification of pottery wares found in
   medieval Nubian sites   115
6 List of variables included in Nubian pottery ware
   descriptions   119
7 Classification of Nubian and Egyptian decorative
   styles   121
8 Outline classification of glazed wares found in
   medieval Nubian sites   123
9 Potential purposes in artifact classification   159
10 Kinds of archaeological classifications and their
   purposes   216

THE ARCHAEOLOGIST'S
PREFACE

For better or worse, this book represents something of an experiment. It is, so far as we know, one of the first attempts to achieve a genuine, two-way dialogue between archaeology and philosophy – the respective fields of its two authors. (For a predecessor – not concerned specifically with classification – see Kelley and Hanen 1988.)

It has been a common practice in recent years for archaeologists to borrow concepts and analytical tools from the philosophy of science, and apply them to their own field of endeavor (cf. Fritz and Plog 1970; Martin 1971; Watson, LeBlanc, and Redman 1971; Hill and Evans 1972; Kelley and Hanen 1988). However, this usage has often been both selective and uncritical. That is, the archaeologists have borrowed certain tools while ignoring others, and they have frequently overlooked the fact that the concepts they borrowed were the subject of controversy within the field of philosophy itself (cf. Kelley and Hanen 1988; WYA n.d. 2). Moreover, and more importantly, communication was strictly in one direction: from philosophy to archaeology.

In the present book we have tried to initiate a more genuine dialogue. We believe that, if the archaeologist has much to learn from the philosopher of science, the reverse is necessarily also true. In addition to applying philosophical concepts to the practice of archaeology, therefore, we have tried at various points to show how the practices of the field archaeologist reflect upon current controversies and issues in the philosophy of science. Our book is consequently written both for archaeologists and for philosophers; indeed we hope that it may be of interest to scholars in many other fields in which classification plays a key role.

The effort to produce a genuinely cross-disciplinary work is not without its hazards. Contrary to what is sometimes asserted, the boundaries between scholarly disciplines are not merely the result of academic turf battles and compromises. To a very considerable extent they are linguistic boundaries. The anthropologist, the philosopher, the sociologist, and the psychologist may be and frequently are debating the same issues, but they are using fundamentally different vocabularies in doing so. Unless they happen to be fluent in two or more of these "languages," scholars in the different disciplines may never be quite sure how much they understand and/or agree with each other.

Precisely because of the linguistic problem, the writing of this book has been a far more difficult task than the authors first imagined. It has taken years of dialogue for us to discover the full extent of our agreement on particular issues, and it has taken additional years to decide on the right words in which to communicate our ideas both to archaeologists and to philosophers. To make sure we are understood by both parties in the dialogue, we have had unavoidably to introduce various explanatory passages as well as an extensive glossary (Appendix A).

There may well be readers who will find all of this cumbersome, and who will wish that we had addressed ourselves exclusively to one audience or the other. Undoubtedly, a simpler and clearer book would have resulted. We feel strongly, however, that our respective fields of archaeology and philosophy have reached a point where they need each other – not just as a source of concepts to be uncritically borrowed, but as a basis for enlarged self-understanding. Whether our first effort in that direction succeeds or fails can be judged only by our readers, but we believe in any case that the effort has been necessary.

Specific objectives

More specifically, our book has a number of concrete objectives that can be briefly stated:

1 We hope to clear away some of the conceptual confusion surrounding the processes of classification, insofar as it results from inadequate or inadequately defined vocabulary.

2 We hope to show that the concept of a "type" is a far more complex matter than is usually supposed. In the case of archaeology it has separate physical, mental and representational dimensions, none of which is wholly determined by any other.

3 We want to insist that the making and use of typologies can never be an automatic or a wholly objective process. Typologies are created to serve human purposes, which strongly affect the ways in which they are made and used.

4 We want to explore some of the diversity in classificatory systems in relation to the different purposes they serve.

5 We want to argue the need for practicality and cost-
effectiveness in archaeological classifications.

Some non-objectives

Because the theory and the practice of classification are beset by many misunderstandings, it is also important to state at the outset some of the things
that our book is not:

1. Although it is written by an archaeologist and a philosopher
of science, this book does not reflect the orthodox or currently fashionable
view of classification in archaeology, philosophy of science, or any other
discipline that is known to us. Both of the authors are in fact regarded as
mavericks in their respective fields. From time to time we meet like-
minded scholars, in our own disciplines and in others, but so far as we know
they are not in the majority anywhere. We therefore claim to speak with
authority for no one but ourselves.

The most obvious point of difference between the present authors and
most of their colleagues is that our views on the subject of classification are
thoroughly eclectic. Not only are they a distillation of ideas derived from
our separate disciplines, but they have been influenced by the rather
diverse and unorthodox interests that each of us has pursued within those
disciplines.

2. Our book is mainly about the practice and not about the
theory of archaeological classification, as it is currently understood. To
emphasize this fundamentally important distinction we can do no better
than to quote the recent words of Robert Dunnell (1986: 150): "two
features emerge as characteristic of the contemporary classification literature: (1) this literature is concerned, almost exclusively, with technique
and method to the virtual exclusion of the *raison d'être* of classification; and
(2) while there is a clear commitment to a single general model of archaeological classification (within which there is considerable technical debate),
in-use classification is entirely different and of a much earlier vintage.
Nowhere . . . is the archaeological record organized and understood in
terms supplied by the means debated in the contemporary programmatic
literature. The 'theoretical' literature has diverged from practice to such a
degree that the two are now unrelated."

The reasons for this discrepancy between theory and practice are not
far to seek. For the last twenty years theoretical writing on the subject
of archaeological classification has concerned itself very largely with
computerized programs of one sort or another. These programs are fun to
play with (cf. Rodrigues de Areia 1985: 404); they are much more

methodologically intriguing than are old-fashioned, semi-intuitive classification methods. They are also invaluable for producing frequency seriations and informational taxonomies, as we will see in Chapter 17. Nevertheless, computers can only order the data that is fed into them; that is, they can only classify material that is already in hand. They cannot, at least up to now, produce an "open" typology (see Chapter 18) that is continually applicable to newly excavated material (cf. Margolis 1987: 91, 115), which is the first requirement of the field archaeologist. The present generation of computers also cannot perform two functions that are essential in all practical typologies: they cannot make purely qualitative distinctions, and they cannot make purely arbitrary judgments (cf. *ibid.*: 3).

Field archaeologists must therefore continue for the most part to employ the "in-use classifications . . . of a much earlier vintage," to which Dunnell (1986: 150) referred. It is these classifications, and the ways in which they are developed and used, that are the subject of our book. We hope therefore that field archaeologists will find much that is familiar in these pages, and perhaps find food for thought with reference to their own problems and procedures. On the other hand, pure theoreticians may find less of interest. Only in the last chapters (Part V) do we turn our attention from questions of practice to those of theory.

3. Unlike much of the recent literature on archaeological classification, this is not a programmatic or "how-to" book, although it does include a number of practical suggestions about how to proceed in particular circumstances. In general, however, our book should be regarded as an ethnography of archaeological classification, a study of the various ways in which field archaeologists go about making and using classifications to meet their different needs. Classification methods, in our view, are essentially tools, and like other tools they are nearly always good for something. Some of them work better for some purposes and some for others, and it may be also that some classification systems work better for certain individuals than for others. Insofar as we engage in evaluation in the present work, it is only evaluation of a highly situational sort. That is, we try to discover what kinds of tools work best for what purposes, and why.

4. Although our approach to classification is empirical and eclectic, we have not attempted to present a complete or a balanced overview of all the different classificatory procedures employed by the archaeologist. Such a comprehensive treatment would entail a far more detailed knowledge of the field than either of us possesses. We have tried at least to mention a good many classificatory approaches, but our discussion is heavily weighted toward the systems that are familiar in the

personal experience of the authors. In discussing the theoretical literature we have also given disproportionate attention to certain issues that are especially important or interesting to us, in particular to the ever-elusive pursuit of "objectivity."

Our discussion, especially in Part V, may be more germane to what archaeologists write about than to what they talk about among themselves. One friend and colleague (George Cowgill, personal communication) has reminded us more than once that archaeologists are not nearly so committed to computerized classifications, even in theory, as we have made out. However, this will not be apparent to anyone whose only knowledge of classificatory procedures comes from the published literature. Be it noted, therefore, that Part V is specifically a critique of what archaeologists say in print, and may or may not be relevant to what they say in private.

5. The point has already been made that our book is not written exclusively either for archaeologists or for philosophers. The practical problems and procedures of archaeological classification furnish a convenient springboard for the discussion of more general issues that will, we hope, be of interest to scholars in all of the different fields in which classifications are made and used, and also to those disciplines like ethnoscience, cognitive psychology, and philosophy of science, in which classifications themselves are a subject of analysis.

6. Finally and emphatically, our book is not meant to be the last word on any subject. We have changed quite a few of our ideas in the course of writing it, and will undoubtedly change others in the course of discussing and defending it. We are hoping to begin a dialogue, not end one.

About the authors

We argue throughout the book that classification is always partly subjective, and our approach to the subject is itself necessarily subjective. Readers therefore need at the outset to know something about the authors and their respective backgrounds and experiences. We are, to begin with, brothers who grew up in the same household, mainly in Arizona and California. For the past thirty years, however, we have pursued markedly different careers in different parts of the world. I will here detail a few particulars about my own background, while my co-author will do the same in the Philosopher's Preface that follows.

I (identified in subsequent text as WYA) have for thirty years been purely a salvage archaeologist, working in areas that were soon to be inundated by man-made reservoirs (see WYA 1973d; 1984). I have conducted excavations in more than 160 sites, ranging in age from paleolithic to late medieval, and in areas from the Napa Valley to the Nile Valley, but the choice of sites was usually dictated by the necessities of salvage and not by any personal interest of mine. I have had to develop classifications of pottery (WYA 1962d; 1964a; 1986a), of house architecture (not yet published), of church architecture (WYA 1965a), and of Nubian cultural phases (WYA 1964b: 241–7) simply to get on with the jobs of excavation and publication, and not because of any particular interest either in the material being classified or in the processes of classification itself. Most of my work has been done in countries that do not permit the export of antiquities, even for study, and I have therefore been obliged to carry on the tasks of excavation and the analysis and classification of the excavated material simultaneously. Finally, most of my field work has been carried out under conditions of severe time restraint, and usually of financial restraint as well. These circumstances, by no means unfamiliar to field archaeologists of earlier generations, will account for the pragmatic outlook and the extreme concern for practicality and cost-effectiveness that are reflected in the present work.

It is relevant to mention also that I was trained as an ethnologist rather than as an archaeologist (see WYA 1963), and that I have in addition a longtime interest in languages and linguistics. The essentially cognitive approach to classification that is offered in this book owes much more to the literatures of ethnology and linguistics than it does to the literature of archaeology, where the issue of cognition is almost wholly ignored. It probably owes even more to the fact that I have at one time or another been fluent in half a dozen languages, including Navajo and Arabic as well as modern European languages. Like all polyglots I am keenly appreciative of the interrelationship between language and cognition, of the arbitrariness of categorical systems, and the untranslatability of many categorical concepts from one language to another.

In a recent work, Elman Service (1985: 289–313) has categorized ethnologists as falling into two "moieties," as follows:

Moiety A	**Moiety B**
is characterized by	*is characterized by*
Natural science approach	Humanistic approach
Determinism	Free-willism (or individualism)
Evolutionism	Relativism
Emphasis on social structure	Emphasis on culture
Generalization	Particularism
Comparative method	Holism
Environmentalism	Mentalism
Organismic analogy	Language analogy

To the extent that this dichotomy is valid, it may be further observed that a substantial majority of American ethnologists, at least in the past, have belonged to Moiety B, while the overwhelming majority of archaeologists have always adhered to Moiety A. It is not, for the most part, a matter of conditioning within the respective sub-fields; it is more a reflection of the very different personality types who are attracted respectively to ethnology and to archaeology. Readers of the present work will in any case have no trouble in recognizing that I, as an imperfectly reformed ethnologist, belong with the other ethnologists in Moiety B.

Acknowledgements

Many persons read the manuscript, or parts of it, prior to publication. Two who deserve special mention are Paul Teller, Professor of the Philosophy of Science at the University of Illinois (Chicago), and George Cowgill, Professor of Anthropology at Brandeis University. Many changes, additions, and deletions have been made at their suggestion, although perhaps not as many as either of them would have liked. In any case our book is very much the better for their input. Two other commentators whose suggestions have been beneficial are Alison Wylie, Professor of Philosophy at the University of Western Ontario, and an anonymous reviewer for Cambridge University Press.

While the book was in preparation, both the authors conducted graduate seminars on the subject of classification at their respective universities. I would like especially to thank my archaeology students for their many helpful comments and useful contributions: Frank Bodkin, Bet Ison, Jack Rossen, and Chris Turnbow.

THE PHILOSOPHER'S PREFACE

I (identified in subsequent chapters as EWA) received a BS in electrical engineering and a PhD in philosophy, with a minor in mathematics, at Stanford University. I have been a Fellow of the Behavioral Models Project at Columbia University, Instructor at Wesleyan University, and Professor of Philosophy at the University of California, Berkeley. Aside from philosophy of science I have published papers on mathematical psychology, decision theory, theory of probability, and probabilistic aspects of logic, including a book, *The Logic of Conditionals, an Application of Probability to Deductive Logic* (EWA 1975). In philosophy of science I have studied and written on induction and confirmation, causation, scientific concept formation, theory of measurement, and the foundations of physical topology and geometry, on which I am presently writing a book.

A word should be said about my philosophical development in relation to the present work. My initial orientation was toward the highly abstract and formalistic approach of the logical positivists (empiricists) and their allies, such as Rudolf Carnap, Carl Hempel, and Karl Popper. This approach dominated the philosophy of science in the 1940s and 1950s, and my early work, especially on measurement, was in that tradition. However, my faith in positivism was shaken by the criticisms of Thomas Kuhn (1962), though I did not accept the Kuhnian historicist position (the "dialectic of scientific paradigms") that came to succeed positivism as the dominant trend in the philosophy of science in the 1960s and 1970s. (Aspects of this "revolution in philosophy of science" will be discussed in Chapters 1 and 26.)

Seeking to identify what was missing both in the positivist and in the historicist approaches, I concluded that neither of them took sufficient cognizance of the purposes of scientific endeavor, and particularly of their importance in shaping scientific concepts. Following up that idea, I used mathematical information theory in a paper, "On the nature and purpose of measurement" (EWA 1966), to formulate a theory according to which numerical measurement systems are designed so that the measures they yield will be "maximally informative indices of phenomena." (The same approach is now offered, in regard to systems of classification, in Chapter 21 of the present book.) As will be noted in Chapter 1, informal conversations with my co-author (designated in later chapters as WYA) brought to light the fact that he had, quite independently, arrived at views on the subject of archaeological classification that closely paralleled my own about measurement. Those conversations led ultimately to the research on which a joint article, "Purpose and scientific concept formation" (EWA and WYA 1987), as well as the present book, is based.

An additional word should be said about the chapters in this book (Chapters 12, 21, and 26) that are specifically devoted to philosophical issues. Their aim is to discuss the implications of our views, on the one hand on archaeological typology and on the other hand on general topics and issues in the philosophy of science. Among the latter are included: the nature of concepts in science and their definitions; the existence (or realism) of abstract types; relations between empiricism and the Kuhnian theory of the dialectic, including the possibility of progress in science; and the so-called "problem of pseudoproblems" that arises because of the difficulty of distinguishing between factual claims and definitions in many scientific contexts. These are very diverse topics, each of which is important in its own right, and we obviously cannot give them careful or rigorous treatment in the present brief compass. We aim only to record unsystematic reflections concerning the relationship of each of the themes to our instrumentalist, purpose-oriented views on typology construction and use. The point should also be stressed that these reflections are not put forward as definitive "philosophical positions," but only as "working hypotheses," arrived at in an ongoing search for philosophical solutions to problems of methodology and philosophy that have engaged leading thinkers almost since the dawn of science.

PART I

INTRODUCTORY

The fundamental problem of each science is the establishment of the identity of its phenomena. That the problem still awaits its solution, and that the science of culture still lacks real criteria of identification . . . will hardly be disputed by anyone acquainted with the controversies of anthropology.

Bronislaw Malinowski (1960: 69–70)

I

BEGINNING POINTS

On a summer afternoon in 1983, two brothers – the authors of this book – went for a hike in the California mountains. As usual on the infrequent occasions when we get together, our conversation ranged over matters of common intellectual concern. On this particular afternoon we somehow got onto the topic of scientific typologies, and we discovered for the first time that we share a strong interest and closely similar views on the subject, although approaching it from nearly opposite directions.

Ernest W. Adams (hereinafter EWA) is Professor of the Philosophy of Science at Berkeley. Earlier work in the field of scientific measurement (EWA 1966; Adams and Carlstrom 1979) had led him, by natural extension, to a consideration of typologies, which have some of the attributes of measurement (see Chapter 7). William Y. Adams (hereinafter WYA) is Professor of Anthropology at the University of Kentucky, and for many years has also been a director of archaeological excavations in Egypt and the Sudan. The practical requirements of his work have led him over the years to construct a number of typologies (WYA 1962d; 1964a; 1965a), the best known of which is a classification of medieval Nubian pottery wares (WYA 1986a). This has become the principal instrument for calculating dates of occupation at Nubian archaeological sites, and has been adopted for that purpose by a number of different expeditions (see Gardberg 1970; Scanlon 1970; Säve-Söderbergh 1981).

EWA thus approaches the subject of classification from a wholly philosophic point of view, and WYA from a wholly practical one. Working respectively "downward" and "upward," however, we had arrived at a common level of understanding about the relationship between theory and practice before either of us became aware of it. Yet our perspective is not one that seems to be widely shared by colleagues in either of our disciplines.

The common ground on which we meet is that of praxis: the belief that theory and practice must be interrelated and inter-relevant. By this we mean only that theory must be grounded in practical reality, and that

3

everyday practice must in turn be relevant to some coherent theory. Later (Chapter 5) we will suggest that praxis in the field of classification is analogous to the relationship between language and speech. Here it is enough to point out that praxis is nothing more than the Greek noun from which is derived the adjective pragmatic, and we mean no more by it than that.

We find little of praxis or pragmatism in the literature on typology in our respective fields. Most of it is programmatic, doctrinaire, and far removed from practical reality, concerned with what typologies ought to be rather than with what they are. In this work we intend to consider both issues. We assume that all existing typologies must have been useful to someone for some purpose, and we want to discover how and why this is so.

Ellen and Reason (1979) have recently observed that

> "Classification" is a key concept in contemporary Western thought, figuring prominently in such apparently diverse fields of enquiry as anthropology, artificial intelligence, mathematics, history, biology, sociology, linguistics and philosophy. In each case, "classification" provides a topic for study, a methodological device and an explanatory principle. Where a concept appears to be so generally employed (seems, indeed, so necessary) in such a disparate range of disciplines, there is a clear and pressing need to scrutinize that concept, to put it to the question and to explicate its various uses and usages. (*Ibid.*: vii; see also Ellen 1979: 7)

This is precisely our objective in the present work.

We encounter frequently the assertion that typologies should strive for maximum scientific "objectivity." This does not strike us as a relevant or even a meaningful consideration, applied to what are essentially tools of communication. Useful typologies require intersubjective agreement (consistency), which is not the same thing as objectivity (correctness). We will never know, in many cases, how closely our type concepts correspond to some external reality, but we can discover and measure how closely the concepts of one person correspond to those of another (cf. especially Fish 1978 and Ziman 1978).

We find too that discussion often focuses on what to us are secondary issues, like the distinction between emic and etic types or between formal and functional classification. We will have something to say on these and a good many other questions, but they are not our primary concern. Our thesis is that the overriding considerations in any discussion of typology must be those of purpose and practicality. There is no right or wrong way

4

to classify anything, but there are better and worse ways of achieving specific purposes, once we have decided what those purposes are. By better we mean not only more precise, but also more communicable and more affordable.

We had only a shadowy vision of what lay ahead when we returned from our hike in 1983. We had, however, agreed on a common point of view, and on what we saw as a need to communicate it to our colleagues in philosophy and in anthropology/archaeology. We envisioned two essays written in somewhat different language, addressed to the different interests of the two disciplines. That intention has led, after five years of reading and intermittent dialogue, to a relatively brief and theoretical article for philosophers (EWA and WYA 1987), and to the present much longer work, which is concerned specifically with the theory and practice of artifact classification in archaeology. (For a brief preview of some of our ideas in the present work see also WYA 1988.)

We had not originally intended quite so narrow a focus. It became evident on reflection, however, that artifact typologies have special qualities that set them apart from other archaeological typologies, as well as from typologies in other disciplines. The sheer volume of material that is often involved, as well as the ancillary nature of many typologies (see Chapter 18), make the issues of purpose and practicality especially critical. We believe nevertheless that much of what we have to say has wider relevance, both within and beyond the field of archaeology.

Basic orientations

This is a book about the formation and use of concepts, both in a generic and in a specific sense. Typologies are systems of concept-formation (see Chapter 4), and types are the concepts formed according to those systems, but the words "typology" and "type" are also concepts in themselves. That is to say, they are tools of communication. They are not facts, processes, theories, or laws, though at one time and another they have been mistaken for all those things. (Thereby hang a great many problems that will occupy us in Part V.) Properly understood, typological concepts have no fixed or inherent meaning apart from their use, which varies from typology to typology and from person to person.

It is therefore impossible to talk about types and typologies except in subjective terms. We cannot speak of *the* concepts; we can only speak of *our* concepts. What we are presenting here is our own comprehensive and, we hope, comprehensible view of typologies, based on years of practical experience, individual reflection, and dialogue. We hope through systematic expostulation that at least some colleagues will be won over to our perspective, not on the grounds of its truth but of its utility.

Consequently and necessarily, this book is written throughout in the first person. It is an essay, not a textbook, rule book, or proclamation. The first person pronoun is employed usually in the plural, but occasionally in the singular. In the latter instances, the speaker will be identified by the initials WYA or EWA.

Readers will find that our work reflects no particular school of thought, or ideological commitment. For better or worse we have always been mavericks, preferring to work out our own ideas without much regard for received wisdom. Our approach to classification bears some relationship to the general philosophy of language developed by Ludwig Wittgenstein (see especially Canfield 1981), but he was certainly not the source of our inspiration. We have not attempted to explore in detail the extent of our agreement and disagreement with Wittgenstein, because, unlike him, we are concerned only with one very restricted kind of language, in which the relationship between mental conceptions and physical objects is of primary concern.

Possibly our freethinking outlook was conditioned by our early residence among Navajo Indians, who believe that no one and nothing is all good or all bad, all right or all wrong (Kluckhohn and Leighton 1946: 216–38). We hold much the same view with regard to philosophies and theories. We take it for granted that all social science theories are at best situational truths; they are applicable and useful in some circumstances and not in others. We have to discover for ourselves what utility there is in any given theory in any given circumstances.

Our position is thus a relativistic one. However, our instrumental relativism should not be mistaken for the kind of theoretical relativism that has recently become fashionable in archaeology and anthropology (cf. Bernstein 1983; Hodder 1983; Shanks and Tilley 1987; Wylie 1989). To argue that the utility of a classification can only be judged in relation to some purpose is something very different from arguing that the truth of a scientific observation can only be judged in relation to some theory. We will pursue this issue further in Chapter 26.

Our approach throughout the book is necessarily empirical. Since we are writing about practical typologies, and since, as Dunnell (1986: 150) has aptly observed, "The 'theoretical' literature has diverged from practice to such a degree that the two are now unrelated," we have no recourse but to disregard the literature and concentrate on the practice. This is what we will mainly do in Parts II, III, and IV, where we will look at existing and functioning typologies to try and discover what their characteristics are, how they come into being, and how and why they work. Only in Part V will we enter fully into what has been called the "Typological Debate" (Hill and Evans 1972: 231–2; Hayden 1984: 81; Dunnell 1986: 154–90), comparing our ideas and observations with those of others.

If our approach is empirical, it is also necessarily eclectic. In developing and refining our ideas we have derived a measure of assistance from many sources, including the literature in biology, cognitive psychology, philosophy of science, structural linguistics, semiotics, and structural, functional, and historical anthropology. Each of these has been helpful, but none has provided a comprehensive, informed overview. Whatever overview we present has arisen from our examination of actual, practical typologies.

At the same time we are not suggesting that our perspective is a new one. It is "radical" only in the literal sense of that term, which has to do with getting back to the root of things. We believe that most typologies were created in the beginning to meet some practical need, and that this was fully recognized by the makers. It was only later, when they became aware of the shortcomings in their typologies, that the typologists began looking at their work with a more detached and critical eye. This in itself was originally pragmatic; it was undertaken in the hope of achieving more useful typologies. But what began as a means became, finally, an end in itself, a kind of intellectual parlor game of making and then dissecting typologies. It is this game which is largely responsible for the gap between theory and practice that Dunnell (1986: 150) remarked. But since our own orientation has necessarily had to be practical (at least in the case of WYA), our view remains close to that of the early typologists.

We do not even claim that any of our ideas is new individually. Probably all of them have been expressed before somewhere, by someone. In particular the idea that typologies must have a purpose is not new; it was expressed with extraordinary clarity by W. S. Jevons in 1874 (II: 348–50; see also Brew 1946: 65; Rouse 1960). But the practical implications of that observation have rarely if ever been fully considered. Typologists, it seems, have consistently failed to grasp the connection between the purpose of typologies and the meaning of individual types (see Chapter 24). They have acknowledged the possibility of variable purposes in typologies, while at the same time looking for inherent or "natural" meaning in the types themselves (cf. Griffin 1943: 3, 303, 334–40; Spaulding 1953: 305; Clarke 1968: 187–227).

What we hope to do here is to pull together, and put into sharp focus, a set of related ideas that have been more often stated than explored. Above all, we want to put the issues of purpose and practicality back where they belong: in the forefront of any discussions of scientific typology. Holsinger (1984: 304) has put the matter in the simplest and clearest of terms: "a systematist faced with a mass of information . . . must consider what is the most useful and practical way to organize this information."

Because of our concern with practicality, we will have less to say about epistemology and about logic than have other recent commentators (Dunnell 1971b: 43–86; Watson, LeBlanc, and Redman 1971: 126–35; Whallon 1972; Whallon and Brown 1982; and various individual contributors in the latter volume). It is not that we don't understand the issues involved (EWA is after all a teacher of these subjects), but we question their practical relevance. As we will argue later (Chapter 6), logical typologies are not always useful, and useful typologies are not always logical. We agree with Kaplan (1984: 25) that "The *logic-in-use* of a science is not to be confused with the *reconstructed logic* of the philosophy of science" (emphasis in the original). It might be appropriate also to recall the words of Nils Bohr at this point: "[He] never trusted a purely formal or mathematical approach. 'No, no,' he would say, 'You are not thinking, you are just being logical'" (quoted in Margolis 1987: 1).

We want to make it clear, in sum, that our concern throughout this essay is with practical typologies – a category that may or may not include the complex formulations of Spaulding (1953), Whallon (1972), Read (1974), Christenson and Read (1977), and a host of others. A practical typology in our definition is one that achieves some clearly stated objective with a reasonable economy of time, effort, and resources.

Readers will have no difficulty in recognizing that Chapters 12, 21, 26, and the concluding part of this chapter were written by EWA, and the remainder by WYA. However, the ideas expressed in all the chapters were developed through a continuing dialogue between the two of us.

The validity and value of archaeological typologies

We consider that typologies are tools made for a purpose, and as long as they can be shown to work for that purpose they require no more abstract justification than does a crowbar. Their validity lies ultimately in their value. The point of departure for our analysis will therefore be to recognize that, whatever theoretical literature may assert, there are literally hundreds of practical archaeological typologies in effective daily use. They were and are the backbone of prehistoric archaeology, as Chang (1967: 4) has rightly observed. The reasons for this are worth recalling, for they will not be

immediately evident to non-archaeologists, and they may have been forgotten by some archaeologists as well.

Before it can be useful to the social scientist, human behavioral data
must be placed in defined contexts of time and space. For the ethnologist,
the sociologist, or the political scientist this is usually a matter of simple
observation. For the prehistoric archaeologist it is not. Sites and artifacts
do not date themselves, and chronological ordering is always the archaeologist's first problem. His data must be located in time before they can be
used to reconstruct cultures, to reconstruct history, or to test theories. The
majority of artifact typologies were developed to meet that elementary
but fundamental need. James Ford (1954b: 52), speaking of artifact
typologies, put the matter perfectly thirty-five years ago: "This tool is
designed for the reconstruction of culture history in time and space. *This is
the beginning and not the end of the archaeologist's responsibility*" (emphasis
added).

What archaeologists in the present, radiocarbon age often fail to recognize is that the entire time–space grid of North American prehistory was
erected almost entirely on the basis of artifact typologies. Architectural
remains and burial types also played their part, especially in the Southwest,
but only to the extent that it was possible to classify them in the same way
as artifacts. The same has essentially been true in the study of prehistory on
every other continent.

Spatial and temporal ordering of data is not, is not intended to be, and
should not be mistaken for, explanation (*contra* Fritz and Plog 1970:
407–8). It is wholly pre-theoretical (see Chapter 25). It is the necessary
preliminary step which brings the archaeologist to the point where the
ethnologist, the sociologist, and the political scientist all begin. Failure to
recognize this elementary fact has probably introduced more confusion
into the Typological Debate than any other single factor.

One of the most persistent critics of conventional typologies has been
Lewis Binford (e.g. 1972: 195–207, 252–94). It seems appropriate, therefore, to illustrate our point about temporal ordering with examples from
his own writing. The following is a conspectus of chapters from his *An
Archaeological Perspective* (Binford 1972):

> "Archaeology as anthropology" (pp. 20–32) makes its point
>   with reference to implements of the *Old Copper Complex*.
> "Smudge pits and hide smoking: the use of analogy in archae-
>   ological reasoning" (pp. 33–58) discusses pits found in a
>   small *Mississippian* farmstead.
> "Some comments on historical versus processual archae-

9

ology" (pp. 114–21) critically assesses a theory about the *Classic Maya*.

"Hatchery West: site definition – surface distribution of cultural items" (pp. 163–84) discusses *Embarrass Simple-Stamped* and *Embarrass Cordmarked* pottery types.

"Archaeological systematics and the study of culture process" (pp. 195–207) discusses containers of the *Havana tradition* and the *Scioto tradition*.

"Model building – paradigms, and the current state of Paleolithic research" (pp. 244–94) is about *Mousterian* remains.

"'Red ochre' caches from the Michigan area: a possible case of cultural drift" (pp. 295–313) is about *Late Archaic* cemeteries.

"Indian sites and chipped stone materials in the northern Lake Michigan area" (pp. 346–72) discusses flint artifacts from four *Late Woodland* and *Upper Mississippian* sites.

"An analysis of cremations from three Michigan sites" (pp. 373–82) and "Analysis of a cremated burial from the Riverside cemetery, Menominee County, Michigan" (pp. 383–9) bring us back again to *Late Archaic* burials.

"Galley Pond mound" (pp. 390–420) was of "*Late Woodland affiliation*" (p. 391).

In the above list, every one of the italicized terms is employed routinely and uncritically by Binford, and every one of them designates a culture or culture period that has been defined largely or wholly on the basis of artifact types.

Robert Adams (1984: 14), partially echoing Binford, has written that "except for remote corners and unusual circumstances, the need for descriptive inventories of the remains of human activity during successive epochs is long past." This may be true, but it does not mean that the old-fashioned artifact typologies that brought us to this happy pass are no longer needed. Each new find must still be located within a time and space grid before the data can be used for any other purpose, and that is still being done, and done successfully, with the same old typologies.

Another peculiarity of archaeology is worth noticing at this point. At least in prehistoric archaeology there is a longstanding tradition that recovered data should be published in their entirety. This is emphatically not the case in ethnology and other social sciences, where raw data are usually presented (if at all) only in summary and condensed form. The problem of describing a mass of highly diverse material within a finite number of pages is a very real one for the archaeologist, and a good many typologies have been designed just for this purpose (cf. Krieger 1944: 273; Taylor 1948: 126; Everitt 1974: 4). As we will see in Chapter 13, archaeological typologies may also serve quite a number of other purposes, and for the majority of them they appear to be working satisfactorily. This constitutes, we suggest, the ultimate proof of the pudding.

ISSUES IN THE PHILOSOPHY OF SCIENCE

Thus far we have been concerned to provide a context for our work within the discipline of archaeology. It remains here to say a word about connections between our views on archaeological typology and some general issues in the philosophy of science. We will begin by briefly sketching trends in the subject that have developed in the past seventy-five years.

Theoretical trends

The dominant concern of philosophy of science from the late nineteenth century through the 1950s was with epistemological questions, i.e., with the meaning and justification of scientific claims like "Force equals mass times acceleration," "Biological evolution is determined by natural selection," "Price is a function of supply and demand," and the like. As will be more fully explained in Chapter 26, there was also a dominant epistemology, namely sense empiricism, which held that what distinguishes scientific claims from mere speculation and matters of faith is that they are capable of being justified by appeal to objective observational and experimental data. Though this view has come under severe criticism in recent years, as we will note a little later, it is fair to say that in some form it is still accepted by nearly all working scientists today, especially in the natural sciences. This epistemology also goes along with the view that the fundamental objective of scientific research is to discover and if possible explain the laws of nature, where nature is what the senses reveal to us.

Attempts to clarify the empiricist philosophy of science led to many difficulties, and disagreements about how to deal with them gave rise to different versions of empiricism. One difficulty concerns what really are and are not objective observational data. Some "radical empiricists" like Ernst Mach (1893) and Bertrand Russell in some of his writings (cf. 1919) maintained that the only things we can be perfectly certain of are private sensations. Naturally, few working scientists can accept the demand that scientific claims may be based only on data that are ultimately subjective, and more moderate empiricisms like that of Carnap (1956) only demand justification in terms of "reasonably objective" things such as the results of physical measurements (cf. Bridgman 1927).

Other disagreements arose over the question of how much of science ought to be "provable" by direct observation. Again, radicals like Mach and Russell demanded that all of it should be. Finding that certain laws, such as Newton's laws of motion, were stated in terms of unobservable "absolutes," they attempted to reformulate them in an "empirically acceptable" manner (Mach 1893). Less radical empiricists like Carnap and especially Hempel (1965; 1966) were content to advocate a kind of hypothetico-deductivism, holding that while basic scientific laws need not be susceptible to direct observational testing, it should be possible to deduce consequences from them that are testable, or in terms of which they can be indirectly tested. Hypothetico-deductivism seems to fit well the practice of advanced sciences like physics, and it has been very influential in the social sciences as well in recent decades. Popper (1935; 1963; etc.) can be regarded as an extreme proponent, holding that the main objective of scientific research should be to formulate "conjectures" (hypotheses) and then to strive to "refute" them by showing their inconsistency with observational data. We will comment a little later on empiricism and hypothetico-deductivism with reference to our own views on typology construction, but first we need to take note of the anti-empirical reaction that has arisen since 1960, mainly influenced by the work of Thomas Kuhn (1962; 1970) on scientific revolutions.

Starting from the historical fact that fundamental scientific theories like Newtonian mechanics are never given up simply because they conflict with a few bits of observational data (e.g., the perihelion of the planet Mercury), Kuhn was led to question whether confrontation with sense observation really is the sole or proper test of a scientific theory. Going even beyond that, he questioned whether pure objective data of sense, uninfluenced by the observer's preconceptions, ever play a significant role in theory-testing. For example, "normal" scientific research (cf. Kuhn 1962: 35–42) may involve applying Newton's laws of motion, but this presupposes them to such an extent that the question of their truth or falsity has been answered in advance. In part, the theory is a paradigm that determines how the scientist "sees the world" – in this case as a place controlled by Newton's laws – and to give up the paradigm is to see the world in a different way. Giving up a fundamental theory is therefore a much more radical matter than the empiricists have realized. It involves not only giving up explicit claims like Newton's laws, but also giving up a particular way of looking at the phenomena to which the laws apply. Of course Kuhn's challenge to empirical orthodoxy gives rise to problems of its own, perhaps the chief of which is that of accounting for progress in science.

Chapter 26 will comment extensively on Kuhn's position, but here there is a more recent development to be noted. If there is any discernible post-Kuhnian trend, it is probably a reaction away from overarching philosophy of science in the singular, toward philosophies of particular sciences.

The physical sciences have been philosophically important from ancient Greek times to the present, and they have profoundly influenced the general philosophies of such giants as Plato, Descartes, and Kant, a fact that has been emphasized in recent historical work (cf. Vlastos 1975; Buroker 1978; Wilson 1982; M. Friedman 1983; etc.). Lately, however, there has been a development of distinctive philosophies of other fields, such as biology (Hull 1974), economics (A. Nelson 1986), mathematics (Chihara 1973; Benacerraf and Putnam 1983), and quite recently anthropology (Salmon 1982), as specialities within the general field of philosophy. Each focuses on methodological issues that arise within a particular substantive discipline – for example, the proper definition of a biological species, which will be discussed frequently throughout this work – and as much as possible these issues are approached from the same perspective as that held by the regular practitioners of the disciplines. Philosophical specialists therefore strive to acquaint themselves with the details of ongoing research in the different disciplines, even perhaps hoping that they may themselves make a contribution in a particular field, and they tend to accept the different aims and standards of the various disciplines in a way that contrasts quite markedly with the detached judgmental attitudes characteristic of earlier *a priorist* philosophers of science. If the modern philosopher of science can nevertheless hope to make a special contribution, it is by virtue of the broader if less detailed perspectives offered by philosophy, and possibly a familiarity with other sciences, in contrast to the more narrowly particular perspectives of the biologist, economist, mathematician, or anthropologist. This is what we hope may be gained as the outcome of our collaboration in the present work, and we turn now to a brief introduction of our views in relation to the issues that we have just discussed.

Instrumentalism: nature and artifice in typology construction

Our general philosophy of archaeological typology may be stated as follows. Whether or not there are such things as natural kinds or types in a subject domain, we reject the idea that the aim of typology construction is necessarily to characterize them. The Medieval Nubian Pottery Typology, which will serve in Part III as the major case study illustrating our views on

archaeological typology, was not constructed with the objective of classifying pottery fragments (sherds) into natural types, but rather with the
hope and expectation that making certain discriminations among the
pottery sherds found in a given archaeological location (provenience) can
provide a good indication of the date of the provenience. This illustrates
our general view in regard to deliberately constructed scientific typologies:
they are conceptual instruments. Like physical instruments, they are
designed and used for particular scientific purposes – sometimes as "indicators" of something quite external to themselves (see especially Chapter
18 and Chapter 21) – and they are to be evaluated in terms of their effectiveness in serving those purposes.

Typological instrumentalism involves a special view of the roles of
nature and of artifice in making a typology. Figuratively put, nature
supplies the materials which the typologist then "shapes" to serve the
purposes for which the instrument is to be used. Nature may or may not
supply obvious types, and these may or may not be unique, but in any case
the typologist will use only those that suit his purposes (see Chapter 13).
In the case of the Nubian Pottery Typology, nature (or, more correctly,
ancient culture) provided the potsherds, but WYA subdivided them into
types in such a way that dates can be estimated on the basis of the sherd
types found in any given provenience. As it happened, the most obvious
"kinds" that nature provides – those distinguished from each other on the
basis of coloration – are of little use for WYA's purposes, since in Nubia
color criteria are of little use for dating.

In keeping with the general trend away from any single overarching
philosophy, our instrumental view of archaeological typology is not offered
as a general philosophy of science. It nevertheless bears on some of the
more general issues that were discussed a little earlier, as will become evident in later chapters. A few of the key points may be briefly indicated here.

Concepts and plural purposes

Empiricism has tended to see scientific concepts only as building blocks for
theories or hypotheses, and it assumes that if they are deliberately induced,
rather than being simple "givens," this must be for the purpose of theory-
construction. Ernest Nagel made this point explicitly with regard to
systems of measurement, to which classifications are in many ways comparable (see especially Chapters 12 and 21): "Consequently, if we inquire
why we measure in physics, the answer will be that if we do measure, and
measure in certain ways, then it will be possible to establish the equations
and theories that are the goal of inquiry" (Nagel 1961: 123).

If we were to substitute "classify" for "measure," and "archaeology" for "physics," we would have a classic empiricist philosophy of archaeological classification. Obviously the Nubian Pottery Typology does not conform to such a philosophy, and we see no reason why it should. We are not saying that archaeology should not aim at equations and theories, but rather that these are not its only legitimate goals, and moreover that its concepts should be adapted to and appropriate for the goals which it has set itself. We will expand on this issue of plural purposes, in relation to systems of classification, in Part IV, and especially in Chapter 13.

Definition

This critically important topic is discussed at length, from a philosophical perspective, in Chapter 12. Briefly, we interpret the thesis that "definitions define, and to be scientific they should be precise" as saying that definitions instruct people in the use of conceptual instruments, and they should be precise enough so that two or more people can use the same instrument with a degree of consistency sufficient for the purposes for which the instrument was designed. But we note at the same time that instruction in the use of concepts need not be entirely verbal; especially in archaeology it generally involves also a lot of hands-on laboratory training. Moreover, the definitions are seldom if ever precise to the extent of specifying necessary and sufficient conditions for membership in any type; we argue in Part III that to insist on developing and following such definitions would in many practical situations be counterproductive. Precision and objectivity have their uses, but these have to be demonstrated with respect to specific purposes; they are not ends in themselves. The issue will further occupy us in Chapter 21.

Realism

A philosophical question regarding the nature of the types formulated for archaeological purposes has to do with the sense in which they can be said to be *real*. This relates to the frequently made distinction between natural and artificial types (see Chapter 23). We have already noted that our instrumentalist approach allows roles both to nature and to artifice in type formation.

A somewhat more technical question, discussed more fully in Chapter 12, has to do with the way in which types are counted, or sorted, especially when this involves the possibility of finding entities that do not fit into any of the previously described categories, or types. Open typologies, discussed in Chapter 18, make specific allowance for the discovery of new types, comparable to new biological species, and it would seem to follow from this that the newly discovered types were "out there in nature" all the time. Nevertheless, we argue that scientific typologies (unlike systems of measurement) cannot be designed to accommodate anything and every-thing; that is, they do not have "container-spaces," or pigeonholes, not only for all existing entities, but also for all other entities that could poss-ibly exist. In the case of quantitative measurement there are generally theories that delimit the class of possibilities to be measured; for example the laws of physics which imply that everything that ever happened, will happen, or *could* happen would have to fit into a "slot" in the time-frame of physical theory. But there are no comparable theories that delimit the class of possible artifact types that might be discovered, even in so seem-ingly limited a field as that of arrowheads. Several thousand different arrowhead types have actually been designated in different parts of the world, and a single typology which could accommodate them all, as well as all other conceivable types not yet discovered, would include an infinity of types. And, that there is no absolute "space" of all possible arrowhead types, analogous to that of all possible times, means that there are no theoretical criteria of existence for arrowhead types like those for times and places in physical space.

Observation and nature

The ability to use type-concepts in practical situations (that is, in typing and sorting; see Chapter 16) is a skill that is imparted partly by verbal instruction and partly by hands-on training under expert supervision. Exercising this skill involves perception and cognition – observation and thought – but our view of these processes is that of "naturalized epistem-ology" (Quine 1969: Chapter 3). If determining that a particular potsherd represents a particular type in the Nubian Typology involves comparing a "sensory input" with a previously existing mental template or gestalt, as some classifiers have claimed, this is a psychological fact to be established *a posteriori*, not something that is essential to classification or to "grasping a concept."

A note on terminology

Because of the ambiguity of so much conceptual terminology (see especially Chapter 24), we are faced with the necessity either of inventing a whole new conceptual vocabulary or of using a great many terms which, for others, may have meanings different from those that we give them. We have chosen the latter alternative as the lesser of two evils; that is, as the least disruptive to the orderly communication of ideas. We must however make it absolutely clear that our use of many terms does not correspond to that of other authors, or even to usages that are more or less standard in certain disciplines other than our own. We have set forth our own definitions at various points in the book, and they are listed comprehensively in the Glossary (Appendix A).

Readers are therefore cautioned against attaching any meanings to our terms other than those that we ourselves have given them. This is particularly true of words like dialectic, gestalt, and praxis, which in our usage do not carry the same theoretical or ideological loading which they have in some other work. (In order to emphasize this point, we spell these words without capitalization or italics.)

Throughout the book we have striven for as much terminological rigor and consistency as seems necessary to make our meaning clear, without being unduly pedantic. Thus, we have not insisted on using precisely the same word to mean precisely the same thing on all occasions. Excessive verbal rigor is not only stylistically objectionable; it often impedes the smooth flow of thought and in effect "hides the forest behind the trees." Only in the Glossary (Appendix A) have we attempted to formulate rigorous definitions, and the reader should refer to these at any point where the meaning of any word in the text is not clear.

A note on documentation

Since this is intended as a "think-piece" rather than as a work of scholarship, we will not be particularly concerned about the intellectual pedigrees of the ideas expressed. We will, however, make reference to the work of others to the extent that we are aware of it. Our apologies go to any other authors who may have said the same things, and whose work we have overlooked.

For didactic reasons it seems desirable to explain the system of reference citations that we have adopted. A reference preceded by "see" will identify a place – either in this work or in another – where the subject under discussion is more fully treated. The prefix "cf." should be read as "see incidentally." It will identify a place where the reader will find ideas similar but usually not identical to our own. For the most part these were not the actual source of our ideas, and we are not attempting to shift credit or blame for them. "*Contra*" will mean "for a contrasting view see." A citation without a prefix will identify the direct source of information, ideas, or quotations presented by us; in these cases credit or blame belongs to the authors cited.

2

INTRODUCTORY THESES

This chapter will state briefly the major theses that are to be elaborated in later chapters. It will serve at the same time as an introductory guide to the remaining parts of the book, so that readers with particular interests may judge for themselves which chapters are and are not germane to them. Since there is no point in describing what has presumably already been read, we will begin our review with Part II. In the paragraphs that follow, the numbers that precede each heading are chapter numbers.

Part II The nature of types and typologies
Part II is occupied with preliminary considerations about the nature of human concept formation, the organization of concepts into languages, classifications, and typologies, the special structural features of typologies, and the nature of types and type concepts individually.

3 Dimensions and elements of "typehood." We have at the outset to establish at least a working definition of what we mean by the word "type," although we are not yet ready to offer a formal definition. Accordingly we begin Chapter 3 by considering the different usages of the word in scientific literature, observing that it refers sometimes to a group of physical entities, sometimes to our ideas about a group of entities, and sometimes to the words and/or pictures in which we express those ideas. We conclude that all of these usages are legitimate, and that a type in the fullest sense must therefore be recognized as having separate but interrelated material, mental, and representational dimensions, each of which involves several more specific elements. We then proceed to explore in more detail these elements of "typehood," which we designate as type concepts, type descriptions, type definitions, type labels, type names, type categories, and type members. All but one or two of these elements are necessary con-

stituents of every useful type. The relationship between them is not, however, a fixed one, with the result that types as wholes are mutable. In the
latter part of the chapter we consider, in addition, two essential properties
that are characteristic of all useful types: those of identity, or identifiability, and meaning relevant to some purpose. We point out that most
physical entities have both individual identity and typological identity, and
they may in addition have both individual meanings and typological
meanings.

4 Perceptual and conceptual foundations. We believe that scientific thought is not qualitatively different from other thought, and we therefore begin with a general consideration of what is known about how human
minds function to formulate, organize, and use concepts in general. We
distinguish between sensory perceptions, sensory images, gestalts, concepts, words, categories, classes, and types, successively involving the
mental processes of pattern recognition, imprintation, association, symbolization, abstraction, classification, and segregation. We argue that a
classification is a special, restricted kind of language, and that a typology is
a special, restricted kind of classification – specifically, one made for sorting entities. A typology therefore differs from other classifications in that it
always has some practical purpose in addition to that of simply communication.

5 The dialectics of type concept formation. In this chapter we trace
the "natural history" of type concepts and typologies. In practical
typologies we suggest that the first type concepts are often largely intuitive;
they may be influenced both by conventional wisdom and by the circumstances of our first encounters with the material under study. Later, our
concepts will consciously or unconsciously change as we begin systematically to differentiate types from other types, and to give them formal
expression. They may change even more through the practical experience
of sorting new material. Throughout, there is a continual dialectic or feedback between the objects and our ideas about them, and this process will
never end as long as there is new material to be sorted. In conclusion we
underscore the inescapable necessity of hands-on experience in learning to
use typologies effectively.

6 The nature of types. Having discussed the various ways in
which type concepts come into being, we now turn to a consideration of
their actual nature. We suggest that they are so complex as to defy rigorous

characterization: they are partly intuitive and partly rational, partly natural and partly artificial, partly essential and partly instrumental. We go on to point out that most archaeological typologies are polythetic, so that there are no fixed criteria of "typehood," and that archaeological types are usually distinguished by norms or central tendencies rather than by distinct boundaries. In conclusion we suggest that the justification for types does not lie in how they were made but in whether or not they work for some specific purpose. This does not necessarily mean that we understand *why* they work; often we can demonstrate empirically that a typology works for some purpose without knowing why.

7 The structure of typologies. Here we argue that a typology is not merely a congeries of types; it is a *system* of types. As such it has inherent systemic features, not all of which are presupposed by the nature or purpose of the individual types themselves. We first consider what these features are, and then go on to suggest that they may be partly a reflection of inherited mental templates that are common to the human species and many other creatures as well. This leads us to a brief consideration of structuralist theories of classification, and their potential relevance to the study of scientific classifications. At the conclusion of the chapter we take up briefly the much misunderstood question of the relationship between classification and measurement.

8 A synthetic definition of typology and type. Here we synthesize much of what has been said in the four preceding chapters into a single comprehensive definition that is both functional and structural. The definition is then analyzed in terms of the significance of each of its constituent parts.

Part III Typology in action: the Medieval Nubian Pottery Typology

Here we introduce, explain, and critically analyze a particular artifact typology that will later serve to exemplify many of the points that will be developed in Part IV. The Medieval Nubian Pottery Typology was developed by WYA over a thirty-year period, and is still evolving.

9 Origin and development of the Nubian Typology. This chapter details the historical circumstances which led to the development of the Medieval Nubian Typology, and the subsequent steps and missteps in its development.

10 Basic features of the Nubian Typology. This chapter explains the features of the Medieval Nubian Typology in its current state of development as of 1989.

11 The uses of the Nubian Typology. Here we explain in detail how the Medieval Nubian Typology is used to date archaeological deposits, and then go on to discuss more briefly some secondary uses of the typology.

12 Philosophical implications. Here we consider how the ideas presented in Part II, as well as the data presented in Part III, bear upon certain current interests and controversies in the philosophy of science. The issues specifically discussed are those of conceptual instrumentalism, identity and meaning, the reality of types and other abstract concepts, and the relationship between classification and measurement.

Part IV Pragmatics of archaeological typology
Part IV is the pragmatic heart of our work. Here we take a strictly empirical approach to scientific classifications: not attempting to develop abstract principles about what they are or how they should be made, but seeing what kinds of generalizations can be derived from the consideration of actual, extant typologies. We refer repeatedly to the Nubian Pottery Typology for illustration, but many other artifact typologies are also considered.

13 The starting point: purpose. In this chapter we return to our central thesis, that typologies are sorting systems made for one or more specific purposes. We discuss several kinds of purposes that may be served by artifact typologies, and how these affect the nature of the typologies themselves. We make an initial distinction between what we call basic and instrumental purposes. Basic purposes involve an attempt to learn or to express something about the material being classified. They may be either descriptive, comparative, or analytical, and analytical purposes are further subdivided into intrinsic, interpretive, and historical categories. Instrumental purposes are served when we classify material for some purpose not directly related to the material itself; they may be either ancillary or incidental. At the conclusion of the chapter we discuss the possibility of making typologies for multiple purposes.

14 The determinants of types: variables and attributes. It is our purpose that determines the selection of variables and attributes that we use in making typologies. In this chapter we first distinguish between variables and attributes, and then go on to discuss three different kinds of variables and attributes that are often incorporated in artifact typologies. These are intrinsic, contextual, and inferential variables and attributes. We point out that types are not defined by individual attributes but by combinations of attributes, and we discuss different kinds of attribute clusters and their significance. We suggest that, because types must have both identity and meaning, artifact types are usually defined by a combination of intrinsic attributes and either contextual or inferential attributes.

15 The making of types: formulation, designation and description. In Chapters 5 and 6 we discuss, in somewhat abstract and theoretical terms, the origin, development, and communication of type concepts. In Chapter 15 we return to the same issues from a more pragmatic perspective. We talk about the different processes through which archaeological types may come into being (formulation), about how and when we decide to give a type "official" status (designation), and about how we go about describing a type once it has been designated (description). We make the essential point that useful descriptions must go far beyond the minimum requirements of definition, because the attributes that are used to define a type may not be very conspicuous, and therefore may not be the most useful ones for recognizing individual members of the type. We therefore suggest that useful type descriptions involve what we call overdetermination; they include every attribute that might be useful for the recognition of individual specimens of the type, whether or not those attributes are diagnostic. In the concluding section we discuss the various points at which arbitrary decision-making is required in the formulation, designation, and description of types.

16 The use of types: typing and sorting. In this chapter we discuss the problems and procedures involved in type attribution; that is, in the application of type concepts to particular objects (typing) and to groups of objects (sorting). We point out that in these attributions we are not simply "recognizing" types or members of types; we are recognizing the resemblance between particular objects and particular type concepts that we have in our heads, or on paper. Since resemblance is always a matter of degree, and also a matter of individual judgment, precision in the definition and description of types will not eliminate problems in their attribution. Typing and sorting are in fact processes that involve continual, arbitrary decision-making. We suggest that the position of the artifact sorter is not essentially different from that of the baseball umpire, who has minutely specified rules to guide him but still must make continual arbitrary decisions. At the end of the chapter we discuss three possible "philosophies of umpiring" which are relevant to artifact sorting.

17 The ordering of types: taxonomy and seriation. After types have been formulated they can be manipulated in various ways for various purposes. Two of the most common ways are by taxonomy (hierarchic ordering) and seriation (linear ordering). We argue that in archaeology these processes are nearly always independent of, and subsequent to, the actual process of classifying, and therefore do not affect the formulation or definition of types themselves. Taxonomic ordering can theoretically be done either by lumping types into larger categories or by splitting them into smaller ones, but in practical taxonomies the former process is by far the more common. On the other hand computerized taxonomies are often made by a continuous splitting process, which is likely to produce "types" having little utility. Seriation, unlike taxonomy, is not in itself a classificatory process. In archaeology it is usually a matter of arranging types in chronological order. However, the most interesting and useful archaeological seriations do not involve types but type frequencies; that is, they are seriations of percentage figures. At the conclusion of the chapter we suggest that statistics have a much larger and more legitimate role to play in taxonomic ordering and in seriation than they do in the actual formulation of types.

18 Variation and variability in archaeological classification. Here we describe some of the different kinds of archaeological classifications that are actually in use. We first recall the basic structural distinctions between classifications, typologies, and taxonomies, pointing out that some archaeological classifications are and some are not typologies, and that some are and some are not taxonomies. We then go on to consider various kinds of archaeological classifications – phenetic, stylistic, chronological, spatial, functional, emic, and "cultural" – in relation to the purposes they serve. Finally, we discuss some additional factors, unrelated to purpose, that can affect the development and use of archaeological classifications.

19 The bottom line: practicality. Here we argue that the necessity of some purpose in typologies also implies a need for practicality, or in other words cost-effectiveness. Both classifying and sorting are time-consuming operations, which become time-wasting if they do not produce usable results. We discuss separately the issues of practicality in classifying and in sorting, and we conclude that in neither procedure need we aim for a higher degree of accuracy than can be shown to serve the purposes for which the typology was made.

20 Principles of practical typology. Here we draw together and summarize the points that have been developed in the preceding seven chapters, in a series of twenty-eight didactic principles.

21 Information-theoretic formulations. In this chapter we attempt to express many of the ideas developed in Part IV in formal language, in order to demonstrate how they relate to a number of current issues in the field of information theory.

Part V Classification, explanation, and theory
In the first four sections we have presented our own ideas and procedures, without much reference to what others have written on the subject of archaeological classification. In this concluding section we review and critique the work of others both from a historical and from a theoretical perspective, at the same time endeavoring to place our own work within the larger context of what has been called the Typological Debate. This introduces a certain change of focus, since we turn from a consideration of actual artifact classifications to a consideration of theoretical writings about them. Because there is a substantial gap between theory and practice, the issues that are discussed in Part V are to a considerable extent "paper issues," having little relevance to what goes on in practice in the field.

22 The Typological Debate. Here we present a brief conspectus of theoretical and methodological writing about artifact classification, mostly by American prehistorians, since the beginning of the twentieth century. We show how the theory but not the practice of classification has been affected by successive theoretical and methodological paradigms: first the classificatory, then the configurationist, then the nomothetic, and finally the electronic.

23 Issues and non-issues in the Typological Debate. Here we single out for discussion some of the issues that have been raised in the course of the Typological Debate. Among these are the issues of "natural" vs "artificial" classification, of lumping vs. splitting, of induction vs. deduction, of emic vs. etic classification, of formal vs. functional classification, of object clustering vs. attribute clustering, and a number of more particularized issues. We suggest that some of these are genuine issues relating to the differing purposes and circumstances of classification, and some are spurious issues arising from terminological ambiguity or from a misunderstanding of the basic nature of concept formation and classification. We conclude with a consideration of the appropriate roles of statistics and of computers in the classificatory process.

24 Conceptual problems. In the early years of the Typological Debate, ambiguity often resulted from the lack of an adequately formulated conceptual vocabulary. Too few words had to be employed to mean too many things. In the more recent past a great deal of new terminology has been introduced, but misunderstandings still arise from a failure to make basic conceptual distinctions. In this chapter we try to identify specific misunderstandings whose basis is conceptual rather than theoretical.

25 The use and abuse of theory. In this chapter we begin with a consideration of the nature of scientific paradigms in the social sciences. We suggest that, unlike the situation described by Kuhn (1962) in the natural sciences, they are largely independent of methodology. Paradigm shifts take place not through methodological advances or discoveries but because interest shifts between paradigms which emphasize explanation, prediction, or understanding. This is well illustrated in the case of the successively dominant classificatory, configurationist, and nomothetic paradigms in twentieth-century American archaeology, of which the first emphasized prediction, the second understanding, and the third explanation. We argue that the configurationist and nomothetic paradigms really had little theoretical relevance to classification, because classification is essentially a process of definition. It cannot simultaneously provide either understanding or explanation except in a tautologous sense. We conclude that classification, like speech, is essentially a pre-scientific rather than a scientific undertaking, if by science we mean the search for explanatory principles.

26 Paradigms and progress. In this concluding chapter we challenge the notion, made popular by Kuhn (1962), that the evolution of science is not commensurate with progress. Specifically we suggest that the majority of scientific concepts are actually independent of paradigms, not paradigm-dependent as Kuhn suggested, and we believe that it is possible to measure progress insofar as it involves the formulation of more effective concepts for achieving certain recognized purposes that are actually common to all science. We conclude with a discussion of what Carnap (1927) called pseudoproblems, which arise from a failure to distinguish between facts and concepts or interpretations.

PART II

THE NATURE OF TYPES AND TYPOLOGIES

The clarification of concepts . . . directly gauges scientific progress.

Robert H. Lowie (1937: 281)

3

DIMENSIONS AND ELEMENTS OF "TYPEHOOD"

Since our book is about typologies and types, we should in theory begin by explaining what we mean by the two terms. However, this is much more easily said than done. We will suggest in later pages (especially Chapter 6) that types are among the most complex of all human ideas; so much so that they often defy formal definition (cf. Klejn 1982: 35–6). In addition, a typology has peculiarities and complexities of its own (see Chapter 7). Although by definition it is a system of types, it is more than just the sum of its parts.

We will leave aside until Chapter 7 the question of what is a typology, and will concentrate here on the question of what is a type. Some scientists would probably argue that it is a group of similar things, others that it is an idea or group of ideas about the similarity of things, still others that it is a form of words describing things and their similarity (cf. Dunnell 1986: 191–3). If our discussion is to encompass all of the different meanings given to the word "type" in the scientific literature, however, we must begin by recognizing that all three of the usages described above are legitimate. That is, a type in the fullest sense consists of things, plus our ideas about them, plus the words and/or pictures in which we express those ideas (see especially Leach 1976: 17–22).

When we use the term "Tsegi polychrome," for example, it is more than likely that we are thinking on some occasions of the type concept, on others primarily of the type members, and on still others primarily of the type description. When we say "Tsegi polychrome is essentially a stylistic variant of Kayenta polychrome" we are clearly thinking of the type concept; when we say "You can recognize Tsegi polychrome by its red and black designs on an orange slip" we are thinking mainly in terms of the type description; when we say "That bowl is Tsegi polychrome, not Kayenta polychrome" we are thinking of the type category; when we say "Put the Tsegi polychrome sherds in the third drawer" we are thinking of the type members.

We may say, therefore, that a type involves a combination of material, mental, and representational (verbal or pictorial) dimensions, each of which in turn involves a number of specific elements of "typehood." In our view the idea of a type cannot be fully understood except as the sum of these elements. In trying to understand what a type is, we will begin by identifying and defining its individual constituent elements. We will then go on to consider, in addition, two essential properties that are characteristic of all useful types.

The essential elements of "typehood"

The mental, physical, and representational elements of "typehood" that will be discussed here and elsewhere in the book are type concepts, type descriptions, type definitions, type labels, type names, type categories, and type members. For the moment we will give only brief, preliminary definitions of these elements, most of which will be more fully discussed in later chapters.

Type concept. A type concept is the purely mental aspect of "typehood." It is a body of ideas about the nature and characteristics of a group of entities which make it possible for us to think of them in a collective way and under a collective label. In archaeology the type concept will nearly always involve two components: a mental picture of what the type members will look like (type identity), and ideas about where the members are likely to be found, what function they may have performed, and other associations and inferences (type meaning). The nature of type concepts will be much more fully considered in Chapters 4, 5, and 6.

Type description. If a type concept is to be shared between two or more individuals, it must first be communicated in the form of a type description. This is a verbal and/or pictorial representation of the type concept which depicts as many of its known characteristics as possible. Type descriptions will be more fully discussed in Chapters 6 and 15.

Type definition. Every type necessarily has a diagnostic attribute or diagnostic attribute cluster; that is, a recognizable quality or qualities that set it apart from all other types. We therefore say that every type is theoretically capable of having a type definition: a statement or depiction of its diagnostic features which is sufficient to distinguish it verbally and/or pictorially from all other types. In archaeology, as we will see in Chapter 15, most types are never given a formal or explicit definition, even though

Table 1. *The essential elements of "typehood"*

Mental elements	Physical elements	Representational elements
Type concept	Type members	Explicit type definition
Type category		Type description
Implicit type definition		Type name
		Type label

it should theoretically be possible to do so. We are therefore obliged to say that most archaeological types have an unstated or implicit definition. Type definitions are more fully discussed in Chapters 6 and 15.

Type label. Although it is not a theoretical necessity, useful types are nearly always given an identifying label consisting of a letter, number, word, or words. These labels make it possible to communicate the type concept from one person to another merely by stating, writing, or exhibiting the label, without having to repeat the full type description. In our usage a type label differs from a type name in that it is purely arbitrary, and does not involve any component of description. Thus, any label we like can be given to any type (cf. Dunnell 1971b: 58–9). In the Medieval Nubian Pottery Typology, "W14" is the label attached to the pottery ware that we have described in Appendix B of the present book.

Type name. A type name performs the same function as a type label; that is, it provides a shorthand means for the communication of a type concept from one person to another. However, it differs from a type label in that it involves a certain element of description, and therefore is not wholly arbitrary. "Kayenta black-on-white" is an example of a type name widely employed in the American Southwest (see Colton and Hargrave 1937: 217–18), in which "black-on-white" describes a specific identifying feature of the type. Consciously or unconsciously, type names may influence the choice of entities that are subsequently assigned to the type (see Chapter 10); therefore, unlike type labels, they must be chosen with considerable care (cf. Foucault 1973: 139).

In most typological systems, the individual types are given either labels or names, but not both. In the Medieval Nubian Pottery Typology and certain other systems, however, types are given both labels and names. The ware (type) which is described in Appendix B has the label "W14" and the name "Terminal Christian white ware." For more on labeling and naming see Chapter 10.

Type descriptions, type definitions, type labels, and type names are, collectively, the representational aspects of "typehood."

Type category. According to our usage, every type is by definition a sorting category: that is, it is a theoretical "pigeonhole" into which entities (type members) can be placed in order to differentiate them in some meaningful way from other entities which are members of other types (see Chapter 4). We cannot appropriately say that entities are placed in a type concept, type description, or type definition; we therefore refer to the "pigeonhole" aspect of any type as the type category.

Type members. A type member is an entity that has been identified as exemplifying the characteristics of a particular type, and has therefore been put into that type category. In archaeological classifications, type members are nearly always artifacts or fragments of artifacts. They are, collectively, the physical aspect of "typehood."

The nature of entities

For the sake of conceptual clarity it seems desirable to say something at this point about the nature of the things that are classified and sorted in a typology (see Chapter 4). We have referred to these before they are classified as entities, and after they are classified as type members. It will be obvious that they are not necessarily physical objects. The classification of musical compositions into symphonies, concertos, sonatas, and the like is a genuine typology, and the classified entities have a physical (that is, auditory) dimension, but they cannot properly be called objects. In addition, there are classifications of things like philosophies and literary *genres* which have no physical dimension at all.

Even where physical objects are involved, as in archaeology, it may be argued that we are not classifying the objects but some kind of mental or physical representation of them. In house and grave typologies, for example, it is sometimes only the plan of the house or grave that is classified, and not the complete building or interment. These plans cannot properly be referred to as objects, since they are two-dimensional representations. The same is essentially true when we classify pictographs, or rock drawings.

The issue is somewhat more complex in the case of artifact typologies. Here common sense would suggest that we are classifying and sorting real, three-dimensional objects. It can nevertheless be argued that, in the processes of classifying and sorting, our mind's eye does not really see the complete object, but only those external aspects of it which bear some resemblance to other objects, and which therefore give it a type identity. In short, what we are classifying are not really things but incomplete mental representations of them, having typological identity but not individual identity (see below).

The relationship between physical objects and their representations is interesting philosophically, and will be explored from that perspective in Chapter 12. However, it is not of practical consequence to the present discussion. We will use the term entity to designate whatever is classified and sorted, without considering whether this refers to objects, to their representations, or to both. In the case of artifact typologies the classified entities (type members) can for our purposes be considered as physical objects, and we have therefore referred to them as the physical aspect of "typehood."

The relationship between types and their components
According to our view, a useful archaeological type must have all of the mental, physical, and representational components that we listed earlier. That is, it must involve a concept, a description, a stated or implied definition, a label and/or name, a categorical identity, and actual, physical members. A mental conception of a type (i.e. a type concept) for which no physical exemplars have been found is what we call an unrealized type, while a collection of similar objects which have been grouped together and labeled, but for which no type concept or description has been formulated, is an unformulated type. We will suggest in later chapters that computer clustering programs often produce unrealized types, while a few old-fashioned, intuitive archaeologists operate with unformulated types. In neither case do these types have practical utility, at least for anyone but the makers. In our view they are not types in the fullest sense of the word.

It follows from the above that, from our point of view, every type is both discovered and invented. The physical members of the type (at least in the case of archaeological types) are discovered, while the mental conception and the description of the type are formulated, or in other words invented, by human minds. From this perspective there can be no such thing as an "undiscovered type," in the fullest sense. There are only undiscovered type members, which may belong either to already formulated types or to types that have not yet been formulated. In the latter case we may speak of unformulated types, consisting of undiscovered members.

It should be evident by now that the relationship between a type and its constituent elements is not a simple one. In the case of types and type members, the relationship is somewhat analogous to that between a human society and its members. Every society has members, but the whole is something more than the sum of the parts, as sociologists have long insisted (e.g. Durkheim 1898). There is a sense of collective identity which is both more and less than the sum of the individual members' identities, and the society as a whole behaves in ways that are not always reflected in the behavior of individual members.

Summarizing what we have thus far said about types, we may repeat that each type (or at least each archaeological type) is composed of a group of things, plus our ideas about the things as a group, plus the words and/or pictures in which those ideas are expressed. The relationship between these different aspects of "typehood" is not an immutable one, such that any one of them is wholly determined by any other. The physical entities incorporated in any type do not change, but our ideas about them – our conception of their collective identity – may change either as we come to study them in more detail, or as we add more entities to the original collection. The words in which we express our ideas may also change, as the ideas themselves change or simply because we think of better ways in which to express them (see Leach 1976: 19–22). It is also true that we can relabel or rename our types, without necessarily affecting either the type concept or the type description.

We have to recognize therefore that types as wholes are mutable, even though their physical members are not. This characteristic will be discussed at much greater length in Chapter 5.

The essential properties of types

In addition to the elements that we have just discussed, useful types must also possess two essential properties: those of identity and meaning. These terms must likewise be briefly defined in the present chapter, for they are critical to much of the argument that we will offer later about the practicality and purpose of types.

Identity. We say that a thing has identity when it is consistently identifiable; that is, when it has distinctive visible, tactile, or other sensory properties (criteria of identity) which make it distinguishable from all other things, on the basis of sensory evidence. We will see a little later that individual entities, or type members, usually have both individual identity and typological identity, while types as wholes have what we call type identity. These terms will be more fully defined in the next section.

Meaning. We will say that a thing is meaningful (has meaning) when it has consistent, known associations above and beyond the denotata (criteria) of its identity. That is, we know that the thing always behaves in a certain way or occurs in certain contexts, even though this cannot be determined merely by looking at it. Meaning, then, refers to the association between things and our ideas about them. It should be clear in this context that we are not concerned with the meaning of words as such (semantics), but with the meanings attached to things. Questions of semantics, although philosophically interesting, have no immediate relevance to our theories about classification; they will, however, be briefly considered in Chapter 12.

As in the case of identity, individual entities, or type members, may have both individual meanings and typological meanings, while types as wholes have what we call type meanings. While an entity can have only one individual and one typological identity, however, any entity or type can have more than one meaning. It is also possible for an entity or type to have a meaning that is not known. These circumstances oblige us to introduce two additional conceptual terms: those of significance and relevance.

Significance. We will say that a thing is significant when for one reason or another we know that it has meaning, even though we may not know what the meaning is. For example, if we find a pottery type exhibiting highly complex and unusual decoration, we will usually be justified in assuming that it was made only during some limited period of time in the past, and is therefore chronologically significant. However, we will not know its chronological meaning until we have determined the actual dates of its manufacture.

For purposes of this discussion we can speak of three different kinds of significance: intuitive, empirical, and statistical. A thing has intuitive significance for us if it makes a sensory impression so sharp that we instinctively decide that it must have some meaning. As we will see in a moment, these impressions are what we call gestalts. A thing has empirical significance if we have discovered through experience that it has meaning, and specifically what its meaning is. It has statistical significance if it has two or more attributes occurring together so consistently that we know that their co-occurrence cannot be due to chance. We therefore deduce that some causal factor has been at work, even though we may not know what it is (cf. Salmon 1982: 131–2).

Relevance. We will say that a thing is relevant when it has a known meaning with reference to some specific purpose, which in our usage always means the purpose for which a particular typology was made. A pottery type which is known to have been used for transporting wine is a relevant type with reference to a functional pottery classification (see Chapter 18), but it is not relevant with reference to a chronological classification unless we have also determined the dates of its manufacture.

It is necessary to stress that the properties of identity and meaning that we have been discussing here are essential properties of useful types, but not necessarily of all types. It is possible in theory to conceive of types having either no identity or no meaning. For example, a pottery type consisting of all the vessels made at the site of Pueblo Bonito between A.D. 1000 and 1025 would be enormously meaningful, if there were any way of identifying such vessels. Unfortunately there are no known criteria of identity for these vessels, and we therefore have to refer to the "type" in question as an unidentifiable, or occult, type. On the other hand we could, if we wished, postulate a pottery type made up of sherds of a particular shape. The members of this "type" would be readily identifiable by their shape, but would almost certainly have no discoverable meaning. We would therefore have to refer to them as comprising a meaningless type. It is hardly necessary to repeat that neither occult types nor meaningless types possess any practical utility for the field archaeologist.

Individual and typological identities

The concepts of identity, meaning, significance, and relevance are all applicable either to individual things (entities) or to groups of things (types). The relationships between individual and group identity, and between individual and group meanings, must be clarified here. As we will see in Chapter 24, the failure to distinguish between individual and typological identities, and even more between individual and typological meanings, has been a source of considerable confusion in the development of typological theory.

Individual identity. At least in the natural world, few physical things are identical in every detail with any other physical thing. In other words, nearly every physical entity has certain properties that make it distinguishable from all other entities. The sum of these properties constitutes its individual identity.

Typological identity. Every classified entity has certain properties that identify it as a member of a type, and which at the same time distinguish it from the members of other types. The sum of the properties that
identify any entity as a type member constitutes its typological identity. An
entity may have more than one typological identity only if it belongs to
different types in two or more different typologies.

Individual meaning. Most things have meanings attached to
them as individual entities, which are not shared in any consistent way with
other entities. For example, a pottery vessel may be found buried in a grave.
This circumstance gives the vessel an individual meaning as a grave offering, but does not at the same time identify it as a member of any particular
pottery type. The vessel may have other individual meanings as well, if, for
example, it was deliberately broken in a particular way. Many and perhaps
most entities have more than one individual meaning.

Typological meaning. Every classified entity has certain meanings that attach to it because it has been identified as a member of a particular type. For example, a particular pottery vessel may have been bought
from a commercial dealer, who can give no information about the time of
its manufacture. If, however, the vessel can be assigned to a type which is
known to have been made between A.D. 1200 and 1300, then we assume
that the individual vessel was also produced during that interval of time.
This is a typological meaning. An entity can have several typological meanings, either because the type to which it belongs has several type meanings
(see below), or because the entity belongs to different types in two or more
different typologies.

We are obliged to use slightly different terms when we speak of the
collective identities and meanings of types as wholes, in contrast to the
identities and meanings of their individual members. We will speak in
these instances of type identities and type meanings.

Type identity. Type identity refers to the sum of all the diagnostic characteristics of a type that can be described or illustrated, and that
make it possible to formulate a type description different from all other
type descriptions. Type identity is not, precisely speaking, the sum of all
the typological identities of individual type members, for the type concept
and its identifying features must be formulated before individual entities
can be assigned to it. That is, it is the identifying features (type identity) of

the type concept as a whole that determine the typological identities of the members.

Type meaning refers to any collective meaning or meanings that attach to a type concept; that is, anything we know about the type which cannot be determined simply by looking at its members. A type, as well as its individual members, may have several meanings. For example, we may know that a pottery ware was made at a particular factory, that it was made between certain dates, that it was made by specialized craftsmen, and that it was regularly traded over a particular area. All of these are type meanings. Usually there will be one or more type meanings that are specifically relevant to the purpose for which the typology was made; e.g. the dates of manufacture for a pottery ware are specifically relevant to a typology made for dating purposes. We will refer to any type meaning which is relevant to the purpose of a typology as type relevance.

4

PERCEPTUAL AND CONCEPTUAL FOUNDATIONS

In Chapter 3 we discussed the physical, mental, and representational elements that go into the making of a type. Of these it is the mental elements that are the most problematical, and also, surprisingly, the least considered in the literature on typologies. As Lakoff (1984: 22) observes, "the classic theory of categories is not a cognitive theory. It is a theory about things as they are in the world, not about how the mind makes sense of the world." He goes on to remark: "I do not know why the . . . theory of categories should be an Aristotelian one. But it is an issue that cognitive scientists need to address" (*ibid.*: 26).

The mental dimensions of typehood will be our concern in the next two chapters. In the present chapter we will discuss the relationship between types and other, related mental constructs: concepts, categories, and classes. Our purpose here is not to develop a theory of knowledge or of classification, but simply to establish working definitions for a great many terms that we will employ later in the book. Much of what we say here is not critical to the arguments that we will present later in regard to the use of types; our purpose is simply to make our meanings clear. We must stress once again that our definitions do not necessarily coincide with those of other authors (see Chapter 1).

Types and scientific thought

Science is defined more by its purposes (ends) than by its methods (means). There is no generally accepted, orthodox definition of what is and is not science, and by the same token the boundaries between science and non-science are difficult to draw. In our modern industrialized world there is a large, self-labeled category of Science (with a capital S), but in everyday life there is probably a great deal of additional knowledge-seeking, experimentation, and ratiocination that is sufficiently rigorous that it deserves to be called scientific (cf. Ellen 1979: 5–7). In traditional and primitive societies, where there is no self-labeled category of Science, there

39

has been much scholarly disagreement as to what should and should not be called by that name (Lowie 1924: 136–52; Malinowski 1948: 25–36; Tylor 1958: 112–36; J. Needham 1969; Lévy-Bruhl 1985).

It follows from the above that there can be no sharp distinction between scientific thinking and other kinds of thinking. Whatever our problems may be, we have only the same human mental equipment with which to attack them. Traditionally, in scientific thought, we use only a certain part of our mental equipment – the rational as opposed to the mystical – but that is true also in many areas of everyday activity. Moreover, in science we certainly do not disregard intuition. Many scientific insights have begun as flashes of intuition, the source of which we are later at a loss to identify (Vygotsky 1962: 82–118; Hempel 1966: 15–18; Margolis 1987). The intuitions merely signify that our minds have made some kind of connection between events or phenomena at a level below that of conscious reflection.

What is true of scientific thought in general is true of classificatory thought in particular. All of the world's peoples classify nearly everything in their experience, for every human language involves a large measure of classification – of animals, plants, people, and every kind of inanimate thing (Jevons 1874, II: 344). We will refer to these everyday classifications, which are deeply embedded in the structure of everyday language, as vernacular or folk classifications. So-called scientific classifications are not qualitatively different from vernacular classifications (cf. Ellen 1979: 5–7; Canfield 1981: 23); indeed, the circumstances attending their inception are often virtually the same in the two cases (cf. Lakoff 1984: 24–6; also Chapter 5). Classifications in this respect are not different from other kinds of language. In and of themselves they are not inherently either scientific or non-scientific; we may describe them rather as pre-scientific. That is, they are a necessary tool which must be present before many kinds of scientific endeavor can be carried out. Classifications may be said to *become* scientific when they are put effectively to scientific uses.

What is true of classifications is, of course, true also of their constituent classes, or types. Precisely the same type may be put either to scientific or to non-scientific uses, and it may accordingly be designated either as a scientific type or as a vernacular type. In archaeology, for example, types of arrowheads are often used as criteria of identity for prehistoric "cultures," or for the dating of prehistoric sites. These are generally accepted as scientific purposes, and the arrowhead types themselves may therefore be considered scientific. On the other hand private collectors of arrowheads will often divide them into morphologically similar groups (i.e. essentially types) in order to mount them in an aesthetically pleasing way on a display board. Their groupings may be identical with those of the professional archaeologist, but since the purpose of the grouping is non-scientific, the types themselves must be considered non-scientific.

In order to serve scientific purposes, types must usually be described somewhat more precisely, and/or differentiated somewhat more rigorously than is true in the case of vernacular classification. To this extent we may say that there is a difference between scientific types and vernacular types, but it is obviously a difference in degree and not in kind. Throughout the remainder of this book we will make no further effort to differentiate between scientific types and vernacular types.

The mental steps to "typehood"

Since scientific thought is not qualitatively different from other thought, it behoves us to begin by considering certain basic features that are common to all human cognition, and that contribute to the formation of type concepts. We saw in Chapter 3 that type concepts are not precisely synonymous with types, but they are one of the essential components of what we have called "typehood."

Type concepts are, in our view, the products of a succession of perceptual and conceptual processes, involving increasing degrees of abstraction and categorization. The processes we will discuss are those that we call recognition, imprintation, association, symbolization, abstraction, classification, and segregation. These processes combine in the formation of various mental constructs which we call sensory perceptions, sensory images, gestalts, concepts, words, categories, classes, and types. Since our concern in this book is ultimately with archaeological typologies, we will consider here only the cognition, symbolization, and classification of material things; that is, visible or tangible entities.

Sensory perceptions involve only the single mental process of pattern recognition (cf. especially Margolis 1987: 1–8). For each of us individually, a sensory perception takes place whenever our minds are able to separate out an object, person, act, or feeling from the undifferentiated stream of sensory experience, and to focus on it independently of its surroundings.

Sensory images. Sensory perception may cease as soon as the stimulating object or experience has been removed, but a sensory image often remains in the mind, and can be recalled at a later time. (It should be evident here that we are not speaking of images purely in a visual sense; there can also be auditory, tactile, and/or olfactory images.) The mental process involved is that of imprintation. This is usually a necessary first step in concept formation, especially where conceptions of material things are concerned. However, in and of itself a sensory image has identity but no meaning, as we defined those terms in Chapter 3. That is, a sensory image is something we can recognize, but it does not necessarily have any associations for us above and beyond the features of its identity. Hence it is not a true concept in our sense.

In the world of everyday thought we doubt if there are many sensory images that are not also concepts, except perhaps in the minds of very young infants. Our associative powers are so strong that we are apt to attach some kind of meaning to almost anything we can consistently recognize; conversely, we don't bother to recognize things that have no meaning for us. A case in point is our dealings with our fellow humans: we seldom bother to imprint their names or faces on our memories unless there is some reason to do so.

The distinction between sensory images and concepts is nevertheless worth making in principle, because artificial intelligence is quite capable of identifying attribute combinations or object combinations that are recognizable but have no meaning. We will suggest later (Chapter 23) that many computer-generated "classes" and "types" are in this category.

Gestalts. A gestalt, in our usage, is a sensory image so sharp and distinct that we invest it with immediate, intuitive significance, simply because of its distinctness. We are here speaking of what we call intuitive gestalts, as opposed to acquired gestalts which we will discuss in Chapter 5. We may say therefore that intuitive gestalts have identity and significance, but, at least initially, they have no specifiable meaning.

On this point we are in partial disagreement with the structuralist view of Gestalt psychologists (e.g. Köhler 1940; 1947), who hold that Gestalts are the result of inherent mental templates common to all mankind. They further suggest that Gestalts have for all of us a common associative meaning, which is pre-programmed into our minds, so to speak. This may be true in a limited number of instances; for example, there seem to be associations with certain colors that are common to all or nearly all peoples (V. Turner 1967: 59–92). We believe, however, that for the most part gestalt-formation varies from person to person and from culture to culture, and that the largest number of gestalts have, in the beginning, no meaning apart from their identity. To emphasize that our usage of this term is not the same as that of Gestalt psychologists, we spell it throughout this work without its capital G.

We do agree with the psychologists that gestalts are often, though by no means always, the beginning step in concept-formation. (We will argue in Chapter 5 that this is true not only in everyday thought, but also in scientific classifications.) According to our usage, gestalts become concepts when we are able to attach definite associative meanings to them.

Concepts, then, are sensory images to which we attach some meaning above and beyond the denotata of their identity. (We will not be concerned for the moment with abstract concepts that have no sensory identity.) They are formed through the combination of recognition and association. Concepts are the essential building blocks of all human thought (Jevons 1874, II: 346; Vygotsky 1962; Johnson-Laird and Wason 1977a: 169).

The processes of concept-formation have been extensively studied by experimental psychologists, especially among children and adolescents (e.g. Ach 1921; Piaget 1926; 1928; 1929; etc.; Vygotsky 1962; Johnson-Laird and Wason 1977b), but they are still far from clearly understood (cf. especially Vygotsky 1962; Johnson-Laird and Wason 1977a; Margolis 1987). It is evident, however, that the process is not a uniform one; concepts can be acquired in a number of different ways. An initial distinction can be made between concepts that we learn through formal instruction or precept, and those that take form spontaneously through our individual powers of observation and association (Vygotsky 1962: 86). More often than not spontaneous concepts are formed unconsciously; hence the difficulty in studying them. As we suggested earlier, we believe that spontaneous concepts often begin with gestalts, to which we subsequently attach associative meanings.

Words and language. If concepts are the essential building-blocks of thought, words are the essential building-blocks of communication. Spontaneous concepts may be usable by their originators without any formal definition or labeling, although how far thought can progress in the absence of language is debatable (Sapir 1921: 14–17; Vygotsky 1962: 58–9; Cole and Scribner 1974: 39–60). It is evident in any case that our concepts cannot be shared with any second person until we have developed some way of communicating them, and that way nearly always involves some kind of shorthand labeling. The process involved is that of symbolic expression, or symbolizing.

43

In ordinary or natural language, labeled concepts are synonymous with words. That is, every word is a label for a concept at some level of abstraction. Sometimes a part either of the identity or of the meaning of a concept may be incorporated in the label (e.g. "whitewash," "hatbox"). The examples just cited also illustrate how words may be run together to form descriptive labels for concepts involving a combination of other concepts. This kind of polymorphic labeling is very common in formal languages such as scientific classifications, in which the classes are sometimes given quite complex identifying labels. In no case, however, does the label convey the full inventory either of defining characteristics or of associated meanings (cf. Dunnell 1971b: 58–9).

We may say therefore that words have the three characteristics of identity, meaning, and labeling, each of which must be learned independently of the others. We will pursue this issue further in the next chapter.

A language (or more properly a lexicon) is simply the sum total of all the labeled concepts (words) used and understood by any individual or group. It is basically a congeries of words, without boundaries, without rules for generating new words (except phonological rules), and without much internal consistency. It is capable of infinite extension in any direction, to accommodate new experiences, and the addition of new words does not necessarily affect the definition or the meaning of existing ones. There are no consistent rules of concept formation or naming, except for phonological rules that limit the sound combinations that may be used in naming. There is a very high degree of overlap in meaning between different words; sometimes different words have precisely the same meaning, and sometimes the same word has a variety of meanings. Finally, the various words are at all different levels of abstraction from the most concrete to the most abstract, and there is no formal differentiation of words according to their level of abstraction. All of these are characteristics that distinguish a language from a classification in the strict sense.

Categories. Most, but not quite all, words involve some degree of abstraction. They are labels applied to two or more things which, in a given context, have precisely the same meaning for us, but which are not identical in all of their characteristics. We give the things a common name on the basis of common features which we consider important, ignoring other, divergent features which we do not consider important. Words involving some degree of abstraction are not merely labeled concepts; they are labeled categories. The main exceptions are proper names that apply

44

to one thing or to one person only, so that no abstraction or generalization is involved.

Abstraction may create problems of recognition that do not arise in the case of gestalts and concrete concepts. Since the entities in any category have some but not all of their characteristics in common, we have to learn to see them selectively, so to speak, focusing upon the characteristics which are the determinants of category membership while ignoring those that are not (cf. Foucault 1973: 132–3). The process of abstraction tends to make meanings clearer while it makes identities fuzzier, so that the higher the level of abstraction, the greater is the possibility for error or ambiguity in category recognition. It is possible to differentiate much more clearly between *Pinus ponderosa* and *Pinus edulis* than it is between a tree and a shrub, for example.

Classes and classification. A language, we said, is a congeries of labeled concepts, most of which are categories involving some degree of abstraction. A classification, however, is a matched set of partially contrasting categories, roughly at the same level or levels of abstraction, which exist in what has been called "balanced opposition" to one another. We will refer to the process of making a classification as classifying. Note, therefore, that in this book "classification" does not refer to a process, but only to the result of the classifying process. We will refer to the individual concepts in a classification as classes.

A classification differs from a natural language in a number of important respects (cf. Foucault 1973: 134). First, it is finite. Every classification is a classification of some things and not of others. The boundaries of what is classified may be determined in any of a variety of ways, and may be based either on internal or on external criteria. Internal criteria are those discoverable by examination of the things being classified; on this basis we may develop a classification of all pottery or of all stone objects, for example. External criteria are those relating to the context of the things being classified; on this basis we may classify all of the objects found in a particular site, or made during a particular era, or in the possession of a particular museum. (We will see in Chapter 14 that most archaeological classifications involve a combination of internal and external criteria.) The boundaries of a classification are usually rather flexible, allowing for the inclusion of new classes, sometimes involving new criteria of identity.

While the identity of classes is absolute, their meaning (unlike that of words in a natural language) is relative. That is, it is possible to lay down absolute criteria of identity for any class, but the class has meaning only in relation to other classes in the same system (cf. Dunnell 1971b: 56–8). Thus, there is no such thing as a one-class classification. Part of the significance of Class A is simply that it is not Class B, C, or D.

This means that classes, unlike many categories in natural language, have negative as well as positive defining criteria. Class A_1 is included in Classification A because it has the attributes that are common to all members of Classification A, but it is distinguished from Class A_2 because it lacks the defining characteristics of Class A_2.

Another way of making the same point is to say that classes have both internal cohesion and external isolation (Cormack 1971: 329), in contrast to the labeled categories in a natural language which are distinguished on the basis of internal cohesion alone. As an example of the latter, the standard textbook definition of anthropology is "the study of man," a characterization that is accurate so far as it goes, but is quite insufficient to set anthropology apart from sociology, psychology, political science, or history. A *classification* of social sciences would have to define anthropology much more explicitly and exclusively.

The requirement of internal cohesion and external isolation means that, in theory, classes have both central tendencies and boundaries. In practice, however, the former are usually much more clearly recognizable and more important than the latter (cf. Clarke 1968: 196). So long as they serve only the purpose of communication, classifications (like natural languages) can sustain a certain degree of ambiguity. Thus the boundaries between classes (as for example between color categories) are often far from sharp, and there may be entities that do not fall very obviously into any of the named categories. When nothing practical is at stake, however, we are content to say "sort of a brownish yellow," and hope that this conjures up an image in the hearer's mind that is reasonably close to our own.

In a classification there are necessarily some generative rules – at least rules of thumb – for forming new classes. The attributes chosen and not chosen in defining new classes will have to be at least partially the same as those used in defining the existing classes. Usually, too, there are rules of thumb in regard to class nomenclature, so that the class labels have a certain degree of semantic correspondence.

There is one other important point to be made about classifications, in contrast to natural language. Either the constituent classes are all considered to be at more or less the same level of abstraction, or else differences in level of abstraction are indicated in a formal hierarchy (e.g. species grouped into genera and genera into orders). Biologists and some other scientists are inclined to think of hierarchy as an essential feature of classifications (cf. Mayr 1942: 3–17; Simpson 1945: 14–17; Beckner 1959: 55–80), but this is true only in the case of genetic classifications. There are a great many non-genetic classifications (including most arrowhead typologies, for example) that involve only one level of abstraction (cf. Ellen and Reason 1979: 5, 12–14). We will refer to classifications having a hierarchic dimension as taxonomies, and will discuss them further in Chapter 17.

In sum and in conclusion, we may say that classes are categories having the additional feature of membership in a formal set. (For more on the linguistic aspects of classification see Foucault 1973: 125–65.)

Types and typology. Scientific literature often does not distinguish between classifications and typologies. To us, this distinction is crucial. In our usage, a typology is a particular kind of classification: one designed not merely for categorizing and labeling things, but for segregating them into discrete groups which correspond to our class categories and labels. This process of segregation we call sorting; the things that are classified and sorted we call entities; the categorical groupings into which they are sorted we call types. In brief and in sum, a typology is a particular kind of classification, made for the sorting of entities. A type, unlike other kinds of classes, is also a sorting category.

Before we can proceed further we must first stress the distinction between classifying and sorting, for this is crucial to much of our later argument. Classifying is, very simply, the act of creating categories; sorting is the act of putting things into them after they have been created. One is a process of definition, the other of attribution. The respective activities involved in classifying and in sorting will be discussed in Chapters 15 and 16, and we will see there that the practical problems involved are quite different in the two cases.

Our point for the moment is that classifications which are created for the purpose of sorting – that is, typologies – must have systemic features that are not necessary (though they may be present) in other classifications. First of all it must be clear what is and is not to be sorted; hence the boundaries of the system as a whole must be clearly specified. Second, each object that is sorted must go somewhere; hence the system of categories (types) must be comprehensive. Finally, each entity can be put in one and only one place; hence the types must be mutually exclusive. As a practical necessity in sorting, we have to invest our type categories with sharp boundaries even though no such boundaries may be discoverable empirically. The mental process involved is that of segregation, or partitioning.

Table 2. *Defining properties of sensory images, concepts, words, categories, classes, and types*

Properties shown in Roman type, *associated mental processes in italics*

Sensory images	have *involve*	Identity *recognition*					
Concepts	"	"	+Meaning *association*				
Words	"	"	"	+ Labeling *symboliz-ation*			
Categories	"	"	"	"	+ Abstraction *abstraction*		
Classes	"	"	"	"	"	+ Set member-ship *classifi-cation*	
Types	"	"	"	"	"	"	+ Bounded-ness *segre-gation*

Types and purposes

The sorting factor which is implicit in typologies and types leads us to a final important consideration: typologies and their constituent types, unlike many other classifications, are always made for some purpose or purposes in addition to that of simple communication. The activity of sorting is unnecessary for simple communicative purposes, since we can always communicate our ideas about groups of things without physically clustering or numerically tallying the things themselves.

The proximate purpose of typologies and types is, then, to permit the sorting of entities. Obviously, however, the activity of sorting is not carried out for its own sake; it is done for any of a number of more fundamental purposes such as group comparison or statistical manipulation (see Chapter 13). Our point here is that typologies, unlike many other classifications, are always made for some purpose, which must necessarily be the purpose of some person or persons. In typologies, therefore, subjectivity is inherent and inevitable. It is the purpose of the classifier that dictates the choice of variables and attributes that are to be considered in the typology, and that choice in turn determines the nature of the types that result. A type is therefore set apart from other kinds of classes by the additional features of

Table 3. *Properties of lexicons, classifications, and typologies*

	Bound-aries[1]	Partitions[2]	Abstrac-tion	Defi-nitions	Ambi-guity	Systemic features	Purpose
Lexicons	none	very fuzzy	variable	incon-sistent	high	congeries	communi-cation
Classifi-cations	flexible	somewhat fuzzy	constant	fairly consistent	inter-mediate	set	communi-cation
Typ-ologies	sharp	sharp	constant	consistent	low	system	communi-cation +

[1] Boundaries of system as a whole
[2] Partitions between words, classes, or types

boundedness and purpose. The special systemic features of typologies will be much more fully considered in Chapter 7.

A final important point is that typologies, unlike many other classifications, are always to some extent experimental, at least in their formative stages. They are designed to work for a specific purpose, above and beyond that of communication; whether or not they really do work can usually be determined only through experience (cf. Simpson 1945: 13). This is a point to which we will return again and again in later pages.

In Table 2 we have attempted to show schematically the defining features of sensory images, concepts, words, categories, classes, and types, as well as the mental processes involved in the formation of each. In Table 3 we have contrasted the different characteristics of lexicons, classifications, and typologies. In the next two chapters we will pursue further the relationships between language, classification, and typology.

5

THE DIALECTICS OF TYPE FORMULATION

In the last two chapters we were concerned mainly with establishing definitions, and we discussed types in more or less abstract and theoretical terms. Here we will adopt a more practical perspective, and will explore the actual processes of human thought and activity through which types come into being, or are formulated. We will suggest that the formulation of any type involves a continual feedback, or dialectic, between its physical, mental, and communicative aspects, which we discussed in Chapter 4. At least in open typologies, types evolve through use and experience like the words in any other language (cf. especially Smoke 1932; Vygotsky 1962: 124–30). (In Chapter 18 we will define an open typology as one that is designed to accommodate new finds as well as material already in hand. The great majority of practical typologies are of this kind.) We will also suggest that, like the words in any language, the use and meaning of types has to be learned, and the type labels, identities, and meanings have to be learned independently of one another (cf. Margolis 1987: 48–9).

Ferdinand de Saussure (1966) was the first to recognize that language involves the two aspects which he called *langue* and *parole*. The approximate English equivalents are "language" and "speech," but the conceptual distinction is more clear-cut in French. *Langue* is the cognitive aspect of language: the set of names, rules, and meanings that each of us carries in his head. *Parole* is the performance aspect, denoting the sum of our individual speech acts. De Saussure recognized that there is a continual feedback between structure and performance. *Langue* largely shapes our *parole*, but at the same time we continually reshape the language in the process of using it.

What is true of language generally is also true in the restricted languages of classification and typology (cf. Foucault 1973: 125–65). In the case of the latter, *langue* consists of the underlying structure of the typology, its purpose, the variables and attributes that have been selected in accordance with that purpose, the rules for generating types on the basis of those variables and attributes, and the idealized type conceptions that have been generated thereby. *Parole*, in the case of types, actually involves two different kinds of performance. First, as in all languages, there is communicative performance. Our type concepts have to be put into words before they can be communicated to others (and to a considerable extent even to ourselves), and this process of verbalization itself affects the concepts. We will refer to this as type representation. But in the case of types there is also sorting performance: an ongoing dialogue between ourselves and the artifacts, so to speak. That dialogue may affect our type concepts even more than does the communicative performance.

In this chapter we will review the various steps or stages in the process of type-concept formation. In open typologies it is, we suggest, a continually ongoing process, with no theoretical ending point.

Foreknowledge

Probably no one would undertake to classify anything without some previous ideas about the material in hand, and this foreknowledge may play an important part in the formation of type concepts (cf. Hempel 1966: 13; Hill and Evans 1972: 251–5; Gardin 1980: 82). Foreknowledge may suggest at the outset what are and are not significant variables to be looked at; for example color in the case of pottery but not in the case of projectile points. It may also suggest which variables are and are not practicably classifiable; for example, decorative designs in the medieval Nubian pottery wares but not in the early Egyptian glazed wares (see WYA 1986a: 585–6). Foreknowledge can, at the same time, be incorrect or misleading. WYA could probably not have undertaken the classification of the medieval Nubian wares without the prior knowledge gained in the study of Southwestern pottery (see WYA and N. K. Adams 1959: 17–26), but this knowledge also led to some incorrect assumptions about the variables to be looked at in the study of Nubian pottery (see Chapter 9).

Because of foreknowledge, or conventional wisdom, we suspect that many typologies may contain "soft spots" in the form of unstated and untested assumptions. Very often there is no clear understanding of why particular variables are considered or not considered (cf. Dunnell 1971b: 139–40). Tempering material may be included in pottery type descriptions simply because "archaeologists have found that it's important," without ascertaining whether or not it shows patterned variability in the material being studied in a particular classification. Other typologists interested in the same material are likely to possess the same conventional wisdom, and soft spots may therefore go undetected for years, perhaps until they are spotted by a critic from outside the field. Usually, we imagine, the untested assumptions will be found on examination to be valid, but there may be cases when they are not.

Purpose

The numerous and varied purposes which typologies and type concepts may serve will be discussed in Chapter 13. Here we will anticipate the discussion only to the extent of suggesting that there is surely no typology in existence that serves no purpose at all. Indeed Vygotsky (1962: 54–5) has suggested that this is true of concepts in general; they are always in some way purpose-related. The purpose of the typologist may at times be so embedded in implicit knowledge, or traditional methodology, that he is not consciously aware of it; in other cases it may be so idiosyncratic that it is apparent to the typologist but to no one else.

Consciously or unconsciously, purpose always will, or should, affect the direction that a typology takes (see Sokal 1977: 188–90). It will determine not only the variables that are and are not to be looked at, but also the kinds of attribute clusters that are and are not considered significant (see Chapter 14). The more clearly the typologist is aware of his purpose, the more rationally and systematically he will be able to select variables and to designate types that will be relevant to that purpose. But purposes must not only be conscious; they must also be clearly specific. One of the difficulties besetting recent efforts to classify ancient Egyptian pottery is not that the typologists have no purpose, but that they have too many (cf. Anonymous 1975; Bourriau 1985). They are trying to answer a lot of different and unrelated questions with the same set of types (cf. Brew 1946: 64; Dunnell 1971a: 115; Hill and Evans 1972: 235; Brown 1982: 180).

Collections

Every typology necessarily starts with a collection of material to be classified. The archaeologist can begin the actual process of classifying either by grouping together objects or by grouping together attributes (cf. Cowgill 1982; Hodson 1982; Spaulding 1982; Voorrips 1982: 111; Whallon and Brown 1982: xvi–xvii), but unless he first has some material in hand he will not know what attributes are available to be grouped. Moreover, even if his types are determined initially by some abstract process of attribute grouping, they must in the end be tried out on real objects. The ultimate use of typologies, after all, is not for sorting attributes but for sorting objects.

Collections of material to be classified can originate in all kinds of ways, often involving a considerable element of chance. Regardless of how they have come about, however, initial collections will probably have a major influence on the development of type concepts. It is the variables and attributes observable in this material that necessarily form the basis for our initial type descriptions, and type descriptions, once formulated, can be slow to change. This is probably more true in the case of variables than it is of attributes, since the differences between variables are qualitative rather than quantitative. (In Chapter 14 we will define a variable as some property that is manifest in a number of different ways in the material being classified, and an attribute as one of the specific ways in which it is manifest. "Red" is one of the attributes of the variable "color.")

In our initial collection there may be certain features that do not vary; for example we may find that all of our pottery has a matte finish. We will therefore decide that surface finish is an invariant rather than a variable (see Chapter 14), and will not include it in our type descriptions. But later additions to the collection may include some sherds that are polished or burnished, indicating that there is, after all, variability in surface finish. Having previously excluded this feature from our descriptions, however, we may be slow to recognize that it must be added. On the other hand we will probably have no difficulty in adding new color attributes to our earlier list, or new vessel shapes to our earlier corpus, when new material requires this.

Since initial collections can put an indelible stamp on type concepts, it is important to know as much as possible about their source and their significance. For the archaeologist this can pose a very real problem. He may be working with material from his own excavations, but just as often he is working with museum collections assembled over a long period of time, from a variety of sources, and under a variety of circumstances. It is probable that aesthetic or other judgmental considerations have affected the collecting process in some cases, though to what extent will probably not be known. If aesthetic appeal was considered, then the classifier may be presented with a set of nearly "ideal" type specimens which do not at all reflect the true variability of the material. As a general principle we can observe that the significance of a type depends on the significance of the collection from which it was determined.

Gestalts

When we examine our initial collection of material, it is likely that a few intuitive types will "jump out at us" in the form of intuitive gestalts, as we defined that term in Chapter 3. These are clusters of objects so distinctive that we are sure immediately that they must be significant, even though we have not yet consciously determined what their distinctive features are. In all probability these will become our first types, and the foundation blocks in our typology (cf. Rouse 1939: 11; Gilmour 1940; Krieger 1944: 279–80; Hill and Evans 1972: 235; Gardin 1980: 11; Watson, LeBlanc, and Redman 1984: 203). In this respect we suggest that, in their origins, scientific typologies may not be very much different from folk typologies (cf. especially Berlin 1973; Hunn 1976; Ellen 1979: 5–7).

We do not suggest, as did the German morphological school of classification, that all types disclose themselves through gestalts, or that all gestalts correspond to "real" types (see Riedl 1983). They are merely the most convenient starting points for a process of differentiation that we will discuss in the next section.

In our usage (though not that of Gestalt psychologists or of the German morphological school) gestalts can be acquired as well as intuitive. Types that we have originally determined through a process of conscious analysis acquire a gestalt when we have learned to recognize them at a glance – something that comes about in time through the processes of handling and sorting (cf. especially Margolis 1987: 48–9). We may say that, when they acquire gestalts, our types have in some sense become "real" to us. We will suggest later (Chapter 16) that type gestalts, whether intuitive or acquired, are a practical necessity in large-scale sorting operations.

Differentiation

When types disclose themselves to us in the form of gestalts, the differences between them are so intuitively obvious that we are not likely to analyze them in terms of specific features of dissimilarity. A group of types designated in this manner may be said to make up a congeries, but not a classification. When we have recognized a sufficient number of intuitive types, however, we are sure to begin perceiving also what are the specific features of similarity and dissimilarity between them – the invariants and the variables, as we will designate them in Chapter 14. As we do so our type concepts will come increasingly to focus on features of dissimilarity rather than of similarity. It is through this process of differentiation that our types acquire the important dimension of set-membership (see Chapter 4), and our congeries becomes a classification (cf. also Foucault 1973: 141–3).

Differentiation leads us, consciously or unconsciously, to revise our original type concepts so as to emphasize the differences between types. At the same time, by revealing what are and are not significant variables, it provides a basis for the recognition of new types that did not disclose themselves through gestalts. We suggest that in many typologies the original types began with gestalts, while later types were added through a process of increasingly conscious and systematic differentiation. That is, we begin with a specific, finite assemblage of material to be classified, and from this we first remove the "obvious" types that reveal themselves through gestalts (cf. Deetz 1967: 49–50). Usually we can only proceed so far in this manner, after which we still have a sizable unclassified residue of material which does not obviously "classify itself." Before proceeding further we must now take a closer and more analytical look at our gestalt-types, to see what it is that makes them distinctive. We then attempt to classify the remainder of the material in terms of these same variables (*ibid.*). If we are unable to do so, we are likely to begin considering some additional features that did not figure in our gestalt-concepts, but that came to our attention in the study of the unclassified material (cf. also Daugherty 1978: 169–75). If these new features turn out to be useful (i.e. to show consistent patterning), then we must go back to the original types to see how the newly recognized features are represented there.

It may be noted that, when classification proceeds according to the process of differentiation that has been described here, the role of purpose becomes increasingly clear and increasingly important as the differentiation process continues. When the initial types are formulated intuitively – that is, disclosed by intuitive gestalts – they are usually unaffected by any conscious sense of purpose. In the later stages, when differentiation becomes more rational and systematic, purpose increasingly dictates the choice of variables and attributes to be considered in type formulation.

Differentiation is of course the basic principle in many computer-generated taxonomies, which are formulated by continuous stepwise partitioning (Sokal and Sneath 1963: 48–59; Dunnell 1971b: 98–102; Doran and Hodson 1975: 173–86). In practical typologies, however, the process is rarely that consistent or that automatic.

Representation

At some point in the classifying process – before, during, or after differentiation – it becomes necessary to put our type concepts into a communicable form, by the use of words, pictures, diagrams, or some combination of those things (cf. Foucault 1973: 132–9). This is the process that we call type representation (cf. Gardin 1980: 31–6). Its objective is not to find the most accurate way of representing some nature-given or god-given "reality," for to the typologist "reality" is measured simply in the satisfactory attainment of his objectives. The purpose of representation is to ensure accuracy in relative rather than in absolute terms; that is, to ensure consistency of use. As Foucault (1973: 132) observes, it is a question of bringing our words as closely as possible into harmony with what we think we perceive.

Consistency in the use of language, as Jakobson observed, has an intra-subjective and an intersubjective dimension (see Waugh 1976: 17). The former refers to how consistently each of us as individuals uses the same word to mean the same thing; the latter refers to how consistently groups of people use the same word to mean the same thing (cf. Fish 1978). Both of these aspects are relevant to the development and refinement of type concepts. It is necessary to recall, however, that in the use of typologies we are concerned with consistency in two different areas: in the type concepts that we carry in our heads, and in our sorting decisions.

Undoubtedly there are archaeologists who operate for years with intuitive type concepts that they have never bothered to represent formally in words or pictures. Such concepts are of course usable by no one but their originators, and their reliability even to the originators is somewhat ques-tionable (cf. Vygotsky 1962: 79–80). The Nubian experience of WYA (see Chapter 9) suggests that representation plays a major part in refining the type concepts of the originator himself; that is, it leads to a substantial increase in intrasubjective consistency. The practice in Nubia is to formu-late a complete provisional type description and illustrations for each new pottery ware (type), covering all of the variables listed in Table 5, as soon as the ware has been recognized. In the process it is usually found that some aspects of our initial gestalt are unreliable; that is, some features are less consistently present than a first glance suggested. At the same time representation reveals other features that have not met the eye at first glance.

Representation is of course a critical necessity if the typology is to be used by anyone other than the maker. Since two people rarely see the same material, intuitively, in quite the same way, intersubjective consistency is always potentially a more serious problem than is intrasubjective consist-ency: the potential inconsistency of the individual user is multiplied by the number of different users of the typology. In practical typologies this prob-lem is never fully overcome, but it can be minimized by giving types the most detailed and specific representation that is possible. We will refer to this in Chapter 14 as overdetermination.

In open typologies, initial representations cannot be final, for new material will always suggest refinements and modifications.

Modification through use

The evolutionary developments that we have described up to now all take place in the process of classifying our initial collection of material. Up to this point there is no operational distinction between classifying and sorting, for our classification itself is made by sorting. There hopefully comes a time, however, when we are sufficiently satisfied with our differentiation and description of types, so that we are ready to put them to use in sorting new material, and this inaugurates a new phase in the type dialectic.

New material is never precisely like what we have seen before; it brings both new types and new variants of old types to our attention. As Margolis (1987: 91) observes, "we learn by adapting and tuning patterns we already know to new situations" (see also *ibid.*: 115). Successive experience is likely to reveal fewer and fewer new types, but more and more unsuspected variants of existing ones. Consequently we will probably have to keep on revising our type descriptions as long as we keep on sorting (cf. Vygotsky 1962: 124–30). As the cognitive psychologist Smoke (1932: 5) long ago observed, "As one learns more and more about dogs, his concept of 'dog' becomes increasingly rich, not a closer approximation of some bare 'element'."

Another factor also comes into play at this point: we become aware that the problems involved in sorting are not precisely the same as those involved in type determination. Even the "inventors" of type concepts have to learn to apply them in the sorting of actual objects, and the features that are most useful for this, especially in rapid sorting, are not necessarily those that are most definitive of the types. In time and through experimentation we will develop procedures that permit maximally efficient sorting (cf. J. A. Ford 1962: 15, 18–20; Shepard 1965: 306; Thomas 1972; Whallon 1972: 15), and as we do so our type concepts are likely to change so as to give greater emphasis to features of recognition as opposed to features of definition. This issue will be more fully explored in Chapter 16.

Acquisition of secondary purposes

We have made it clear in earlier discussion that typologies should have a clearly understood purpose, and that they should usually not try to satisfy more than one purpose. It will often happen nevertheless that types that were designated for one purpose will be found useful for others. This will probably be most true of types defined on the basis of a large number of variables, or involving a clustering of a large number of attributes, since different purposes are reflected in the selection of different variables and attributes for classification (see Chapter 14). These types will exhibit the optimum combination of internal cohesion and external isolation, and thus will give the greatest appearance of "naturalness" (see Chapter 23).

As we will suggest in Chapter 13, multiple purposes are most effectively and most legitimately served by the taxonomic (that is, hierarchic) clustering of types rather than by modification of the original type of definitions. Various kinds of relationships – genetic, chronological, or functional – can be indicated by different taxonomic clusterings of the same types, or at different hierarchic levels in the same taxonomy. In the Medieval Nubian Pottery Typology, wares that were originally devised for dating purposes were later grouped into families to indicate their spatial relationships and into ware groups to indicate their genetic relationships (see Chapter 10). These groupings, however, have not involved any redefinition of the individual wares, and it is not necessary to know them in order to use the wares for the original and primary purpose of dating.

Secondary purposes, then, will most likely give added meanings to our types without affecting our conceptions of their identity. However, this is not wholly true with regard to extrinsic, contextual, or functional attributes (see Chapter 14). For example, if pottery types are devised purely for purposes of dating, then the place of their origin is irrelevant and can be omitted from the type descriptions. But if we later find that the types were made in different places, and can be used to measure the volume of trade between regions (an important secondary purpose of the Nubian types, as described in Chapter 11), then places of manufacture and geographical distributions become significant extrinsic features of identity.

Once in a great while, the primary purpose of a classification may itself change over time. The classic example is the Linnean biological taxonomy, which began as a purely morphological classification and became, after Darwin, a phylogenetic one (Mayr 1942: 108–13; Simpson 1945: 4; Sears 1950: 51; Shepard 1965: 308). Any such change should ideally require at least a reconsideration of the definition of each individual type, but typological inertia may prevent such revisions from taking place in practice. In the case of the Linnean taxonomy, the change from a morphological to a phylogenetic basis appears to have created problems and ambiguity that persist to the present day (cf. Diver 1940; Simpson 1945: 4–5; Mayr 1949; Dunnell 1971b: 66–8; Holsinger 1984).

An important point to note in conclusion is that types, like other words, are in the public domain; they do not remain the exclusive property of their originators. If they prove to have any utility they will eventually pass into the general scientific discourse, and thereafter may acquire new definitions, meanings, and even purposes that were neither intended nor desired by the original makers. It is very doubtful, for example, that Linnaeus would have approved of the transformation of his taxonomy from a morphological to a phylogenetic basis (Mayr 1942: 108–13; Simpson 1945: 4).

The necessity of learning

We have tried to suggest in these pages that the making and use of type concepts involves a never-ending process of learning, just as does the use of words in a natural language. In language we are constantly discovering new circumstances in which to use our existing vocabulary, and at the same time we continually encounter new and appropriate usages in the speech and writing of others. But with typologies we have in addition to learn to sort, and skill in this usage can no more be learned from "grammars" and "dictionaries" than can the use of any other language. Precisely formulated type descriptions and illustrations can be helpful and even necessary, but at the same time there is no substitute for hands-on practice. As J. A. Ford (1962: 15) put it, "There is no magical archaeological machine that may be fed potsherds and, at the turning of a crank, produce valid types neatly arranged in chronological order. There is no substitute for thorough study of the material and the monkey-like procedure of learning what we want to know by trial and error" (cf. also Shepard 1965: 306; Thomas 1972; Whallon 1972: 15). As Ford clearly implied, the learning process is just as incumbent on the originators of types as it is on those who begin using them later. It should further be observed that some people will always have a better aptitude for type-learning than will others, just as some people have a more natural facility for languages. (In Nubia WYA has observed a marked variation in aptitude among different sherd-sorters, and a few otherwise intelligent individuals have proved altogether incapable of learning the types.)

It remains only to note that the labels, identity, and meaning of types must be learned independently of one another, for none of them is wholly implicit in the others. Moreover, three different kinds of learning are involved. The learning of labels is essentially mnemonic or rote, like our initial learning of most words in a natural language. Labels are of course the easiest components of types to learn, and also the least likely to change afterward (unless we find that our original type labels were descriptively inaccurate or inappropriate). The learning of identities on the other hand is a continual process of revision; each time we alter our conceptions of identity we have to unlearn the old ones. We may also change our understanding of the meaning of types, but more often we simply learn new meanings without discarding the old ones, so that the learning process is one of cumulation.

The classificatory dialectic

Typologies are apt to be presented in the literature as *faits accomplis*, if not as received wisdom (cf. Dunnell 1971b: 139; Gardin 1980: 81). We are seldom told how they were made, although now and then we can catch a glimpse of their developmental stages (for example by following the published work of Hargrave and Colton over a period of years; see Hargrave 1932; Colton and Hargrave 1937; Colton 1955; 1956; 1958). We suspect, however, that most practical typologies have evolved in somewhat the fashion that we have envisaged here (cf. also Gilmour 1940; Mayr 1942: 11–17; Krieger 1944: 279–82; Deetz 1967: 49–52). The classifiers have started with a body of material in hand, have had to organize it for some practical and immediate purpose, have reflected on the various possible ways of going about this, have hit on a system that seemed to work (cf. especially Jevons 1874, II: 364–6; Deetz 1967: 49–52), and have ended by erecting an inverted pyramid of concept and theory on the relatively small empirical base of their own experience. Certainly the same holds true in the present book, whose empirical base is the Medieval Nubian Pottery Typology to be described in detail in Part III. Indeed, we doubt that much useful scientific theory or methodology has ever been generated in any other way.

The process that we have been describing throughout this chapter is one of continuing dialectic, or feedback, between our type concepts and our objects (cf. Vygotsky 1962: 79–80, 124). It is also, therefore, a feedback between induction and deduction (see Chapters 6 and 24; also Harris 1980: 8; Watson 1986: 451). In reality it does not matter how the process starts, by object clustering or by attribute clustering (Cowgill 1982; Hodson 1982; Spaulding 1982; Voorrips 1982: 111; Whallon and Brown 1982: xvi–xvii). If we begin with object clusters we will soon have to give them formal representation, and at this point they become in effect attribute clusters, since the type descriptions are stated in terms of attributes. On the basis of those descriptions we will add new material to the original type clusters, and this will eventually require a new description of the enlarged group to take account of newly observed features. If we begin with attribute clusters we will sooner or later have to apply them to the sorting of real objects, and again our notions of what are and are not significant variables, attributes, and attribute clusters are likely to change.

(For the comparable process in biological classification see Mayr 1942: 11–17; Gilmour 1951: 402; in chemistry see Jevons 1874, II: 365–6.)

The evolution of type concepts also involves continuous, simultaneous lumping and splitting. Each time we create a type we are lumping together some objects that are not identical in every detail, and at the same time splitting them off from all other types.

The characteristics as well as the problems of a practical typology can be likened to those in a system of mail sorting. Let us suppose that we have to receive and sort mail for an unknown number of people who are personally unfamiliar to us. The first day's delivery brings a hundred letters, all addressed to the same six individuals: John Doe, Jane Roe, George Smith, Ann Brown, David Jones, and Mary Johnson. So far there is no problem: we put up six boxes, and put the mail in them. The next day's mail brings another hundred letters, half of which are addressed to the same six individuals. Another twenty-five letters are addressed to William Davis, Susan Jordan, and Frederick Anderson, necessitating three new boxes. But then there are twenty-five letters addressed to John H. Doe, G. T. Smith, Miss Ann Brown, and so on. Now begin the problems: new boxes, or new mail in old boxes? If the latter, then we have obviously got to revise the criteria by which we put mail into particular boxes. As the process continues from day to day we will discover fewer and fewer new names, but more and more variants of the existing ones, and each time we will have to decide anew whether to redefine the criteria for existing boxes or to put up new ones. Our problems will be compounded from time to time by such things as misspellings, incomplete addresses, and illegible handwriting. We may even have to face the ultimate sorting problem: a letter addressed to two or more of our individuals.

So long as we go on sorting, either letters or artifacts, the dialectical process will never end. Each new collection will bring some objects that are not quite like anything we have seen before. They must somehow be fitted into the system, but the system itself will also have to be adapted so that they can be. In short and in sum, useful types are necessarily mutable, and useful typologies are always to some extent experimental. As Simpson (1945: 13) puts it, "classification [i.e. typology] is and should be in a state of constant flux."

Learning and communication

The dialectic process that we have been describing here can also be viewed as a dialectic between learning and communication. Before we can classify any material we have first to study it, and we learn about the material and its variability in the course of that study. We then attempt to communicate what we have learned in the form of a classification or typology.

It might be argued that we would learn just as much whether or not we chose to communicate it, but this is never true in practice. Our ideas and perceptions are sharpened and clarified in the process of trying to communicate them, and in many cases this will impel us to go back and reexamine the material itself. Classifying thus involves a continual feedback between learning and communication. It is nevertheless important, for theoretical reasons, to maintain a distinction between the two processes. We will say, in terms of our definitions in Chapter 4, that classifying is a learning and communicating process, but a classification is purely a communicative device (cf. Simpson 1945: 13). The importance of this distinction will appear in the last chapters of our book, when we talk about the relationship between classification and theory.

6

THE NATURE OF TYPES

In the last chapter we saw how types come into being. Here we will consider more fully what their properties are, once they have been formulated. It should be evident from the previous discussion that they are among the most complex of all human mental constructs (cf. Jevons 1874, II: 425–6); so much so that it is often impossible to give them precise or rigorous definition (cf. Simpson 1945: 15–16; Vygotsky 1962: 79).

A preliminary note on terminology
The processes of type formation that we described in the last chapter are in the broadest sense processes of definition. Yet, as we will see presently, archaeological types are almost never defined in the rigorous or formal way required by philosophers and logicians. Consequently, we must be careful in our use of the terms "define" and "definition" in the present work.

We will speak of a type as being defined by certain attributes, if and only if the possession of those attributes is both a necessary and a sufficient condition for the existence of the type. We will say that a definition is a recognized or unrecognized aspect, or component, of every type, in the sense that every type must necessarily have a unique combination of features (diagnostic attributes) that is potentially capable of formal definition. To avoid terminological confusion, we will refer to the process of consciously formulating or expressing a definition as defining. (Note, therefore, that in our usage "defining" refers to a process, "definition" refers to the result of the process.) This will not imply that most type concepts actually came into being through a process of defining, for definitions in archaeology are much more often implicit than explicit. We therefore say that a type is *defined* by its combination of diagnostic attributes, but it is *formulated* and *designated* by the typologist.

We will use formulation (rather than defining) to describe any of the various processes by which type concepts actually come into being – whether by attribute clustering, object clustering, stepwise differentiation, or taxonomic splitting (cf. Dunnell 1971b: 76–84). Designation will refer to the culminating act in type-concept formulation, when we decide that a type is sufficiently "real" or sufficiently useful to deserve a name and a place in the typological system. Once this has happened the type will usually be given formal representation in words and/or pictures, and we will refer to this as description. As we will see presently, the formal representations of archaeological types are nearly always maximal descriptions and not definitions in any rigorous sense. Finally, when types have been named and described, they are used to sort entities, and we will refer to this as type attribution. These processes and their practical consequences will be more fully discussed in Chapters 15 and 16.

The definition paradox

To classify is, in the broadest sense, to define. That is, entities are grouped together on the basis of shared characteristics, and then are given a collective label and description that enables the group or any of its individual members to be recognized, and at the same time to be differentiated from other groups. Yet very few types are ever defined in a formal or rigorous sense, nor is it possible to state in abstract terms exactly what a type is (cf. Klejn 1982: 18–19). Individually, types are given verbal representation in the form of extended and detailed descriptions rather than formal definitions. Collectively, it is not possible to state what constitutes a type because the criteria of "typehood" are not uniform; they vary from system to system, and even from type to type in the same system. We will discuss this factor and its significance a little later.

It is important to notice that the problems of defining types in the abstract and in individual cases are not the same. At this point we can observe a fundamental difference between the typological debates that have flourished among biologists and among archaeologists. The biologists have been concerned primarily with the issue of what, in the abstract, constitutes a species (Dobzhansky 1937; Huxley 1940; Mayr 1942: 102–22; Simpson 1945: 15–16); they have argued less often about whether Canis familiaris or Felis leo are or are not legitimate species. On the other hand debates among archaeologists, at least until the recent past, have much more often been over the legitimacy of individual types (cf. Gladwin 1943: 49–54; Brew 1946: viii) rather than over the type concept itself.

There has been, at times, an assumption that the problem of defining "type" and the problems of defining "types" are two aspects of the same thing, and that solving the first will automatically take care of the second (cf. Wheat, Gifford, and Wasley 1958: 38; Clarke 1968: 187; Whallon

64

1972). At least in practical typologies this is not the case. While rigor of description is undoubtedly important, no amount of rigor in specifying in the abstract what constitutes a type will necessarily make it easier to decide in particular cases if a group of objects is sufficiently different from other groups of objects to merit designation as a separate type. As we have written elsewhere (EWA and WYA 1987: 17),

> one expects only a rather loose connection between general type definitions and the individual type concepts that fall under them. For example, one would not expect a change in the definition of *biological species* to lead to a radical change in the description of *Eschscholtzia californica*, or in the laboratory and/or field techniques that are used to identify this plant. In fact one could argue that the shoe is on the other foot: it is the individual species concept that is primary and any changes that are proposed at the more abstract level of *species in general* must not radically tamper with the individual species distinctions that are now recognized. [emphasis in the original]

Why are types so hard to define? This question has troubled philosophers and scientists for more than a hundred years (cf. Jevons 1874, II: 344–426; Simpson 1945: 15–16; Lakoff 1984: 22–6). It lies at the heart of the Typological Debate that perennially flourishes among archaeologists, and that we will be discussing in Chapter 22. In the course of the debate there have been many programmatic statements about what types are and how they should be made, yet no uniform set of rules or procedures has proved capable of generating uniformly useful typologies for all different purposes (cf. Dunnell 1986: 150).

In earlier chapters we have already hinted at some of the sources of ambiguity. We noted in Chapter 4 that one of the essential features of typologies is that of comprehensiveness, or universality. Within any specified set of boundaries (ceramics, lithics, etc.) we insist that if anything is to be classified, everything must be classified. More often than not this will prove feasible in practice only if we do not try to classify everything according to precisely the same criteria. Whatever rules of determination or inclusion we may choose, it is probable that they will prove useful in classifying some objects and not others.

In Chapter 5 we suggested that many typologies are generated by a process of stepwise differentiation, beginning with a few intuitively obvious types and proceeding to the differentiation of other types by an increasingly formal analysis of attributes. It is precisely this approach to classification which leads, in most cases, to the use of shifting criteria of type differentiation. At each stage of the differentiation process (except the last) there will remain a certain residue of material that has not yet been classified, precisely because it is not classifiable according to the criteria that have so far been applied (cf. also Deetz 1967: 50). If this material is to be classified at all, it will therefore require the introduction of new criteria of differentiation. We may say as a general rule, therefore, that each stage in the differentiation process may involve the introduction of one or more new variables or attributes. The end product is a polythetic classification, in which types are identified on the basis of a certain overall set of variables and attributes, but no one variable or attribute is necessary for the definition of any type. This point will be further elaborated in a later section.

The important point to notice is that, according to the procedure we have described here, types are commonly generated by differentiation, not by definition. The term "definition" can be applied only to those specific features of any type which serve to distinguish it from all other types. Yet we rarely specify precisely what these are, partly because they are so variable from type to type and partly because our type concepts are continually changing through use (see Chapter 5). Moreover, definitions in the strict and rigorous sense will usually serve no useful purpose. The practicalities of sorting require that a type be described as fully as possible, not that it be formally defined. This and related issues will be further explored in Chapter 15, and need not occupy us longer here.

The complexity of type concepts

The difficulty of defining types in the abstract is, above all else, an indication of their extreme complexity (cf. Klejn 1982: 35–6). We may suggest that they are neither wholly intuitive nor wholly rational, neither wholly inductive nor wholly deductive, neither wholly natural nor wholly artificial, neither wholly essential nor wholly instrumental. To a large extent these are four ways of saying the same thing, but for the sake of analytical clarity we will address the issues separately in the pages that follow. We will then go on to consider other variables and enigmatic features that add to the difficulty of giving a precise definition of types, either individually or collectively.

Intuition and reason. We suggested in Chapter 5 that the earliest types in any practical typology are likely to be intuitively obvious, while later types are added by increasingly conscious analysis (cf. Margolis 1987: 73). As this process continues, the original types will themselves be subjected to formal analysis, and may be somewhat redefined. It is probable

66

nevertheless that in most typologies there are certain types that remain largely intuitive. These are the types that we recognize first and describe in terms of attributes afterward, as distinguished from types that are not recognized until after significant attribute clusters have been identified. On this basis we could in theory distinguish between intuitive and "constructed" types, but the distinction is not really hard-and-fast. It would be more nearly accurate to say that in any typology there are likely to be varying degrees of intuitiveness among the different types.

Induction and deduction. W. S. Jevons (1874, II: 346) described the process of classification as one of "perfect induction." At the opposite extreme, some "New Archaeologists" have insisted that to be scientifically legitimate, types must be formulated deductively (Fritz and Plog 1970: 407–8; Hill and Evans 1972: 252–68; Read 1974). In Chapter 5 we have already stated our conviction that the evolution of any type concept actually involves a continual feedback between induction and deduction (see also Binford 1972: 118–19; Salmon 1976; Gardin 1980: 88; Harris 1980: 8; Watson 1986: 451). This issue (or rather, non-issue) will be further discussed in Chapter 23, and need not detain us longer here.

Discovery and invention. The oldest of all typological debates is that between the proponents of "natural" and "artificial" classification (cf. Jevons 1874, II: 348–50). The former group insist that types are made by nature, and that we merely discover them. They have described this process as one of "finding the joints in nature" (Spaulding 1982: 11). Proponents of "artificial" classification on the other hand hold that types are invented rather than discovered, as we draw an arbitrary grid over the seamless fabric of nature for some purpose of our own (cf. Brew 1946: 44–66; J. A. Ford 1954b).

If either of these views were wholly correct, it would be an easy matter both to define what types are and to say how they should be made. If types were wholly natural, we would merely have to develop appropriate discovery procedures. (Many adherents of natural typology insist that these already exist, in the form of tests for the statistical significance of attribute clusters. See, e.g., Spaulding 1953; 1960; 1982; Watson, LeBlanc, and Redman 1971: 126–34.) If types were wholly artificial, on the other hand, we could develop any procedures we liked for the clustering of attributes into types. The methodology of paradigmatic classification (Dunnell 1971b: 70–6) employs this principle.

In the real world of practical typologies, however, all types are to a degree natural and to a degree artificial, which means also that they are partly discovered and partly invented (see Willey and Phillips 1958: 13; Lakoff 1984: 22; Holland and Quinn 1987: 3 and also Chapter 5). We can say as a general rule that nature (or culture) creates modalities, but we, the typologists, choose among them those that are informative for any particular purpose of our own. It is also we who have to draw arbitrary boundaries between modalities, if they are to be used as sorting categories, where often enough there are no such boundaries in nature. But the degree of naturalness, like the degree of intuitiveness, varies from type to type in the same system (cf. Ellen 1979: 8–12). The Nubian Pottery Typology (Chapter 10) includes certain wares, like H7, that are both grossly obvious and sharply bounded; that is, they do not significantly intergrade with any other ware. There are other wares, like R21, whose criteria of identity are so subtle that they are recognizable only by an expert, and they intergrade with earlier and later wares to such an extent that the makers themselves may have been unaware of the differences.

The measure of "naturalness" in any given type is, in essence, the degree to which it works for any given purpose. When we say that a type "works," or serves a purpose, we nearly always mean that it co-occurs or co-varies with something external to itself. A pottery type is found only during a certain time period, or a presumed ritual object is found only in certain locations, or a tool type only occurs in association with certain other tool types. The more consistently this is true, the more clearly it indicates that there is "something going on"; i.e. that there is an inherent order in the data that has not simply been imposed by us. In other words, co-occurrence between two or more things is evidence of the "reality," or naturalness, of the things themselves. We have to note, however, that this is a variable and not an absolute proposition. The strength or consistency of association between things is itself highly variable (cf. Thomas 1978: 233–5), and we may say in consequence that types are variable in their degree of "naturalness."

Being and doing. The process of dividing a corpus of material into finer and finer subdivisions can theoretically proceed until each entity in the corpus is a separate type. Thus, every typological system is potentially capable of generating far more types than it actually includes. Among the innumerable possible types, we retain those that are useful for our purposes and ignore those that are not. When a typology is formulated without reference to any specific purpose, it nearly always generates far too many types to be useful or meaningful (cf. Dunnell 1971b: 97–8).

68

We must state here once again that types have the two essential features of identity and meaning (see Chapter 3). Identity is established by intrinsic features, and meaning by extrinsic features (see Chapter 14). Consequently, in practical typologies, decisions to retain or to exclude types cannot be based on intrinsic features alone. This might suggest a purely instrumental approach to the problem of type determination – an assertion that types are determined not by what they are but by what they do. It could be said that, within any given typology, a type is whatever works for the purpose of that typology.

Once again, the reality is not that simple. In the first place, types must usually be formulated before their usefulness can be tested. That is, they must first be formulated on the basis of intrinsic features alone, and only then can we discover if their particular cluster of intrinsic attributes co-occurs with any extrinsic attributes in which we are interested. (Once in a great while the reverse is true; we begin with a group of entities having a known common provenience, and then attempt to determine if they share any intrinsic features in common. See Gardin 1980: 87–9.) Moreover, as we suggested in the last section, if the types are found to "work" consistently for any purpose, it must mean that they have some degree of "reality" or "naturalness." We have therefore to acknowledge that types are partly essential and partly instrumental; they are determined partly by what they are and partly by what they do (cf. Sokal 1977: 187–95).

In our usage, the instrumentality of a type is proportional to its relevance to the purposes of the typology of which it is a member. Like the other qualities of types that we have been discussing, this is something that can vary from type to type, even within the same system. In the Nubian Pottery Typology, for example, the utility Ware U5 is distinctive and easily recognized, but it is so ubiquitous in Nubian sites between A.D. 500 and 1500 that it has little value for dating purposes (see Appendix C). It is therefore easily recognized as an essential type, but it has little utility as an instrumental type. At the opposite extreme, the Post-Classic Ware R21 is very difficult to distinguish from several related wares, but when it can be recognized it is invaluable for dating because it was made entirely in the twelfth century. It is difficult to recognize as an essential type, but has great value as an instrumental type.

The polythetic feature

The concept of polythetic classification was one of the major contributions of the "New Systematics" in biology, which took shape in the 1930s and 1940s (see especially Huxley 1940). (Biologists commonly employ the term "polytypic" rather than "polythetic," but the meaning is the same.) After wrestling with the species concept for more than a century (see Mayr 1942: 102–22), the biologists came to recognize that, as Huxley (1940: 11) put it simply, "There is no single criterion of species." A generation later archaeologists began to realize that the same is true of most artifact classifications, and especially of pottery classifications (*contra* Watson, LeBlanc, and Redman 1984: 8).

The polythetic feature has been thus described by Clarke (1968: 190):

> . . . it is possible to define a group of entities in terms of a set of properties such that
>
> (1) Each entity possesses a large but unspecified number of the particular set of properties.
>
> (2) Each property in the given set is possessed by large numbers of these individuals.
>
> (3) No property in the given set is necessarily possessed by every individual in the aggregate.
>
> By the terms of the third condition no single property or attribute is necessary for the membership of a polythetic group. (Compare also Beckner 1959: 22.)

As a result of these peculiarities it is not possible to specify either necessary or sufficient conditions for "typehood" in a polythetic classification – another feature which makes an abstract definition of type virtually impossible.

In an earlier section we suggested that polythetic classifications are a consequence of the stepwise differentiation procedures by which typologies are often formulated. However, this does not answer the fundamental question: why are polythetic types necessary? They seem to defy the rules of formal logic that systematists often demand (cf. Dunnell 1971b: 43–86; Read 1974), yet both in biology and in archaeology it has proven impossible to get along without them.

Part of the answer, as we suggested earlier, lies in the comprehensive nature of typologies. Within any given set of limits, everything must be classified into units that we can somehow treat as equivalent (cf. Chapters 4 and 7), but this can very rarely be done according to any one set of fixed criteria. Another part of the answer lies in the instrumental function of typologies. It will often be found that many different kinds of tools will suffice for the same job, and we will retain all of those that do, even though they were not always designed according to the same principles.

(For a discussion of the significance of polythetic classification in other fields of anthropology see R. Needham 1975.)

70

Centers and boundaries

The oldest and seemingly the most "natural" of all scientific typologies is the Linnean classification of genera and species (Linnaeus 1735). Consciously or unconsciously it has served as the model for systematists in many other fields of science (Jevons 1874, II: 348–9; Brew 1946: 46–64), and the mammalian species, in particular, is probably every scientist's ideal of what a type should be (cf. Krieger 1960: 141; Foucault 1973: 132). There has been, as a result, a tendency to equate "naturalness" with boundedness; that is, to assume that the most "real" or natural type is the one with the most sharply defined boundaries. There is in fact no scientific basis for such an equation (cf. Rosch 1973; 1975). It might be correct to say that sharp and intuitively obvious boundaries are *a priori* evidence of "naturalness"; it is not correct to say that the absence of such boundaries denotes a lack of "naturalness" (see especially Klejn 1982: 58–64). Very few other biological phenomena, and still fewer social and cultural phenomena, are as clearly bounded as are mammalian species, for the simple reason that they do not reproduce sexually and do not inherit their traits genetically. (But even among biologists the definition of species does not appear as sharp today as it once did; see, e.g., Holsinger 1984.)

In reality, as Cormack (1971: 329) observed, types are nearly always defined by some combination of internal cohesion and external isolation; that is, they are defined both by some kind of modality and by some kind of boundaries. As Simpson (1945: 21) observed, "Diagnosis is the art and practice of distinguishing between things. Definition is the art and practice of setting limits to things. Both enter into taxonomy and it is unusual to distinguish between the two, but they are essentially different and their complementary rules should be clearly understood." However, the relative importance of these two determinants of "typehood" varies from typology to typology and from type to type. Some types have a good deal of internal variability, such that a number of rather diverse entities are included in the same type category. Occasionally there are even bimodal types, having no one central tendency but exhibiting instead two (or even more) fairly consistent variants. There are also, of course, types which have no clearly defined boundaries, but which intergrade with other types to such an extent that the classifier or sorter must make an arbitrary decision as to where the boundaries lie. This is particularly true in archaeological classification, since culture often does not create sharp boundaries.

There is, obviously, a kind of negative correlation between internal cohesion and external isolation as determinants of type identity. The fuzzier are the type boundaries, the clearer must be the modality or central tendency, and vice versa. As we have just noted, modalities are usually much more conspicuous than are boundaries in the definition of archaeological types, and in particular of artifact types (cf. Jevons 1874, II: 411–14; Clarke 1968: 189–90; *contra* Dunnell 1971b: 45). It must be stressed again, however, that this can vary from type to type, even in the same typology.

Whether types are defined primarily by modalities or primarily by boundaries, it is true in either case that they may exhibit a good deal of internal variability. In these cases the type definition and type description are necessarily idealized concepts (cf. Shepard 1965: 317; Keighley 1973: 133; see also Rosch 1973; 1975; Klejn 1982: 49–50) referring to an ideal type specimen: one which exemplifies in the fullest degree all of the diagnostic and descriptive attributes of the type. (Some archaeologists have actually created special, archival collections consisting entirely of such ideal specimens, which are usually referred to as type specimens. See Colton and Hargrave 1937: *passim*.) A great many type members will of course deviate from the type ideal, or norm, in one way or another and to one degree or another. In fact, Simpson (1945: 29) observed that "It is a natural but mistaken assumption that types [i.e. type specimens] are somehow typical . . . of the groups in which they are placed." This furnishes another good reason for avoiding the use of formally stated or rigorous type definitions: they may create a false expectation of conformity (cf. Shepard 1965: 317; Keighley 1973: 133). For practical utility, type descriptions should list both norms and expectable deviations from the norm; that is, they should state what kinds of variation can be expected, and up to what limits. (A discussion of variability is included in all of the medieval Nubian ware descriptions, of which an example is given in Appendix B.)

It should be obvious from the foregoing that it is only the norms of types that must be mutually exclusive by definition, rather than by arbitrary decision (see Chapters 4 and 7). The norm for any type cannot for obvious reasons be identical to the norm for any other type, but individual specimens can fall between the norms in such a way that we must decide arbitrarily which of the norms they most closely resemble, and sort them into the most appropriate type category accordingly. An inevitable consequence is that precision of type definition can never entirely solve the practical problems of sorting. We will pursue this issue further in Chapter 16.

Sets and fuzzy sets

We have suggested in the preceding section that most artifact types correspond to what elsewhere have been called fuzzy sets (Zadeh 1965;

1971; Kay and McDaniel 1978; Kempton 1978). In his pioneering article on fuzzy sets, Zadeh (1965: 338) wrote that "More often than not, the classes of objects encountered in the real physical world do not have precisely defined criteria of membership. Yet, the fact remains that . . . imprecisely defined 'classes' play an important role in human thinking, particularly in the domains of pattern recognition, communication of information, and abstraction." Clearly all of these observations are applicable to artifact types.

Fuzzy sets are contrasted with "ordinary sets," in which membership is an absolute, yes-or-no proposition. In fuzzy sets it is argued that there are measurable degrees of membership. On this basis fuzzy set theorists have developed rather complex mathematical formulas or "laws," which enable them to measure degrees of membership and thus to quantify imprecise data in a seemingly precise way (Zadeh 1971; Kay and McDaniel 1978: 621–38).

We can agree in principle with the concept of degrees of membership, or degrees of fit as we would prefer to say. It is tantamount to suggesting that there may be a variable degree of closeness between the material, mental, and representational dimensions of "typehood" (see Chapter 3). At the same time, we find that fuzzy set theory has little practical utility for the archaeologist. Apart from the fact that some of its mathematical "laws" are philosophically suspect (cf. Weston 1987), there is the practical difficulty of developing quantitative measures for the association of any artifact with any given type. Even more difficult would be the task of applying such measures, if we had them, to the sorting of masses of material within any reasonable period of time. As we will suggest in the next chapter, any procedure that introduces mathematical or statistical procedures in the sorting operation is not likely to be of much use to the field archaeologist. (However, for an application of fuzzy set theory to the classification of modern pottery see Kempton 1978.)

In the end, the archaeologist is forced to treat his artifact classes as "ordinary sets," even though he knows that they are fuzzy. That is, potsherds or projectile points must be assigned to type categories on a yes-or-no basis, without reference to how well they exemplify the ideal type characteristics. This is precisely the practical archaeologist's dilemma, which will occupy us further in Part IV.

Typology, logic, and theory

The foregoing discussion should suggest that the processes involved in the formulation of practical typologies are seldom wholly logical, according to the canons of formal logic, while wholly logical typologies are seldom very useful (cf. also Rosch 1973; 1975). Types are justified by what Kaplan (1984: 25) has called "logic-in-use," rather than by abstract principles. While there must necessarily be some fundamental logic underlying our type concepts, if they work consistently for any purpose, it is often the case that we do not know what it is.

This leads to a critically important concluding observation: we often know that our types work for particular purposes without knowing why they work. For example, we know that many types of artifacts, or particular attributes, show chronological patterning, while others do not, but we do not know why this is so. We only know through consistent experience that they work for our announced purpose of site dating. Wittgenstein made essentially the same point in arguing that reasons are not causes (cf. Canfield 1981: 13).

A particularly cogent example is furnished by the dating procedures followed at Qasr Ibrim and other Nubian sites. As in many other archaeological dating operations, dates are calculated for particular deposits not on the basis of wares present and absent, but on the basis of percentages of the wares that are present (see Chapter 11). In order for this system to work, there must have been uniform deposition of refuse all over the site at any particular moment in time, so that the same proportions of decorated, utility, and imported wares were dumped in one area as in another. Such a situation runs counter not only to common-sense expectations but to actual archaeological findings in other parts of the world (Millon 1973; Whallon 1973; 1974; Hietala 1984), yet we can show over and over again, in sites throughout Nubia, that there was in fact uniformity of deposition (WYA 1986b: 32–3; WYA n.d.: 1). As a result we know that our dating system works without having any idea why it works.

Many New Archaeologists have insisted that types, like everything else in archaeology, must have theoretical justification (Binford 1968: 16–27). There is nothing inherently wrong in insisting on some kind of justification; indeed the fact that types work for any given purpose (i.e. that they co-occur consistently with something else) is *a priori* evidence that some causal factor is at work. But it is wrong to assert that we must be able to state the theoretical justification for our types. To know that they work, it is not necessary to know why they work, even though this would of course be scientifically desirable.

Many parallel examples can be cited from the natural sciences, most of which can predict far more than they can currently explain. "The chemist and geneticist were able to build theories with many observable consequences decades before they could observe an atom or a gene, or say anything at all about what an atom or a gene might really be like" (Margolis 1987: 1). Even for such commonplace and utterly predictable processes as freezing and thawing, "there is no accurate, universal (or universally accepted) theory of freezing, or indeed of first-order phase transitions in general" (Haymet 1987: 1076). Or again, 'One-sixth of the value of all goods manufactured in the United States involves catalytic processes. However, in spite of this dramatic economic impact, little is known about this broad subject at the molecular level" (Goodman and Houston 1987: 403).

We will discuss the relationship between typology and theory much more fully in the final chapters of this book.

7

THE STRUCTURE OF
TYPOLOGIES

In Chapter 3 we made the point that a lexicon is a *congeries* of words, a classification is a *set* of classes, but a typology is a *system* of types. What we mean by this is that a typology has systemic or structural features that are not entirely dictated by the nature of the constituent types, just as a language has structural features that are not dictated by its lexicon (cf. Waugh 1976: 20). In this chapter we will consider first what are the structural features of a typology, and then how they come about and what (if any) purpose they serve. The features that we will specifically discuss are those of boundedness and comprehensiveness of the typology itself, and the mutual exclusiveness, consistency of definition, equivalence, equidistance, and independence of the constituent types.

Basic structural features

Boundedness. In any classification that is to be used for sorting entities (that is to say, a typology), it must be clear at the outset what is and is not to be sorted. Hence typologies (unlike some other classifications) have quite rigidly specified and inflexible boundaries. Moreover, because sorted material is often subjected to statistical manipulations, the outer boundaries of the system cannot be adjusted to include new material which was formerly excluded, without invalidating any statistical operations that were previously performed.

Typological boundaries may be defined on the basis of either internal or external criteria, or both (see Chapter 14). In order to minimize ambiguity, most archaeological typologies are bounded by both internal and external criteria. That is, they are classifications of a specific kind of material (internal criteria) made and/or used in a specific part of the world during a specific interval of time (external criteria). The Medieval Nubian Pottery Typology that will occupy us later (Chapters 9–11) is a classification of ceramic vessels used (though not necessarily made) between the

76

First and Fourth Cataracts of the Nile in the interval between A.D. 100 and 1600.

Comprehensiveness. In a sorting system there must be a category for every item sorted. This will nearly always require that there be a residual, "none of the above" category for items that do not fit any of the other categories (cf. Cowgill 1982: 33–4). This is not at all a meaningless or a useless designation. In any statistical manipulation the importance of Type A is determined by the ratio of objects in it to objects not in it, and the latter will include objects in the residual Type X. At the Nubian site of Qasr Ibrim, the fluctuating percentage of potsherds in Type X enables us to distinguish Ptolemaic from Roman occupation levels even though the sherd percentages in all other categories are nearly constant (see WYA 1985: 13–14; 1986b: 44; and Chapter 11).

Practicality in sorting may not be the only explanation for comprehensiveness in typological systems. We will observe later in the chapter that typologies belong to a general class of categorical systems called segmentary systems, and that comprehensiveness, or universality, is a feature of all such systems.

Mutual exclusiveness. It cannot be stated too often that artifact types are not precisely comparable to biological species. The great majority of artifact types are identified by clearly distinct central tendencies, or norms, but not by clearly distinct boundaries (see Chapter 6). More often than not there is intergradation between one artifact type and another, and we must arbitrarily decide where to draw the line between them. It is nevertheless self-evident that no object can be put in two places at the same time, and hence types in a sorting system must be formulated in such a way that no object can belong simultaneously in two categories. This means that all types must, for sorting purposes, have clearly specified boundaries, whatever the realities of nature or of culture may have been. A typology in other words is a set of pigeon-holes, or sorting categories. But typological boundaries are a practical requirement of the sorting process, not a reflection of nature's or of God's order. We will pursue this issue more fully in Chapter 23.

It is also important to note that precision of description will lessen but will not eliminate ambiguity in the sorting process. Our type definitions (cf. Chapter 6) refer to central tendencies, or in other words ideal type specimens, of which real-life exemplars are relatively rare (cf. also Rosch 1973; 1975). Most of the objects that we sort, at least in archaeology, are fragmentary, worn, or for some other reason lack the full spectrum of attributes involved in the type description. Moreover, it is easy to specify in principle that Type A is red while Type B is orange, but if there is a continuum of variation between them we will still have to decide arbitrarily what to do with red-orange specimens. The issues of type description vs. type attribution (classifying vs. sorting) will be much more fully considered in Chapters 15 and 16.

Consistency of definition follows automatically from the requirement of mutually exclusive types. All types in any system must be formulated on the basis of the same set of criteria (variables), to eliminate any possibility of overlapping definitions. (For a detailed discussion of type formulation and definition see Chapter 15.) An elementary example of inconsistent definition is furnished by the four "flavors" of ice cream that used to be sold by a well-known soda fountain in the Republic of Sudan: "chocolate," "strawberry," "vanilla," and "green." Since three were defined on the basis of flavor and one on the basis of color, the possibility of overlap was theoretically if not actually present. (Green was pistachio flavored.)

Paradoxically, the foregoing does not mean that all the types in any typology are defined by precisely the same criteria, but only that they are defined on the basis of a common set of criteria. As we will see in Chapter 18, many typologies, including the majority of artifact typologies, are polythetic. Type determinations are based on a specific, constant set of variables, or denotata of identity, but no one of these is necessarily involved in the determination of any given type. Type A may be defined by variables w, x, and y, Type B by variables w, x, and z, Type C by variables w, y, and z, and Type D by variables x, y, and z. All four types are defined by the set of variables w-x-y-z, but no one of them is essential. On the other hand there are presumably other variables, r-s-t-u, which are present in all the types but are not introduced into the definitions. For example all projectile points have color of some kind, but color is very rarely a defining variable in projectile point typologies.

Equivalence of types. Here we encounter one of the most interesting and unexpected features of basic or one-level typologies (as distinct from taxonomies, in which the types are hierarchically clustered). All of the types within any typology are treated as being theoretically equal in importance, regardless of what we may know to the contrary. To begin with, they are described according to the same descriptive protocol, with the same degree of rigor and specificity, whether they have 100 members or 10,000. In the sorting process, moreover, any particular object is assumed to have a chance of belonging to any of the possible type categories, regardless of how many or how few objects may previously have been placed in these categories. (This is conceptually tantamount to the observation that the chances of "heads" and of "tails" are exactly equal for any given flip of a coin, regardless of how many times "heads" or "tails" have come up in previous flips.) Finally, the relevance of any particular type, for the purposes of its typology, is usually not in any way proportional to the number of its members. In archaeology, the dating of a particular site can hang on the presence or absence of a pottery type having no more than 100 members, while much more abundant types may be less important for dating purposes.

Equivalence of types is a necessary assumption if typological data are to be subjected to many kinds of statistical manipulations. However, this practical consideration does not appear to provide a complete explanation for what Vygotsky (1962: 112–16) has called the "law of equivalence of concepts." Recent experiments, both in developmental psychology and in ethnoscience, have suggested that human groups tend consistently to classify things within the same domain (birds, plants, colors, etc.) at one primary, or salient, level of abstraction, even though the level may not be the same from one society to another or from one classificatory domain to another (Rosch et al. 1976; Daugherty 1978). Later in the chapter we will suggest that there may be a very old and deeply rooted basis for this conception that "all types are potentially equal."

The practical consequences of the "law of equivalence" are well illustrated in the case of the Tellico Dam controversy in Tennessee. This multi-million dollar reclamation scheme, which had already consumed large sums in the planning, was nearly abandoned in the face of objections from environmentalists. They pointed out that the dam would destroy the environment of the snail darter (*Percina tanasi*), a tiny, unique species of fish found only in the Little Tennessee river. Controversy naturally raged over whether human interests should be sacrificed to the interests of fish (see Palm 1979; Norman 1981), but it is interesting to notice some of the questions that were apparently *not* asked. Would the preservation of this particular population of fish have been considered so important if they had not been classified as a species? Is the snail darter really so very different from the forty-odd other American darters, even though for scientific purposes we have designated it as a separate species? Finally and most significantly, is the extinction of the snail darter to be equated with the

79

extinction of the blue whale or the Siberian tiger? For environmentalists, it seems, the answer to all three questions was the same: an endangered species is an endangered species, regardless of size or distinctiveness.

Equidistance of types. As we suggested in Chapter 5, a typology may be likened to a set of mail pigeonholes. Regardless of where these may be physically located, there is no suggestion that the mail in Box A is more similar to the mail in Box B than it is to the mail in Box Z. A basic (one-level) typology cannot indicate degrees of relationship. All types are treated as equally similar to and equally distinct from one another, regardless of the number of their shared characteristics. It is possible to indicate degrees of relationship only by introducing one or more higher taxonomic levels into the classification. This is a fundamental necessity in genetic classifications, but not in morphological, historical, or functional classifications. We will suggest in Chapter 17 that taxonomic ordering is frequently an incidental or a secondary feature in artifact classifications.

It follows from the above that types are essentially qualitative (cf. Dunnell 1971b: 52–6). As Lévi-Strauss (1953: 528) puts it, "there is no necessary connection between *measure* and *structure*." Measurement can be introduced into typologies only in the form of nominal or incremental data. A continuum of length variability, for example, may be broken up into arbitrary increments of "long (over 20 cm)," "medium (10–20 cm)," and "short (under 10 cm)," but it is impossible to define types on the basis of specific, individual lengths without resulting in an infinity of types.

Independence of types. A final obvious point is that the existence of any type, or its presence in any collection being sorted, is not predicated on the existence of any other type. In the sorting procedure, Type A has an equal chance of being present whether or not Types B, C, or Z are present.

The segmentary principle

How shall we account for the structural features which appear to be common to all typologies? Some of them, like boundedness, comprehensiveness, and mutual exclusiveness of units, are obvious necessities of the sorting process. However, this is less evidently true in the case of equivalence of types, equidistance of types, and independence of types. What is extraordinary about these features is that they exist in defiance of common sense and of our actual knowledge of cases. We know in reality that in any given system some types are much more important than others, that some types are much more like each other than they are like other types, and that if Type A is present, it is much more probable that Type B will be present than would be the case if Type A were not present.

We might be inclined to treat these latter features as statistical necessities, in that they are necessary assumptions if typological data are to be subjected to most kinds of statistical manipulations. Units that are to be used for measurement and comparison must themselves be constant. However, this does not appear to furnish a complete answer, for the features in question were present in classificatory systems long before the introduction of statistical procedures (cf. Lévi-Strauss 1966: 138–9). Equivalence of units, equidistance of units, and independence of units are not features exclusively of modern, scientific typologies. They are the legacies of a very ancient and very pervasive kind of classification, which has usually been characterized as cellular or segmentary. The latter term is better known among anthropologists, and will be employed here.

The unique and seemingly paradoxical feature of these systems is that they are sets of complementary, mutually exclusive units based purely on qualitative criteria (cf. Lévi-Strauss 1953: 528–9). Normally it requires some form of quantification or measurement to produce mutually exclusive units, since no number is the same as any other number in the same series (integer, fraction, percentage, etc.). But cells, segments, and artifact types have the simultaneous features of equivalence of units, equidistance of units, and independence of units, which means that numbers can play no part in their determination.

It was the great sociologist-anthropologist Emile Durkheim (1893) who gave us the concept of segmentation. He pointed out the tendency of all human societies to organize themselves into units of comparable structure, which exist in a state of "balanced opposition" to one another. The forms that these units may take are highly variable from society to society; they may include groupings as disparate as the bands of primitive hunter-gatherers, the villages of horticultural peasants, the lineages and tribes of pastoralists, the city-states of ancient Sumer, Greece, and Yucatán, and the nation-states of the modern world. What is important is that within any given system the form of the organizational units tends very strongly toward uniformity: each unit strives to emulate its competitors, and to have the things that its competitors have. This propensity has led Abu-Lughod (1989: 280–7) to speak, albeit somewhat satirically, of *Homo segmentarius* (see also Dresch 1986).

Modern social anthropologists have sometimes regarded segmentation as process rather than as structure: a continual fissioning of society into smaller and smaller units (Barnes 1954: 47–54; Middleton and Tait 1958:

7–8). However, this is not a necessary feature of segmentary theory, nor was it part of Durkheim's original formulation (Durkheim 1947: 1–10; see also Fortes and Evans-Pritchard 1940: 13–14; Radcliffe-Brown and Forde 1950: 39–43). It is true that complex societies may be segmented at several different levels (provinces, counties, cities, etc.), but these are not always the products of a fissioning process. Sometimes the larger units result from the confederation of smaller ones (like the United States from the original thirteen colonies), and sometimes there are wholly different lines of segmentation (as for example between kinship units and territorial units). The important feature of segmentation is simply the propensity of all human societies to organize themselves into comparable units.

Studies of animal ethology have made it plain that this propensity is by no means confined to *Homo sapiens*. Normative forms of the "family," or social clustering, vary enormously from one animal species to another (cf. Rowell 1967: 219–35; Hinde 1979: 295–315; Wrangham 1979: 336), from the loosely organized troop of baboons through the patriarchal pride of lions and the matriarchal herd of elephants, to the lifelong monogamous pairing of geese and swans, but each species has only a single normative unit of organization.

Sociobiologists and other social materialists find explanation for all this in the factor of competition (Chalmers 1980: 185–95; Richard and Schulman 1982: 240–9). Consciously or unconsciously, all living creatures are seen to be in competition with their fellows of the same species, and competitive advantage lies in having everything your neighbors have. The forty-year arms race between the United States and Russia presents an obvious modern example of this kind of thinking.

For our purposes it is, perhaps fortunately, unnecessary to pursue the issue of why segmentation takes place; it is sufficient to recognize that it is a universal feature of human and animal social organization. The important point for us is that segmentary organization is very explicitly a form of typological classification. It is a comprehensive scheme for sorting all of the individuals within a given population (community, tribe, nation, or whatever) into a set of mutually exclusive categories, such that each individual has a theoretical chance of belonging to one and only one.

This is, fundamentally, our way of mapping the social universe. We rarely deal with our fellow humans as isolates. In some sense or another we treat them as members of larger sets, and before relations can proceed very far we have to know where their affinities and allegiances lie (cf. Dresch 1986). Thus, exploratory rituals of greeting always involve the discovery of group identity: "Where are you from?", "What is your clan?", "Are you

American or English?", etc. These inquiries often serve no immediate practical purpose, but they establish for each of us a classificatory identity without which we are to some extent a non-person. (Try, for example, to cross an international frontier without a passport, and you will discover that it is impossible not to have a national identity.)

The social groupings we are discussing here are classificatory units having the same basic attributes that we have ascribed to types. As a matter of practical necessity they have, like artifact types, the properties of boundedness, comprehensiveness, and exclusivity of units. But they also have, within limits that we will discuss in a moment, the properties of equivalence of units, equidistance of units, and independence of units. "All men are equal before the law" expresses this principle at the lowest and most specific level, but we may note additionally that (at least until very recently) the rights and obligations are the same in all marriages, all states have two votes in the United States Senate, and all nations have an equal voice in the United Nations General Assembly. Canada is not obliged to vote in the same way as the United States or England because of cultural or historical affinities, nor is it necessary for the United States or England to vote before Canada can vote. Examples of this kind of thinking in the social and political spheres could be multiplied indefinitely.

One of the features common to all typologies and all segmentary systems is that of comprehensiveness, or universality. That is, there must be a place (and only one place) for everyone or everything somewhere within the system. Individuals or things that do not readily fit into any of the existing categories are a threat to the system itself, and they are likely to be excluded from classification through some process of veneration or execration which in effect declares them to be non-persons or non-things (see especially Douglas 1966; also Douglas 1975: 27–46 and Bulmer 1967). It is unlikely that this propensity can be explained on pragmatic grounds alone. More probably it is evidence of a universal but subconscious mind-set, a feeling that if anything is to be classified, everything must be classified. We have already noted (Chapter 6) that this feature of enforced comprehensiveness is responsible for some of the ambiguity that is common in artifact typologies.

The problem of hierarchy

Louis Dumont (1970) and his followers have argued that hierarchical ranking is as universal a feature of human social organization as is segmentary classification, and ethologists have found the same to be true in many animal species (Hinde 1979: 310–13; Chalmers 1980: 160–84;

Richard and Schulman 1982: 236–9). Obviously, this poses a problem for our analysis. How can we reconcile hierarchical ranking with the principle of equivalence of units?

We can at least simplify the issue by distinguishing between classificatory (taxonomic) ranking and social ranking. Classificatory ranking takes place when the lowest and most specific units in a system are combined into larger and more inclusive units on the basis of shared characteristics. It may also occur, though less commonly, when large units are split into smaller sub-units (cf. Chapter 17). In this book we refer to such multi-level classifications as taxonomies. They are common alike in scientific classifications and in folk classifications (cf. Berlin 1976), and we will discuss them at some length in Chapter 17.

Classificatory rankings are non-evaluative, and do not invalidate the principles of equivalence of units, equidistance of units, or independence of units at any given taxonomic level. Members of the genus *Felis* are much more numerous than are members of the genus *Canis*, but there is no suggestion that the two genera are consequently of different biological importance. At the species level, there is no implication that *Canis latrans* (the coyote) is more similar to *Canis aureus* (the jackal) than it is to *Canis familiaris* (the dog), though this appears superficially to be true.

Classificatory ranking is not a feature exclusively of scientific and folk taxonomies; it is also found in many social systems. Families may be grouped into lineages, lineages into clans, and so on. As in other taxonomies these groupings are not, in and of themselves, evaluative; they do not undermine the principle of equivalence of units. A family or a clan may be poor in numbers or in resources at a given moment in time, but it may later become large or rich. It can therefore potentially "trade places," so to speak, with any other family or clan in the society.

Social ranking, as we have defined it, differs from classificatory ranking in two important respects. First, it is evaluative, introducing quite explicitly the principle that not all people and groups are equal. Second, it is, strictly speaking, a process of seriation rather than of classification (cf. Chapter 17). Individuals or groups are rated along a linear scale from prestigious to despised, according to some accepted evaluative principle.

It may be, as Dumont (1970) has insisted, that ranking is as universal a human propensity as is classification. The two principles are nevertheless conceptually independent, even though they may be employed in combination (cf. Leach 1976: 53–4). In many human societies, theoretically including our own, individuals are ranked on some scale of individual merit, without reference to the groups to which they belong. In some tribal societies there are prestigious individuals but no prestigious clans. In formally stratified societies ranking is indeed applied to classificatory groups (prestigious lineages, clans, races, etc.), but it always and necessarily follows classification. Individuals are not assigned to a clan or race because they are prestigious; they are assigned prestige because of their clan or race.

We may note, then, that structure is not a product of ranking; it necessarily precedes ranking. But it is also true that ranking is not a product of classificatory structure. It is the result of applying to the structural units some evaluative principle which is external to the structure itself.

The combination of segmentary classification and evaluative ranking is not confined to human social systems; it is common to many classificatory systems. Many folk taxonomies have an evaluative component, and so, for example, do the classifications of art historians. From our perspective, the single factor which most distinguishes scientific typologies from other classifications is the conscious elimination of evaluation and evaluative ranking.

This did not come about suddenly, but by degrees. Early archaeological classifications involved a large component of aesthetic judgment. According to Daniel (1964: 74) it was General Pitt Rivers who "exorcised taste from archaeology," and who deserves to be recognized as the father of scientific artifact classification. It may be questioned, however, if the demon is fully exorcised even yet. There is still a tendency to think in terms of "ideal types," and therefore to select as "type specimens" the most perfectly symmetrical arrowhead or the most precisely decorated sherd of a particular ware, even though these may be statistically atypical (cf. Shepard 1965: 317; Rosch 1973; 1975; Klejn 1982: 49–50).

As a concluding generalization we would suggest that scientific typologies have inherited from our pre-scientific past the propensity for segmentary classification, while largely eliminating the propensity for evaluative ranking. Interestingly, Durkheim and Mauss made essentially the same point in 1903: "the primordial forms of the society impose on the people a classification that they are subsequently to impose on the rest of nature" (Durkheim and Mauss 1903, paraphrased in Service 1985: 140).

The symbolic dimension

We noted in Chapter 3 that classificatory units are always named, and at least to that extent are given symbolic expression. However, structural and social anthropologists long ago discovered that categorical systems are often invested with a degree of symbolic significance extending far beyond the mere requirements of labeling. In particular categorical boundaries are invested with a high degree of sacredness – they are legitimized and defended by all kinds of myth and ritual (Douglas 1966; 1970: 173–201; 1975: 27–46; V. Turner 1967; 1969; Leach 1972; 1976: 33–6). When we consider that the oldest and most universal of all human classificatory systems are social systems (that is, classifications of ourselves), the rationale for symbolic boundary maintenance becomes obvious enough. This is what Leach (1976: 33–6) has characterized as "the symbolic ordering of a man-made world." From the same perspective, Greenwood (1984: 45–6) points out "the close linkage between systems of classification and systems of morality. Any alteration in the major classifications of a cultural system nearly always implies alterations in moral systems as well. Put another way, there are no morally insignificant classifications."

As Durkheim (1912) long ago observed, all forms of human social ordering require some kind of divine legitimation. What is extraordinary, however, is that symbolic loading is also found in many kinds of classificatory systems that have little or nothing to do with social organization (cf. especially Douglas 1973: 118–93). To eat the wrong food, to use the wrong tool, to kill the wrong animal, may bring divine retribution as surely as to marry the wrong woman.

Why this insistence on the sacredness of categories? The present authors are neither structuralists nor cognitive psychologists, and the best that our understanding will permit is a rather speculative guess. We can, however, begin with the well-established premise that all human belief requires some kind of legitimation (cf. Gellner 1974). When legitimation is not provided by the evidence of our own senses it must rest on some other authority. In childhood that is likely to be the word of someone we trust, but few of us continue in adult life to place implicit trust in the word of any fellow mortal. We require a higher authority, whose name is God or Science or something in between. This authority may speak to us in a variety of ways, perhaps most commonly through mythology.

The less our beliefs are empirically verifiable, the more they require some other form of legitimation. In the pre-scientific era, such legitimation could hardly come from other than divine sources. We might accept it from the mouth of a fellow human, but only if he was authorized to speak for the gods.

Categorical systems would appear to furnish a classic example of beliefs that require divine legitimation. Once in a while our senses may have recognized some actual seams in nature, or "natural classes"; much more often we have had to impose arbitrary boundaries on the seamless fabric of nature for the sake of cognition and communication. But it would be an

86

unbearable psychic burden, as well as a monstrous inconvenience, if we had to give rational justification for our use of every categorical word in the language. Mythology relieves us of that burden by the reassurance that our categories, although seemingly arbitrary, are in reality god-given. Mythology does not merely legitimize social systems; it legitimizes language itself (see Leach 1976: 35–6).

Is the scientific mind emancipated from such considerations? Only to a degree, we believe. All scientists are human beings, and the majority of them are ordinary human beings. Their beliefs require legitimation as much as do those of primitive tribesmen, the difference being only that when possible they accept scientific rather than divine legitimation. Scientific principles and procedures have indeed provided legitimation for many beliefs that were once attributed to the gods, but by and large classificatory categories are not among them. Thus the continuing, elusive search for "objectivity" or "reality" in scientific classifications may proceed from the same need for legitimation that produced the mythologies of yesteryear. We cannot, it seems, take upon ourselves the responsibility of imposing order on nature, though this assuredly is what our classifications are doing.

We are suggesting, then, that the locus of the elusive "reality" so long sought by scientific typologists is probably largely in their (and our) own minds. In some degree it may be the product of mental processes that we have inherited from our pre-human ancestors. In unconscious ways that are little understood, but that seem to be common to all humanity, we have imposed a necessary coherence and order on the tangled web of experience and sensation (see especially Leach 1976). (Leslie White [1949: 284–5] long ago offered virtually the same argument in regard to mathematical "reality." He undertook to show "on the one hand, why the belief in the independent existence of mathematical truths has seemed so plausible and convincing for so many centuries, and on the other, to show that all of mathematics is nothing more than a particular kind of primary behavior." White's arguments have not, it must be added, found much favor among mathematicians.)

This is not to suggest either that there is no natural order, or that it exists but is beyond our capacity to verify. We do insist, however, that natural order is not necessarily equivalent to typological order. We suggested in Chapter 6 that nature produces regularities, but more often than not it is human minds that draw boundaries between them. Moreover, the requirements of communication (as well as many other purposes that we will discuss in Chapter 13) oblige us to impose far more classificatory order on our experience than we can attribute to nature. We may therefore conclude (as indeed did W. S. Jevons in 1874 [II: 351–3]), that every classification is to some extent natural and to some extent arbitrary. The extent of "naturalness" will vary not only from classification to classification, but also and conspicuously from type to type within the same typology (cf. Ellen 1979: 8–20; also Chapter 6).

By recognizing that typologies are made by us, for our own purposes, we may hopefully be liberated from the deceptions of mythology and the often time-wasting search for "reality." It is our purpose that dictates the choice of variables and attributes to be classified, and that choice in turn determines the shape, boundaries, and meaning of our types. Effectiveness for their intended purpose, not divine will or natural order, is their ultimate legitimation.

Classification and measurement

A word must be said in conclusion about the important but much misunderstood relationship between classification and measurement (cf. also Dunnell 1986: 151–2). In discussing this issue we must first recall the distinction we made earlier in the chapter, between typologies and taxonomies. A typology is a basic set of mutually exclusive categories, at the same level of abstraction, and a taxonomy is a clustering of basic types into larger and more inclusive units, or taxa. At least in archaeology the role of quantitative measurement is usually small in the formulation of types and typologies, but much larger in the formulation of taxonomies.

In some disciplines there may be purely quantitative typologies. That is, differences between types can be expressed in terms of interval or ratio scales of measurement (but for a discussion of ambiguity in the use of these terms see Chapters 12 and 14). In the periodic table of the elements, for example, the differences between chemical elements are all theoretically capable of expression in quantitative terms. This is emphatically not true in archaeology and most other disciplines, in which differences between types are essentially qualitative (Lévi-Strauss 1953: 528; Dunnell 1971b: 52–6). Put in the simplest terms, archaeological types are mostly "apples and oranges," they cannot be derived from one another by processes of quantification or measurement. If they could be, it would be necessary to define only one type in each system, after which the others could be derived from it by mathematical formulas.

The only role that quantitative measurement ordinarily plays in the formulation of basic types is in determining whether a particular group of attributes (e.g. fine clay paste, red surface color, and incised zigzag decoration in the case of pottery) occurs together with sufficient frequency so that they can be thought of as collectively defining a type. As we will see in Chapter 14, there are various statistical measures of randomness and nonrandomness that can be helpful in deciding this question, although nonrandomness is itself a complex issue which is subject to varied interpretations (Jos. Ford 1983; Kolata 1986). We will also see, however, that a nonrandom association of attributes is a necessary but not a sufficient condition for designation of a type (Chapter 14).

Although typological classification is not measurement, it is functionally analogous to measurement in one important respect. That is, typologies provide a systematic basis for the qualitative discrimination of things in the same way that systems of measurement provide a basis for their quantitative discrimination. Typologies might therefore be thought of as constituting a kind of qualitative mathematics. As Lévi-Strauss (1953: 528) observed:

> Structural studies are, in the social sciences, the indirect out-
> come of modern developments in mathematics which have
> given increasing importance to the qualitative point of view
> in contradistinction to the quantitative point of view of
> traditional mathematics. Therefore, it has become possible,
> in fields such as mathematical logic, set-theory, group-
> theory, and topology, to develop a rigorous approach to
> problems which do not admit of a metrical solution.

It is also to be noted that groups of type members are often used as units of measurement. As we will see in Chapter 13, one of the most common reasons for sorting artifacts into discrete groups (types) is to permit quantitative and statistical comparisons between the groups, in terms of their relative frequency of occurrence in different situations. The whole methodology of frequency seriation, which is basic to a great deal of archaeological dating (see Chapter 17), is based on such comparisons. We might go on to suggest, therefore, that it is precisely because types are to be compared quantitatively that they must be defined qualitatively; that is, they must be qualitatively distinct.

Taxonomies, like seriations, are designed to indicate the relationships between types, once the types themselves have been formulated (see Chapter 17). These relationships can be of many kinds: historical, morphological, functional, or whatever. In a great many cases, however, relationships are assumed on the basis of degrees of similarity between types. That is, the types that appear the most similar are assumed to be the most closely related, and are grouped into higher taxa accordingly. Thus measurement can play a very large role in the clustering of types into larger taxonomic units.

In sum, then, archaeological types are qualitatively distinct units which are often compared quantitatively. Measurement therefore plays only a small role in the formulation of types, but a much larger role in their subsequent use.

8

A SYNTHETIC DEFINITION
OF TYPOLOGY AND TYPE

The various concepts that were discussed in the three preceding chapters may now be synthesized into a single, synthetic definition of "typology" and "type." This will necessarily be a cumbersome formulation, since a large number of individual concepts is involved. Following the example of Geertz (1966: 4) in his famous definition of religion, we will first state the definition, then break it down into its constituent elements, then analyze each element for its significance.

> *Definition*
> A typology is a conceptual system made by partitioning a specified field of entities into a comprehensive set of mutually exclusive types, according to a set of common criteria dictated by the purpose of the typologist. Within any typology, each type is a category created by the typologist, into which he can place discrete entities having specific identifying character- istics, to distinguish them from entities having other charac- teristics, in a way that is meaningful to the purpose of the typology.

The definition can now be analyzed in terms of the following com- ponents: (1) A typology is a *conceptual system* (2) made by *partitioning* (3) a *specified field* of entities (4) into a *comprehensive set* (5) of *mutually exclusive* types (6) according to a set of *common criteria* (7) dictated by the *purpose* (8) of the *typologist*. (9) Within *any typology* (10) each type is a *category* (11) *created* by the typologist (12) into which he can place *discrete entities* (13) having specific *identifying characteristics* (14) to *distinguish* them from entities having other characteristics (15) in a way that is *meaningful* (16) to the *purpose* of the typology. (Italics identify the key concept to be analyzed in each of the numbered components.)

Analysis of the definition

(1) A typology is a *conceptual system* . . . We made the point in Chapter 4 that types are (among other things) concepts, and in Chapter 7 we added that a typology is a system with structural features that are not entirely predicated by the characteristics of the types themselves. Typology and types are of course wholly interdependent concepts. There is no typology without types, and there are no types except with reference to some specific typology.

(2) . . . made by *partitioning* . . . Since every typology applies to a specified field of entities (see below), and since every typology includes more than one type, it follows *a priori* that every typology involves a partitioning of the field of entities in question. This does not mean that a typology is made exclusively by a splitting process, as in many computer-generated taxonomies (Sokal and Sneath 1963; Dunnell 1971b: 98–102). In real life, typology-making usually involves continuous and simultaneous processes of combining and separating. That is, entities with like characteristics are lumped together, and at the same time are split off from the remaining corpus of entities having different characteristics. This is the differentiation process that we discussed in Chapter 5.

(3) . . . of a *specified field* of entities . . . Since a typology is a sorting system, it must be clear at the outset what is and is not to be sorted, as was indicated in Chapter 7.

(4) . . . into a *comprehensive set* . . . In a sorting system it is also necessary that there be a category for every entity sorted, even though this may necessitate a residual, "none of the above" category.

(5) . . . of *mutually exclusive* types . . . Entities to be sorted are indivisible, hence can go into one and only one category.

(6) . . . according to a set of *common criteria* . . . Type norms cannot be mutually exclusive unless they are defined throughout by the same set of criteria; that is, by a uniform choice of variables to be considered and not to be considered. If pottery types are formulated on the basis of color in some cases but not in others, and on the basis of vessel form in some cases but not in others, the result will almost certainly be cross-cutting types that are not mutually exclusive. This does not mean that all types must be formulated on the basis of precisely the same *individual* criteria; only on the basis of the same *set* of criteria. As we observed in Chapter 6, many artifact typologies are polythetic, so that types may be formulated on the basis of any of a variety of attribute combinations. But the attributes must always be drawn from the same, pre-selected group of variables.

(7) . . . dictated by the *purpose* . . . The purpose of the typology will

determine which variables are to be considered and not considered in the designation of types. Many artifact types have been made for purposes of chronological estimation (see Chapters 11 and 13), and in these cases the variables selected will be those with known or presumed chronological significance. If reconstruction of prehistoric activity patterns is the purpose of the typology, then the variables selected will be those with presumed functional significance. It is this purpose, whatever it may be, that gives meaning to the individual types generated within the system, as we defined meaning in Chapter 3. When defining variables are selected with no specific purpose in mind, the resulting types will have no specifiable meaning (cf. Dunnell 1971b: 98).

(8) . . . of the *typologist*. The selection of variables to be considered and to be ignored in classification is almost never self-evident. It must be relevant to a purpose, and that purpose is necessarily somebody's purpose. It is because of the purpose factor that all typologies are to some degree instrumental and subjective, as we observed in Chapter 3 and Chapter 5.

(9) Within *any typology* . . . Every type is necessarily a member of a typology, and it has meaning only with reference to other members in the same typology (cf. Dunnell 1971b: 56–8). The same morphological type may occasionally occur in two or more typologies (this is conspicuously true of arrowhead types in the eastern United States), but in these cases the meanings of the type are potentially different in each typology.

(10) . . . each type is a *category* . . . That is, each type is a concept potentially applicable to two or more individual entities, which are not necessarily identical in all of their characteristics.

(11) . . . *created* by the typologist . . . Most archaeologists would probably agree that typologies are made by typologists, as we suggested in no. (8). At the same time, many of them have argued that types themselves are "natural" (Krieger 1944; Spaulding 1953: 305; Clarke 1968: 196; Thomas 1972). It is therefore necessary to stress the point that types as well as typologies are made by the typologist. The issue of "natural" vs. "artificial" classification (see Chapter 6) is not involved here. There may indeed be self-defining, clearly bounded units in nature (e.g. some mammalian species), and even occasionally among artifact groups, but the decision to include or not to include these units in a sorting system is always that of the typologist. No practical typology includes more than a fraction of the total number of types that could theoretically be generated according to its rules of "typehood."

(12) . . . into which he can place *discrete entities* . . . Sorting always implies some process of manipulation, and the things to be sorted must be

physically discrete if they are to be put into one and only one category. It is not always the entities to be classified that are manipulated (e.g. in the case of house types); sometimes it is merely data sheets or punch cards, or even photographs.

(13) . . . having specific *identifying characteristics* . . . Types have the two essential properties of identity and meaning (see Chapter 3). A type with no identifying characteristics would have no practical utility, even though in theory it might be enormously meaningful. We could for example think of a type comprising all of the pottery made at Pueblo Bonito in A.D. 1000. We could obviously learn an enormous amount from the study of such a type if there were any practical way of identifying it; unfortunately, at least for the moment, there is not.

(14) . . . to *distinguish* them from entities having other characteristics . . . Cormack (1971: 329) has observed that types are characterized by "internal cohesion and external isolation." This recognizes the fact that all types are members of typologies, and they have their identity and meaning partly with reference to other types in the same system. They are distinguished both by what they are and by what they are not.

(15) . . . in a way that is *meaningful* . . . We are not going to differentiate types, no matter how morphologically distinct they are, if the distinction will not serve the purposes of our classification. For example there is enormous sexual dimorphism in some bird species; so much so that the males of different species sometimes appear, superficially, more similar to each other than they do to the females of their own species (Simpson 1945: 9–11). But this difference is ignored in Linnean classification, whose purpose is to define intrafertile species. A still more gross example might be cited in the case of phonograph records, where the most obvious difference is between 10" and 12" records. Few music libraries are likely to take this into account in their classifications.

(16) . . . to the *purpose* of the typology. This brings us back finally, as everything does, to the issue of purpose. It is the purpose of the typology that gives meaning to the individual types, and it is on the basis of such meaning (or lack of it) that we decide whether or not to distinguish one type from another.

Practical typologies

The definition we have offered above applies in theory to all typologies, whether practical or impractical. Our book, however, is specifically about practical typologies, and this obliges us to add one further qualification: a practical typology consists only of realized types, not of potential ones. In our mailbox analogy in Chapter 5, we noted that an artifact typology may be likened to a set of mailboxes that we have put up. Obviously we are not going to put up a box for John Smith until some mail for John Smith actually arrives. Once we have done so, however, the box will be there for future mail as well as for mail currently in hand, and we will have to decide whether or not to put into it mail addressed to J. S. Smith, Jack Smith, and so on.

A practical typology therefore cannot be made by paradigmatic attribute clustering (cf. Dunnell 1971b: 70–6). In paradigmatic classification, every unique attribute cluster is defined in advance as a type, whether or not it has actual exemplars. But a typology involving no more than four attributes, each of which could be either present or absent, would already have sixteen different potential attribute clusters. In a typology involving as many variables as are normally studied by archaeologists, the number of possible combinations would be beyond calculation. A practical typology, therefore, will include no types until there are entities to fit them. This is one reason why, as we saw in Chapter 5, archaeological type concepts usually begin with artifact clusters.

PART III

TYPOLOGY IN ACTION: THE MEDIEVAL NUBIAN POTTERY TYPOLOGY

Scientific procedures are not gadgets preconceived and thrust into reality in the hope of a catch. They evolve and are applied spontaneously as problems arise in the mind of the thinker.

Robert H. Lowie (1937: 280)

9

ORIGIN AND DEVELOPMENT
OF THE NUBIAN TYPOLOGY

The authors of this book are familiar, in theory or in practice, with quite a number of typologies, and so presumably are most readers. Since we hope to reach a wide and varied audience, however, we cannot be sure that all or even most of our readers will be familiar with the same examples of the *genre*. Rather than illustrate our points with examples from a number of different typologies, we have chosen to describe in detail one particular typology, which will provide many of the illustrative examples we will discuss in subsequent chapters. The typology chosen is WYA's Classification of Medieval Nubian Pottery Wares (WYA 1986a), hereinafter called the Nubian Pottery Typology.

This seemingly egocentric procedure can be defended on several grounds. The typology is a fairly complex one, with enough internal variability to illustrate most of the points we want to make. It was developed for a specific purpose, and its utility in serving that purpose can be not only described but measured. Most importantly of all, one author (WYA) is familiar in detail not only with the typology but with its family history and secrets. This makes it possible to consider how the scheme first arose, and the hits and misses of its development – a privilege we are not often given in discussions of typologies (cf. Dunnell 1971b: 139; Gardin 1980: 81).

Much that is said in this and the next two chapters will already be familiar to field archaeologists, and especially to those who are accustomed to work with pottery. It nevertheless seems desirable to provide a fairly detailed description of classificatory and sorting procedures for the benefit of those (hoped-for) readers who have not personally been involved in these arcane rituals. Throughout the discussion that follows, the pronoun "I" refers to WYA.

Circumstances of origin
When I went to Nubia to undertake salvage excavations in 1959, I knew nothing whatever about medieval Nubian pottery. Neither, as it turned

99

out, did any of the other archaeologists then active in the region. By pure accident the first site I chose to dig (called the Faras Potteries) was a factory where pottery had been mass-produced between about A.D. 600 and 900 (WYA 1961). The site was clearly stratified, and the pottery in the bottom layers was conspicuously different from that at the top. It was therefore evident that if I could learn systematically to differentiate the pottery wares from the different levels at Faras, they might furnish a useful tool for dating any other medieval Nubian sites in which the same wares might later be found (cf. WYA 1970a: 111).

Without any ceramic material to work with, there was obviously no possibility of constructing a typology before the excavation of the Faras Potteries began, nor was there time to do so while the work was in actual progress. I could only put aside the collected pottery fragments (sherds) for later investigation. But the sherds were accumulating at the rate of about 1,000 per day, and I had no containers in which to store them except for the carrying baskets that were also needed in the excavations. Before long a serious shortage of baskets developed, and it became a practical necessity to do something about reducing the sherd population. Out of that humble and pragmatic necessity the Nubian Pottery Typology was born.

Among the accumulated sherds there were some intuitively obvious "types" that stood out quite markedly from the rest of the material, and which I felt that I could nearly always recognize at a glance. One of these was an undecorated utility ware, used mainly for wine amphorae, that had been produced in enormous quantities. I took a large sample of this ware (i.e. type) out of the baskets, analyzed each of the sherds in terms of its constituent attributes, and was able to establish that all of the selected sherds did indeed share a very large number of attributes. I then proceeded to write a formal description of the ware (now designated as Ware U5 – see Table 5), listing as many of its regularly occurring characteristics as I could identify. Finally I pulled out all of the remaining sherds that matched this description from the baskets, counted and tallied them, and dumped them out into a "Ware U5 pile." I was able to do the same with two or three other intuitively obvious types while the excavations were still in progress, and in this way was able to liberate enough baskets to get me through the excavation season (WYA 1975: 82).

The initial Nubian Typology

Once started down the rocky road to typology, there was no turning back. Unfortunately, the first wares that I was able to recognize did not prove to be very temporally significant. They were found from bottom to top of the

Faras Potteries site, meaning that they had been made during the whole of its 300-year history. If my ceramic studies were to have any practical value, beyond liberating baskets and shelf space, I would have to learn to differentiate those wares that did not occur throughout the whole of the Faras Potteries site; i.e. those occurring only in the bottom, in the middle, or in the top layers. These wares could then be arranged in a chronological sequence, reflecting their stratigraphic occurrence in the site. The task of analyzing and classifying the chronologically significant wares from Faras occupied me during the summer months between my first and second excavation seasons in Nubia.

At this point I was, and indeed still am, a field archaeologist and not a ceramologist (cf. WYA 1981a). In my earlier excavations in the American Southwest I had given little attention or thought to pottery, and none at all to its classification. I was not interested in it as a technological or artistic medium, and I found the extant typologies of Colton (Colton and Hargrave 1937; Colton 1955; 1956; 1958) and others quite sufficient for any purposes of mine. It was only when I arrived in Nubia, and was faced with the practical challenge of organizing an archaeological salvage campaign in *terra incognita* (see WYA 1968b; Säve-Söderbergh 1987: 193–6), that I was forced as a practical necessity to enter into the field of pottery analysis for myself.

As of 1959 more than two-thirds of all the known sites in Sudanese Nubia (the area of the Sudan to be flooded by the Aswan High Dam) dated from the Christian Nubian period, between about A.D. 600 and 1500. Most of the sites did not appear to have been occupied for more than two or three centuries, but there was no basis on which to arrange them in a chronological sequence. Our strategy in the salvage campaign, however, was to draw a sample of sites from each period of history (generally encompassing two or three centuries each), to provide a basis for the reconstruction of Nubian cultural development from beginning to end (WYA 1962a; 1966: 161–2; 1968b). Some method for the chronological ordering of sites was therefore a critical necessity, and, as usual in archaeology, pottery provided the key (cf. Ford and Willey 1949: 40; Rouse 1960: 319–21; 1970: 10; Hole and Heizer 1965: 121–2; Sabloff and Smith 1969: 179).

My reason for studying pottery was therefore clearly evident at the outset, and it remained so throughout the Nubian salvage campaign. I wanted to discover all of the ceramic varieties that were temporally significant (i.e. that had been made during a definable period of time), and could therefore serve as a basis for the dating of any sites in which they might be found. Given the pressure of time and other duties, I wanted as much as possible to ignore all varieties that did not serve that purpose. What this meant in practice was that I wanted to define types on the basis only of temporally significant attributes: fabrics or vessel forms or decorative styles whose distributions in time could be plotted. But this was, and still is, more easily said than done. I had already discovered that I could not make *a priori* assumptions about what individual attributes were and were not temporally patterned, and for the same reason I could not make *a priori* assumptions about what clusters of attributes were and were not significant. Hence I had to adopt the operating principle, "split first, then lump" (cf. WYA 1975: 88; Doran and Hodson 1975: 166–7).

In other words, types had to be provisionally designated, and given identifying numbers, before their spatial and temporal distributions could be investigated. Only later could they be eliminated from the system, if they proved to have no chronological significance. This happened most commonly when two distinguishable but closely similar types proved to have precisely the same distribution in time and space; they could then be combined under a single type description and number. Less commonly, a sharply distinct "type" was represented only by a few sherds (perhaps all from the same vessel) at a single site, and was never subsequently encountered elsewhere. Eventually it would be eliminated as a type on the grounds of statistical insignificance.

The foregoing discussion should make it clear that extrinsic as well as intrinsic evidence contributed to the final designation of types. No cluster of intrinsic attributes (fabric, form, color, decoration, etc.) was given separate designation as a type if its distribution in time and space was found to be identical to that of another, similar cluster of attributes. This necessarily means that distributions in time and space are themselves among the defining attributes of Nubian pottery types; they are what we have elsewhere called extrinsic variables (see Chapter 14).

Over time, the Nubian Pottery Typology acquired secondary purposes in addition to that of dating sites. One such purpose that soon became apparent was that of aiding in the cataloguing of whole vessels, which were recovered in great numbers from the Faras Potteries. It is self-evident that many characteristics of pottery vessels – particularly those of shape and decoration – cannot be adequately described in words, nor in many cases do they show up clearly in photographs. They can of course be effectively represented in drawings of various kinds, but the laborious execution of several drawings of each individual vessel was a task far beyond my resources of time and talent. In the long run, the most efficient way of cataloguing vessels – that is, of recording on paper the minimum necessary information about each vessel – was to develop typologies of form and design, so that one drawing and description could stand for many vessels. Any particular vessel might then be recorded simply as belonging to Form F16 and exhibiting decoration in Style N.VIA, comprising an upper wall frieze of Elements H3-2 and H3-3 in alternation, and a waist frieze of Elements K2-2 and K2-3 in alternation, as illustrated in Figure 8 (Chapter 11).

This enterprise carried me onto new ground, so to speak; from the analysis and recording of sherds to the analysis and recording of whole vessels (see also Chapter 11). As a result various refinements were introduced into the typology that would not have been necessary purely for the analysis of sherd material, or purely for dating. These added features included the complex sub-classifications of vessel forms and of decoration that will be described in Chapter 11.

In time I became interested also in the economic and in the historical possibilities in the ceramic data, as they reflected on the circulation of goods and on the evolution of styles. For these purposes I began recording other attributes of the pottery that would not necessarily have been useful for dating; for example, variations in fabric that would identify different sources of origin. Dating nevertheless remains the primary objective of the Nubian Typology, and the basis on which wares that appear similar are or are not differentiated from one another. I continue to make some typological distinctions that are probably of no significance for any purpose other than that of dating, which in some cases means making distinctions that the makers and users of the pottery would themselves have considered insignificant.

I need not describe in detail the further progress of my classification of the Faras material. Basically it involved a continuation of my initial procedure: recognizing and defining one type at a time, removing it from the pile, and turning my attention to the diminishing residuum of unclassified sherds. As I did so, and became increasingly aware of which attributes did and did not cluster meaningfully, I naturally developed a growing sense of what to look for.

In the beginning I was strongly influenced, in the choice of variables, by typologies I was previously familiar with in the American Southwest. These provided a useful point of departure; in fact I doubt that I could have undertaken the classification of the Nubian wares without this foundation to build on. But it took me some time to appreciate the fact that the variables that are important in differentiating pottery wares in the Southwest are not necessarily important in Nubia, or vice versa. I was, in hindsight, surprisingly slow to recognize that some of my wares were hand-made while others were wheel-made, since this distinction did not exist in the aboriginal Southwest. Eventually the lesson came home that I could make no *a priori* assumptions, but must treat every variable characteristic as potentially significant until I could prove that it was not (that is, that it did not co-occur regularly with any other variable).

I came gradually to recognize that the defining variables in medieval Nubian pottery fell into five distinct categories, which I designated as method of construction, fabric (characteristics of the paste), vessel forms, color, and decoration. Each of these involved a cluster of partially inter-dependent variables; for example, a change in certain aspects of decoration would necessitate, or accompany, changes in other aspects as well. But variability within any one of the five major domains would not necessarily affect any of the others. The five domains were designated by me as universes or domains of variability. (As noted earlier, extrinsic evidence of distribution in time and space was also taken into account in the designation of pottery types. This constituted an additional, sixth domain of variability.)

In the process of classifying I found it necessary to develop formal sub-classifications in several of my domains of variability. In due time I recognized and named five recurring fabric combinations, eighty-one forms which were grouped into eighteen form classes, and about 130 individual designs which were clustered into ten styles. Method of construction was classified as hand-made or wheel-made, and color as black, brown, red, orange, pink, yellow, white, or natural (i.e. the unmodified clay color). On the basis of recurring combinations of attributes in the five basic domains (that is, one method of construction, one fabric type, a recurring group of forms, one or two colors, and one decorative style) I found that I could consistently recognize twenty-seven pottery types in the sherd collections from the Faras Potteries. But because the word "type" has been used by Nile Valley archaeologists almost exclusively to designate vessel forms, I decided to substitute the term "ware" in my classification, and I have continued this usage down to the present.

As can be seen, the original version of the Nubian Pottery Typology was the result purely of a differentiation process (cf. Foucault 1973: 141–3). I concentrated on differences rather than similarities, and did not attempt to discover any relationships among my twenty-seven wares, or to group them into higher taxonomic categories. At this point I had a typology but not a taxonomy, according to the usages employed here (see Chapter 17).

As of 1960 there were more than fifty known medieval sites awaiting excavation in Sudanese Nubia, and several of these had been requested as excavation concessions by European and American archaeological missions. With this in mind I hastened to publish my initial typology as an aid to others working in the medieval field, both in Egypt and in the Sudan (WYA 1962d). It was clearly labeled as provisional, but inevitably some colleagues treated it as received wisdom, and some of them have faulted me for subsequently altering it.

Subsequent evolution of the typology

In 1961 and 1962 the continuing excavation of medieval sites brought much new material to hand (see especially WYA 1962b), and extended the time range of my investigations backward in time to around A.D. 200, and forward to around 1100 (cf. WYA 1964b: 241–7). This of course contributed many new wares from the early and late centuries, and even some additional wares from the period coeval with the Faras Potteries, which had not been found at Faras itself. At the same time, however, four of my twenty-seven originally designated wares turned out to be statistically non-significant, and were eliminated from the system. I could not find them at any site other than Faras, and the total collection of sherds was too small to be of account. I have since adopted the rule of thumb that wares must be represented by sherds from more than one vessel, and, if the total collection of sherds is under 100, they must be from more than one site.

By 1963 I had expanded the Nubian Typology to include forty-one wares. I had also come to recognize two new groups of attributes, or domains of variability, as potentially significant in the classification of the Nubian wares. The first of these was surface finish (which was usually either polished or matte), and the second was relief decoration, which I had not previously treated independently from painted decoration. Some wares were now differentiated from each other on the basis of surface finish alone, although this was found to be significant only at certain periods in Nubian history.

I had also begun to look at similarities as well as differences among my wares, and for the first time I grouped them into larger categories which I called ware groups. As I originally conceived them, ware groups were defined by a common fabric, style, and method of construction; that is, the wares in any given group were characterized by a similar method of construction (hand-made or wheel-made), a similar fabric, and a similar style of decoration. I assumed that each ware group represented, in a general way, pottery made by the same group of people in the same area, using the same methods and materials. By the introduction of this second taxonomic level, the original typology had now become also a taxonomy, according to the usages employed here.

By 1963 the published, preliminary classification of twenty-seven wares (WYA 1962d) was being widely consulted by other expeditions, although by this time I was already aware of its limitations and imperfections. It seemed important to alert the expeditions to recent developments and changes, but, in view of the rapid evolution and probable future growth of the scheme, another publication seemed unwise. Instead I produced in typescript a 250-page *Field Manual of Christian Nubian Pottery Wares*, which was made available in manuscript form to a number of interested expeditions (WYA MS-1). Some copies of it are evidently still circulating, for it continues to be cited from time to time in the literature (e.g. Schneider 1975: 37–8; Shinnie and Shinnie 1978: 56).

In 1963 and 1964, excavation of the magnificently stratified mound site of Meinarti (WYA 1964b: 222–39; 1965b; 1968c) provided me with a whole series of new and well-defined wares, covering the period between A.D. 1100 and 1500. Because of its enormous volume, the Meinarti material also greatly enhanced my familiarity with the earlier wares. (The site had been inhabited from about 200 to 1500.) By the conclusion of this excavation I had recognized and defined most of the wares that are included today in the Nubian Pottery Typology, although work at Kulubnarti in 1969 (WYA 1970b) added a few more wares from the period 1500–1600.

Apart from the description of some new wares and the revised description of some old ones, the main innovation in the Nubian Pottery Typology since 1963 has been the introduction of a new taxonomic level, the pottery family. Families are distinguished from each other on the basis of fabric and method of construction alone (see Table 4). They represent pottery which, on distributional evidence, I know to have been made by the same people in the same area, using the same materials and techniques, over a long period of time. (In fact, the three most important families were in continuous production throughout the period from 200 to 1500.) The more long-enduring families are now subdivided into successive ware groups, representing intervals in the history of each family when particular norms of form and decoration were in vogue. In other words, ware groups have the defining characteristics of fabric and method of construction, which are common to the families to which they belong, and the additional defining characteristics of vessel form and decorative style, which distinguish one ware group from another in the same family (see Table 4).

Table 4. *Defining variables in Nubian pottery families, ware groups, and wares*

	Method of construction	Fabric	Surface treatment	Vessel forms	Colors	Painted decoration	Relief decoration
Families	x	x					
Ware groups	x	x		*		*	*
Wares	x	x	+	*	+	*	*

x Defining characteristics of families and their constituent ware groups and wares
* Additional defining characteristics of ware groups in each family
+ Additional defining characteristics of wares in each ware group

The average duration of Nubian ware groups was about two and a half centuries, although they persisted much longer in the conservative hand-made wares than in the competitive, market-oriented wheel-made wares (see Figure 4).

In one family (Family L; see Table 5), comprising mass-produced Egyptian transport wares, variability was primarily spatial rather than temporal. That is, vessels of much the same type were made at a number of different localities, using the same techniques but slightly different materials. I have accordingly subdivided this family into sub-families rather than into ware groups, since they were all in existence concurrently rather than sequentially. Sub-families are distinguished from each other by minor differences in fabric, and sometimes also in vessel forms, rather than by stylistic characteristics.

Wares are still the basic building blocks of the Nubian Typology. Within any given ware group or sub-family, the individual wares represent con-current, deliberately produced variation, primarily in the use of color and/or surface finish. In Nubia there was always some demand for white-slipped and some demand for red-slipped vessels, as well as a continuing need for various kinds of utility vessels that were usually not slipped. Consequently most ware groups will be found to include, at a minimum, a white-slipped ware, a red-slipped ware, and an unslipped utility ware. At some periods, but not others, we also find yellow-slipped and orange-slipped wares. At some periods a further distinction can be made between polished and matte-finished wares, which otherwise exhibit the same styles and colors. Defining characteristics of families, ware groups, and wares are shown schematically in Table 4.

Introduction of the family concept gave to the classification, for the first time, a genetic dimension. All of the wares in any one family can be seen, figuratively speaking, as descendants of a common ancestor or ancestors, and the various ware groups in each family represent successive stages in its evolution. It should be noted, however, that the taxonomic levels of family and ware group were added to the system for secondary, primarily historical purposes; they are unnecessary for the original purpose of dating sites. Dates for any deposit can be calculated simply by knowing the percentages of different wares present and absent, without knowing to what families or groups they belong. The procedures involved will be more fully explained in Chapter 11.

By 1970 excavation in Nubia had largely ceased, and most of the area that had been threatened with inundation was in fact under water. Since I did not anticipate much further development of the pottery typology, I felt safe in publishing it once again in the form which it had then reached (WYA 1973c). There were at that time ninety-eight wares, grouped into seven families having a total of sixteen ware groups among them. The scheme had become sufficiently elaborated that it was scheduled for publication in two successive issues of *Kush*, the Journal of the Sudan Antiquities Service. Unfortunately, the journal suspended publication before the second instalment could appear.

Since 1972 I have been engaged biennially in excavations at Qasr Ibrim, a large site in Egyptian Nubia. Here, assisted for the first time by a sizable team, I have been able significantly to improve my field procedures for recording pottery. Every potsherd from every excavation unit throughout the site is now systematically collected, cleaned, and recorded on a tally sheet according to its ware (Plumley, Adams, and Crowfoot 1977: 39–41). The total of sherds recorded in this fashion comes to over 150,000 in a typical season, and to well over a million since the excavations began. Such a volume of material has, of course, allowed for the further refinement of some ware descriptions, and the special circumstances of preservation at Qasr Ibrim have allowed a more precise calculation of dates for many wares than was previously possible.

The excavations as Qasr Ibrim have also, for the first time, carried me back into deposits substantially earlier than A.D. 200, for the site had been occupied since the days of the Egyptian Pharaohs. More than thirty previously unfamiliar wares have come to light, and have been subjected to provisional classification in the same way as were the medieval wares twenty years earlier. I have now prepared, and have distributed in manuscript form, a preliminary manual of twenty-eight Ptolemaic and Roman wares, made between 100 B.C. and A.D. 200 (WYA MS-2). My collaborator Pamela Rose is at work on the first stages of a classification of still earlier wares, extending back to around 750 B.C.

All of my earlier publications were necessarily synopses, presenting only abbreviated ware descriptions and a few pages of sample illustrations. However, I have long been urged by UNESCO and by the Sudan Antiquities Service to publish the typology in full, with complete ware descriptions and illustrations. This project was frustrated for many years by lack of funds, but in 1986 the full, two-volume *Ceramic Industries of Medieval Nubia* finally appeared (WYA 1986a). Here each individual ware is given from three to five pages of verbal description, as well as several pages illustrating most of the known vessel forms, with typical decoration. There are separate descriptions and illustrations of vessel forms, decorative styles, and other variable features. This work can be consulted by anyone wishing to confirm or to amplify what is said here.

IO

BASIC FEATURES OF THE
NUBIAN TYPOLOGY

In spite of its massiveness, I have insisted that *Ceramic Industries of Medieval Nubia* (WYA 1986a) is not and cannot be the "last word" on Nubian pottery; it is merely the latest and most detailed in a continuing series of progress reports. The ongoing excavations at Qasr Ibrim are sure to contribute new information, and possibly also new wares, and hopefully future excavations in the Sudan will do the same. It is still also possible that some wares will be eliminated, since the significance of some of my finer distinctions remains suspect. I will here briefly recapitulate the scheme as it exists at the moment, without in any way suggesting that it has attained its final form.

The Nubian Typology in 1989

The Nubian Pottery Classification for the period A.D. 200–1600 today contains 101 wares, grouped into the same seven families and sixteen ware groups that were mentioned in the last chapter. The scheme bears a close but not total resemblance to the familiar type-variety system employed in the American Southwest and Mesoamerica (Wheat, Gifford, and Wasley 1958; Smith, Willey, and Gifford 1960; Sabloff and Smith 1969). The complete listing of wares, ware groups, and families is given in Table 5. Each ware has been formally described in terms of seventy variable features, as listed in Table 6 (WYA 1986a: 411–597). Following the description of intrinsic features there is, for each ware, an estimation of the probable completeness and reliability of the description, and a discussion of the spatial and temporal distribution and historical relationships of the ware. The description concludes with a list of references to works in which the ware has been discussed or (much more commonly) illustrated. For illustrative purposes, a typical ware description and illustrations are presented in Appendix B.

The variables of form, of painted decoration, and of relief decoration are described in separate, formal sub-classifications. The form classification now includes about 650 different normative vessel shapes found in different wares, and these are grouped into twenty-seven mostly functional form classes (WYA 1986a: 108–83). All of the vessel forms are illustrated, as shown in the specimen form illustrations included here (Figure 1). More than 2,600 individual decorative designs have also been recognized and illustrated, and these have been grouped into thirty-nine styles, as listed in Table 7. Figure 2 shows a typical page of style illustrations. The style typology is itself highly complex; it involves such cross-cutting variables as decorative elements (kinds of decoration that may be found on different parts of a vessel), decorative programs (varying combinations of elements), decorative fields (areas that normally are and are not decorated on different vessel forms), decorative motifs (classified as shown in Figure 3), and styles (combinations of motifs). Boldness or fineness of lines, and precision or casualness in the execution of designs, are also considered in the classification of styles. (For a fuller explanation of the scheme see WYA 1986a: 213–392.)

Adequacy of the current typology

Like all classificatory schemes, the Medieval Nubian Pottery Typology does not "fit the data" equally well at all points. The Meroitic wares, made between about A.D. 200 and 400, are sufficiently different from all of the later wares so that I originally included them in a separate classification altogether (WYA 1964a). They seem to have been made simultaneously at a lot of different factories, some of which followed quite individualistic traditions in regard to both vessel forms and decoration. There is, as a result, a good deal more concurrent variability in the Meroitic wares than there is later. Following the principle of "split first, then lump," I originally designated no fewer than twenty-five different Meroitic wares. However, some of the distinctions I was making (e.g. between burnished, polished, and matte surface finish) proved to have no chronological significance during this particular period of history. Again following my own guidance of eliminating anything that was not useful for dating, I collapsed the original classification of twenty-five wares into no more than thirteen when I combined the Meroitic and Christian classifications in 1963 (WYA MS-1). Now, however, some of my Meroitic wares are so diversified that they are hard to characterize, since they exhibit no very obvious modality. Following my own principles, I began with too many wares and ended with too few, but I still have not found a really satisfactory solution to this dilemma.

The glazed wares present a classificatory problem of another kind.

Class G: Small pots and bottles

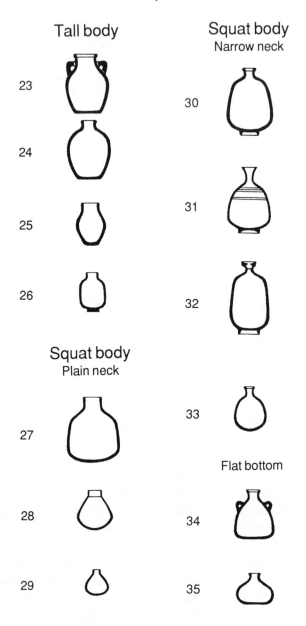

Figure 1 The Medieval Nubian Pottery Typology: specimen page of vessel
form illustrations. The page shows a group of vessels in Form Class
G (small pots and bottles).

Style NVB: Post-Classic Christian Style, southern variant

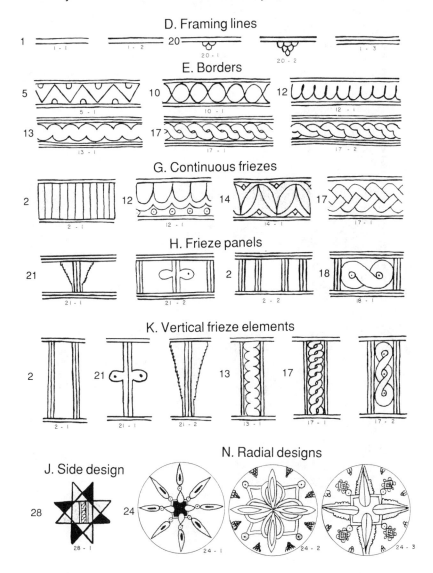

Figure 2 The Medieval Nubian Pottery Typology: specimen page of decorative style illustrations, Style N.VB. Numbers to the left of each design or group of designs are keyed to the classification of motifs (Figure 3).

Classification of X-Group and Christian Nubian decorative motifs

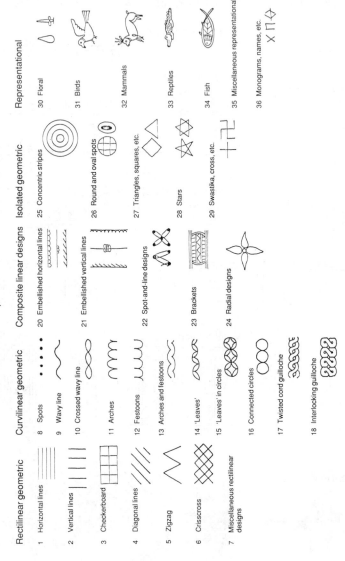

Figure 3 The Medieval Nubian Pottery Typology: classification of decorative motifs.

Table 5. *Outline classification of pottery wares found in medieval Nubian sites*

Indigenous wares

Family D Nubian hand-made (domestic) wares
Ware group D.I: Meroitic domestic wares

Ware H1	Early domestic plain utility ware
H9	Meroitic burnished domestic ware
H11	Meroitic fine black domestic ware
H12	Meroitic painted domestic ware
H18	X-Group red-on-white domestic ware

Ware Group D.II: X-Group and Early Christian domestic wares

Ware H1	(continues unchanged from Ware Group D.I)
H13	Transitional white-on-red domestic ware
H18	(continues unchanged from Ware Group D.I)
H2	Earlier Christian red-topped domestic ware
H3	Earlier Christian red domestic ware

Ware Group D.III: Later Christian domestic wares

Ware H4	Later Christian plain utility ware
H5	Later Christian red domestic ware
H8	Later Christian black domestic ware
H6	Late Christian incised red domestic ware
H7	Late Christian painted red domestic ware
H14	Late Christian painted white domestic ware

Ware Group D.IV: Post-Christian domestic wares

Ware H4	(continues unchanged from Ware Group D.III)
H5	(continues unchanged from Ware Group D.III)
H15	Post-Christian schist-tempered plain domestic ware
H16	Post-Christian schist-tempered red domestic ware
H17	Modern red-topped domestic ware

Family M Meroitic and X-Group fine ("eggshell") wares

Ware R35	Meroitic fine red ware
W26	Meroitic fine white ware
W27	Meroitic pale pink ware
W30	X-Group fine white ware

Family N Nubian ordinary wheel-made wares
Ware Group N.I: Meroitic ordinary wares

Ware R32	Meroitic ordinary red ware
R33	Meroitic striped ware
R34	Meroitic imitation Roman ware
W25	Meroitic ordinary white ware

Table 5 (*cont.*)

Ware Group N.II: X-Group wares
Ware R25	Early X-Group brown ware (also in Family T)
R1	Classic X-Group red ware
R2	Transitional red ware
R10	Transitional orange ware
W11	X-Group decorated white ware (also in Family T)
W29	X-Group ordinary white ware

Ware Group N.III: Early Christian wares
Ware R10	(continues unchanged from Ware Group N.II)
R3	Early Christian matte red ware
R5	Early Christian polished red ware
W1	Early Christian peach ware
W2	Early Christian matte white ware
W9	Early Christian polished white ware

Ware Group N.IV: Classic Christian wares
Ware R7	Classic Christian fine red ware
R23	Classic Christian heavy red ware
W5	Classic Christian fine white ware
W6	Classic Christian matte yellow ware
W10	Classic Christian polished yellow ware
W7	Classic Christian heavy white ware

Ware Group N.V: Post-Classic Christian wares
Ware R21	Post-Classic Christian polished orange ware
R22	Post-Classic Christian matte red ware
R36	Post-Classic Christian southern red ware
W20	Post-Classic Christian polished yellow ware
W23	Post-Classic Christian matte white ware
W21	Post-Classic Christian southern yellow ware
W7	(continues unchanged from Ware Group N.IV)

Ware Group N.VI: Late Christian wares
Ware R11	Late Christian polished orange ware
R17	Late Christian matte red ware
R19	Late Christian heavy decorated ware
W15	Late Christian matte white ware
W16	Late Christian polished yellow ware

Table 5. (*cont.*)

Ware Group N. VII: Terminal Christian wares
Ware R20	Terminal Christian heavy red ware
R26	Terminal Christian polished orange ware
R27	Terminal Christian dull orange ware
R28	Terminal Christian decorated orange ware
W14	Terminal Christian decorated white ware
W18	Terminal Christian thin white ware
W31	Terminal Christian brown-on-white ware

Ware Group NU: Nubian coarse utility wares
Ware U1	Pre-Christian brown utility ware
U5	Christian red utility ware
U10	Later Christian pink utility ware
U14	Later Christian slipped utility ware
U23	Later Christian hard buff utility ware
U24	Later Christian hard red utility ware

Imported wares

Family A Aswan wares

Ware Group A. I: Graeco-Roman Aswan wares
Ware R30	Aswan Graeco-Roman ordinary red ware
R31	Aswan Graeco-Roman flaky pink ware
R37	Aswan Graeco-Roman polished red ware
W24	Aswan Graeco-Roman ordinary cream ware
W32	Aswan Graeco-Roman fine cream ware

Ware Group A. II: Byzantine Aswan wares
Ware R4	Aswan Byzantine polished red ware
R14	Aswan Byzantine decorated pink ware
W3	Aswan Byzantine cream ware
U2	Aswan Byzantine pink utility ware

Ware Group A. III: Early Islamic Aswan wares
Ware R12	Aswan Early Islamic decorated red ware
R13	Aswan Islamic plain red ware
W22	Aswan Early Islamic white ware
U8	Aswan Early Islamic red utility ware

Ware Group A. IV: Medieval Aswan wares
Ware R13	(continues unchanged from Ware Group A.III)
R24	Aswan medieval decorated red ware
W12	Aswan medieval white ware
U6	Aswan medieval grey utility ware
Group G.V	Aswan medieval glazed utility ware[1]

Table 5. (*cont.*)

Family T Middle Egyptian ("Theban") mud wares

Ware R25   Early X-Group brown ware (also in Ware Group N.II)

W11   X-Group decorated white ware (also in Ware Group N.II)

W28   Middle Egyptian plain white ware

U4   Middle Egyptian brown utility ware

Family E Lower Egyptian mud wares

Ware   U20   Mameluke thin utility ware

U21   Mameluke heavy utility ware

Group G.IV Mameluke glazed wares[1]

Family L Egyptian drab utility wares

Sub-family LB: Ballas wares

Ware U16   Roman Ballas ware

U9   Ballas ribbed utility ware

U12   Ballas drab utility ware

Sub-family LF: Fostat wares

Ware U13   Fostat ordinary utility ware

U19   Fostat decorated utility ware

Group G.III Dull glazed wares (also in Sub-family LG)[1]

Sub-family LG: Egyptian buff wares of uncertain provenience

Ware U17   Buff utility ware with a drab surface

Group G.I   Earlier gloss glazed wares

G.III Dull glazed wares (also in Sub-family LF)[1]

Sub-family LS: "Saqqara" wares

Ware U3   "Saqqara" buff amphora ware

U15   "Saqqara" scored utility ware

Unclassified

Ware U18   Micaceous brown utility ware

Group G.II Later gloss glazed wares[1]

[1] For fuller classification of the glazed wares see Table 8

Table 6. *List of variables included in Nubian pottery ware descriptions*

Intrinsic variables

Method of construction

Fabric
  Paste
  Density
  Texture
  Color
  Carbon streak
  Hardness
  Fracture
  Solid temper
  Organic temper
  Fabric variability

Surface treatment
  Covering
  Finish
  Texture
  Configuration
  Variability in surface treatment

Vessel forms
  Most common forms
  Other forms
  Doubtful forms
  Vessel sizes
  Rim characteristics
  Base characteristics
  Handles
  Wall thickness
  Quality of execution
  Form variability

Colors
  Natural color
  Slip or wash color
  Primary decorative color(s)
  Secondary decorative color
  Color of rim stripe
  Color variability

Painted decoration
  Frequency
  Principal style(s)
  Other style(s)
  Most common decorative elements
  Other decorative elements
  Program of exterior decoration
  Program of interior decoration
  Quality of execution
  Fineness of delineation
  Decorative variability

Relief decoration
  Frequency
  Types
  Decorative programs
  Maker's marks
  Owner's graffiti
  Decorative variability

Extrinsic variables

Contextual variables
  Earliest date of appearance
  Main dates of manufacture
  Main dates of importation of Egyptian wares
  Dates of continued use of vessels after cessation of manufacture
  Dates of persistence of sherds in archaeological deposits
  Archaeological contexts where regularly found
  Centers of production
  Areas of geographical distribution

Table 6 (*cont.*)

Extrinsic variables (*cont.*)
Abundance or scarcity of the ware
Historical relationship to other wares
Contextual association with other wares
Index clusters in which found (see Chapter 12)

Evaluation of the ware description itself
Sufficiency of sherd material as basis for ware description
Sufficiency of whole vessels as basis for ware description
Estimated completeness of the description
Standardization or variability of the ware
Known variability of the ware over time
Known variability of the ware from area to area
Intergradation with other wares
Most nearly diagnostic features
Problems in definition or recognition

References

Table 7. *Classification of Nubian and Egyptian decorative styles*

General styles
 I   Red, orange, or pink slip only
 II White, cream, or yellow slip only
 III Red exterior, white interior
 IV Brown or black slip only
 V   Slip and rim stripe only
 VI Slip and plain body stripes only
 X   No slip or decoration

Horizon styles
 D.I   Meroitic domestic style
 D.II Early Christian domestic style
 D.III Later Christian domestic style

 N.IA Meroitic fancy style
 N.IB Meroitic striped style
 N.IC Meroitic naturalistic style
 N.IIA Classic X-Group style
 N.IIB X-Group white ware style
 N.IIC Transitional style
 N.III Early Christian style
 N.IVA Classic Christian fancy style
 N.IVB Classic Christian geometric style
 N.VA Post-Classic Christian style
 N.VB Post-Classic Christian style, southern variant
 N.VIA Late Christian fancy style
 N.VIB Late Christian inscribed style
 N.VII Terminal Christian style

 A.IA   Aswan Hellenistic style
 A.IB   Aswan Roman style
 A.II   Aswan Byzantine style
 A.IIIA Aswan Early Islamic style
 A.IIIB Aswan spot-and-line style
 A.IV   Aswan medieval style

Individual styles
 H13 Ware H13 decoration
 R7 Ware R7 decoration
 R10 Ware R10 decoration
 R20 Ware R20 decoration
 R25 Ware R25 decoration
 R26 Ware R26 decoration
 R31 Ware R31 decoration
 R33 Ware R33 decoration

 W18 Ware W18 decoration
 W31 Ware W31 decoration

Egyptian glazes began appearing in Nubia around A.D. 950, and by 1200 we find them comprising about 5 per cent of the total sherd population. Glazing makes possible the use of a whole range of colors that cannot otherwise be produced, and at least ten different decorative colors are found among the Egyptian glazes. As many as five colors can sometimes be found on the same vessel. In these circumstances color alone cannot be used to differentiate individual wares in the same way as with the unglazed Nubian wares; the total number of wares would be unmanageably large. Decoration presents a further problem, because lead glaze (used almost exclusively before about 1100, and sporadically thereafter) causes designs to blur and run during firing. Making a virtue of necessity, the Egyptian potters developed a variety of abstract swirl and splash designs that defy classification.

I have as a result developed a separate, rather complex typology of the glazes, comprising forty-six wares in five groups (see Table 8). (The glazed wares are treated collectively as a single family.) Ware groups here are differentiated primarily on the basis of fabric, which in some cases is associated also with distinctive vessel forms, colors, and glazing material (lead, tin, or alkaline). For dating purposes it has not been found necessary to count individual glazed wares, but only the total number of sherds of each ware group, in any excavation unit. Hence it is only glazed ware groups, and not individual wares, that appear on our sherd tally sheets (Figure 6 in Chapter 11) and in Table 5.

Like many other archaeological classifications, the Nubian Pottery Typology actually combines classification and seriation, as we define those terms here (see Chapters 4 and 17). The classification *per se* is a morphological one, in which wares are combined into ware groups, and ware groups into families, on the basis of visibly shared characteristics. But a chronological dimension is added through a process of seriation – the ordering of ware groups into developmental sequences, or chains of filiation, partly on the basis of external, chronological evidence. However, the Nubian Typology should not be mistaken for a true genetic classification, in which chains of filiation are postulated on the basis of shared attributes alone (as in biological and linguistic taxonomies). Genetic classifications usually exhibit a ramified character as they proceed downward through time (that is, single ancestors commonly have multiple offspring), whereas the sequence of ware groups in each Nubian family is strictly linear, as illustrated in Figure 4.

For all its complexity, the Nubian Pottery Typology remains full of soft spots and imprecision. These are, in some measure, the legacy of its

Table 8. *Outline classification of glazed wares found in medieval Nubia*

Group G.I: Earlier gloss wares (Sub-family LG)

A Monochrome	B Polychrome – lead glaze	C Polychrome – tin glaze
1 Yellow	1 Green on yellow	1 Yellow on white
2 Pale green	2 Green and brown on white	
3 Dark green	3 "Fayyumi" five-color	
4 Aquamarine		
5 Wine		

Group G.II: Later gloss wares (unclassified)

A Monochrome undecorated	B Monochrome carved	C Polychrome flat	D Polychrome silhouette
1 Yellow	1 Yellow	1 Black on green	1 White under green
2 Pale green	2 Pale green	2 Green on white (?)	
3 Dark green	3 Dark green	3 Blue on white	
4 Pale blue	4 Pale blue	4 Black and blue on white	
5 Aquamarine	5 Aquamarine		
6 Dark blue	6 Dark blue		
7 Wine	7 Wine		

Group G.III: Dull wares (sub-families LF and LG)

A Monochrome	B Polychrome
1 White	1 Brown on drab
2 Yellow`	2 Blue on drab
3 Yellow-green	3 Black on green
4 Light blue	4 Green on white
5 Drab	
6 Brown ·	

Group G.IV: Mameluke wares (Family E)

A Monochrome	B Sgraffiato painted	C Fancy painted
1 Yellow ochre	1 Brown on yellow	1 Fancy painted
2 Light green	2 Black on green	
3 Dark green		
4 Dark brown		

peculiar origins and history. Our field seasons in Nubia were typically of seven to nine months' duration each year, and during most of that time we lived in mud houses without electricity or plumbing. Our "trowels" during the first season were hand-forged from broken car springs, and a carpenter's folding rule was our only measuring instrument. We made glue from any plastic we could get our hands on, dissolved in acetone obtained from a local clinic.

The "we" refers almost exclusively to my wife and myself, for during the better part of seven years we had no other technical assistance. Besides counting potsherds we had to supervise the labor force (up to 250 men, in the excavations at Meinarti), to write field notes, to take and develop photographs, to draw plans and cross-sections, and to catalogue artifacts (cf. WYA 1962c). These were the circumstances in which the Nubian Pottery Typology was nurtured, and they will perhaps explain some of its idiosyncrasies. Above all they should explain the extreme preoccupation with practicality and convenience which the reader will find reflected in these pages.

I do not suppose that most typologies will be made and used in circumstances as primitive as those obtaining in Nubia (which, if anything, have become worse rather than better in the last twenty years). But I also do not suppose that they will be made and used under conditions as favorable as those that prevail on many North American digs, with their on-site laboratory and computer facilities and their armies of graduate and undergraduate assistants. Over 80 percent of the world's archaeology is done outside North America, in circumstances that fall somewhere between the extremes of Meinarti and Kampsville. I suggest, as a practical conclusion, that typological procedures must be appropriate to the field situations in which they are likely to be used.

Ware nomenclature

A word should be said in conclusion about the system of ware nomenclature employed in the Nubian Typology. Nomenclature in theory is a purely arbitrary matter, external to the typology itself. In practice, however, we have suggested (Chapters 3 and 5) that type names are one of the legitimate constituents of "typehood, " and they may affect the type concept itself. As such, type names may either facilitate or impede the intersubjective communication of type concepts (cf. Dunnell 1971b: 58–9).

I have avoided the common practice of naming pottery types after places (usually their places of first discovery), because this can be historically misleading. Place names understandably give the impression that the type was made at the place for which it is named, and this is very often not the case. New types are likely to be discovered somewhere at the outer fringes of their area of distribution, far from their main centers of production.

Ware nomenclature, like everything else about the Nubian Typology, has evolved over time. The names that I now use are designed to do two things: first to place the ware within a family or ware group (thereby identifying its fabric, and in many cases its stylistic properties), and second to differentiate it from other wares in the same family or group. Every ware name is, in effect, a mini-definition which is designed to capture in as few words as possible the essential features of the ware concept (cf. Foucault 1973: 139).

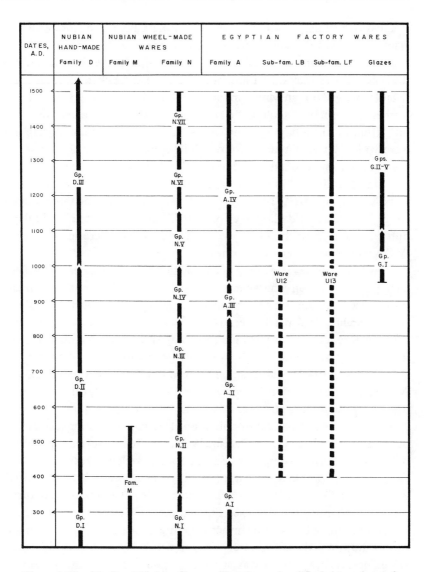

Figure 4 The Medieval Nubian Pottery Typology: simplified chronology of
ware groups in seven main pottery families. Chronology reads
upward.

This can be illustrated in the case of Terminal Christian decorated white ware (Ware W14), whose description is given in Appendix B. First, absence of the word "domestic" in the ware name locates it by default in the wheel-made wares, and absence of the word "Aswan" locates it by default in the Nubian wheel-made wares. Absence of the word "fine" further locates it by default in the Nubian ordinary wares, made from Nile mud (that is, in Family N). The words "Terminal Christian" locate the ware within Nubian Ware Group N.VII, suggesting a particular set of vessel forms and also a decorative style (Style N.VII) that are characteristic of this group. "White" will identify the slip color and at the same time will distinguish Ware W14 from the red ware (R20) and the three orange wares (R26, R27, and R28) in Group N.VII, and "decorated" will finally differentiate it from the other two white wares in the group (W18 and W31), which do not have elaborate decoration.

Ware names have necessarily been changed from time to time to reflect changes in defining characteristics, and only a few names remain unchanged from the original version of the typology. It is partly because of this instability, and partly because the ware names are too long and cumbersome for use in most field recording situations, that all wares are identified by numbers as well as by names. In the original typology I simply assigned them Arabic numerals from 1 to 27 (WYA 1962d: 272–6). As the typology expanded, however, it became increasingly difficult for me to keep the identifying numbers straight in my head. For purely mnemonic convenience, I subdivided the population of wares into arbitrary categories of hand-made (prefix H), and various wheel-made categories comprising red, orange, or pink-slipped wares (prefix R), yellow, cream or white-slipped wares (prefix W), unslipped utility wares (prefix U), and glazed wares (prefix G). It will be noted that the defining characteristics of these categories are not wholly consistent: method of construction in one case, slip color in three cases, and surface covering in one case. As a pragmatic matter, however, these five categories can nearly always be distinguished at a glance. As my purpose was purely mnemonic, this was the overriding consideration. The highest identifying number assigned to any ware is now 35 (Ware R35 in the group of red-slipped wares), and I find that I can commit this many numbers in each category to memory.

Since the early renumbering just described, I have kept the ware numbers unchanged through all subsequent revisions of the typology. It is clearly necessary to have one fixed and unchanging reference point for each ware, so that recorded data from earlier and later seasons can be compared without having to resort to cumbersome conversion tables.

It follows inevitably that the ware numbers proceed in no logical order, as will be apparent to readers of Table 5. They simply reflect the order of discovery of the wares in each category, which is a matter of accident. Sharp readers may also have noticed that there are gaps in the sequence of numbers; for example, there are no Wares R6, R8, R9, or W4. These were provisionally designated wares that have since been eliminated from the typology.

II

THE USES OF THE NUBIAN TYPOLOGY

The two previous chapters were concerned, respectively, with the classifi-catory and with the descriptive procedures involved in the making of the Nubian Typology. It remains here to consider the recording procedures that are involved in its use; that is, in the practical application of the typology to the study of actual ceramic material. While the classificatory and descriptive procedures are, as we saw, rather complex and detailed, we will observe here that the recording procedures are correspondingly simple.

The word "correspondingly" is used advisedly, for there is a negative relationship between descriptive and recording complexity. That is, the more detailed and specific is the information encoded in type descriptions, the less such information need be recorded for individual specimens. The mere assignment of a sherd or vessel to Ware W14 (see Appendix B) is enough to describe its method of construction, fabric, surface finish, and colors, as well as to indicate the range of possible vessel forms and decor-ative designs.

The material to be studied
The archaeologist typically finds pottery in two quite different forms: as sherds (fragments) and as complete vessels. The differences between these two kinds of ceramic remains are more than just a matter of completeness; they involve also the kinds of information that can be derived from the two sources. Whole pots are usually found in some place where they were intended to be, while sherds usually are not. They have come to their final resting places through successive accidents of breakage, discard, and possibly redeposition. As a result, it is only pots that consistently allow us to make functional inferences about the contexts in which they are found; for example, that a particular room was used for grain or wine storage. On the other hand whole pots are so rare in most habitation sites that they are

of very limited value for dating purposes; there are simply not enough of them. It is the tremendous proliferation of sherds in most occupation deposits that gives them their unparalleled value for dating, as we will see a little later.

In sum, whole pots and sherds are useful to the archaeologist for different purposes (see especially WYA 1987; n.d.3). In some circumstances there might even be justification for developing wholly different classifications in the two cases. For example, an archaeologist interested in functional reconstructions, and therefore working primarily with whole vessels, might want to develop a typology based exclusively on vessel form – a practice that in fact is fairly common among Egyptologists (e.g. Petrie 1905: pls xxx–xxxiv; Mond and Myers 1934, III: pls. cxxvii–cliv). On the other hand an archaeologist interested exclusively in dating might develop a typology in which form was ignored altogether, since vessel form cannot be precisely determined in the great majority of sherds.

The Nubian Typology is however designed for the recording both of sherds and of whole vessels, as we saw in Chapter 9. The original and primary purpose was for dating, and the system was therefore developed quite specifically with sherds in mind. Over time, however, it developed secondary purposes, some of which involved the recording and study of whole vessels. The present scheme consequently includes some categories of information that are important primarily in the study of sherds, and others that are important primarily in the study of whole pots. But while the typology itself is the same in the two cases, the recording procedures are not. In this chapter we will be mainly concerned with the recording of sherds for dating purposes, since this was the typology's *raison d'être*, but a few words will also be said about other purposes, and about the recording of whole vessels.

Sorting and recording potsherds

Like everything else about the Nubian Typology, sorting and recording procedures have evolved and changed over the years. This is a reflection partly of changing circumstances and needs, and partly of the increasing experience of the sorters. At the Faras Potteries, Meinarti, and other large sites excavated before 1969, extreme shortage of personnel made it a practical impossibility to sort and tally all of the potsherds recovered. Decorated wares were collected and tallied, but the more numerous utility wares were simply noted as present or absent for each excavation unit. In the Kulubnarti excavations of 1969 (WYA 1970b), the presence of student assistants made it possible for the first time to make a complete tally of all sherds, and the same procedure has been followed since at Qasr Ibrim (WYA n.d.1; Plumley, Adams, and Crowfoot 1977: 39).

At Qasr Ibrim sorting must be done on a daily basis, for our excavation strategy calls for stripping the site level by level. Microlevels are differentiated very largely by their ceramic content, and this makes necessary a close and continuous monitoring of the sherd collections (WYA 1986b; n.d.3). Because "today's sherds may determine tomorrow's excavations," it has been the general practice for excavation supervisors to do their own sherd analysis. Sorting is done in the afternoons between about 3:00 and 6:00 p.m.; that is, after the conclusion of digging and before sundown. Experience has shown that effective sorting cannot be done by artificial light; at least not by the feeble light shed by our electric generators.

The first step in sorting is to dump all of the sherds from any one excavation unit into a single pile. Sherds are collected on the site in baskets, which have unit identification tags attached to them. A typical excavation unit will produce two or three baskets of sherds; say, 500 to 1,000 individual sherds, though some units have produced as few as fifty or as many as 3,000 sherds. We have found that sherd sorting is most rapidly and effectively done if we sit on the ground rather than at tables, because a great deal of space is needed to subdivide each pile of sherds into its constituent wares.

Sorting always involves at least two stages, and quite commonly three. In the first stage, sherds are sorted into a few broad categories that are instantly recognizable; most commonly the hand-made wares, the Nubian wheel-made utility wares, the Nubian wheel-made decorated wares, the Aswan wares, and all other imported wares. This initial sorting will yield piles of very unequal size; the important thing, however, is that the groupings can be distinguished at a glance. Five to ten minutes are usually sufficient for the initial sorting of any collection. The categories to be distinguished will actually vary somewhat according to the material being sorted. For example, glazed wares or certain kinds of Egyptian wine amphorae may be separated during the first sorting if they are present in quantity.

The second stage involves subdivision of the five or so initial piles into their constituent wares. This is normally done in a sequence which begins with the easiest category first. The hand-made wares will not comprise more than 5 to 10 per cent of a typical collection, and there are seldom more than four or five individual wares present. The wheel-made utility wares will almost certainly be much more numerous – often 60 to 70 per cent of the total sherd collection – but again there are not likely to be more than three or four individual wares present. The rationale for proceeding from the simplest to the most complex is simply that of liberating sorting space as quickly as possible. The more wares are present, the more space is needed to sort them into separate piles. Sorting and removing the hand-made and the utility wares frees up at the beginning the space they occupy, leaving room for the piles of the much more numerous Nubian decorated wares. These will nearly always be sorted last, and they often require two additional sorting stages: first into ware groups, and then into individual wares. The complete sorting and tallying of 500 sherds, by experienced sorters, will normally take about twenty minutes.

Sherd totals are recorded on tally sheets, illustrated in Figures 5 and 6. Nubian wares, both hand-made and wheel-made, are recorded on one side of the sheet, and imported wares on the other. It will be noted that on the tally sheets there are blank spaces both to the right and to the left of the ware identification numbers. The spaces to the right are for the entry of raw tallies; that is, actual counts of sherds of each ware. When these have been completed they are converted into percentage figures, relative to the total number of sherds collected from the unit, and these are then entered in the spaces to the left of the ware numbers. Later the percentage figures are transferred onto index cluster cards (Figure 7), which serve to highlight the particular percentage figures that are important for dating purposes. The actual dating procedures will be more fully detailed in the next section.

The sorting and recording procedures allow for several different levels of indeterminacy. On the basis of stylistic and/or form characteristics, some sherds can be assigned to a ware group but not to an individual ware. These sherds are simply tallied opposite the number of the appropriate ware group. Weathered sherds, which have lost their original surface color and decoration, can still often be assigned to a family on the basis of fabric characteristics and method of construction; these can be entered opposite the appropriate family name. Finally there will always be some sherds that quite evidently do not belong to any of the 101 wares in the typology; these must be tallied under the heading "unidentified wares" (cf. Cowgill 1982: 33–4).

Percentages of unidentified wares, as well as of identified ones, can be important for dating. For example, we have found that the different Ptolemaic and Roman occupation levels at Qasr Ibrim (c. 100 B.C.–A.D. 100) yield pretty much the same pottery wares in the same proportions, except that in the Ptolemaic levels the volume of unidentifiable wares is usually only 1 to 2 percent, while in the Roman levels it is consistently around 8 per cent (WYA MS-2). There are other microdifferences as well,

___1976___ Season   N= _323_   Code _XC 2_
___2-26___ Date   1n= _.31_   Notebook __WYA III B__

UNIT: _EC-217-H_ ——— POTTERY TALLY - 1
     Room 1-3   Level: _Floor 3 to Floor 4_

Nubian-made wares

10 FAMILY D _____

——— GROUP D.I _____
——— H1 _____
——— H9 _____
——— H11 _____
——— H12 _____
——— H18 _____

10 GROUP D.II _____
6 H1 _19_
——— H2 _____
——— H3 _____
2 H13 _7_
2 H18 _8_

——— GROUP D.III _____
——— H4 _____
——— H5 _____
——— H6 _____
——— H7 burnished _____
——— H7 Coarse _____
——— H8 _____
——— H14 _____

——— GROUP D.IV _____
——— H15 _____
——— H16 _____
——— H17 _____

1 FAMILY M _____
——— R35 _____
1 W26 _3_
——— W27 _____
——— W30 _____

71 FAMILY N _____

2 GROUP N.I _____
——— R32 _____
——— R33 _____
——— R34 _____
1 W25 _3_
1 W29 _3_

51 GROUP N.II _____
48 R1 _155_
3 R2 _9_
——— R10 _____
——— R25 _____
——— W11 _____
——— W29 _____

14 GROUP N.III _____
——— R3 _____
6 R5 _18_
1 R10 _4_
——— W1 _____
6 W2 _20_
1 W9 _3_

——— GROUP N.IV _____
——— R7 _____
——— R23 _____
——— W5 _____
——— W6 Style N.IVA _____
——— W6 Style N.IVB _____
——— W10 Style N.IVA _____
——— W10 Style N.IVB _____
——— W7 _____

——— GROUP N.V _____
——— R21 _____
——— R22 _____
——— R36 _____
——— W20 _____
——— W21 _____
——— W23 _____

——— GROUP N.VI _____
——— R11 _____
——— R17 _____
——— R19 _____
——— W15 _____
——— W16 _____

——— GROUP N.VII _____
——— R20 _____
——— R26 _____
——— R27 _____
——— R28 _____
——— W14 _____
——— W18 _____
——— W31 _____

4 GROUP NU _____
3 U1 _11_
1 U5 _4_
——— U10 _____
——— U14 _____
——— U23 _____
——— U24 _____

Figure 5 Specimen Nubian sherd tally sheet, side 1 (domestic wares). Raw tallies are entered to the right of each ware or group number; corresponding percentage figures to the left. The total population of the sherd collection is entered at top, center.

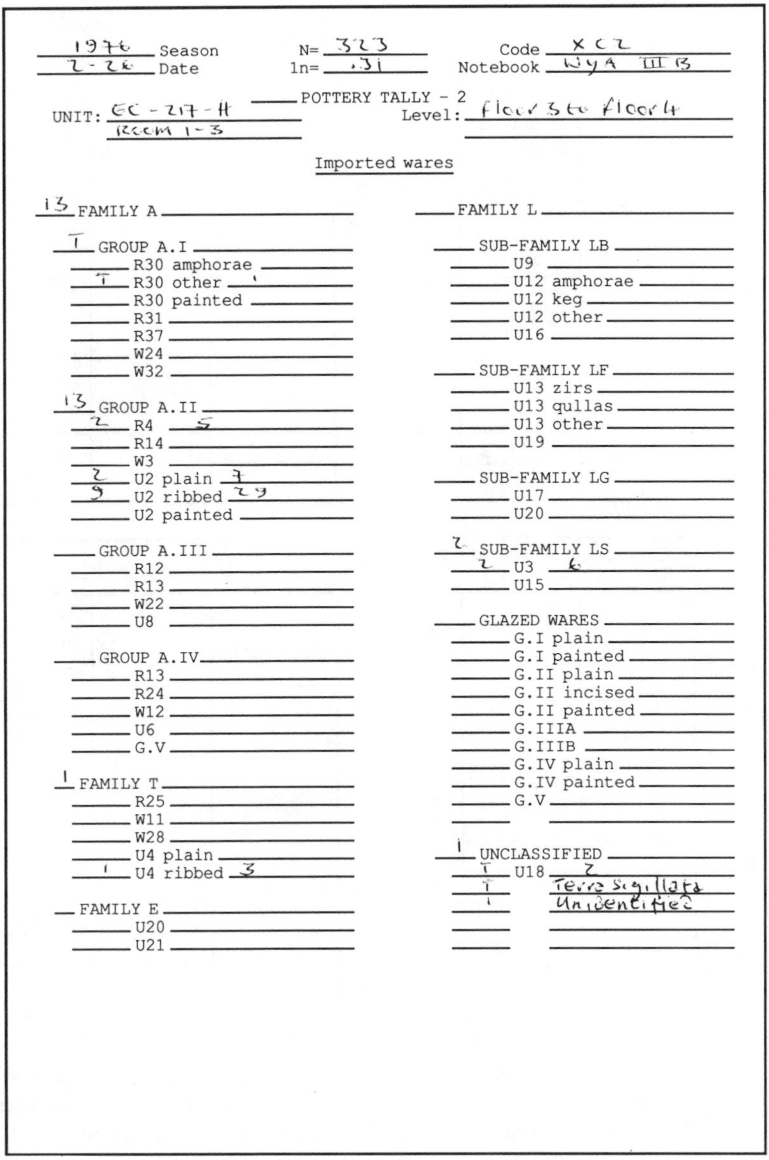

```
1976 Season          N= 323          Code  X C 2
2-26 Date            1n= .31         Notebook  WyA  III 13
                      ──── POTTERY TALLY - 2
UNIT:  EC - 217 - H              Level:  floor 3 to floor 4
       Room 1-3
```

Imported wares

13 FAMILY A _____   ____ FAMILY L _____

  1 GROUP A.I _____   ____ SUB-FAMILY LB _____
  ____ R30 amphorae ____   ____ U9 ____
  1 R30 other '   ____ U12 amphorae ____
  ____ R30 painted ____   ____ U12 keg ____
  ____ R31 ____   ____ U12 other ____
  ____ R37 ____   ____ U16 ____
  ____ W24 ____
  ____ W32 ____   ____ SUB-FAMILY LF _____
                                        ____ U13 zirs ____
  13 GROUP A.II _____   ____ U13 qullas ____
  2 R4 5   ____ U13 other ____
  ____ R14 ____   ____ U19 ____
  ____ W3 ____
  2 U2 plain 7   ____ SUB-FAMILY LG _____
  9 U2 ribbed 29   ____ U17 ____
  ____ U2 painted ____   ____ U20 ____

  ____ GROUP A.III _____   2 SUB-FAMILY LS _____
  ____ R12 ____   2 U3 6
  ____ R13 ____   ____ U15 ____
  ____ W22 ____
  ____ U8 ____   ____ GLAZED WARES _____
                                        ____ G.I plain ____
  ____ GROUP A.IV _____   ____ G.I painted ____
  ____ R13 ____   ____ G.II plain ____
  ____ R24 ____   ____ G.II incised ____
  ____ W12 ____   ____ G.II painted ____
  ____ U6 ____   ____ G.IIIA ____
  ____ G.V ____   ____ G.IIIB ____
                                        ____ G.IV plain ____
  1 FAMILY T _____   ____ G.IV painted ____
  ____ R25 ____   ____ G.V ____
  ____ W11 ____   ____
  ____ W28 ____
  ____ U4 plain ____   1 UNCLASSIFIED _____
  1 U4 ribbed 3   1 U18 2
                                        1 Terra sigillata
  ____ FAMILY E _____   1 Unidentified
  ____ U20 ____
  ____ U21 ____

Figure 6 Specimen Nubian sherd tally sheet, side 2 (imported wares). For
explanation see Figure 5 caption.

House EC 2-5			Room 2		Floor 4 to Floor 5		EC		
D 5	D.I	i	A11	1	A	19	A.II	19	R4	4
	D.II	4	Etc	4					R14	
			H13						W3	1
	M	3	A11	3					U2 pln	6
M+N 68	N.II	48	Etc	41					U2 rib	6
			R2	T					U2 ptd	
			R10	5			A.III		A11	
	N.III 14		R3+R5	3	Misc		T	3	Etc	
			W1	T					U4	3
			W2	10					U9	
			W9	T					U3	T
	N.IV		A11						?	
N?	NU	5	U1	4	Disturbed		Early		N= 553	
			U5	T			Late	1	100/N= 18%	

House B-35			Room 2		Fill to Floor 1		B		
	D.II		A11		A	3	A.IV	3	Etc	
	D.III 61		H4	49					U6	3
			H5	9					G.V	
D 69			H6				E	i	U20+U21	i
			H7+H14	2					U12	
			H8	1	Misc		L	T	U13	T
	D.IV 9		H15	7					?	
			H16	1					G.II	T
	N.VI	1	A11	1	G			i	G.III	
	N.VII	1	A11	i					G.IV	T
N 26	NU 24		U5	18					G?	
			U10	5	Disturbed		Early		N= 272	
			Etc	i					100/N= 37%	
	N?									

Figure 7 Specimen Nubian sherd index cluster cards. Percentage figures from sherd tally sheets (Figures 5–6) are somewhat condensed and then are transferred to these cards, to facilitate the comparison of units in the field, without the aid of a computer. The upper card is used for excavation units of the Early Christian period (*c.* A.D. 600–850), and the lower card for excavation units of the Islamic period (after A.D. 1500). (Other cards are used for earlier and for intervening periods.) Each card lists all of the wares made during a particular period, as well as all wares from the immediately preceding and following periods. Sherds from still earlier or still later periods are listed under the headings "Early" and "Late," at lower right.

but the percentage of unidentifiable pottery wares (mostly fragments of unusual and unfamiliar wine amphorae) can alone be crucial in distinguishing Ptolemaic from Roman deposits. The historical explanation for this difference is simple: the far-flung Roman trade network brought to Nubia a great many exotic wines – and hence exotic wine amphorae – that were never seen before or afterward, and that are too diversified for us to classify. These show up on the sherd tally sheets as high counts of "unidentified wares."

Dating pottery wares

Dating archaeological deposits by their ceramic content is necessarily a two-stage procedure. First we must date the pottery wares themselves, mainly on the basis of their association with other things that can be specifically dated. In prehistoric archaeology this usually means charcoal or other material susceptible to radiocarbon analysis. In medieval Nubia it has depended rather on the finding of pottery in association with coins, inscriptions, and other self-dating objects (WYA 1986a: 603–6). The site of Qasr Ibrim, which has never been subjected to the destructive effects of moisture, has yielded scores of dated documents, and these have been an invaluable aid in the dating of many pottery wares which have been found in the same deposits.

We have to be clear, however, about what we are and are not dating, and here again it is important to keep our purposes in mind. The entities we are finding, studying, and dating are accidental and unintentional fragments, not whole pots. Once upon a time they were pots, and each had its own history of manufacture, use, breakage, and discard, but we can recover very little of that history from the contexts in which the sherds are eventually found. The places where we find them are probably not the places where they were made, used, or even broken; they may not even be the places where they were originally discarded. The dates that we calculate for sherds, on the basis of their associations, are therefore not interpretable *a priori* as the dates during which the original pots were being made and used. They specify only the dates of those archaeological deposits in which the sherds will predictably be found, for whatever reason. In some cases it may be because the wares were actually being made and used when the deposits were laid down; in others it may be that the vessels were no longer being made, but many "heirloom" vessels were still in use; in still other cases it may be that the vessels were no longer either made or used, but broken pieces of them were still abundant on the refuse-strewn ground surfaces. (For fuller discussion see WYA 1987 and n.d.3.) I therefore refer to all datings of pottery wares which are based on their occurrence in particular deposits as their "dates of occurrence" rather than as their dates of manufacture or use.

Because of the unusual conditions at Qasr Ibrim, where many whole pots as well as sherds are preserved in the refuse deposits, it has been possible for the first time to calculate a series of different dates for many of the Nubian wares. These include dates of first appearance, main dates of manufacture (or importation, in the case of exotic wares), dates for the persistence of vessels after their production had ceased, and dates for the large-scale persistence of sherds after the presumed breakage of the last whole vessel (see Appendix C). These separate datings are important for historical and economic studies, but they are of course irrelevant for the overriding purpose of dating archaeological deposits. When we transfer the dates from any given pottery ware to the deposits in which it is found, the only dates we can legitimately consider are the "outside dates"; that is, between the earliest known appearance of the ware and the final date for the disappearance of its sherds.

Dating deposits by their sherd content

Once "outside dates" have been calculated for the various wares, it is a simple and straightforward matter to transfer them to any archaeological deposits in which the wares are found. A single ware will yield only a very imprecise dating, since the "outside dates" for most Nubian wares span a period of four centuries or more (cf. Appendix C). But an assortment of wares, each with its own set of calculated dates, will yield a much more precise determination. In any given deposit, the *terminus post quem* (earliest possible date) will be the earliest date for the latest ware present, and the *terminus ante quem* (latest possible date) will be the latest date for the earliest ware present. Nubian occupation deposits will typically be found to contain twenty or more wares, and their occurrence in combination will allow a dating of the deposit within an increment of one to two centuries.

The comprehensive nature of our recording at Qasr Ibrim has enabled us, since 1980, to develop a considerably more precise method of ceramic dating. We have calculated, for each fifty-year interval of occupation, not only the wares present or absent but their frequency of occurrence, in proportion to the total population of sherds at that time. This has enabled us, in many but not all cases, to recognize distinctive percentage configurations (index clusters) for each fifty-year period, and we can therefore place deposits within those intervals of time on the basis of their sherd content alone (see WYA n.d.1; n.d.2). The addition of stratigraphic evidence will often allow us to further reduce the interval to twenty-five years, or even less. This is particularly true in the early part of the Middle Ages, when the rate of ceramic change was relatively rapid, so that each generation was using pottery somewhat different from the preceding. Between about A.D. 900 and 1400 things were much more stable (cf. Figure 4), with the result that later medieval pottery wares will usually allow us to date archaeological deposits only within an interval of about 100 years.

The dating procedures that we now employ at Qasr Ibrim provide a classic example of frequency seriation, which will be discussed at length in Chapter 17 (see also J. A. Ford 1962; Rouse 1967: 185–6). The index clusters are not created by the seriation, or chronological ordering, of actual pottery wares, but by the seriation of percentage figures that are not really part of the typology itself.

Up to a point, the logic of frequency seriation, and its use in archaeological dating, is obvious. It merely takes advantage of the fact that at any given point in time, some wares will always be increasing in popularity while others are decreasing, so that after fifty years their proportional frequencies will have changed even though the same overall set of wares may still be in use. However, the method of ceramic dating employed at Qasr Ibrim also involves a second and more controversial assumption: that of uniform deposition, not only throughout the five-acre site of Qasr Ibrim but at other Nubian sites as well (see also Rouse 1967: 186). In other words we assume that, at any given moment in time, sherds of all the different pottery wares then in use were being deposited in about the same proportions everywhere on the site, as well as in other sites of the same age. This assumption may perhaps be challenged by those who have undertaken sophisticated analyses of prehistoric activity based on the uneven distribution of pottery wares, as for example at Teotihuacán (Millon 1973: 40–1; Cowgill, Altschul, and Sload 1984). In Nubia, however, we have demonstrated the reality of uniform deposition, not only at Qasr Ibrim but in a dozen other sites, with statistical data from over 1,000 individual localities (see Appendix D). This evidence has been presented and discussed elsewhere (WYA n.d.1), and will not occupy us further here.

In medieval Nubian archaeology it is important to notice that we are not dating sites, but very small units (microcomponents) within sites. At Qasr Ibrim since 1972 we have excavated more than 100 houses, each of which had on the average five rooms, with five or more distinguishable levels of occupation in each room. In other words we are collecting sherds, and calculating dates, for twenty-five different deposits in an average house, to say nothing of additional deposits in streets and plazas outside the houses. Some of these localities are so disturbed that the data are of no use to us, but we have actually obtained usable ceramic dates from more than 2,000 separate find-spots on the site. These considerations must be kept in mind when we talk, later on, about practicality and cost-effectiveness (esp. Chapter 19). We need dating at this level of specificity – house by house and room by room – in order to achieve our objective of reconstructing the natural history of the community as accurately as possible throughout its 3,000-year history. But neither we nor any other expedition could pay for so large a number of radiocarbon dates; hence our overwhelming reliance on pottery.

On previous digs I did all of the pottery analysis myself, so that the problem of intersubjective consistency did not arise. For a long time I was the only one who could use the Nubian Pottery Typology effectively, for, in spite of the circulation of my earlier publications, others could not or would not invest the time necessary to learn the types. It was, in their view, more cost-effective to hire me to analyze their pottery for them, and over the years this resulted in consultantships during which I studied Nubian pottery collections in Egypt, in several European countries, and in the U.S. and Canada (cf. WYA 1969; 1973b: 227–8; 1978; 1981b). Indeed those studies, giving me access to material from many sites in addition to my own, have contributed measurably to the refinement of my type concepts. At Qasr Ibrim, however, the daily volume of sherd material was from the beginning too large for me to handle alone (since for a number of seasons I was also the excavation director), and it became a critical necessity for me to teach the system to others. Their experiences in learning and using it have contributed importantly to the understandings embodied in this book.

Over the years about a dozen individuals have been involved in the sherd-sorting operations at Qasr Ibrim, with notably varying effectiveness. Experienced sorters have nearly always agreed, ultimately, as to the recognizability and utility of my types, but some have arrived at that point sooner and much more readily than have others. Some individuals quite clearly have a natural gift for what I call gestalt acquisition, and can learn to differentiate the wares after a surprisingly short experience of actually handling them. Others require agonizing repetition and frequent reference to the written type descriptions and drawings before they can sort confidently. One or two individuals, who have shown a high degree of intelligence in other aspects of their work, have proved incapable of mastering the system altogether; that is, they have never acquired enough type gestalts so that they could sort with the degree of speed that our circumstances require. I conclude from these observations that learning to use a pottery typology is much like learning any other language: some have a natural gift for it, some can learn with enough practice, and a few can seemingly never get the hang of it.

Other uses and procedures

Obviously the procedures described thus far are designed for maximum speed and volume in the sorting of sherds, since the recording of each sherd involves no more than the making of a single pencil mark opposite the appropriate ware name. No record is made of vessel form, color, design, or any other individual variable; instead each sherd is assigned to a ware category which automatically implies a certain method of construction, a certain fabric, a certain surface finish, a certain set of colors, and a certain range of possibilities in vessel form and decoration. Recording ceramic data at this level of specificity is sufficient for our primary purpose of dating, as we have just seen. Since vessel form and design norms are, by definition, coterminous in time with the wares in which they are found, the recording of vessel form and design data for each individual sherd (even if they could be recognized) would not permit a more precise dating than is possible by recording ware data alone.

The method of tallying sherds by ware has also proved sufficient for most kinds of economic studies. We can trace most of the Nubian and Egyptian wares to their specific places or regions of origin, and can therefore measure the volume of interregional trade as reflected in the percentages of different exotic wares at different periods. We can even measure the fluctuating consumption of imported commodities like wine and honey, since these were shipped in distinctive ceramic containers whose sherds are easily recognized. For example, Wares U2, U3, U4, and U18 (cf. Table 5, Chapter 10) were all used largely or entirely for wine amphorae, coming in the first instance from Aswan, in the second from Middle Egypt, in the third from Lower (northern) Egypt, and in the fourth from across the Mediterranean.

Clearly, however, the mere recording of ware tallies is not sufficient for all purposes or for all kinds of studies. For example, it will not allow us to undertake functional studies based on vessel forms, since vessel form data are not recorded in the case of sherds. Insofar as we have undertaken such studies, they have been based on information from whole vessels only.

As we noted in Chapter 9, our method of tallying sherds is insufficient for the task of cataloguing whole vessels, where details of vessel form and decoration, as well as nuances of color and finish, must be accurately recorded. For this purpose we have developed a separate pottery catalogue card, illustrated in Figure 8. Here, the entries under "Form" and "Style" allow us to draw upon the sub-classifications of vessel forms and of decorative styles, which do not figure in the recording of sherds. Catalogue cards are filled out not only for all complete and restorable vessels, but for all fragments which are large enough for the complete original vessel shape and decoration to be visualized. The filling out of these cards is of course a time-consuming proposition, and would not be possible if whole vessels occurred with anything like the same frequency as do sherds. In fact, the number of vessels catalogued during a typical season at Qasr Ibrim is only about 300.

Catalogue cards, rather than sherd tally sheets, have provided the basis for various historical and stylistic studies, tracing the origins and development of vessel forms and decoration through time (cf. WYA 1970a; 1973a; 1981c). I have to stress, however, that neither the studies so far undertaken nor the records that are currently kept begin to exhaust the possibilities for the study of Nubian pottery. The expeditions with which I have been associated have never enjoyed the luxury of a ceramologist who could devote himself largely or exclusively to the study of the pottery (cf. WYA 1981a). Such a person could follow up many lines of stylistic, functional, or technological investigation that have not so far been undertaken, but to do so he would first have to develop additional recording procedures not currently used by us.

Concluding points

For purposes of the discussion in Parts IV and V, two concluding points should be made about the dating procedures described in this chapter. They will only be asserted here, since they have been empirically demonstrated elsewhere (WYA 1985; 1986b; n.d.1). The first is that, with all its imprecision and inconsistency, the Nubian Typology *works*, for the purpose of dating for which it was originally devised. It has achieved a far more precise dating of medieval sites and deposits than was previously possible, or would be possible today by any other affordable means. It has not yielded results that are equally precise for all periods and all deposits, but it has never yielded results that could be empirically falsified (e.g. when ceramic evidence "predicted" a different dating than did stratigraphy or the finding of actual dated objects). At the site of Qasr Ibrim, which has yielded many dated or datable inscriptions (see Plumley 1966: 9–11; Plumley and Adams 1974: 236–8; Plumley 1975: 7; Plumley, Adams, and

Christian	POTTERY	Vase	$\frac{Q1-64}{21}$

Portion: Complete
Condition: Intact
Height: 125 mm.   Diam. 110 mm.   mm.

Ware: R II   Group: N. VI

Form: F16   Fairly tall
Rim: Everted, rounded   Base: out-flared rivs

Slip: Red-orange
Primary dec: Black
Secondary dec: —

Style: N VI A
Design elements: 2 contiguous friezes
upper well: Frieze of element H3-2 alternating with H33
Waist: Frieze of element K2-3 alternating with K2-2

Surfaces: Polished
Relief dec: None

(a)

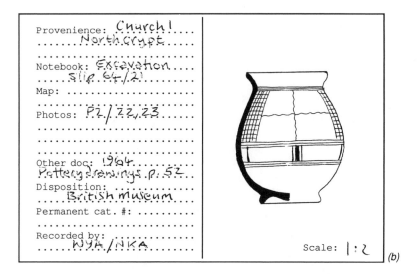

Provenience: Church 1
              North crypt

Notebook: Excavation
          Slip 64/21
Map:

Photos: P.1./22,23

Other doc: 1964
Pottery drawings p. 52
Disposition:
          British museum
Permanent cat. #:

Recorded by:
          WYA/NKA

Scale: 1:2

(b)

Figure 8 Specimen Nubian pottery catalogue card; front (a) and back (b) sides.

Crowfoot 1977: 44–5; Anderson and Adams 1979: 40–1; Adams, Alexander, and Allen 1983: 48–9, 55; Alexander and Driskell 1985: 13), the dates have been found almost without exception to fall within the interval of time "predicted" by the pottery wares found in the same deposits. In addition, a number of informal blind tests have shown that ceramic dating consistently agreed with observed stratigraphy at Qasr Ibrim and other Nubian sites (cf. WYA 1986a: 633; WYA n.d.1).

The second point is that the system would not work, or at least would not work as well as it does, without the classificatory procedures that are described in Chapters 9 and 10. Every ware contributes something to the dating process (otherwise it would not be retained in the classification). In order to do so, every ware must be described in excruciating detail, if two or more users of the system are to achieve a satisfactory level of inter-subjective agreement. The question of what constitutes an acceptably detailed description will be considered in Chapter 15; what constitutes an acceptable level of agreement will occupy us in Chapter 16.

PHILOSOPHICAL
IMPLICATIONS

We will now consider some corollaries of the philosophy of conceptual instrumentalism that was outlined in Chapter 1. To begin with, it involves a wholly pragmatic view of the role that definitions play in scientific typologies. This in turn has implications for more general philosophical issues, and in particular for the presently much-debated question of whether types are "real." We will end the chapter by commenting briefly on that issue, and also on certain similarities and differences between typologies and systems of measurement. Here as elsewhere our philosophical comments must be fairly brief, and cannot fully explore the issues that we raise, much less resolve them. Our main concern is to show the interconnection between our views on archaeological typology, and on more general philosophical problems.

Definiteness and definitions
The philosophy of conceptual instrumentalism that was set forth in Chapter 1 holds that typologies and other systems of deliberately constructed concepts in the sciences are instruments that are designed for specific purposes, and they are to be evaluated in terms of their effectiveness in serving those purposes. It is implicit in this philosophy that definiteness in the concepts is not an end in itself, and should only be insisted upon to the extent that it serves the purposes for which the instrument was created. This holds true of any feature in a typology that can vary in definiteness, including type concepts, and the types themselves. For instance, the centers, boundaries, and external isolation discussed in Chapter 6 (and again in Chapter 21) only serve to give types practical definiteness; that is, they aid the sorter in the quick recognition and differentiation of types under archaeological field conditions. Nevertheless, they are not essential features of typehood. If a system of potsherd classification were to yield accurate provenience-dates even though the types lacked centers, boundaries, or isolation (as

indeed is true of some of the Nubian pottery types), there would be no reason to deny its status as a typology.

Similar considerations apply to type definitions, descriptions, and formulations, as we discussed these in Chapter 3. (In the remainder of this chapter we will gloss all three of them under the term "definitions.") We hold that the role of definitions is instrumental; that is, they are useful to the extent that they help students to learn and to use the typology for its intended purpose. We therefore disagree with other philosophers in regard to the degree of precision that is required in type definitions. Empiricists, in particular, have held that in order to ensure the testability of theories that are stated in terms of particular concepts, the concepts themselves should be precisely defined (cf. Hempel 1952: 21; 1966: 91). But for us testability has not the same importance as it has for empiricists; we hold only that definitions should give sufficiently precise instruction in the use of concepts that students can learn to use the instrument (i.e. the typology) effectively for its intended purpose.

This leads us to a consideration of the kinds of instruction that are actually employed in teaching the use of an archaeological typology. We will illustrate with examples drawn from the Nubian Pottery Typology, as discussed in the three preceding chapters. (For fuller discussion of the role of instruction see also EWA and WYA 1987: 425–6.)

The primary written instruction for the Nubian Pottery Typology is the published manual (WYA 1986a), though, as we will see, it is not the only vehicle of instruction. The nearest things to orthodox definitions that appear in the manual are the ware descriptions that describe the wares, or pottery types, in the Nubian Typology. (An example is reprinted below as Appendix B.) An examination of the published description of Ware W14 (Appendix B) will make it evident that this is not a definition in the logician's sense of giving necessary and sufficient conditions for the application of a term (cf. Suppes 1957: 151–73). It departs from the logical ideal in two ways: (1) it is vague, and (2) it overdetermines, or overdescribes, the ware that it supposedly defines. We will comment briefly on both of these characteristics here, and will return to them again in Chapter 21.

Vagueness in the ware descriptions is illustrated by the fact that they are stated in less precise terms than they might be. For example, the description of Ware W14 gives the fabric density as simply "medium," though obviously it could have been more precisely specified, for example by giving a numerical ratio of weight to volume for one cm^3 of the pottery fabric. This vagueness contributes to the fact that pottery sorters, using the

Nubian or any other pottery typology, attain less than total agreement as to the correct typing of the sherds that they deal with. However, according to our instrumentalist philosophy this is not a fault, because correct type-identification is not an end in itself. More precise ware definitions might indeed lead to a higher degree of intersubjective agreement among sorters, but this would not necessarily lead to the calculation of more accurate or more informative provenience-dates; that is, more accuracy would not necessarily make the typology more effective in serving its intended purpose. Indeed it might be counterproductive, if the delays entailed by applying precise criteria of identity for each sherd were to slow down the sorting process to such an extent that excavators could not obtain a prompt reading on the sherd content of their excavated deposits. (This in fact has proven to be the case in some field applications of the Nubian Pottery Typology.) In sum, objectivity in the sense of intersubjective agreement among sorters is only desirable to the extent that it contributes to the purpose for which the typology was developed; it is not an end in itself. This again conflicts with common ideas about scientific methodology (cf. Hempel 1966: 11), and will be further discussed in Chapter 21.

Overdetermination in the ware descriptions is illustrated by the fact that these list far more attributes, or characteristics, than are logically necessary to recognize the ware being described, and to distinguish it from other wares. One consequence is that it is rare to find any one sherd that exactly fits every detail of the published description – another indication that the descriptions are not definitions in the logician's sense. But the descriptions are those verbal and pictorial formulations that have been found most useful in instructing sorters in how to make effective use of the ware concepts, in a way that logical definitions could not. The latter, as we have already suggested, would slow down the sorting process without leading to the calculation of more accurate provenience-dates. Thus, logical and precise definitions are not offered in the Nubian Typology because they would serve no useful purpose.

As we suggested earlier, the published manual (WYA 1986a) is not the only vehicle through which the type concepts of the Nubian Pottery Typology are acquired, and indeed it can never be sufficient in and of itself. Hands-on training through field or laboratory practice is also essential. In this training students learn to sort potsherds proficiently, a process that really involves two elements: first, that they learn to recognize most of the wares instantly, and without recourse to the written manual, and second, that their ware identifications agree with those of the experts at least most of the time. These are the qualities that are required when the Nubian

Typology is put to use under field conditions, and it is clear that they cannot be imparted by written or oral instructions alone. Thus, the published manual is best regarded as an *aide-mémoire* in a learning process that also has an essential non-verbal component.

Type concepts, identity, and meaning

We turn now to some brief observations about the things that are defined by type definitions, namely concepts and their associated components of identity and meaning. Our illustrations here will be drawn from the field of biology.

Consider *Canis familiaris*, the domestic dog (Linnaeus 1735). In our view two skills are involved in acquiring the concept of this species: (1) the ability to identify members of the species, and (2) the knowledge of what it means to be one. (We will here ignore the difference between meaning and significance that was developed in Chapter 3.) A word will be said about each below, but first we must stress that our focus is on the skills involved in having the concept, not on what the concept is. Moreover, whatever the concept is (and even whether or not it exists), it should not be equated with the type for which it stands. As we saw in Chapter 3, a type is composed of many elements, of which the type concept is one, and the type members are another.

We will also assert that it is possible for a person to identify a *Canis familiaris*, and to know what it means to be one, without knowing the meaning of the Latin words *Canis* and *familiaris*. Therefore, having the concept is not essentially a linguistic attainment, and knowing its meaning is not equivalent to knowing the meaning of a linguistic expression, that is, of a set of verbal communication symbols. This is tantamount to saying that the type concept can be acquired independently of any type name or type label. (Of course the words *Canis familiaris* have a special meaning for zoologists, related to the meaning of the general concept "dog," but the two meanings are not precisely the same.)

Now let us consider identity and meaning in more detail. Type identification, or typing, refers to the procedures used to establish that an individual, or entity, is a member of a particular species or type, thus establishing its typological identity (i.e., who or what it *is* in classificatory terms). Since we assume that a person can have a species concept without necessarily being able to express it in any particular form of words, the type identification procedures are not the same as those used for verifying statements such as "This animal is *Canis familiaris*," even though identity-establishing procedures are involved in both cases. Nor, clearly, are they procedures for establishing so-called numerical identity, that a dog observed on one occasion is the same as the dog observed on another; nor do they verify a statement like "This dog is Fido." It may be important to determine the numerical sameness or difference of two or more entities that are classified, for example, when classified data are to be analyzed statistically, but this is a matter of establishing individual identities and not type identities, according to the distinction we made in Chapter 3. It is a pre-classificational operation that is independent of the ability to identify the types to which the individuals belong.

Note also that we are concerned at all times with practical rather than "in principle" procedures that might make impossible demands on the sorter, such as looking into an individual's past or future. It is for practical purposes, not for theoretical purposes, that we often find it important to distinguish diagnostic attributes, or signs, from less certain indicators of type identity (cf. Dunnell 1971b: 70–6). For the biologist skeletal structure and dentition may be diagnostic of the dog species, but less sure indications can include any practically observable signs, such as that the animal barks and wags its tail. (Indeed many of us have successfully identified dogs, even at great distances or at night, on the basis of just these two signs.) But diagnostic attributes should not be confused with logically necessary and sufficient conditions since, as we previously noted, there need not be any explicitly stated necessary and sufficient conditions of type identity. This brings us back to our central point, that objectivity, in the sense of intersubjective agreement in type identifications, is desirable only to the extent that it serves the purpose for which the types were created (see also Chapter 21).

At this point something must be said about the mental images, or gestalts, involved in type identification, as discussed in Chapters 4 and 5. Our grounds for the claims made about them in those chapters are based on the testimony of classifiers and sorters, who assert that they often form multi-modal gestalts (that is, impressions which may be based on any of several attributes, and possibly involving more than one sense modality) of the types that they deal with, and who assert also that these gestalts are necessary for efficient sorting (cf. J. A. Ford 1962: 15). While the gestalts evidently have practical utility, we must nevertheless stress that our instrumental philosophy is largely independent of any psychological dimension. This is not to say that sorting animals by species or potsherds by wares does not involve sensory and cognitive capabilities, but we do not want to go so far as to claim that the sorting process necessarily involves comparing sensory inputs against mental images. There is currently a debate on this issue among cognitive scientists, as between representationalists and anti-representationalists (see Bloch 1981 and Stitch 1983), but we need not enter into it here since it does not affect the main methodological theses that we are developing.

We turn now to the meanings associated with a type or species like *Canis familiaris*, which involve both type meanings and typological meanings, as discussed in Chapter 3. The important point is that both are closely related to what Grice (1957; 1969) calls natural meanings, which are derived *a posteriori* from our experience with nature, as opposed to the non-natural or conventional meanings that attach to words or signs simply "by agreement." Thus, the non-conventional or natural meaning of a falling barometer is that rain is on the way, and the natural meanings of types comprise those facts about them that a person familiar with the type or species could be expected to possess. In the case of *Canis familiaris* this involves both more and less than a first-hand acquaintance with members of the species, and the ability to identify them. On the one hand, it is possible to know general facts about the animals, such as that they bark, and that many peoples in the world will not eat them, without any prior acquaintance with dogs, so that knowing all or part of the species meaning does not require actual familiarity with the individuals belonging to it. On the other hand one may be acquainted with and able to identify canines without knowing anything about their skeletal structure, dentition, habits, history, or worldwide distribution, and therefore without knowing the species meaning of *Canis familiaris*. In the archaeological case, knowing the type meaning of a ware and the typological meanings of its members is tantamount to having a general familiarity with the contents of the published ware description (WYA 1986a), including the dates that have been calculated for it.

Parenthetically, we may note that our discussion here has some bearing on the widely discussed distinction between scientific concepts and folk concepts (cf. Berlin and Kay 1969; Berlin 1973). Scientific concepts do not necessarily differ from folk concepts in terms of what they describe, but rather in how they describe it. Thus, there might be a scientific concept corresponding to the term *Canis familiaris* that applies to precisely the same animals as does the layperson's concept of "dog," but the concepts themselves differ because the layperson familiar at first hand with dogs will not possess the knowledge about their defining attributes of skeletal structure and dentition that will be of fundamental importance to the professional zoologist.

General type definitions and the discovery of types
We turn now to a conceptual distinction that we have not previously discussed, between open and closed typologies. Scientific typologies that are "designed for long wear" and not for limited situational use (as is the case with many typologies generated by cluster analysis – see Chapter 23) may make explicit provision for additions, modifications, and deletions. These can include rules for the naming of new types (cf. Colton 1953: 51–8), and also generalized class definitions such as the "interbreeding population" definition that is often given for biological species (cf. Mayr 1982: 273). Such rules and class definitions are associated with open typologies, to be discussed in Chapter 18, and also with the splitting and lumping processes that are involved in the evolution of typologies, as we saw in Chapter 5 (see also Chapters 21, 23, and 24). For the present we are concerned with the fact that general type definitions allow for the addition of new types, as would be necessitated by the discovery of an animal species that did not interbreed with any previously known species. The possibility of discovering types that are "out there in nature" has implications for the long-standing controversy as to whether these "abstract things" – species and types – can really be said to exist, and if so what their nature is. This so-called issue of realism is of concern both in general philosophy and in the philosophy of science, and we hope that the general reader will excuse a short digression here to put it into philosophical perspective.

The existence and nature of types
From ancient Greek times to the present there have been philosophical debates concerning the existence and nature of universals as well as particulars, for example in regard to the color "red" as an abstraction from all red things, or the species "dog" as an abstraction from all particular dogs. Realists, as would be expected, have held that these abstractions are real, and that they are different from the particular things that "fall under" or "partake of" them; that is, the species "dog" is not the same as any particular dog (cf. Loux 1970 and Woozley 1949). Nominalists, on the other hand, have held that abstract words and phrases like "the dog" are not proper names that stand for particular things, but rather they function logically as general terms (see Moody 1967). Moreover, the debates about biological species show that even among realists there are disagreements as to the sorts of things that species are. (There are also debates among archaeologists as to what certain pottery types "are," but we will confine our discussion for the moment to biological species because most of the controversy between realists and nominalists in the last twenty years has

revolved around them. Later we will show that the issue of realism does not apply to archaeological types in the same way as it does to biological species.)

Most writers on the controversy over biological species have adopted one or another of the versions of realism. Some, including Hull (1978) and Ghiselin (1966), hold that species are individuals of a rather special kind; e.g. the species *Canis familiaris* is a "thing" that came into existence at a given time, has a history, and may eventually become extinct, even though the species is different from any individual canine. Others have held that species are classes, *Canis familiaris* being the class of all dogs. Others again (e.g. Burma 1949) argue that species are mental constructs, perhaps ideas or gestalts, which are mind-dependent, in the sense that they would not exist if people did not have the ideas or gestalts in their minds. But we will argue that, so long as we disregard the possibility of discovering new species, nothing in the considerations so far advanced obliges us to suppose that species labels like *Canis familiaris* are names for anything real. *Prima facie* it is the possibility of discovering new species or types that carries ontological commitment; that is, it presupposes that there is some real thing "out there" which, when it is discovered, will constitute a species (cf. also Chapters 1 and 4, and Quine 1953). Even here, however, we will argue that the issue is not a simple one.

Let us begin with a negative point: that the mere use of a word or phrase as the subject of a sentence does not necessarily imply that it names or describes any particular thing. For instance, to assert "The dodo is extinct" does not mean that an individual thing called "the dodo" has the property of extinctness; it merely asserts that there are no more living dodos. It is a better approximation to follow Quine (1953) in holding that it is instantiation from generalization (that is, deriving specific instances from broader generalizations) that necessarily entails ontological commitment. Thus, reasoning that "All of the avian species originally on Mauritius are extinct, the dodo was such a species, therefore the dodo is extinct" would commit us to the belief that the species of dodos once existed but is now extinct. But this is still problematical unless we allow for the discovery of new species.

If it were true that no new species were to be found in a region, it is plausible that the avian species to be found in it could be counted and generalized about simply by exploring the region, bird manual in hand, and checking off all of the species descriptions that are instantiated by birds that fit the description. In other words we can count and generalize about species by counting and generalizing about species descriptions and the birds that fit them, as long as there are no birds that don't fit any previously formulated description. But if such a bird is encountered we may be inclined to say that a new species is discovered, and this necessarily implies that the species had to exist prior to its discovery. More than anything else that has been said thus far, this refutes the notion that species are merely mental constructs. The nature of types or species as described in Chapter 3 includes a subjective or at least a conceptual element as well as an objective one, but it is the objective component "in the world" whose existence is established when a new species is described.

The example of the Nubian Pottery Typology shows, however, that even the possibility of finding new individuals not belonging to any known type does not always and necessarily commit us to acknowledging the existence, or reality, of types. This requires some further comment, before we conclude the discussion of the reality of types.

On a typical Nubian dig, nearly every basket of sherds includes at least one or two specimens that do not conform to any of the 101 published ware descriptions in the Nubian Typology. The sorters will tabulate such sherds in the "none of the above" category that is included on every sherd-tally sheet (see Chapter 11 and WYA 1986a: 622), but they will not immediately conclude that a new pottery ware has been discovered. To do so would be to acknowledge the need for an immediate enlargement of the typology. But the Nubian Typology, while allowing for various kinds of evolutionary changes (which may or may not be additive in nature), provides no systematic rules for the addition of new types. This is a consequence of the fact that the typology includes no rigorous definitions either of individual wares or of what constitutes a ware in general; we have already shown that such definitions would serve no useful purpose. In other words there are no uniform criteria of typehood, because the classification is polythetic, as was noted in Chapter 6.

The fact that there is no precise concept of what is a ware, in the abstract, means also that we cannot know precisely what it means to say that two sherds are members of the same ware. In most but not all cases it will mean that they share the same pottery fabric; in most cases it will mean also that they share the same surface colors; in a great many cases it will mean that they share the same general style of decoration; but none of these is essential to membership in every one of the 101 Nubian wares. Lacking criteria of contypicality that could determine whether two or more sherds are of the same or of different wares, there is no way of identifying and counting the total number of wares that are represented in any given collection except by identifying and counting all of the ware descriptions that are instantiated; that is, that have members present in the collection. But this system breaks down when it comes to counting sherds that do not fit any of the 101 familiar wares. If we assert that every sherd must belong to some ware, even though it may not yet have been formulated (and indeed may never be formulated, for lack of sufficient examples), then we are saying that we cannot necessarily count the total number of wares present in any collection; we can only count the number of previously discovered and described wares. The upshot of this unsystematic observation is that even among classification systems the realism issue can take different forms, depending on the criteria of type identity that are included and not included in them. Moreover, since these criteria are associated with definitions of types and of contypicality, and since these are developed for practical purposes, it follows that the realism issue is itself relative to specific purposes. In spite of this relativity, however, we next suggest that criteria of species and type existence have something in common that distinguishes them from quantitative concepts.

Quality and quantity: the scale-type issue

All criteria of species existence or of type existence (that is, of the reality of species or types) seem to have one feature in common, namely, that a type cannot be said to exist unless it is instantiated by actual members of the type. This is necessarily true in schemes like the Nubian Pottery Typology, which lack any abstract definition of what constitutes a type; in these cases the type concepts can only be abstracted from data pertaining to actual entities. But even when general type definitions and criteria of contypicality are given, it appears that uninstantiated types (or unrealized types as we termed them in Chapter 7) are not accorded the status of being "real." This is demonstrated in the biological case by such creatures as unicorns and dragons, which can be very concretely imagined and pictured but which are not considered to be real. The requirement of instantiation is an important point of contrast between qualitative and quantitative concepts. We will start with some general observations.

Systems of measurement in science are like typologies in that they are deliberately constructed conceptual instruments, one of whose principal uses is to give informative indices of phenomena. (This view and its implications are set forth in EWA 1966; see also Chapter 21 herein.) However, it by no means follows that typologies and sophisticated physical measurement systems fit into a neat continuum, with typologies and other classification systems constituting nominal scales at one end of the continuum, and length, mass, time, etc. constituting interval scales, ratio scales, and possibly even stricter scales at the other end (cf. Stevens 1959: 25). The differences between scale types, with their associated ideas about transformations and meaningfulness, will be discussed presently, but we will begin by noting how quantitative measures define "container spaces" while typologies do not.

Consider the measurement of time. The laws of physics, which purport to describe the evolution of the entire universe from the Big Bang onward, give us reason to believe that all events that ever happened, or will or could happen, fit into the temporal order of physical theory. Thus the temporal order constitutes a "container space" because it has "places" in it where any possible occurrence could be fitted. This is what enables us to transfinitely count the instants of time (that is, it enables us to place them in relationship or correspondence with some infinite set, such as the set of real numbers), not by counting events that instantiate them, but by counting the times at which such events *could* occur. For instance, if Caesar had not been assassinated he would have died at a later time, which implies the theoretical existence of an abstract time-slot into which his death would have fitted.

But there are no laws analogous to those of physics which set well-defined limits on the biological species that might at some time make their appearance on earth, and therefore it is not possible to set limits on and to count the species in a "species container" that might encompass them all. The best that the Linnean system and other typologies can do is to be comprehensive, by making sure that they include pigeonholes for all of the entities that are likely to be encountered in practice.

We may return now to the issue of scale types. S. S. Stevens, who first developed the concept of scale types, held that systems of classification constitute nominal scales while standard physical measures constitute interval and ratio scales. The important practical consequence, for followers of Stevens, is that certain things can be meaningfully said about physical measures that are not meaningful with respect to classifications, and certain statistical treatments can permissibly be applied to data about physical measurement that are not permissibly applied to classificational data. For example, it is meaningful to say that event x is nearer in time to y than it is to z, but according to the implications of Stevens' theory it would not be meaningful to say that animal x is "nearer in species" to y than to z. Also, it is permissible to take arithmetic means of temporal measures but not to average numbers that represent typological data.

That it is meaningful to speak of temporal nearness but not of biological nearness supposedly follows from the fact that while relative time-differences are "invariant under permissible transformations of the time scale," there are no analogous "species differences" that are invariant under permissible transformations of a nominal scale (see Adams, Fagot, and Robinson 1965; Narens 1985). An example that will be developed below has to do with the species *Canis familiaris* (the dog), *Canis latrans* (the coyote), and *Elephas maximus* (the Indian elephant). If the Linnean species classification were a nominal scale, then it would be permissible to interchange these labels, since they are entirely arbitrary. However, we would like to argue that while there is some validity to the strictures that Stevens and his followers have placed on what can be meaningfully said, and what statistical operations are permissible, they also involve a serious confusion (for original discussion of this topic see EWA 1966).

We may begin with a negative point. Stevens to the contrary, it obviously *is* meaningful to hold that *Canis familiaris* is closer to *Canis latrans* than to *Elephas maximus*. One might argue that this only shows that the biological classification is a taxonomy and not a one-level typology (cf. Chapter 17), so that the constituent types are not equidistant in the sense argued in Chapter 7. The point, however, is not whether the types generated in a scientific typology are equidistant in any absolute sense, but whether the relative distances that they manifest along their various attribute dimensions (color, size, shape, etc.) have any meaning for the purposes for which the typology was devised. This is the practical importance of meaningfulness, and it is something determined in the first instance not by what type of scale is employed, but by what is the purpose of classifying or measuring the data in the first place. For instance, if size differences among Nubian potsherds were found to be correlated with differences in the time of manufacture of the original vessels, then these differences would be meaningful for provenience-date estimation, and knowing this would be a part of the meaning attached to each of the described pottery wares. But since such differences do not co-vary with any other important attribute, they do not serve the purposes for which the Nubian Typology was designed, and they have consequently been ignored. This does not mean, however, that the differences do not exist, or that they might not be meaningful for some other purpose.

The general implication of these reflections is to suggest once again that scientific concepts which are often held to be absolute are in fact relative to the purposes of the scientist. Here we suggest that the concepts of scale type, permissible transformation, and meaningfulness all fall into this category.

PART IV

PRAGMATICS OF ARCHAEOLOGICAL TYPOLOGY

In anthropology there is little to be gained by pushing conceptual distinctions very far, and some risk of sterility,
because phenomena intergrade endlessly, especially in so
highly plastic a thing as culture. A broad definition, centering
on the core of meaning involved rather than aiming at hair-
line logical definition at its edges, is therefore ordinarily the
most useful.

A. L. Kroeber (1964: 234)

Page 156 blank

I 3

THE STARTING POINT:
PURPOSE

Critics have been heard to complain that for archaeologists typologies are a kind of fetish, and that classification may become an end in itself (Kluckhohn 1939: 338; Bennett 1943: 208; Hill and Evans 1972: 231, 267; Vierra 1982: 164; Hayden 1984: 81). This view seems to imply that some typologies serve no useful purpose. Usefulness, however, is very much in the eye of the beholder. As individuals we constantly encounter typologies that are of no use to us in our own work; for example, WYA has never found a bead typology that adequately describes the beads from his own excavations in Nubia. It is evident nevertheless that the many existing Nubian and Egyptian bead typologies (e.g. Reisner 1923b: 106–27; Steindorff 1935: 46–50; Emery 1938: pls. 43–4) served the practical needs of their makers, in that they permitted the description of a large and diverse body of material within a limited number of pages (cf. Everitt 1974: 4).

If a typology appears to serve no obvious purpose, it probably means only that the typologist neglected to specify what his purpose was. This seems to be a fairly common failing (cf. Gardin 1980: 81). It may also be that the typology-maker was himself not consciously aware of his purpose, something that is perhaps also common (cf. Klejn 1982: 51–4). But we doubt that there are any typologies for which the maker had no purpose at all, either consciously or unconsciously. We suspect in fact that typologies are rendered useless much more often by having too many purposes than by having none – a point to which we will return later.

It should be sufficient to recall here that a typology, according to our definition (Chapter 4), is a "pigeonhole" classification made specifically for the sorting of entities. Obviously, no one undertakes the time-consuming and frequently stressful activity of sorting (cf. Chapter 16) just for the fun of it. The proximate purpose of sorting is usually to permit the enumerative, comparative, or statistical treatment of type data; to discover in one way or another what is the quantitative relationship between objects of different types. Is Type A more abundant than Type B? Is Type C absent when Type D is present? Does the proportion of Type E increase or decrease when Type F increases? However, these immediate inquiries are only means to other and more theoretically interesting ends, rather than ends in themselves. In this chapter we will be concerned with the various ultimate ends – both theoretical and practical – that a typology may serve.

Even those of us who are regularly active in the field of classification may sometimes forget how many different purposes a classification may legitimately serve. It is impossible to review them all within the scope of this chapter, but we would like at least to consider some of the most common purposes that are served by artifact typologies (see also Steward 1954; Rouse 1960; Shepard 1965: 316; Hill and Evans 1972: 244–9; Klejn 1982: 51–4; Hayden 1984: 82). Our concern for the moment is only with different kinds of purposes, not specifically with different kinds of classifications. In Chapter 14 we will go on to indicate how different purposes are reflected in the choice of different variables and attributes to be considered in formulating types, and in Chapter 18 we will review some of the different kinds of classifications that result, in part, from those choices.

KINDS OF PURPOSES

At least in the classification of artifacts we can make an initial distinction between what we will call basic and instrumental purposes. Basic purposes are served when we want to say or to learn something about the material being classified; instrumental purposes are involved when we want the classified material to tell us about something else (e.g. the date of an archaeological site), or to solve some practical problem. Basic purposes may be descriptive, comparative, or analytical, and the last of these categories can be further subdivided with reference to a number of different goals: intrinsic, interpretive, or historical. Instrumental purposes can also be subdivided into ancillary and incidental categories. Table 9 presents a kind of classification of the different purposes that artifact typologies may serve, and that will be discussed in the present chapter. Note that according to our definitions the table offers a classification and not a typology (cf. Chapter 4), inasmuch as the different purposes are by no means mutually exclusive.

BASIC PURPOSES

As we have just noted, basic purposes may be descriptive, comparative, or analytical.

Table 9. *Potential purposes in artifact classification*

Basic purposes	Instrumental purposes
Descriptive	Ancillary
Comparative	Incidental
Analytical	
Interpretive	*Multiple purposes*
Historical	

Descriptive purposes

Economy or convenience of description is one of the most common and most important reasons for undertaking a classification. At the conclusion of a dig the archaeologist is likely to be confronted with a mass of excavated material that must somehow be described and/or illustrated within a limited number of pages, and that does not merit artifact-by-artifact treatment (cf. Krieger 1944: 272–3; Taylor 1948: 176; Everitt 1974: 4). The only practical solution is to describe the artifacts in groups, which is to say in classes. Virtually all of the bead typologies in the Egyptian literature (e.g. Reisner 1923b: 106–27; Steindorff 1935: 46–50; Emery 1938: pls. 43–4), and a good many of the pottery typologies (e.g. Reisner 1923a: 42–7; Mond and Myers 1934: 84–90; pls. CXXXIV–CLIV), were evidently developed to meet this need. The sub-classification of vessel forms that is incorporated in the Nubian Pottery Typology (Chapter 10) is another such "typology of descriptive convenience" (WYA 1986a: 89–183). It is not a generative typology based on combinations of attributes, but a grouping together of observed form modalities in such a way that form data can be conveniently introduced into the various pottery ware descriptions.

Descriptive typologies are essentially morphological; that is, they are based on visible attributes (see Chapter 18). They are more likely to be closed typologies than open ones, in that they are devised for the classification and sorting of material already in hand, without much consideration for additional material that may be gathered in the future. (The important distinction between closed and open typologies will be further discussed in Chapter 18.)

Comparative purposes

Another common purpose in classification is to permit the formal comparison of material from different sites, different areas, or different periods (cf. Griffin 1943; Krieger 1944: 273; Deetz 1967: 51; Sokal 1977: 188–9). If the comparison is to be quantitative or statistical, prior classification is essential. A very large number of pottery classifications appear to have been made for this purpose. Unlike the majority of descriptive classifications, comparative classifications must almost necessarily be open. That is, they must be designed to accommodate new finds as well as material already in hand.

Although both description and comparison are essentially communicative purposes, they can at times be in conflict. When writing up his material for publication, the archaeologist may find that no extant typology suitably describes the artifacts he has uncovered, so that the demands of accurate description would dictate the making of a new typology. On the other hand, comparison with material already in the literature might equally demand the use of an extant typology. There is no fully satisfactory way of resolving this dilemma, which WYA has confronted more than once in his own work. The archaeologist must either classify his material in two different ways, or he must decide whether descriptive accuracy or inter-site comparability is the more important goal in any given situation.

Descriptive and comparative typologies are both essentially morphological, but with the important distinction that descriptive typologies are usually based only on a single collection, while comparative typologies are made specifically in order to compare several collections.

Analytical purposes

Many classifications are undertaken not so much for communicative purposes as to enlarge our knowledge or understanding of the material under study. We will refer to these as analytical purposes. As we noted earlier, they can be of several kinds. Here we will consider three kinds of analytical purposes, which we will designate as intrinsic, interpretive, and historical. It is necessary to reiterate that these categories are not always mutually exclusive.

Intrinsic purposes. Archaeology necessarily begins with the recovery and study of material objects, and in earlier centuries this was considered reason enough for carrying out excavations (cf. Ceram 1951; de Paor 1967: 11–24). More recently, anthropological archaeologists and prehistorians have generally insisted that their primary interest is not in things but in their makers and users, the recovery of things being a means to an end rather than an end in itself. There are nevertheless many scholars whose interest in the past is still focused primarily on the products of the past. Their number would include a good many art historians and museum people, as well as specialists in the study of particular materials such as pottery, textiles, or coins. In the same category would be certain archaeologists who specialize in the study of recent and well-documented periods of history; for example, medievalists and Islamicists.

Art historians and other scholars with a primary interest in objects have developed many classifications that are useful for their own purposes. It is obvious, however, that their purposes in doing so must be somewhat different from those of scholars with a primary interest in people. They are proportionately more interested in differential features of the things themselves, and less interested in the social and economic contexts in which the things were made and used. Their classifications consequently give more attention to what we have elsewhere called intrinsic variables and attributes, and less attention to contextual variables and attributes (see Chapter 14). Since the primary objective of these specialists is to learn as much as possible about the material they study, we will refer to their purposes in classification as intrinsic purposes.

Intrinsic purposes can themselves be of many kinds. In addition to studying simply the morphological variability of artifacts, scholars may hope to learn when they were made, where they were made, how they were made, or why they were made. Each of these questions provides an intrinsic purpose for classification, and each leads to a different kind of classification based on the study of different attributes. In Chapter 18 we will characterize these respectively as chronological, spatial, technological and functional classifications.

In the case of pottery, for example, stylistic attributes will usually provide the primary basis for chronological classification, since these are the attributes that are most likely to vary over time. Constituency attributes (clay, temper, etc.) provide the most common basis for spatial classification, since these give the best evidence of where vessels were made. Technological attributes (method of construction, firing temperature and atmosphere, etc.) are the obvious basis for technological classification, while vessel form attributes are the most reliable basis for functional classification, since they often suggest the use to which vessels were put. It should be noted by the way that any classification of pottery which is made for intrinsic purposes will probably be a classification of complete pots rather than of sherds – an important distinction to which we will return a little later.

Interpretive purposes. Anthropological archaeologists have usually insisted that their primary interest is not in the things they uncover but in the makers and users of those things. For them it is an article of faith that classification of artifacts leads to basic understandings about the people who used them (Krieger 1944; Spaulding 1953: 305; Chang 1967; Heider 1967; Read 1982). Functional classification and emic classification are both expressions of this idea. The former aims to discover something about the activity sets of the artifact makers, and the latter something about their mental templates, or perceptions (Deetz 1967: 45; Watson, LeBlanc, and Redman 1984: 208–10). These were the reasons most commonly given for artifact classifications that were developed in the 1940s and 1950s (see Chapter 22). Classification is also presumed to yield important cultural information about technology, economics, and social organization. Deetz' analysis of Arikara ceramics (Deetz 1965) was the first of a series of studies that were intended to discover principles of prehistoric social organization on the basis of stylistic features and their distribution (Longacre 1964; 1970; Hill 1966; 1970; McPherron 1967b; Plog 1980), although the results were more ingenious than convincing. Nevertheless, it is probable that most prehistorians still consider that interpretive purposes are the most important reason for undertaking classifications.

Historical purposes. By historical we mean simply the study of development and change over time or space. A great many artifact classifications have been undertaken for the purpose of analyzing the changes that have taken place in particular manufactures in the course of centuries. This is particularly true in the case of pottery classifications, most of which have a specifically chronological dimension. In these systems the differentiation of types is partly sequential, each type being the successor of earlier types and/or the predecessor of later ones in the same typology. We refer to such systems as chronological classifications (Chapter 18). There are in addition classifications meant primarily to express cultural variability in space; we refer to these as spatial classifications.

As we will see in a moment, a great many historical classifications of pottery have been devised for instrumental rather than for basic purposes. That is, they have not been developed because of any interest in the pottery itself, but because of its utility as a basis for dating other materials. However, this is less true in regard to historical classifications of material other than pottery, and it is not universally true even of pottery typologies (e.g. Dragendorff 1898; Hayes 1972; and the whole monumental *Corpus Vasorum Antiquorum*). In the various fields of historical archaeology there are classifications of all kinds of artifacts, as well as of architecture, that have not been undertaken for any instrumental purpose, but merely to discover and to express historical trajectories of development. In the Medieval Nubian Pottery Typology, the grouping of wares into ware groups (see Chapter 10) falls into this category. Use of the typology for its primary purpose of dating does not require any knowledge of the system of ware groups; they serve merely to express, for anyone who is interested, the pattern of historical relationships among the wares.

INSTRUMENTAL PURPOSES

It is often necessary or desirable to classify artifacts for reasons of convenience or utility that are unconnected with any interest in the artifacts themselves. One common reason is to aid in the dating or in the functional interpretation of deposits in which the classified artifacts were found; another is for convenience of storage or data coding. We will refer to these respectively as ancillary and as incidental purposes.

Ancillary purposes

The oldest and the most ubiquitous of all archaeological typologies are those involving pottery and those involving certain kinds of lithic artifacts (handaxes, projectile points, etc.). Pottery and lithic types were designated in the beginning primarily as an aid to the identification and dating of deposits in which the types were found, and this continues to be their most important function today (see Chapter 1). Embodied in this usage is the concept of the "index fossil," developed by William Smith at the beginning of the nineteenth century (Daniel 1964: 34). It was Smith who first noticed that geological formations, even when not in stratigraphic context, can be accurately placed within a time sequence on the basis of certain of the fossils found within them, which came to be known as index fossils. Not long afterward, stone, bronze, and iron cutting tools were found to serve as useful "index fossils" for dating the later stages of European prehistory (Daniel 1950: 41; Hayden 1984: 81), and various types of handaxes and other crude stone tools proved to be equally useful for temporally ordering the earlier stages of prehistory (Daniel 1950: 103–11). By the time of Schliemann and Petrie, a hundred years ago, the special possibilities for chronological ordering on the basis of pottery types and styles had also been recognized (see Daniel 1950: 141–5). Since timescaling was then and still is the most critical problem in archaeology, it was inevitable that pottery and lithic typologies, in particular, should be developed simply to provide the archaeologist with an appropriate set of "index fossils" (cf. J. A. Ford 1954b: 52; Childe 1956: 59; Rouse 1972: 126; Brown 1982: 181). This was the avowed primary purpose of the Nubian Pottery Typology, as noted in Chapter 11.

We observed in Chapter 1 that the prehistoric "cultures" in most parts of the world have long since been arranged into basic time and space grids on the basis of pottery and other typologies. Consequently, it is sometimes argued that the early typologies have now done their work, and should be discarded in favor of new typologies made for new purposes (cf. Binford 1965; Clarke 1968: 189–91; Hill and Evans 1972: 254–68). It must be recalled, however, that while the time and space grids are firmly in place, each new site and each new find must still be fitted into them, and for that purpose the old ancillary typologies remain as essential as ever. When a site is discovered in the borderland between the Anasazi and Mogollon areas of the Southwest, it is still likely to be assigned to one or the other culture group on the basis of pottery and house types devised more than fifty years ago.

Another ancillary purpose in artifact classification, though a more controversial one, is that of ethnic identification (Rouse 1965; 1967: 61–101; Ford, Schroeder, and Peckham 1972). In the absence of any direct evidence of who was who in prehistoric times, we have had to decide arbitrarily that artifact types – which usually means pottery types or projectile point types – are to be identified with discrete peoples. When we have two or more pottery types predominating in different sites at the same time and in the same region (for example, Kayenta and Mesa Verde types in the lower San Juan drainage), we conclude that two different peoples were coexisting (see W. Y. and N. K. Adams 1959: 26–8). It would be tautological to say that pottery types are devised for purposes of ethnic identification, when in actual usage our pottery types are, *a priori*, ethnic markers. But it is correct to say that pottery and other types are *used* as ethnic identifiers. This practice is common in all fields of prehistoric archaeology, in both the New and Old Worlds.

Many other ancillary purposes are exemplified by the classifications developed in the recent past by advocates of so-called New Archaeology (see Chapter 22). New classifications of lithics have been devised to enhance our understanding of environmental adaptations (Binford 1972: 244–94; Read 1974; 1982), while some highly ingenious pottery classifications have been developed specifically for the reconstruction of patterns of social organization (Deetz 1967; 1968; Longacre 1964; 1970; Hill 1966; 1970; Plog 1980).

Incidental purposes

It should not be forgotten, finally, that classification may be worthwhile simply as a practical convenience. One of the most common, though least acknowledged, classificatory purposes is mnemonic, to help us remember things that we would otherwise forget (cf. Sokal 1977: 188). There are many experimental studies to show that the human intelligence is capable of remembering only a limited number of things in any one category; beyond that point it becomes a practical necessity to group the things into different categories (G. Miller 1956; Wallace 1961). The system of ware numeration in the Nubian Pottery Typology – separately numbering the hand-made, red, white, glazed, and utility wares, so that the number in each category does not exceed forty – is an example of such grouping made for purely mnemonic purposes. Its only utility is to help the typologist remember the designations for particular wares, without having constantly to look them up (see also Chapter 10).

Storage systems provide another example of classification undertaken for practical convenience. Some museums store their undisplayed collections by accession number or by place of finding, but the largest number probably store them according to some in-house system of classification involving period of manufacture, cultural context, type of material, manufacturing technology, or some combination of those things. The same principle applies of course to the storage and retrieval of verbal or pictorial data (cf. Sokal 1977: 188).

MULTIPLE PURPOSES

The most useful typology for any given purpose is undoubtedly the one which was devised with that purpose most specifically in mind. On the other hand there are probably not many typologies that serve, and can serve, only one purpose. The "natural history" of the Nubian Pottery Typology, detailed in Chapter 9, shows how secondary purposes were picked up along the way, even though they were not envisioned at the start. In a good many cases, too, it is apparent that typologists had more than one purpose in mind from the beginning. This is not inappropriate in theory, but it can become a stumbling block in practice. Many typologies, we believe, have limited utility not because they have no specified purpose but because they have too many. As Hill and Evans (1972: 236) have noted, "Many archaeologists seem . . . to have a propensity for wanting to develop single, all-purpose taxonomic systems, and then wanting to stick to them."

The problem of multiple agendas is well exemplified in the current efforts to develop a comprehensive classification of ancient Egyptian pottery (see Sauneron 1975) – an admittedly recalcitrant body of material that defies easy and intuitive ordering. At least a dozen scholars are separately engaged in this enterprise, but few of them appear to be entirely clear in regard to their purpose. Some are trying to learn about the pottery itself, some to discover its places of origin, some to reconstruct economic activities, and some to develop tools for dating (cf. Anonymous 1975; Bourriau 1985). Until these various purposes are sorted out and prioritized, it is doubtful that the current efforts at classification will result in anything very useful (cf. WYA 1981a).

In fairness to the would-be classifiers of Egyptian pottery it must be acknowledged that ambiguity of purpose is an especially common problem in pottery classifications, perhaps more so than in other fields of archaeological classification. One source of difficulty is simply that pottery is potentially capable of telling us so many different things, depending partly on how it is classified. It can serve both the basic purposes of reconstructing cultures and their history and the ancillary purposes of dating and identifying sites.

Another special problem arises from the fact that so much ceramic material is recovered in small fragments, or sherds, which may or may not tell us very much about the pots to which they once belonged. The typologist therefore faces an initial decision as to whether he wishes to classify pots or sherds. If his classificatory purpose is analytical (that is, inherent, interpretive, or historical), he will probably want to develop a typology of pots, and to treat each sherd only as a fragmentary representative of something larger. In this case equal value need not be attached to all sherds; their value will be measured in proportion to how much information they give about the original pot. Vessel form will almost certainly be a major factor in type determination, since it is the chief indicator of function. But if the typologist's purpose is historical, as in the case of the Nubian Pottery Typology, then the classification will presumably be based on sherds, and vessel form will be treated as relatively unimportant in type determination. A number of pottery typologies, including the incipient Egyptian typology, seem to be plagued by a failure to decide whether the classified entities are to be pots or sherds.

The problem of multiple and conflicting agendas may also arise when theory unduly influences practice, as it rather commonly does in prehistoric archaeology. As we will see in Chapter 22, there has been a major paradigm shift in the study of prehistoric archaeology every generation or so, and the proponents of new paradigms are likely to insist that classifications must now serve the newly identified theoretical interests. The difficulty is that they must at the same time continue serving the old needs of chronological and spatial ordering. As a result, there may be an effort to adapt old typologies to new needs for which they are not appropriate. This propensity was particularly evident in the 1940s and 1950s, when the configurationist paradigm became predominant (see Chapter 22). Most of the typologies then in use had been developed for site-dating purposes, but archaeologists now began to insist that they should also provide emic or functional insights (Rouse 1939: 10–23; Krieger 1944: 272; Spaulding 1953: 305). The relationship, or lack of relationship, between archaeological theory and typological practice will be much more fully explored in Chapter 25.

There are several possible solutions to the problem of multiple agendas. Brew's solution (1946: 65) was a separate typology for every purpose, though it is evident that he was speaking somewhat hyperbolically (but cf. also Jevons 1874, II: 349; Simpson 1945: 13). The suggestion is nevertheless a practicable one if we apply it to taxonomic (i.e. hierarchic) ordering rather than to basic, one-level typologies. That is, it may not be practicable to partition the same body of material into different basic types for different purposes, but the same basic types can be taxonomically clustered in all kinds of ways to express different kinds of relationships. Moreover, taxonomies can be so constructed that they serve different purposes at different levels, as was shown in the case of the Nubian Pottery Typology. In the latter scheme the family level serves primarily to express spatial relationships, the ware group level to express chronological relationships, while the ware level serves primarily for the ancillary purpose of dating sites and deposits – the purpose for which the whole system was originally devised. (For fuller discussion see Chapters 9–11.)

We will suggest in Chapter 17 that taxonomic ordering is probably the most effective way of introducing multiple agendas into a classification without involving a conflict of purposes. There can nevertheless be multiple purposes even in one-level typologies. In these cases the important thing is to have a clearly defined scale of priorities. That is, some one purpose should be recognized as paramount, and every type in the system should be characterized so that it maximally serves that purpose. In the case of the Nubian Pottery Typology, the paramount purpose was dating. Maximum attention was therefore given to features with discoverable chronological significance, whether or not they had any other significance. The result is that all of the Nubian types are useful for dating, while only some of them are useful also for interpretive, historical or other purposes.

Purpose, attribute selection, and type selection

Although a clearly understood purpose is the appropriate starting point for any practical typology, the relationship between purposes and types is not always a simple and direct one. That is, purposes will not entirely dictate the choice of variables and attributes, resulting in the formulation of certain specific kinds of types (cf. Chapter 14). As we saw in Chapter 3, types must have the two essential qualities of identity and meaning, and purpose is relevant only to the second of these. In most practical typologies, however, the identity of types must be established before it can be determined whether they are meaningful or not; this requires in the beginning the designation of provisional types based only on the most distinctive criteria of identity. Such criteria are, of course, independent of any purpose except that of distinguishing the types themselves. In addition, the polythetic nature of most artifact typologies means that almost any attribute may be involved in the definition of *some* types. Consequently, purpose is likely to play a more important role in the selection of types for final inclusion in the typology than it does in the selection of variables and attributes to be used in the initial formulation of the types. This issue will be fully explored in Chapter 15.

In addition to criteria of identity and meaning, there are other, practical factors that also affect the making and use of types, and that will be discussed in Chapter 18. We may therefore say that purpose is only the first of several variable factors that affect the way in which types are made and used. Some of the other factors will be considered in the next chapters. Only after all of the various determining factors have been discussed can we consider, in Chapter 18, the different kinds of typologies and classifications that are actually made and used by archaeologists.

I4

THE DETERMINANTS OF TYPES:
VARIABLES AND ATTRIBUTES

As we saw in Chapter 4, any classification is basically a set of categories. In scientific classifications, the key to formulating such categories is selectivity. That is, scientific classifications are always based on a consideration of some features but not of others, a selection of certain variables and attributes from a wider field of possibilities. What is involved, as Foucault (1973: 132–3) observes, is a deliberate narrowing of the scientist's field of vision, so that certain kinds or domains of information are systematically excluded; for example, color in the case of most stone tool types. It was the introduction of this factor of selectivity which made possible the pioneering classifications of Linnaeus (1735) and other natural scientists of the eighteenth century, whereas their predecessors had aimed at all-inclusive and non-selective descriptions of each biological species that in effect made classification impossible (cf. Foucault 1973: 125–65).

In the last chapter we saw how different purposes affect the choice of features to be considered and not to be considered in making typologies (cf. also Whallon 1982). Here we want to take a closer look at the features themselves. We will categorize them under three headings: invariants, variables, and attributes. Throughout this chapter it is important to bear in mind our distinction between type concepts and type members (see Chapter 3), and to realize that we are talking about the attributes of types (i.e. concepts), and not necessarily about the attributes of individual objects. The relationship between type attributes and object attributes will be considered further at the end of the chapter.

The distinction between variables and attributes was not consistently made in earlier typological literature, and the result was a good deal of conceptual ambiguity (see Chapter 24). Since the distinction is essential to us in this chapter, it must be stated at the outset. This is most readily done by a simple example: "color" is a variable, and "red" is an attribute of the variable "color." An attribute is a definable aspect of a particular variable; that is, one of the states that it can assume.

Invariants

Invariants are the constant features that are common to all members of a typology. They are, in other words, the defining features of the typology itself. They are of course invariant only with respect to any particular typology, for these are precisely the features that distinguish one typology from another. (Hence our preference for the term "invariant" in place of "constant.") In the Medieval Nubian Pottery Typology the invariants are "medieval," "Nubian," and "pottery." Here pottery is an intrinsic feature, while medieval and Nubian are contextual features. We will suggest later in this chapter that most archaeological typologies involve a combination either of intrinsic and contextual features or of intrinsic and inferential features.

Invariants should of course be read as part of the total characterization of each type in the system. Thus there might be pottery types found in other parts of the world which happen to be morphologically identical to some of the Nubian types, but they would not nevertheless be identified as members of the Nubian typology because they do not exhibit the necessary additional features of "medieval" and/or "Nubian."

Variables

Variables might better be characterized as dimensions of variability. They designate properties that are manifest in one way or another in all of the types in a typology, but not always in the same way or to the same degree. Every physical thing has at least the minimum properties of size and weight, and most have also shape and color, but each of these things can be manifest in many different ways. Most cultural products, as well as most living things, exhibit a great many other and more specific variable features as well. In this section we will be concerned with certain basic characteristics that are common to all variables in all classifications.

Universality of variables. All of the variables selected for inclusion in a typology are, in the broadest sense, manifest in each of its individual types. They may, however, be manifest by being absent. In many arrowhead typologies, for example, the presence or absence of tangs or side notches is a significant feature. In the Nubian Pottery Typology, such properties of vessel form as ring bases, handles, and modeled rims are classified in terms of a variety of specific forms, plus a "zero form" (absent).

Because archaeologists deal so often with fragmentary or damaged material, it is often the case that variables are not manifest in individual specimens, even though they are features of the type to which the specimen belongs. This is particularly true in the case of many pottery typologies. They are designed for the sorting almost exclusively of fragmentary material, yet the variables that are included are variables of the original whole pots, not of the sherds being sorted. We do not know of any system in which average sherd size or average sherd shape is included as a significant feature, although in theory either one could be. On the other hand our type descriptions may include variables like decoration that are not manifest in particular sherds, because they happen to come from undecorated portions of the original vessel. This rather paradoxical feature is one of the reasons for what we call overdetermination in pottery type descriptions (see Chapter 15).

Qualitative difference of variables. The differences between variables in the same typology are necessarily qualitative rather than quantitative, since they are separate dimensions of variability. That is, any one of them can vary without affecting any of the others. There is, for example, no fixed quantitative relationship between length, width, and height, even though they often co-vary.

Logical independence of variables. Variables are not always physically independent of each other; the presence of one variable often presupposes the presence of another, and change in one may result in change in another. In the physical world, for example, the presence of either size, weight, or density always presupposes the other two, and change in any one will automatically affect at least one of the other two. But we always have the choice of including or excluding any variable for our own classificatory purposes, regardless of its linkage with other variables. In arrowhead typologies it is common to include length and width but to exclude thickness, while color and weight are nearly always disregarded. We can therefore observe that the decision to include any particular variable in a classification does not predetermine the inclusion of any other, even when two variables are physically interrelated. This is what we mean by speaking of the logical independence of variables.

Selection for meaning. A few scientific purists have claimed to eliminate subjectivity from their classifications by taking account of all possible variables (e.g. Sabloff and Smith 1969); in particular this claim has often been made for computer-generated cluster analyses (see Doran and Hodson 1975: 158–86; Voorrips 1982: 111). In the classification of cultural phenomena, however, the consideration of all variables is a practical impossibility (cf. Dunnell 1971a: 117). The Medieval Nubian Pottery Typology is more comprehensive than most, involving forty-seven different intrinsic variables and a large number of individual attributes under each one (see Table 5), but it still disregards a great deal of variability. Decoration, in particular, is dealt with in a very summary fashion; literally hundreds of additional observations could be made.

The point has already been stressed several times that in practical typologies there must be a selection of variables, and that selection is ideally determined by our purposes in making the typology (cf. also Rouse 1960: 313; Dunnell 1971a: 117; Hill and Evans 1972: 237, 245–52; Watson, LeBlanc, and Redman 1984: 210–11). In the Nubian Pottery Typology, the meaningful consideration for the selection of variables is that of finite distribution in time and space. That is, the attributes of each variable incorporated in the typology must, individually, have temporal distributions less than the totality of "medieval" or else spatial distributions less than the totality of "Nubia" (or both). Variables like sherd size and weight, that do not show patterned distributions in time and space, are excluded.

The more we are clear in advance what our classificatory purposes are, the more we are likely to select variables that are meaningful to them, and on the basis of that selection to produce useful types. We will refer to variables that are chosen for inclusion in a typology as significant variables.

Attributes

Attributes designate recognizably different measurements or aspects within the same field (or along the same dimension) of variability. They differ from variables in several important respects. In each type there can be only one attribute per variable, the differences between attributes are primarily quantitative rather than qualitative, attributes are frequently interdependent, and they are usually selected by the typologist as criteria of identity rather than as criteria of meaning. We will here examine each of these features in a little more detail.

Exclusivity of attributes. While all significant variables are, either positively or negatively, present in each entity that is classified, there can be only one attribute of each variable. In a given object the relationship between attributes is one of mutual exclusivity, so that the presence of one attribute automatically precludes the presence of any other attributes of the same variable. It is self-evident that an object cannot be simultaneously thin and thick, soft and hard, or 10 and 20 cm long.

When two attributes seem to be present simultaneously – for example both red and black decoration on Nubian pottery wares – the combination is itself an attribute, separate both from red and from black occurring individually. There is for example a ware (W11) distinguished precisely by its possession of both red and black decoration, which serves to differentiate it from a similar ware having only black decoration (W9), and from another ware which may have either black or red, but never both (W2). Similarly when vessel wall thickness is described as medium to thick, this is an attribute different from either medium or thick. Thus, if a sufficiently large aggregation of sherds does not exhibit variability in wall thickness, those sherds probably do not belong to the type described as having medium to thick walls. Attributes of the kind just described are, obviously, manifest only in groups of entities and not in individual ones, an issue to which we will return later in the chapter.

Quantitative difference of attributes. While differences between variables are qualitative, those between attributes of the same variable are primarily quantitative, or at least they are capable of some kind of metric expression. Most variations of size and shape can be expressed by some measurement or combination of measurements, and even color can be analyzed in terms of light wavelengths (or described in terms of the Munsell system of color notation). Because they are quantitatively differentiated, attributes are treated as something fixed even though they may in reality include within themselves a good deal of variability. Thus we may break up a continuum of thickness variability into a series of arbitrarily designated segments which we call thin, medium, and thick, or we may subdivide a continuum of color variability into increments called red, orange, and yellow, treating each of these as unitary.

Interdependence of attributes. While variables are conceptually independent, attributes are not. They are interdependent both in a negative and in a positive sense. On the negative side, the presence of one attribute of a variable automatically means that the others are absent. On the positive side, the presence of an attribute of one variable may predetermine particular attributes of other variables. In the case of Nubian pottery fabrics, the selection of certain clays will result automatically in particular features of color, hardness, and texture. But this is not true of all clays; hence the variables of paste (clay, marl, or mud), fabric color, hardness, and texture must be considered independent of each other even though some of their individual attributes are not.

Selection for identity. We select or ignore variables on the basis of whether or not they will be useful for the purposes of our typology. On the other hand we select attributes within any variable primarily on the basis of whether or not they can be consistently distinguished. This matter can be put very succinctly: variables are criteria of meaning, and attributes are criteria of identity. We will refer to the attributes that have been selected for inclusion in any typology as significant attributes. We will refer to those significant attributes that serve to define any particular type as the diagnostic attributes of that type.

Problems of attribute differentiation

Not only is the relationship between attributes of the same variable usually quantitative, but they often exhibit a continuum of variation with no obvious modalities. In this case we have no choice, if the variable itself is considered significant, but to subdivide the continuum in some purely arbitrary fashion. At least among Western typologists there is a marked propensity to make tripartite divisions (long, medium, and short; hard, medium, and soft, etc.). Possibly this reflects the special status of 3 as a magic number in Judaeo-Christian tradition (three wishes, three witches, three wise men, etc.). More probably it is indicative of the apparently universal human tendency toward binary thinking (Lévi-Strauss 1966: 135–60). That is, we conceptualize attributes in terms of binary opposites (hot and cold, hard and soft, etc.), and add an intermediate position for anything that is not obviously one or the other. A common variant in typologies is the five-fold division which adds, for example, very hard and very soft at the extremes of the scale.

Scales of measurement

Although the differences between attributes are usually capable of some form of quantitative expression, it will be evident that they are not all measurable according to the same scale, nor are they amenable to the same kinds of statistical operations. Following the pioneering work of Stevens (1946), it has become common practice among archaeologists to speak of particular variables as being nominal, ordinal, interval, or ratio variables, meaning that their attributes are differentiated from one another in terms of nominal, ordinal, interval, or ratio scales of measurement. Nominal attribute differences are essentially qualitative; ordinal attribute differences are based on rank ordering (i.e. a kind of seriation) along a linear scale; interval attribute differences involve a uniform, measurable increment of difference between one attribute and another; ratio differences involve quantitative differences in relation to a fixed point, as in the case for example of atmospheres in physics or light years in astronomy (cf. *ibid.*).

The distinctions between these different measurement scales are clear enough in theory, and up to now their use has not occasioned much controversy among archaeologists. In other fields, however, they have become a subject of increasing controversy; it is not at all clear in many cases whether certain variables should be regarded as ordinal or interval, for example (Lord 1953; N. Anderson 1961; Adams, Fagot, and Robinson 1965). Because ideas on this subject seem to be rapidly changing, we have generally avoided the use of the terms nominal, ordinal, interval, and ratio scales in the present work. It is nevertheless worth reiterating that quantitative differences between attributes are not all of the same order. At the same time it should be recalled that the variables involved in artifact classifications are very largely nominal.

Classes and domains of variability
Variables and attributes can obviously be of many kinds. For heuristic purposes of the present discussion we will differentiate among them at two levels, which we will call classes of variables and domains of variability. This distinction applies also to attributes; that is, the class of any variable is also, obviously, the class of all the attributes of that variable.

Classes of variables. Scientific purists have sometimes argued that a fully objective classification should consider only properties (attributes) that are discoverable by examination of the entities being classified (L. Stone 1970; Hodson, Kendall, and Tautu 1971; Doran and Hodson 1975: 99–101). The periodic table of the elements is such a classification, and so, at least in theory, are some biological classifications (cf. Simpson 1945: 7). In the study of cultural materials, however, such universality is rarely possible. (For an attempt, which is now generally considered unsuccessful, see Beck 1973 [originally 1926].) What we call extrinsic evidence plays an important part in nearly all artifact classifications, although this has not often been acknowledged in the literature. (A significant exception is Gardin 1980: 65–8, 84–9; see also Ritchie and MacNeish 1949: 98.) It is only necessary to recall that every artifact typology has specific limits in space and time ("medieval" and "Nubian" in the case of our primary example), and that these invariant features of the typology are also part of the description of every type within the typology. In the study of artifact classifications we can further subdivide extrinsic evidence into what we call contextual and inferential variables. The three classes of variables and attributes that we will discuss here are, therefore, intrinsic, contextual, and inferential variables and attributes.

Intrinsic variables and attributes are all of the significant and recognizable features of the material being studied that are discoverable on examination of the material itself.

Contextual variables and attributes refer to the context in which things occur: they include distributions in space and time, and also associations between the things being classified and other things found with them. These variables, like intrinsic variables, are discoverable empirically, not by the study of the objects but from observation of the contexts in which they occur.

Inferential variables and attributes involve inferences that we ourselves make about the objects we classify. In artifact typologies they usually refer either to the presumed function or to the presumed emic significance of objects (see Chapter 23). It is important to note that these things cannot be discovered empirically. Consequently, no typology which involves inferential variables can lay any claim to objectivity. (However, as we have already shown, neither can any other typology in which there has been any selection of variables.)

Domains of variability. If we look at the forty-seven intrinsic variables that are listed for the Medieval Nubian Pottery Typology (Table 6), we can see that they are grouped under seven headings: method of construction, fabric, surface treatment, vessel forms, colors, painted decoration, and relief decoration. We will refer to these as different domains of variability. The importance of distinguishing them lies in the total independence of each group from all the others. Among the different variables listed under "fabric" there is a considerable interdependence of attributes from variable to variable; we have already observed, for example, that clay may determine hardness, color, and texture. On the other hand the attributes in any of the seven groups are wholly independent of all the attributes in the other groups. Hence, no change in fabric will necessitate change in surface treatment, vessel forms, color, or decoration. The importance of distinguishing between domains of variability will become apparent when we talk about attribute clustering in the next section.

Attribute clusters

It is theoretically possible to make a classification based on only one variable; for example, color. There are many folk classifications of this kind. In Chinese culture, for example, red is intrinsically "good," and all things red have a positive symbolic loading. It goes without saying, however, that there are no practical typologies based on only one variable, and certainly no artifact typologies. Consequently, types are defined not by a single attribute but by a combination, or cluster, of attributes. The recognition of significant and meaningful attribute clusters is a necessary second step in the formulation of types, following upon the selection of the variables and attributes individually. We will refer to the attribute cluster that serves to define any particular type as the diagnostic attribute cluster of that type.

Since in each type there can be only one attribute per variable, diagnostic combinations of attributes necessarily involve attributes of different variables. Not all combinations are of equal value for type definition and recognition, however. To be useful to the typologist, diagnostic attribute clusters must have three characteristics: statistical significance, variable association, and meaningfulness to the purpose of the typology. (For the difference between significance and meaning see Chapter 3.)

Statistical significance. Statistical significance refers to the strength of association between two or more attributes. If they occur together fairly often, but not invariably, we need to know whether their association is likely to be due to some causal factor, or if it may be due to chance. This can be determined by any of a number of statistical procedures, although as a practical matter it is often not necessary. Any association of variables which is frequent enough to catch the observer's eye will almost certainly prove to be statistically significant (cf. Watson, LeBlanc, and Redman 1971: 127; Thomas 1978: 236). Statistical procedures will be more fully discussed in Chapters 17 and 23, and need not detain us further here. We need only make the essential point that statistical significance is a necessary but not a sufficient condition for type designation. On the basis of statistical significance alone, most typologies are capable of generating far more "types" than are useful for any particular purpose (cf. Watson, LeBlanc, and Redman 1984: 204–7; Thomas 1986: 461–3).

Variable association. If we have to eliminate chance in the recognition of significant attribute clusters, we have also to eliminate invariant relationships. Some attributes regularly occur together with others (and therefore have a high degree of statistical significance) simply because one causes the others. This is likely to be true of clusters involving attributes within the same domain, as we defined that term a little earlier. The example of the interdependence of clay, hardness, color, and texture in Nubian pottery fabrics has already been cited. Since these clusters are invariant, their only significance for the archaeologist is statistical. We can say as a general principle, therefore, that clusters involving attributes from different domains (hence, wholly independent variables) are more likely to be meaningful than are clusters of attributes from the same domain. If they occur with any consistency they cannot be due to chance, but they also cannot be due to some fixed and immutable relationship. Gordon Childe (1956: 35) put the matter neatly many years ago: "the significance of a type . . . is proportionate to its improbability."

The practical importance of clusters involving attributes from different domains can be illustrated in the case of the Medieval Nubian Pottery Typology. Each of the three taxonomic levels in this system involves a clustering of attributes from different domains. In the most inclusive taxonomic category, pottery families are defined by the combination of method of construction and fabric attributes; ware groups within each family are defined by the addition of vessel form and decoration attributes; wares within each ware group are defined by the further addition of surface treatment and color attributes. (For fuller explanation see Chapter 10.)

Purposive meaning. In and of themselves, the taxonomic discriminations just described do not serve the primary purpose of the Nubian Pottery Typology, which is that of chronological and spatial ordering. To serve that purpose, it is necessary to introduce additional, contextual attributes into the type descriptions. This is true of virtually all artifact typologies. Because of the requirement that types have both identity and meaning, we can state as a general principle that artifact types require a combination of attributes not only from different domains but of different classes; that is, a combination of intrinsic and extrinsic attributes. The former provide criteria of identity, and the latter criteria of meaning.

The combination of intrinsic with contextual attributes will yield primarily historical typologies and types. Each type is defined by a unique combination of intrinsic attributes that, as a combination, also exhibit a specific, definable distribution in time and space. The obvious value of types formulated in this way is that, once they have been formulated and dated, they serve in their turn to date all other material found in association with them. This is the primary function of the Medieval Nubian and many other pottery typologies, and also of many projectile point typologies. As we saw in Chapter 1, historical typologies of this kind were and continue to be the foundations upon which the whole time–space ordering of world prehistory has been erected.

Combinations of intrinsic and contextual attributes may also produce associative typologies, as for example when we group together all of the pottery types found in a particular part of a site, and then endeavor to discover what (if any) features they have in common. These typologies may be helpful in identifying functionally distinct activity areas within a site, or between one site and another (Whallon 1973; 1974; Hietala 1984).

Combinations of intrinsic and inferential attributes may yield functional or (at least in theory) emic classifications, when we group together objects which are presumed to have performed a common function or to have had a common emic significance. As we will point out in Chapter 23, however, these groupings are properly taxonomic rather than typological in the strict sense, for they group together, at a higher level of classification, artifact types that have already been defined on morphological grounds.

Shifting criteria of "typehood"

Types, as we have just indicated, are differentiated on the basis of unique combinations of attributes, not on the basis of unique individual attributes. When a large number of variables is considered, as in the Nubian and most other pottery typologies, it is obvious that the unique combinations cannot always involve attributes of precisely the same variables. Any unique combination of any two or more attributes may be sufficient to define a type, if in addition this combination is found to have a significant distribution in time and space. To put the matter another way, the uniqueness of types does not lie in any one feature or group of features, and it is therefore impossible to specify either necessary or sufficient conditions for "typehood" in terms of specific features. The uniqueness of one pottery type may lie in its combination of colors and decoration, another in its combination of fabric and forms. In other words, the definition of types depends on variable, or shifting, criteria (Krieger 1944: 273, 278; Clarke 1968: 190; see also Huxley 1940: 11).

"Solving for the unknown"

Gardin (1980: 84–9) has made the interesting observation that when we combine intrinsic and extrinsic attributes we are often "solving for an unknown," so to speak. In the case of historical typologies we usually have at the beginning a set of types that have been differentiated on morphological grounds (e.g. pottery types), with an implied hypothesis that they were also made and used at different periods of time. We then have to discover through survey, stratigraphic excavation, and external dating techniques (radiocarbon, dendrochronology, etc.) whether or not this was really the case, and if so, what is the temporal distribution of each type. This was essentially the procedure in the development of the Nubian Pottery Typology, as described in Chapter 9. Types were provisionally designated on morphological grounds, but if two or more similar types were later found to have the same distribution in time and/or space, they were combined into a single type.

It is also possible, at least in theory, that we might have a group of objects of known date (e.g. from a historic site), with an implied hypothesis that because of their common origin in time and space they probably have other morphological or functional characteristics in common as well. In this case chronology is the known factor, and morphological or functional similarity is the unknown, which we seek to discover by examination of the artifacts themselves. Gardin (1980) has referred to these two approaches to typology-building as "induced" and "deduced," but we question the appropriateness of these terms (see Chapter 23). In later discussion we will refer to the two approaches, and to the types generated by them, as "intrinsically determined" and "extrinsically determined."

Type attributes and object attributes

It is necessary to recall here what we said at the beginning of the chapter, that we have been discussing the attributes of types and not of individual objects. Type concepts are formed on the basis of groups of objects rather than of individual objects, and many of their defining attributes are statistical norms characteristic of the object group as a whole but not of every object individually.

It is important to notice also that some type attributes are only collective and are not particularized; that is, they are manifest in aggregates of objects but not in individual objects. This is most obviously true of contextual attributes such as time and space distribution, which cannot be determined from the study of any single sherd or projectile point. Perhaps less obvious is the factor of "variable variability" (cf. Table 5) between one type and another, which also cannot be observed in individual specimens, but which in the aggregate can be important for type recognition. For example, many Egyptian pottery wares were mass-produced at a single specialized factory, and these vessels tend to be highly standardized in nearly all their characteristics. A group of sherds showing a large amount of diversity (for example in vessel form) should probably not be assigned to one of these factory wares, regardless of the resemblance of individual attributes. On the other hand Nubian wares were often produced simultaneously at several factories, with the result that some of these (e.g. Ware W2) are enormously diversified. Thus, a large group of sherds showing little or no diversity almost certainly should not be assigned to Ware W2.

Perhaps the most significant collective variable in the case of pottery types is vessel form. Most types were made in a considerable variety of forms; their number is usually too large to permit the designation of each form as a separate type. Nubian Ware W2, for example, occurs in 110 known forms (WYA 1986a: 477–9). This group of forms is a collective attribute of Ware W2, and a large group of sherds exhibiting many of these forms, and no other forms, may be assigned to Ware W2 with very considerable confidence. But each individual sherd of course exhibits only one form, and this is rarely sufficiently diagnostic to associate the sherd with any particular ware.

15

THE MAKING OF TYPES: FORMULATION, DESIGNATION AND DESCRIPTION

In Part II we talked in somewhat theoretical terms about how type concepts are formulated and communicated. In this chapter we return to the same issues from a more pragmatic perspective, and with reference especially to the relationship between types and attributes.

Discussion in the last two chapters might suggest that typology-making involves a simple and logical progression from the specification of purpose to the selection of attributes to the formulation of types on the basis of selected attributes. This is indeed the procedure recommended in many programmatic statements (Dunnell 1971b: 70–6; Spaulding 1982). Real-life typologies, however, are seldom made entirely in this way or in any single and simple way. The relationship between attributes and types is, in most typologies, a complex and multi-dimensional one.

As we saw in Chapter 5, the formulation and use of type concepts involves a number of successive stages, or processes. Processes that will concern us in the present chapter are those of formulation, definition, designation, and description. We will see that the relationship between attributes and types is somewhat different in each of the four cases, obliging us to make a distinction between diagnostic (prescriptive) and descriptive attributes. In anticipation of the discussion we may say that attributes are prescriptive of types at one level of analysis, and descriptive at another (cf. Whallon and Brown 1982: xvi).

Type concept formulation

Formulation refers to any of the several processes by which we may arrive at the type concepts that are to be included in any typology. The problems and procedures involved were discussed at some length in Chapters 5 and 6. Here we need only recall that types can be formulated in any of several ways: intuitively or rationally, inductively or deductively, by attribute clustering or object clustering, or some combination of those things. For each type the process of formulation usually involves some degree of discovery and some degree of invention, although this itself varies from type to type. No one method of type formulation is inherently right or wrong, and in fact many practical typologies include types that were formulated in more than one way. Consciously or unconsciously, however, attributes and attribute combinations play an essential role in the formulation of all types, and it is that role that we want to consider here.

We have stated a number of times previously that useful types have the two essential properties of identity and meaning. Both of these things have to be established in the process of type formulation. Identity is absolute; it is established on the basis of attributes and attribute combinations that are found to recur consistently, and that can be consistently recognized. Meaning on the other hand is relative only to the purpose of the typology. When a typology has no expressed or implied purpose, it will usually generate types that have no specifiable meaning (Dunnell 1971b: 97–8).

In the usual process of typology making, identity must be established before meaning. That is, provisional types must be differentiated on purely morphological grounds, and only then can we discover if their distributions are significantly patterned in time and space, or if they co-occur with other cultural remains, or if they are useful in some other way for our classificatory purposes. (For the opposite case see Gardin 1980: 87–8.) If morphologically identifiable types do not prove useful for our purposes, then presumably we will not retain them in the classification.

In the initial search for identifiable types, we will probably have to give some consideration to all of the variables and attributes present in our material, or at least to all those that are readily observable. Unless we have specific foreknowledge that certain attributes never cluster in any consistent way, or are not useful for our purposes, we have no choice but to assume that they may be useful. It is only by studying the circumstances in which each attribute occurs that we can determine whether or not it forms significant clusters, and whether these in turn co-occur with other things that interest us.

If our material proves to be classifiable on the basis of readily observed attributes, it is likely that we will not bother with other attributes that are not readily observable, and that can only be discovered through such cumbersome and time-consuming operations as measurement, weighing, or microscopic examination. We may on the other hand have foreknowledge that some of these procedures are necessary. In pottery classifications, for example, fabric (clay and temper) characteristics are among the most consistently useful determinants of types. It would be unthinkable to make a pottery classification without giving at least initial consideration to these features, even though they cannot usually be recognized and described without the examination of broken pottery surfaces under a hand lens.

It follows from what we have said that, unless we have substantial and reliable foreknowledge, purpose plays little role in the initial formulation of types, which are established on the basis of identity only. Purpose comes into play at a later stage, when we decide which of our identifiable types we do and do not want to retain for particular purposes.

Some archaeologists have claimed to achieve complete objectivity in classification by basing their typologies on all observable attributes, rather than selecting among them (Sabloff and Smith 1969; see also Voorrips 1982: 111). At least in the case of pottery typologies this is, in reality, an impossibility, for the number of potential attribute combinations is beyond calculation (cf. Dunnell 1971a: 117). It would probably be more legitimate to say that the archaeologists considered all attributes before formulating their types, and then selected those that were found to show significant patterning. As we have just suggested, this is frequently a necessary procedure in the initial stages of typology formulation.

Type definition

In Chapter 6 we discussed at some length the paradox of type definition: the fact that classifying is in the broadest sense a process of definition, yet types are very seldom formally or rigorously defined (cf. Klejn 1982: 18–19). It is nevertheless true that every identifiable type has an implicit or unstated definition, in that it must possess a unique combination of attributes, present and absent, that distinguishes it from all other types. Yet our type concepts are constantly changing in the course of use, as we saw in Chapter 5. Some types are redefined, some are split into two or more separate types, and some are combined with other types. We are therefore compelled to add the qualifier that every type has, at least implicitly, a provisional or working definition, at any given moment in time. With increasing experience and the sorting of more and more material we can anticipate that provisional definitions will become more and more fixed and less likely to change, but we can never really say that we have achieved fixed and final definitions as long as there is any material still to be sorted (cf. Simpson 1945: 13). Throughout this work, therefore, the noun "definition" must always be read as "provisional definition."

When we have formulated a series of provisional types, and analyzed them in terms of their distinguishing characteristics, it will usually be found that some attributes show a significant patterning among the types and others do not. In other words, some attributes serve provisionally to define types and others do not. Some of the attributes will not be very consistently recognizable; others will not cluster with other attributes in any consistent way; still others will cluster so uniformly that there is no variation from type to type. The attributes that can serve for type definition are those that form recognizable clusters with a high degree of consistency, but not invariably. We refer to these as significant attributes in the case of typologies, and diagnostic attribute clusters in the case of individual types (see Chapter 14). We therefore say that a type is defined by its unique attribute cluster, which however may or may not be consciously recognized by the typologist. (Thus we say also that the type is *defined* by its attribute cluster, while it is *formulated* by the typologist; see Chapter 6.)

It should be observed that in formulating provisional types we have, in most cases, established only their identity and not their meaning. Up to this point purpose may still have played no important role. Except in cases where we have substantial foreknowledge, purpose will be involved more in the selection of types themselves than in the selection of significant attributes and attribute clusters, as we will see in the next section.

Type selection and designation

It should be apparent from the foregoing that the formulation of provisional types usually constitutes only a first step in the making of a useful typology. The second step consists in the selection of types that are useful for our specific purposes. Every typology that involves a large number of variables or attributes is capable, in theory, of generating an almost infinite number of types on the basis of identity alone, yet practical typologies rarely include more than 100 designated types. This is because a selection has been made among the potential types on the basis of meaning.

In one way or another, consciously or unconsciously, selection is involved in all typology making. Discussion in the typological literature usually refers to the selection of defining attributes that are to be used in type formulation (e.g. Krieger 1944: 276, 284; Rouse 1960: 313; Clarke 1968: 137; Watson, LeBlanc, and Redman 1971: 127; Hill and Evans 1972: 245–52), rather than to the selection of types themselves. However, as we have just seen, there may at the outset be no rational basis for the selection of attributes; we have no choice but to consider most or all of them, and to formulate a large number of provisional types. Thereafter it is not attributes but types that must be selected on the basis of whether or not they are useful for our purposes. In sum, we suggest that the making of practical typologies usually involves first the formulation of provisional types on the basis of criteria of identity, and then the selection of useful types on the basis of criteria of meaning. It is mainly in the second step that purpose plays a determining role.

When a type has proven meaningful and has been accepted, we will probably give it formal legitimation by bestowing on it a name or a number. At this point we may say, metaphorically, that our type has been initiated into membership in the typology. This is the critical step that we call type designation.

Type description

When a type has been accepted and designated, the next step is to describe it. There are field archaeologists who have made use for years of intuitive type concepts that they have never bothered to formalize, but obviously such concepts can be useful only to their makers. If type concepts are to be shared between two or more people, and even more particularly if they are to be used in sorting (see Chapter 16), then it is necessary that they be communicated through some kind of representation (*contra* Wittgenstein; see Canfield 1981: 39). In the case of archaeological typologies this nearly always involves a combination of verbal description and pictorial representation, which may be photographic or diagrammatic or both. For convenience of terminology we will refer to the whole process of representation as one of description, even though non-verbal representations may also be involved.

Type description is never simply tantamount to definition. A formal definition would specify only those attributes or attribute combinations that serve to distinguish a type from all other types. However, every type possesses in addition a large number of attributes that serve to distinguish it from *some* other types, and which are therefore useful in the process of sorting entities (see Chapter 16). These descriptive attributes will also be included in any useful type description. (Our distinction between diagnostic attributes and descriptive attributes corresponds in a general way to Wittgenstein's distinction between criteria and symptoms; see Canfield 1981: 31–9.)

Type descriptions may be relevant either to theoretical or to practical concerns, or both. In the biological sciences, species definitions are often formulated primarily for theoretical purposes. That is, they are formulated in such a way as to justify the designation of a particular group of organisms as a species, according to some abstract principle of species determination. Consequently, species descriptions are likely to include at least an attempt at formal definition, though they are not limited to this. There is also, for many biologists, a sense of obligation to describe as accurately as possible the "reality" of nature, which means a comprehensive description of all attributes of the species.

These considerations generally do not apply to archaeological typologies, whose purposes are largely practical. They are not formulated in order to justify the designation of a particular group of attributes or objects as a type, but only to facilitate the communication and use of the type concept for some practical purpose. Ordinarily there is no effort at formal definition, and no distinction is made between what we have called diagnostic attributes and descriptive attributes.

Archaeological type descriptions serve two main practical purposes: to ensure consistency in the communication of information, and to ensure consistency in the sorting of entities (see Chapter 16). The first of these is a matter of intersubjective agreement – the extent to which all of the users of a typology share the same mental image of each type (for extended discussion see Ziman 1978). The second involves both intrasubjective and intersubjective agreement – the consistency with which any given person, or two or more persons, will sort the same entities in the same way. (For a discussion of consistency problems see Fish 1978.) Obviously, both of these goals are best achieved through the use of maximally comprehensive type descriptions. The more fully a type is described in terms of all its recognizable features, the more likely it is that two or more persons will form the same mental conception of it, and will sort entities in accordance with that conception. There is, in addition, the consideration of practicality or rapidity in sorting (see Chapter 19), which is also facilitated by maximally comprehensive descriptions of types.

A practical type description, then, will include all of the attributes that are involved in the actual definition of the type, as well as all other attributes that may be useful for the typing of specific objects (see Chapter 16). We refer to this process of extended description as overdetermination. It is not necessarily synonymous with total description, for a type may exhibit some features that are useful neither for definition nor for object recognition. These would include invariants, which are common to all types in the system (see Chapter 14), and also attributes that show no consistent patterning, such as color in the case of many lithic tool types.

As we suggested in Chapter 6, archaeological types are usually defined by unique norms rather than by absolute boundaries, and type descriptions are therefore descriptions of norms, or ideal types (cf. Klejn 1982: 49–50). The number of actual specimens that conform closely to the norm will be large in the case of some types and small in the case of others (cf. Shepard

1965: 317; Keighley 1973: 133). To be maximally useful for recognition and sorting, therefore, type descriptions should indicate both norms and known deviations from the norm. Variability is itself a feature that varies from type to type (see Chapter 14).

Type definitions are not, of course, formulated only for the practical purposes of object labeling and sorting. They are usually intended also to provide contextual and/or historical information about the type, and for this reason they may list extrinsic as well as intrinsic attributes of the type. For further discussion of this issue see Chapter 14.

Most of the principles of description that have been discussed in this chapter are exemplified in the medieval Nubian pottery ware descriptions. Each ware is described in terms of forty-seven separate intrinsic character-istics, as detailed in Table 6. Only a few characteristics of each ware are actually diagnostic, but all of them are useful in application; that is, they help us in the task of attaching type identities to particular pots or sherds. There is also an attempt to indicate the nature and the extent of variation in each of the major attribute domains (method of construction, fabric, surface treatment, vessel forms, colors, and decoration). Finally, each ware description includes information about the temporal and spatial distribution of the ware, its place(s) of manufacture, its frequency of occurrence, and its associations. A specimen Nubian ware description is included in Appendix B.

Decision-making in classification

It should be evident by now that a certain amount of arbitrary and subjec-tive decision-making is involved both in the classifying and in the sorting processes. It is undoubtedly this subjectivity that has proven objectionable to scientific purists, and has led to so many attempts at "automatic" classification by means of computers and statistics (cf. Doran and Hodson 1975: 158–86; Brown 1982: 183–5). Yet all attempts to rid classifications of their subjectivity have ended by robbing them also of their utility. The utility of type concepts is enhanced, not diminished, by the very com-plexity that makes them so difficult to define rigorously (see Chapter 6), and that makes decision-making an unavoidable necessity.

There are at least four points at which decision-making is required in the formulation and use of typologies. These are in the selection of variables for type formulation, in the selection of attributes for type formulation, in the actual designation of types, and in the sorting of entities. The criteria on which we base these decisions are not entirely uniform in the four cases, and require further consideration here. (Sorting decisions will, however, be discussed in the next chapter.)

Variable selection. In theory, the choice of variables for type formulation is the most straightforward and the least subjective phase of the classifying process. The variables chosen are those that are known or presumed to be useful for the purposes of the typology, as discussed in Chapters 13 and 14 (see also Rouse 1960: 313; Dunnell 1971a: 117; Hill and Evans 1972: 237, 245–52). If the purpose is for dating, then the variables selected are those that are known to undergo change over time, such as color and decoration in the case of pottery types.

The reality, as always, is not quite so simple. To begin with, we are almost certain to give attention to any feature that, on first inspection, is highly conspicuous and conspicuously varied, whether or not we know it to be significant for our purposes. Color in the case of decorated pottery wares is one such feature; serration in the case of projectile points is another. Selection of these features is simply a matter of reacting to gestalts, as discussed in Chapter 4. Usually our instincts in this regard will prove to be sound, but this cannot be taken for granted.

At a more conscious level of analysis, the selection of a variable on the basis of known or expected significance assumes a good deal of foreknowledge, which we may or may not actually possess. When we do not, we have no choice but to assume that any variable may be significant (i.e. useful for our purposes), until we have demonstrated in practice that it is not. Consequently, as we suggested earlier in the chapter, types must be provisionally designated before their distributions can be studied.

No matter how conscientiously we proceed in the beginning, however, it is unlikely that our initial list of significant variables will remain unchanged. We will probably discover through experience that some variables are not significant or useful after all, but we are likely also to find new significant variables that were previously overlooked. The consequence is that in some cases initially designated types will be discarded or combined with other types, while other initial types will be split into two or more types. Both of these things happened in the development of the Nubian Pottery Typology (see Chapter 9).

It is self-evident that the significance or utility of a variable in one part of the world is no guarantee of its utility in another. It is equally true, though perhaps less obvious, that the significance of a variable at one moment in time does not guarantee its significance at another, even within the same area. In Nubia, the difference between polished and matte surface finish was found to be significant in all of the later pottery wares (that is, differences of surface finish significantly clustered with other characteristics of the pottery), but this was not true in the earliest (Meroitic) period. Consequently, it was necessary to select different variables for type formulation at different periods within the same typology.

Obviously, decisions in regard to variable selection will be most arbitrary and subjective in the beginning phases of typology development. The decisions become more and more informed over time, as guesswork and intuition gradually give way to experience.

Attribute selection. The problems involved in attribute selection are different in several respects from those in variable selection. When we decide that a variable is potentially significant, we automatically decide that each of its attributes is potentially significant. But because the difference between the attributes of any variable is essentially quantitative (see Chapter 14), we may face at the outset a problem of differentiation, or recognition. This can be particularly acute in the case of measurement data, when we may have to decide quite arbitrarily how to subdivide a continuum. In the case of projectile point lengths, for example, shall we make a three-fold division into long, medium, and short, or a five-fold division into very long, long, medium, short, and very short, or some other differentiation?

The fact that a particular variable is found to be significant does not mean *a priori* that all of its distinguishable attributes will be equally significant. This can be readily illustrated in the case of Nubian pottery slip colors. Seven colors (cream, yellow, orange, pink, red, brown, and black) can be consistently differentiated, but only four of these (cream–yellow–orange, pink, red, and brown–black) are always significant. Particularly in the early medieval periods, cream, yellow, and orange are accidental mutations of the same "color," so that any vessel form with a cream slip may also be found with a yellow or orange slip, and with the same patterns of decoration. Moreover, the color of individual vessels may shade from cream on one side to orange on the other. In some of the later periods (Ware Groups N.V and N.VI), however, there is a clear differentiation between cream, yellow, and orange vessels, so that each occurs in vessel forms and with decorative features not found in the other two. We have to recognize, therefore, that there are four significant slip color attributes in the early periods, but six in the later periods, even though the same seven basic colors are present in all the periods.

In sum, the significance of attributes, like the significance of variables, cannot be taken for granted. It varies from area to area and from period to period, and it must be established empirically in each individual case.

Type designation. As we have already suggested in this and in previous chapters, the discovery of significant variables and attributes will not lead automatically to the determination of significant types. Types are defined not by single attributes but by combinations of attributes (see Chapter 14), and the fact that attributes are individually significant does not necessarily mean that all combinations of them are significant. Every typology is theoretically capable of generating thousands of types, if every possible combination of attributes is treated as significant. In the world of reality we have to discover empirically which attribute clusters are significant or useful, just as we do in the case of individual attributes and variables.

In Chapter 14 we discussed three features that identify significant attribute clusters: nonrandomness (statistical significance), variability of association, and meaningfulness for the purposes of the typology. Unfortunately, only the first of these is immediately discoverable. If we have a sufficient body of material in hand, we can apply any of a number of statistical tests to determine whether the association of two or more attributes is too consistent to be due to chance (Spaulding 1953; 1960; 1982; Watson, LeBlanc, and Redman 1971: 127–32; and various contributions in Whallon and Brown 1982). But the issue of randomness or nonrandomness is itself a complex one (Jos. Ford 1983; Kolata 1986), and it is not always clear which of several statistical tests will provide the best evidence of nonrandomness. Sometimes it may be necessary to choose among them more or less arbitrarily (cf. Hempel 1966: 65).

In any case, nonrandomness is a necessary but not a sufficient condition for type designation. We may be certain that two attributes regularly occur together, but we have still to discover if this is because of a dependent relationship between them, so that the presence of one automatically determines the other (cf. Salmon 1982: 131–4). If the association of two or more attributes is found to be absolutely consistent, then of course it will show no variation in time, space, or context, and it will not be useful for most typological purposes. Variability or constancy of trait association can often be determined only after a great deal of material has been studied, or after some kind of technical analysis has determined whether variables are or are not causally related.

We observed in Chapter 14 that archaeological types are usually defined by a combination of intrinsic and extrinsic (contextual or inferential) attributes. In order to have the two essential properties of identity and meaning, a type must show a consistent co-occurrence between internal features, which establish identity, and external features, which establish meaning. However, external features (especially contextual features) are frequently unknown in the beginning phases of typology making. We may therefore be forced to designate provisional types on purely intrinsic grounds, and then to discard them later if they prove to have no distributional or associational significance. The governing principle in these cases should in theory be "split first, then lump" (cf. WYA 1975: 88).

If this procedure were followed systematically, typologies might be expected to become gradually smaller in the course of their development. The reality is usually otherwise; the number of types increases rather than decreases with the passage of time. There are a number of reasons for this seeming anomaly. First and most obviously, new excavations continually bring forth new and previously unsuspected types. Second, sorting experience makes us aware of significant variables and attributes that we had previously overlooked or disregarded, and this may result in the splitting of some of our original types into two or more separate types. Third, the use of typologies is often extended over larger territories or over longer periods of time than those for which they were originally intended. Finally, and unfortunately, there is a tendency to retain type designations once they have appeared in the literature, whether or not they have any proven utility.

For all these reasons, the number of types that are added to a typology over time usually exceeds the number that are deleted. Both processes are likely to occur, however, and both require a measure of arbitrary decision-making.

Apart from the issues of nonrandomness, variable association of traits, and meaningfulness, there are at least two other factors that may require arbitrary decision-making in the process of typology development. One has to do with significant and/or useful degrees of differentiation. If typologies are made by a process of differentiation (see Chapter 5), at what point should it stop? Or if types are made by object or attribute clustering, when are two clusters sufficiently different so that they merit separate type designation? There are clearly no hard-and-fast answers. As a general rule of thumb it may be suggested that types should be differentiated whenever they satisfy the minimum criteria of identity and meaning: when they can be consistently differentiated, and when the difference between them is found to have chronological or spatial or functional significance (cf.

Shepard 1965: 318). But how much consistency is sufficient must necessarily be a matter for individual judgment (cf. Hempel 1966: 65).

There is, finally, the question of how many specimens are necessary to make a type. We suggested in Chapter 7 that practical typologies consist only of realized types and not of potential ones. In other words, to put it in terms of our mailbox analogy (Chapter 5), we will not put up a mailbox for John Smith until some mail for John Smith actually arrives. But how much mail? Since archaeological typologies are normally designed for the description and differentiation of large numbers of artifacts, one letter is not theoretically sufficient to justify a mailbox.

At the same time archaeologists, like other anthropologists, are accustomed to think in terms of norms (cf. Shepard 1965: 317; Keighley 1973: 133). Whenever they find an object that has obviously been intentionally produced, they are likely to attribute this to culturally determined choice rather than to individual choice. As a result, there is a temptation to confer "typehood" on any highly distinctive specimen, or at least on a small collection of distinctive specimens, in the expectation that others like them will sooner or later turn up. This expectation may or may not be fulfilled. Ancient craftsmen, like modern ones, liked to vary the monotony of production by occasional experiments with new forms, which might never subsequently be repeated or copied. The aberrant results of these experiments turn up from time to time to plague all field archaeologists, and each archaeologist has to decide for himself when there are enough specimens to constitute a type. The rule of thumb that has been adopted in regard to Nubian pottery wares is that each ware must be represented by sherds of more than one vessel, preferably coming from vessels of more than one shape, and coming from more than one site (cf. WYA 1986a: 9). There are nevertheless wares in the system that are represented by fewer than fifty sherds altogether, while sherds of others number in the millions.

16

THE USE OF TYPES:
TYPING AND SORTING

In Chapter 4 and Chapter 8 we defined a typology as a system of classification made specifically for the sorting of entities. We cannot state often
enough that classifying (making categories) and sorting (putting things
into them) are two different processes, each involving its own problems (cf.
Jevons 1874, II: 394–6; Kluckhohn 1960: 135–6; Dunnell 1971b: 45;
Vierra 1982: 162–3). The problems encountered in classifying are in the
broadest sense problems of definition; they are partly theoretical (see
Chapter 6), partly procedural, and partly judgmental (see Chapter 15).
The problems in sorting are problems of recognition, and are purely
judgmental. As we have observed several times before, even the inventors
of types have to learn to use them in practice.

It is important at the outset to be clear about what it is we are recognizing in the sorting process. It is not, as is often suggested, a simple matter of
identification (cf. Shepard 1965: 306–22; Clarke 1968: 187–91; Whallon
1972: 15; Voorrips 1982: 116–17), because in archaeology the type
membership of an artifact is often far from obvious. What we are recognizing are the *resemblances* between specific entities and specific type concepts. That is, we are matching entities with concepts, and we have to
decide for each individual entity which of several type concepts it most
nearly resembles, and label it accordingly. Type application therefore
involves the processes of matching and labeling, which we will designate
collectively as type attribution. We will refer to any single act of type attribution – that is, matching of a type concept and label with a single object –
as typing of the object. In certain conditions (which we will discuss later)
the making of type attributions in series will be referred to as sorting.

Definition vs. application
It might be supposed that type formulation and type attribution are two
sides of the same coin; that whatever features are involved in the definition
of any type will also be the basis for recognizing individual members of that

194

type (cf. Shepard 1965: 306; Whallon 1972: 15). In practice this is often not the case. There are several reasons for this seeming paradox, most of which we have already noted in Chapter 6.

First, archaeological types are usually determined by central tendencies, or modalities, rather than by hard-and-fast boundaries (cf. Jevons 1874, II: 411–14; Klejn 1982: 58–64). This means that type descriptions necessarily refer to an idealized conception of the type, which may or may not be reflected in a large number of actual specimens (Simpson 1945: 3–4; Klejn 1982: 49–50). In most archaeological classifications the perfect type specimen is probably more the exception than the rule (cf. Dunnell 1971b: 139–40; Keighley 1973: 133; for the parallel case in biology see Simpson 1945: 28–30). It is therefore never a foregone conclusion that any artifact will clearly and unambiguously exhibit all of the diagnostic attributes of any one type.

Another problem is that diagnostic attributes cannot always be quickly or easily identified. In pottery classifications this is especially true in regard to fabric (paste) characteristics, which can only be examined under a hand lens after making a fresh break in the vessel wall. Fabric is a critical variable in the definition of medieval Nubian pottery wares (cf. Chapter 10), but fortunately most of these wares can also be recognized on the basis of other and less absolutely diagnostic traits, so that the time-consuming process of fabric examination is necessary only in a small number of cases.

Moreover, in large and/or complex classifications the number of absolutely diagnostic attributes for any given type is usually small; the great majority of traits are shared with at least one or two other types. When the matching of objects with types is based only on a small number of attributes, the possibility for error or for disagreement between two sorters is obviously higher than when a large number of attributes is considered.

Finally, in archaeology a great deal of the material that we sort is fragmentary, particularly when we are dealing with ceramics. Our entities are very largely potsherds, but our types are not really types of sherds; they are types of whole pots. This means that specimens often will not exhibit all of the diagnostic attributes that were originally present. Many Nubian wares are defined partly on the basis of decoration, but no decoration is likely to be preserved on sherds from the basal portions of vessels. The same holds true for most characteristics of vessel form, which can usually be recognized only in sherds from the rim or from the base.

It is evident, in sum, that some attributes are more useful in the process of type formulation than they are in the process of application. Fortunately, the reverse is also true (see especially Jevons 1874, II: 394–6). Every type possesses only a few attributes that distinguish it from all other types, but a much larger number of attributes that are helpful in distinguishing it from some other types. The process of sorting is therefore greatly facilitated when type and object matchings are based on as many attributes as possible, and not merely on those attributes which are absolutely diagnostic of types. This is the reason for overdetermination, or maximal description, in type descriptions, which we discussed in the last chapter.

Typing

The most elementary and presumably the most common application of type concepts is simply in the typing of individual objects. As we noted earlier, this is a matter of matching objects against type concepts, and, when an appropriate fit is found, of applying a particular type label to a particular object. The type label, like all labels, then serves as a form of shorthand communication. It tells us that whatever we know to be true of the type in general – its origin, distribution, or function – will be true *a priori* of the specific object which we have labeled.

Archaeologists rely heavily on type labels for abbreviated communication. One obvious usage is in museum displays, where various objects are designated as scrapers, borers, fleshers, and the like – terms which are actually classificatory rather than descriptive. An even more common usage is in published reports, where, for the sake of economy, similar objects are often grouped under a common designation and description, and where individual objects may be "described" merely by identifying them as representatives of previously well-known types. Thus the contents of an Anasazi grave, for example, may be described simply as comprising "a large jar of Tusayan corrugated, an olla of Kayenta black-on-white, and a bowl of Tsegi polychrome," without proceeding to more precise description.

It is important to notice that typing, as we have described it here, is a classificatory procedure but not in all cases a typological procedure, according to the definitions that we laid down in Chapter 4. That is, the labels that are applied to particular objects may actually be class labels rather than type labels, because they are not necessarily mutually exclusive. Labeling an object as a representative of a particular class does not preclude its membership in other classes as well; indeed it is quite common to find the same object described or illustrated more than once in a published report. For example, pottery lamps may appear both in a chapter on pottery and in a chapter on lamps.

Sorting

It follows from what has just been said that a series of individual typings does not necessarily constitute a process of sorting, according to our definition (see Chapter 4). Sorting is always a cumulative and comprehensive activity: a succession of typings carried out on all members of a previously specified body of material (all pottery vessels, all objects from a site, etc.) for a specific purpose above and beyond that of communication (see Chapter 13). Moreover, and most importantly, sorting is a process of successive pigeonholing: the matching of each object with one type category to the exclusion of all other categories.

We have observed in Chapter 13 that the proximate purpose of sorting is usually to permit the enumerative, comparative, or statistical treatment of type data; in one way or another to discover and/or measure the quantitative relationship between different types of entities. It is because of this comparative feature that entities can be placed in one and only one category. However, comparative and statistical manipulations are not ends in themselves, they are means to various other and more theoretical ends. The different ends that may be served by archaeological typologies were discussed in Chapter 13, and need not be reviewed again here. Our concern in this chapter is with the practical problems and procedures involved in sorting, for whatever purpose.

As was pointed out in Chapter 15, there has been a common tendency to assume that problems in sorting can be eliminated by precision in the definition of types (Wheat, Gifford, and Wasley 1958: 38; Clarke 1968: 187–91; Whallon 1972; Voorrips 1982: 116). It should be evident by now that this is an illusion. Sorting problems are reduced not by the formulation of rigorous type definitions but by the formulation of maximally extended descriptions. Even then, the problems are never wholly eliminated. In the world of reality there are always borderline cases and fragmentary specimens, which do not match closely with any one type concept, and which force us to make arbitrary sorting judgments or else to assign the specimens only to broad and partially indeterminate categories; for example to families or to ware groups rather than to individual wares in the Nubian typology (see Chapter 11).

Learning to sort

Comprehensive type descriptions, then, are necessary but not sufficient to ensure effective sorting. The use of typologies, as of other languages, cannot be learned entirely from books. A certain amount of hands-on experience is essential in learning to recognize and to sort types consistently (cf.

197

Shepard 1965: 306; J. A. Ford 1962: 15; Thomas 1972; Whallon 1972: 15). The learning process may be described as one of gestalt acquisition. That is, we learn to recognize at a glance types which we originally had to identify by a conscious process of attribute analysis (cf. Margolis 1987: 48–9). When this happens our types have almost inevitably become to some extent reified. However, we should not make the mistake of assuming that the ability to identify a type at a glance is *a priori* evidence of its "naturalness," as is assumed in Gestalt psychology (Köhler 1940; 1947).

In sum, effective and consistent sorting involves both the memorization of attribute lists and the acquisition of gestalts through hands-on experience. Individual sorters will be found to vary in their ability to do both of these things, just as individuals vary in their ability to learn other kinds of languages. Those with a special aptitude for pattern recognition will probably learn to sort very largely on the basis of gestalts, and without reference to formal type descriptions, while those with less aptitude for pattern recognition will have to rely proportionately more on memorized descriptions. In this respect, different sorters may be likened to different instruments measuring the same thing; for example, the use of different kinds of thermometers to measure temperature.

Sorting procedures

Sorting procedures are likely to vary according to the type and quality of material to be sorted, the time and facilities available, and the proclivities of individual sorters. When rapid and/or large-scale sorting is required, it is important to work out procedures that are both reasonably reliable and reasonably efficient (see Chapter 19). It is also important to follow the same procedures consistently, since procedures themselves can affect individual sorting decisions. When stepwise procedures are followed, for example, they will usually result in a slight increase in the number of specimens that are assigned to the last types to be sorted, whatever they happen to be.

In theory, the ideal or at least the most logical way of sorting would be to follow the same procedure used in the primary sorting of mail; that is, to put up in advance a box for each known type, and then to sort individual specimens in whatever order they come to hand. There are, however, two practical drawbacks to this kind of random sorting procedure. First, it is enormously space-consuming, and may require the sorter to walk back and forth between widely separated sorting bins or areas – a requirement that is not conducive to rapid sorting. Second, each individual sorting decision is final, and there is no subsequent chance to correct initial errors of judgment.

There are various alternatives to a purely random system of sorting. One is to remove all of the members of each type in stepwise succession, beginning with the most easily recognized and proceeding to the most difficult. Another, which is currently followed in Nubia, is to sort in stages, making an initial division into a few gross and easily recognized classes, and then further subdividing these either into individual types or into finer subdivisions, which are then divided into types in a third stage. The sorting procedures currently employed in Nubia are described in detail in Chapter 11.

The use of extrinsic evidence

In principle, type formulations are based on a combination of intrinsic and extrinsic attributes (see Chapter 14), while type attributions (typings) are based on intrinsic evidence alone. There may nevertheless be times in the sorting process when it is possible to make use of external, contextual evidence, providing that it does not result in a process of circular argument. This can be exemplified in the case of the Early Christian Nubian wares. Early Christian deposits yield large numbers of white-slipped sherds which, because of design and color peculiarities, can be confidently assigned to three well-defined wares (W1, W2, and W9). However, the same deposits also yield enormous numbers of polished red sherds which usually have no painted decoration. Except when modeled rims are present, these sherds cannot be unambiguously assigned to any one Nubian ware on the basis of intrinsic features alone. There are polished red wares in most of the Nubian ware groups, dating from different periods in history. However, the red sherds can be unambiguously assigned to only one ware in the Early Christian period, because only one polished red ware (R5) was made and used at that time. When Wares W1, W2, and W9 are present in abundance, therefore, we feel safe in assuming that most of the polished red sherds found in association with them belong to Ware R5. Of course this identification cannot be correct 100 per cent of the time, since all excavation units produce at least a few stray sherds that properly belong to earlier or to later periods (cf. WYA 1986b; WYA 1987: 19–25; WYA n.d.3). For purposes of our statistical analyses, however, it is a much more accurate and more useful identification than would result if we assigned most of the polished red sherds to the "unidentifiable" category, when in fact their identity is more than 95 per cent certain. The typing of any sherd is a matter of calculating probabilities, and contextual evidence may assist in that calculation.

External evidence must of course be used in sorting with appropriate caution. It cannot be used if a chain of circular reasoning would result; if, for example, a deposit were to be dated on the basis of sherd identifications that were themselves dependent on pre-assumptions about their date. Contextual evidence also cannot be used as a basis for assigning a sherd to one ware as opposed to another, if both wares could conceivably occur in the same context. The main, and important, value of contextual evidence is in diminishing the "unidentified" category, permitting reasonably reliable type identifications that could not be made on the basis of intrinsic evidence alone. The question of acceptable degrees of reliability will be further discussed in Chapter 19.

Decision-making in sorting

In Chapter 15 we observed that human judgment, or decision-making, is involved at various points in the formulation of types. Sorting, on the other hand, is a process of continual decision-making.

It should be recalled that in the processes of typing and sorting we are mostly recognizing the resemblances between objects and type concepts, and resemblance is always a matter of degree. Moreover, the perception of resemblance varies greatly from one person to another. In everyday life we often hear arguments as to whether or not one person resembles another – for example, does a child "take after" his father or his mother? Essentially similar arguments can be heard with reference to potsherds. One sorter may say, "This looks like Ware W2 to me"; another will reply, "It looks more like W6 to me"; a third will assert "Of course it's W6; any idiot can see that"; and a fourth will say "It can't be W6; the context is 200 years too early." Anyone who has been on a dig or in an archaeological laboratory for any length of time will have heard many arguments of this kind.

Because of these complicating factors, sorting decisions are the most arbitrary and the most subjective of all typological decisions. Insofar as there are any rules of thumb in the matter, each sorter must develop his own. When a borderline specimen appears equally close to two type norms, how shall we decide into which pigeonhole we will put it? When a specimen is highly incomplete, shall we give it a type identity on the basis of a few features that are present, or shall we put it in the "unidentified" category? If a specimen appears slightly more similar to late medieval than to early medieval norms, but was found in an early medieval context, shall we nevertheless identify it as a late medieval type?

Where large-scale or rapid sorting is involved, the situation of the sorter is not essentially different from that of the baseball umpire. He must make continual, rapid judgments, largely on the basis of instinct, and then have the courage to stick to them. The baseball rulebook (Rule 14.10) may tell the umpire fairly precisely what is a ball and what is a strike, but this is no help at all in making borderline calls. Moreover, the best judgment in the world will not save him from a considerable number of disputed calls, and perhaps one or two full-fledged rhubarbs, in the course of a typical nine-inning game. It is worth noting, by the way, that professional baseball players do not expect consistency of judgment between one umpire and another; they know that individuals differ in their perceptions. What they look for is consistency in the judgment of each individual umpire.

Having invoked the baseball analogy, it seems appropriate that we should conclude this chapter with the parable of the three umpires, who are arguing in their dressing room after a game. The youngest umpire, who has been working behind the plate, is taking considerable criticism for his ball and strike calls, and he asserts heatedly, "Doggone it, I call 'em as I see 'em." An older umpire retorts contemptuously, 'Well, I call 'em as they *are*.' But the old chief umpire winks and says, "They *ain't* nothing till I call 'em." We suggest that three distinct philosophies of classification and sorting are illustrated in this neat parable (for which we are indebted to Stephen Pepper), and any sorter is free to choose among the three of them. There can be no doubt, however, that the chief umpire's view will be most conducive to the sorter's peace of mind.

17

THE ORDERING OF TYPES: TAXONOMY AND SERIATION

We observed in the last chapter that the immediate reason for sorting entities is usually, though not always, to permit some kind of enumerative or statistical comparison between types. This in itself is an intermediate step toward the more fundamental goal of determining relationships between types. However, as we saw in Chapter 7, such relationships cannot be expressed within the structure of basic (one-level) typologies, because of the principles of equivalence of types and equidistance of types. In order to express relationships it is necessary to subject types to some kind of secondary ordering which is independent of the type concepts themselves (cf. Dunnell 1971b: 83).

The two most common procedures in secondary ordering are those of taxonomy and seriation. The former is a process of hierarchic clustering, and the latter of linear ordering. Both taxonomic ordering and seriation are common in archaeological classification, but we have delayed consideration of them until this point because, in the great majority of cases, they are incidental rather than essential features of the classificatory system.

Taxonomy

The term taxonomy, like other words relating to classification, has no generally accepted, precise definition. For many systematists, especially in the biological sciences, it is synonymous with classification itself (e.g. Mayr 1942: 3–17; Sokal and Sneath 1963; see also Brew 1946: 44–66). Our usage, however, is more restricted. We apply the term only to classificatory systems having an explicit hierarchic feature; that is, systems in which basic types are either clustered into larger groups or split into smaller ones, or both.

Most of the time, taxonomic ordering is simply the classification of classes: the clustering of basic types into larger and more inclusive units on the basis of some but not all of their attributes (see Vygotsky 1962: 114).

The classic example of a taxonomy is the Linnean system of biological classification, in which species are clustered into genera, genera into families, and so on up to the level of biological classes (see Mayr 1942: 10). Because they are usually not genetic (see below), taxonomies in archaeology are likely to be much less comprehensive than those in biology; they seldom include more than two or three levels of taxonomic differentiation. We will refer to these levels as taxonomic levels, and to the groupings that occur at each level as taxa (sing. taxon).

Taxonomic ordering is an essential feature of genetic classifications, such as are predominant in biology and linguistics (see Chapter 18). The express purpose of these classifications is to indicate degrees of similarity between species or languages, which are interpreted as evidence of descent from a closer or more distant common ancestor (cf. Simpson 1945: 14–17). On the other hand taxonomic ordering is not a necessary feature of non-genetic classifications, such as are usual in archaeology (see Chapter 18). It is, however, fairly common in pottery typologies, somewhat less so in lithic typologies, and rare in typologies of houses and graves. When present, it is often introduced for some purpose that is secondary to the main purpose of the typology (cf. Dunnell 1971b: 141–4). The grouping of pottery types into series (e.g. Colton and Hargrave 1937: 1–5) is usually done to indicate some kind of presumed historical or cultural relationship between the types, e.g. that they are regional variations on a common theme, or chronologically successive variations on a theme. Taxonomic clusterings of stone and other tool types are much more often made to indicate functional relationships. All projectile point types are clustered together, all of the different scraper types are clustered together, and so on (cf. Taylor 1948: 113–18). The purpose of taxonomic clustering can also be simply mnemonic: it is easier to remember a large number of types if they are hung from a smaller number of mnemonic pegs, so to speak. The system of numeration adopted for the medieval Nubian pottery wares, in which they are grouped into red, white, utility, hand-made, and glazed wares, was adopted purely as a mnemonic aid (see Chapter 11).

Taxonomic ordering can involve either the lumping of original taxa into larger taxa or splitting them into smaller taxa, or both. The type–variety system of pottery classification (Wheat, Gifford, and Wasley 1958) is a two-level taxonomic system in which types are split into varieties. The Medieval Nubian Pottery Typology is a three-level system in which wares are lumped into ware groups and ware groups into families. Of the two processes lumping is by far the more common, both in archaeology and in biology (see Mayr 1942: 8–17).

In the great majority of cases, taxonomy involves the ordering of previously defined units (types, species, languages, etc.) that are treated as immutable. That is, the basic units are either clustered into larger taxa or split into smaller ones, but neither process affects the definition of the original units. Biologists are continually rearranging species into genera and genera into families, without at the same time redefining the species themselves (Simpson 1945: 14–16).

As we suggested in Chapter 13, taxonomic ordering is often the most appropriate way of introducing secondary purposes into a typology, without detriment to the original purpose (cf. Dunnell 1971b: 141–4). Types that were originally designed for dating or identification purposes may, for example, be taxonomically ordered to indicate historical or functional relationships that are interesting to the classifier, but irrelevant for dating or identification. In the Medieval Nubian Pottery Typology, wares are grouped into ware groups in order to indicate their chronological relationships, and into families primarily to indicate their spatial relationships. However, to use any ware for calculating dates it is not necessary to know either the ware group or the family to which it belongs (see Chapter 11).

Since taxonomy usually involves the classification of classes, much of what was said about the making of types in Chapter 15 applies to the higher-level taxa as well. Each level in a taxonomy (or at least in a non-genetic taxonomy) is potentially a separate classification made for a separate purpose, and defining attributes may be selected accordingly. It is obvious, however, that the higher-level taxa must be formulated by the clustering of type attributes and not by the clustering of object attributes, since the members of the higher taxa are themselves types and not objects.

Unlike basic types, higher-level taxa may or may not be involved directly in sorting operations (see Chapter 16). Usually it is types rather than groups of types that are sorted and numerically or statistically compared. If we want to ascertain the proportions of different genera or families in an animal population, we usually have to add up the numbers of the different individual species in each genus or family. Consequently, when they are not employed as sorting categories, the higher taxa in a taxonomic system do not require intrinsic criteria of identity, but only criteria of meaning. We are in effect free to group together any types we like for any purpose we like. We can for example group together all of the pottery wares, or even all of the artifact types, made in the twelfth century into a single taxon, even though these types have no visible common denominator. As a result, purpose usually plays a more direct and more dominant role in taxonomic ordering than it does in the formulation of basic types.

Genetic and non-genetic taxonomies

Archaeologists develop taxonomies in order to indicate various kinds of relationships between types: genetic, historical, functional, or morphological. The different kinds of archaeological taxonomies will be discussed more fully in the next chapter. We need to note here, however, that there is a basic structural difference between genetic taxonomies and all others. It has been much discussed by biologists and physical anthropologists (e.g. Sneath and Sokal 1973: 75–90; Mayr 1981), but has been less often remarked by archaeologists.

As we noted a little earlier, genetic taxonomies are made by grouping together all of the "types" (biological species, members of a language family, etc.) that are presumed to be descended from a common ancestor. The criteria of grouping are, therefore, those features that are presumed to be most indicative of common ancestry, even though these are not necessarily the most visibly conspicuous features. In the classification of animal species they are most commonly features of skeletal structure; in the classification of languages they are likely to be features of grammatical structure. Initial groupings made in this fashion can, if we wish, be combined into larger groups on the basis of presumed descent from a still more remote ancestor (Simpson 1945: 14–17). Genetic taxonomies always have an implied chronological dimension, since some time must be allowed for the evolution of different offspring from a common ancestor. Indeed, in the great majority of cases the presumed ancestor (biological, linguistic, or cultural) is actually extinct. (For a discussion of some of the problems inherent in genetic classification see especially Simpson 1945: 1–33.)

Taxonomic ordering is thus a necessary and inherent feature of genetic classifications, whose express purpose is to show relationships indicative of common ancestry. Taxonomic ordering may also be present, but it is not a necessary or inherent feature, in non-genetic classifications, in which relationships between types may or may not be considered significant. We noted earlier that taxonomic ordering is sometimes introduced into artifact typologies as a secondary feature, to express morphological, historical, or functional relationships between types that are incidental to the main purpose of the classification. These relationships, however, are fundamentally different from genetic relationships, since they are purely synchronic. Pottery varieties in the type–variety system (Wheat, Gifford, and Wasley 1958; Gifford 1960; Smith, Willey, and Gifford 1960) are not separate descendants of an extinct ancestor; they are synchronous variants of a coexisting type.

Complex taxonomies may involve both genetic and non-genetic dimensions. In the Medieval Nubian Pottery Typology, for example, the relationships between wares and between families – the lowest and highest taxonomic orders in the system – are determined morphologically (or phenetically, to use the biologists' term), while the relationships between ware groups within any family are genetic. (For fuller explanation see Chapter 10.)

The practical importance of these distinctions will appear more fully in the next chapter, when we contrast "culture" classification with artifact classification. In conclusion here we can simply note that practically all biological classifications since Darwin have been genetic (Mayr 1942: 102–22; Beckner 1959: 55–80), whereas the great majority of artifact classifications are not. Consequently, analogies between biological classification and artifact classification (cf. Gladwin and Gladwin 1930; Krieger 1960: 141–2) are of limited value, as a few authors have already noted (Brew 1946: 46–66; Ford 1962: 13).

Computerized taxonomies

In the recent past many taxonomies have been developed by means of one or another of the computerized clustering programs that are known collectively as cluster analysis. These programs can be either agglomerative (lumping programs) or divisive (splitting programs). (For an analysis of individual programs see Everitt 1974: 8–24.)

Many of the generalizations that we made earlier do not apply to computer-generated splitting programs, which include many of the algorithms of Numerical Taxonomy (Sokal and Sneath 1963; Clarke 1968: 512–67; Sneath and Sokal 1973; Doran and Hodson 1975: 159–61). In these systems an original assemblage of entities is split into successively finer subdivisions by a continual process of binary division. That is, the original group is split into the two subgroups whose members share the most traits with one another and the fewest traits with the members of the opposite group; each of these groups is further split in two on the same basis, and so on, theoretically *ad infinitum*. The end product of this process is a dendrogram, or continually branching tree diagram, with the final "types" at the ends of the branches (Figure 9).

It will be evident that, in Numerical Taxonomy and other splitting programs, the "types" are not independent of the taxonomic system; they are products of the splitting process itself. Any change in the taxonomic process will automatically result in a redefinition of the types. While types are the beginning point in normal or intuitive taxonomies, in computerized taxonomies made by splitting they are the endpoint of the taxonomic process. As a result, such computer-generated taxa have none of the flexibility and adaptability of ordinary type concepts, nor, in non-genetic classifications, do they have much utility (see Chapter 23). Many computer-generated taxa have identity but lack meaning: one of the two essentials of "typehood" (see Chapter 3; also Dunnell 1971b: 98–102). We therefore refer to these taxa as "types" only in quotation marks. Just as it is possible to have types without taxonomies, so also it is possible to have taxonomies without types, in the full sense of the term as we defined it in Chapter 3.

Seriation
Seriation refers to the linear ordering of entities or types along a single scale, e.g. from largest to smallest or from oldest to newest. It can usually be done only on the basis of a single, measurable variable (but see Cowgill 1972). Thus for example, artifacts may be seriated on the basis of size or of age or even of color (if color is expressed in terms of light wavelengths), but they usually cannot be seriated on the basis of any combination of those things, because ordering on the basis of any one variable will rarely produce a series identical to that obtained by ordering another variable. Entities also cannot be seriated on the basis of purely qualitative variables such as

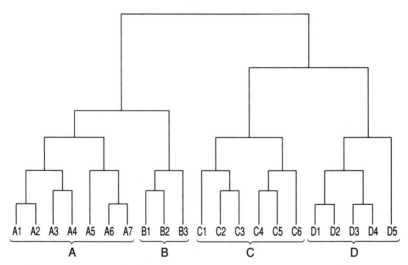

Figure 9 An example of a dendrogram produced by Numerical Taxonomy. An original population is divided into two groups on the basis of maximum number of shared traits, and each subgroup is further subdivided into pairs on the same basis.

207

material (metal, stone, wood, bone, etc.), which provide no basis for rank ordering.

Seriation can obviously be done either with individual entities or with classes. In group photos of artifacts (especially projectile points) we are likely to find them arranged, for aesthetic purposes, in a series from the largest to the smallest. However, archaeological seriation is much more often done with classified than with raw data; that is, it is types and not individual entities that are ordered. Some types have been formulated specifically for purposes of seriation (see, e.g., J. A. Ford 1962). For this reason there is a tendency to think of seriation, like taxonomy, as a form of classification, or at least as closely associated with classification (cf. Brew 1946: 44–66; Rathje and Schiffer 1982: 208–9). This is not strictly accurate, since seriation, unlike taxonomy, does not produce categorical groupings. A seriation expresses certain kinds of relationships among types, but does not group them into larger clusters on the basis of those relationships (cf. Doran and Hodson 1975: 159).

For obvious reasons the great majority of seriations undertaken by archaeologists are chronological: the ordering of artifact types or sites or even whole "cultures" (see Chapter 18) into temporal sequences. Seriation is regularly used to express chronological relationships that have already been determined through such evidence as stratigraphy and radio-carbon dating. However, in the absence of external dating evidence seriation can also be used on occasion to *determine* chronological relationships. In this procedure, which was pioneered by Flinders Petrie in 1899, artifact or grave or house types are placed in what appears to be a logical developmental sequence; for example, pottery types may be arranged in a sequence because their decoration shows an evident pro-gression from simple to complex designs. This method has been found reliable in a good many archaeological cases, in that it has subsequently been confirmed by external evidence (see especially Rouse 1967). Obviously, however, it involves a certain measure of intuition. It also involves an assumption of linear, one-directional cultural development, which is not always the way in which culture actually evolves (cf. Hole and Heizer 1965: 179–80; Dunnell 1970; Cowgill 1972: 381–7).

The use of seriation to determine chronological relationships is often referred to as sequence dating, the term that was originally employed by Petrie (1899). Most discussion of seriation in the archaeological literature refers only to this particular kind of seriation (cf. Hole and Heizer 1965: 177–80; Deetz 1967: 30–3; Rouse 1967; Rathje and Schiffer 1982: 250–3). However, we will here use chronological seriation in a broader sense, to designate any kind of temporal ordering of types, whether based on internal or on external evidence.

Taxonomy and seriation combined

Taxonomy and seriation are not mutually exclusive methods for the ordering of types. The Medieval Nubian Pottery Typology, described in Chapter 10, combines both procedures within the same overall classificatory scheme. The categories of ware group and family each represent a taxonomic grouping of the basic wares at successively higher levels. However, the ware groups in each family are further subjected to chronological seriation; they are represented as following each other in a linear order (see Figure 4). That is, in each family it is assumed that only one ware group was in production at any given time, and its production ceased when the next ware group was initiated, although of course some vessels of earlier groups would continue in use. It is this ware group seriation, rather than the ware taxonomy itself, that introduces a specifically chronological dimension into the Nubian Pottery Typology.

Frequency seriation

The most interesting and the most useful archaeological seriations involve neither artifacts nor types, in a direct way. They are seriations of artifact or type frequencies, or in other words of numbers. The principle involved is that of plotting the changing abundance of different artifact, pottery, or house types, relative to one another, over a period of time.

At any given moment in time some things are always in the process of becoming popular, some are at the height of their popularity, and some are declining in popularity. As a result the relative proportions of different types of things rarely stay the same for very long. The apparently irresistible propensity toward stylistic and/or functional change makes it possible to plot the first appearance, growing popularity, peak of abundance, declining popularity, and final disappearance of pottery or artifact types in the form of "battleship curves" (Figure 10).

It is changing frequencies of occurrence, rather than the absolute presence or absence of artifacts or types, that are most useful to the archaeologist for dating purposes. We can observe in Figure 10, for example, that in the year A.D. 800 Nubian Ware Group N.II was in decline but still fairly prevalent, Group N.III was near the peak of its popularity, and Group N.IV was just making its first appearance. Two hundred years later the same three groups were still present, but Group N.II was now on the point of disappearance, Group N.III was also very scarce, while Group N.IV was now in its heyday. If, therefore, the pottery from a particular site or level includes 15 per cent sherds of Group N.II, 80 per cent sherds of Group N.III, and 5 per cent sherds of Group N.IV, we will have no difficulty in concluding that the deposit in question dates from around the year 800. A deposit yielding 5 per cent sherds of Group N.II, 5 per cent sherds of Group N.III, and 90 per cent sherds of Group N.IV will just as obviously date from around the year 1000. On the other hand if we only noted the presence of the three ware groups, without recording their relative per-centages, we could only say that the two deposits both fell somewhere between A.D. 750 and 1050 without knowing which of them was the earlier.

Note that these calculations will not serve to determine the actual sequence of development of the pottery types (cf. Dunnell 1970: 308–9; Cowgill 1972: 382; Marquardt 1978: 258). If we had at our disposal only the two sherd collections just mentioned, and they came from two differ-ent sites, we could not deduce whether the sequence of popularity went from Type A toward Type C or from Type C toward Type A. To use the method of frequency seriation for the actual dating (or chronological ordering) of sites and deposits, it is first necessary to determine the sequence of the critical types or artifacts on independent grounds (e.g. stratigraphy), and also to calculate the relative frequencies of the types in deposits of known age (cf. especially Marquardt 1978: 258). Once these calculations are made, they can then be applied to collections from other, undated sites, on the assumption that relative popularities of different types or artifacts will be pretty much the same, at any given moment, throughout the area of their use. (For further discussion see Ford 1962; Deetz 1967: 26–30; Dunnell 1970; Rouse 1972: 127–8.)

A relatively simple, non-computerized system of frequency seriation has been developed for the medieval Nubian pottery wares, as described in Chapter 11 (see also WYA 1986a: 601–33, and WYA 1986b). It permits the dating of most Nubian archaeological deposits within an interval of fifty years, on the basis of pottery ware percentages, whereas they could be dated only within a century or two on the basis of wares present or absent, without reference to frequencies.

With the aid of statistics and computers, much more complex and sophisticated frequency seriation programs have been developed in some areas. The number of different statistical programs that have been tried is enormous, and they cannot be reviewed individually here. For discussions of seriational methodology see Robinson 1951; Ford 1962; Kendall 1969; Cowgill 1972; and Marquardt 1978; for practical applications to the dating of archaeological materials see Brainerd 1951; Ford 1962; Kendall

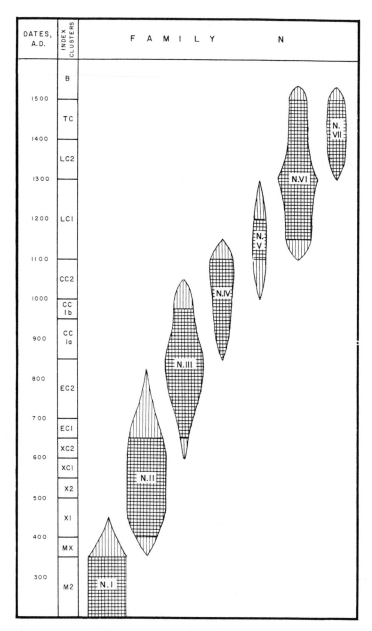

Figure 10 An example of a "battleship graph," showing the sequence of ware groups in Nubian Pottery Family N, and their relative frequencies in relation to each other through time. In each "battleship," cross-hatching indicates the main period of manufacture. Chronology reads upward.

1969; Marks and Robinson 1986. Marquardt (1978: 266–92) gives a particularly useful and detailed historical overview of the development of statistical seriation techniques in archaeology.

The role of statistics and computers

We have observed at a number of points that statistics (and hence computers) have a rather limited role to play in the formulation of types. Diagnostic attribute combinations must, it is true, be statistically significant, but in the case of useful types this is usually intuitively obvious (cf. Watson, LeBlanc, and Redman 1971: 127; Thomas 1978: 236). The situation is quite otherwise in the taxonomic or seriational ordering of types. In these operations we are specifically interested in the relationships between types, and relationships, as we just saw, are frequently determined or expressed statistically. It can be important for many purposes to discover not only the fact of association but the strength (or frequency) of association between two types; for example, do they occur together as regularly as do two other types? Equally important is the strength of association between types and extrinsic, distributional features. Does Type A occur in twelfth-century contexts more consistently than does Type B? If so, it is obviously a more reliable type for dating purposes.

In these circumstances statistics have no substitute. If the statistical procedures are sufficiently complex (as they usually are nowadays), then computers likewise have no substitute. Virtually all of the legitimate contributions to artifact classification that have been made by statistics and computers have in fact involved the ordering of types rather than the formulation of types.

So far as archaeology is concerned, the use of statistical methods appears thus far to have contributed more to the field of seriation than it has to taxonomy. This may be because archaeologists have not, to any significant extent, developed their own taxonomic algorithms. Instead they have borrowed from other disciplines a number of methods (especially Numerical Taxonomy) that are really appropriate mainly to genetic classifications (cf. especially Cormack 1971: 321; Dunnell 1971b: 98–102; Whallon 1972: 16–18; Read 1982: 70; Rodrigues de Areia 1985; WYA n.d.2). Linguists, whose classifications are very largely genetic, have been able to make far more appropriate and effective use of computerized taxonomic methods than have archaeologists (e.g. Dyen 1965; Jorgensen 1969; W. Miller 1984). In the field of seriation, on the other hand, archaeologists have pioneered in the development of new methods, which have proven their value over and over again in field situations (Ford 1962; Ammerman 1971; Marquardt 1978; Marks and Robinson 1986, etc.).

We will have a little more to say about the use of statistics and computers in Chapter 23. However, an extended discussion of them lies far outside the scope and purpose of the present book, and indeed is beyond the technical competence of its authors. A full discussion of these issues would in any case require a book in itself (see, e.g., Everitt 1974; Doran and Hodson 1975; and Orton 1982).

18

VARIATION AND VARIABILITY IN ARCHAEOLOGICAL CLASSIFICATIONS

In previous chapters we have considered a number of factors, theoretical as well as practical, that influence the development of classificatory systems. We are now ready to discuss the different kinds of classifications, typologies, and taxonomies that archaeologists actually make and use, and the reasons why they differ one from another. We will begin by re-emphasizing certain basic structural distinctions that affect many different kinds of classifications. We will then go on to consider some specific kinds of classifications that archaeologists make for different purposes. Finally we will discuss some additional, practical considerations that are unrelated to purpose, but that may result in variation from one classification to another.

Basic structural distinctions

Classification and typology. We indicated in Chapter 4 that, according to our usage, a classification is any contrasting set of categories into which a specific body of material may be subdivided, or partitioned. A typology is a particular kind of classification; one designed for the sorting of entities into categories that are absolutely mutually exclusive. The practical importance of this distinction will appear when we discuss the differences between artifact classifications, which are nearly always typologies, and "culture" classifications, which are not.

Typology and taxonomy. A basic typology has only one level of abstraction or generalization; all of its member types are considered to be equivalent in this respect (see Chapter 7). A taxonomy, in our usage, is a typology or classification having a specifically hierarchic feature, in that the basic types are either clustered into larger taxa or split into smaller ones, or both. We will see presently that some kinds of archaeological classifications are inherently and necessarily taxonomic, some are often but not necessarily taxonomic, and some usually are not taxonomic.

Genetic and non-genetic classification. We saw in Chapter 17 that genetic classifications are necessarily taxonomic, while non-genetic classifications may or may not be. We also saw that there are basic structural differences between the two kinds of taxonomies. The relevance of this distinction to the present discussion lies in the fact that most artifact taxonomies are non-genetic, while "culture" classifications usually have a genetic component.

Basic and instrumental typologies. Basic typologies are made to express or learn something about the material being classified; instrumental typologies are made when we want the material being classified to assist us in some other purpose (see Chapter 13). In archaeology the great majority of instrumental typologies are ancillary; their main purpose is to help us use pottery and artifact types as a means of reconstructing "cultures" or of dating sites.

Archaeologists regularly make and use both basic and ancillary typologies; in fact, the same typology can at times serve both basic and ancillary purposes. There can, however, be significant differences in the ways in which types are formulated and selected (cf. Chapter 15), as well as in the ways in which they are used, in the two cases. The types selected in a basic typology will usually be those with the highest degree of intuitive "naturalness," since our objective in this case is to learn about the material itself. At the outset, purpose will not dictate the selection of any particular attributes in preference to others; we will probably give some attention to all of the attributes that are readily observable. On the other hand, the types in an instrumental typology will not necessarily be intuitively obvious ones, and they may have a relatively high degree of "artificiality" (cf. Ellen 1979: 8–12). The main criterion of selection or exclusion is whether or not the types work for some particular ancillary purpose. In the Nubian Pottery Typology, Wares R21 and R22 are distinguished by stylistic features so subtle that even the makers may have been unaware of them, but they are an invaluable guide, when they can be recognized, to the dating of twelfth-century archaeological deposits. Specific purposes will probably play a more overt and direct role in the formulation of ancillary typologies than in the formulation of basic typologies, both in the selection of attributes to be considered and in the selection of types to be retained.

The distinction between basic and ancillary typologies is probably more important in the field of archaeology than in most others, since archaeology is one of the few disciplines in which classifications are regularly made for purposes (primarily dating) that are wholly extrinsic to the

Table 10. *Kinds of archaeological classification and their purposes*

Kind of classification	Tax-onomic[1]	Kind of purpose[2]		Specific purpose
Phenetic	S	Ba	Descriptive	Economically describe material from one site
		Ba	Comparative	Describe and compare material from different sites
		Ba	Analytical-intrinsic	Learn about nature and variability of material classified
		In	Incidental	Convenience of filing and storage
Stylistic	S	Ba	Analytical-intrinsic	Learn about stylistic evolution
		In	Ancillary	Ethnic and cultural identification
				Chronological ordering of associated materials
				Reconstruction of social and economic patterns
Chronological/ Spatial	S	Ba	Analytical-historical	Learn historical development of material classified
				Learn spatial distribution of material classified
		In	Ancillary	Dating of associated materials and sites
				Use as basis for defining "cultures"
				Chronological seriation of sites and "cultures"
Functional	U	Ba	Analytical-interpretive	Reconstruct activities of makers and users
		In	Ancillary	Identify different activity areas or sites
Emic	R	Ba	Analytical-interpretive	Understand mind-set of makers and users

Table 10 (*cont.*)

Kind of classification	Tax- onomic[1]	Kind of purpose[2]		Specific purpose
"Cultural"	I	Ba	Descriptive	Define and differentiate prehistoric "culture" units
		Ba	Analytical- historical	Seriate "culture" units in successive stages
		In	Ancillary	Construct basic time/space grid for ordering artifacts and sites

[1] Taxonomic: I = inherently; U = usually; S = sometimes; R = rarely
[2] Ba = basic; In = instrumental. For explanation of terms see Chapter 13.

material being classified. Nevertheless, the basic/ancillary distinction appears to have been little noted as such by archaeologists (but see Steward 1954). We can perceive, however, that it clearly underlies the long-running debate between the adherents of "natural" and of "artificial" typology (cf. Klejn 1982: 53). The makers of basic typologies are likely to believe that they are discovering "natural types," while the makers of ancillary typologies are much more likely to suppose that their types are "artificial." As we suggested in Chapter 6, the truth always lies somewhere between these two extremes, although it is variable from type to type. This issue will be further considered in Chapter 23.

KINDS OF ARCHAEOLOGICAL CLASSIFICATIONS

The things that archaeologists most consistently classify are artifacts, designs (on artifacts, temple walls, rock faces, etc.), houses, burials, sites, and "cultures." ("Culture" for the prehistoric archaeologist means material culture, plus whatever else may be inferred from it.) The most common kinds of archaeological classifications, and the purposes they may serve, are enumerated in Table 10, and will be briefly discussed in the next paragraphs. The different kinds of classifications are, of course, no more mutually exclusive than are the different purposes they serve.

Phenetic (morphological) typologies

A phenetic or morphological typology will include all of the types in any given body of material that can be recognized on the basis of intrinsic attribute combinations, whether or not the types show any consistent patterning in their distributions or associations. Type definitions will be based on all intrinsic attributes that regularly cluster, but no consideration will be given to extrinsic (contextual or inferential) attributes (see Chapter 14). Hence, in phenetic types, identity is more or less synonymous with meaning. There is no selection of attributes or of types with reference to any purpose except that of description. However, it will usually be found that highly visible attributes such as size, shape, color, and decoration will play a larger role in the determination of phenetic types than will less conspicuous attributes like material, density, or fineness of finish.

Phenetic classifications are developed primarily for purposes of description and comparison. In published site reports, they often represent the most efficient way of describing and illustrating a large number of individual objects in a limited number of pages (cf. Krieger 1944: 272–3; Everitt 1974: 4). In more general surveys, they are the most effective and often the only way of comparing the finds from one site with those from another (cf. Krieger 1944: 273; Deetz 1967: 51). Persons with a particular interest in certain kinds of artifacts may also develop phenetic classifications simply to discover the extent and kinds of variation exhibited in those materials, whether or not description is intended. Phenetic types can, in addition, be a first step toward taxonomic classifications developed for other purposes, and particularly for functional purposes, as we will see a little later. Finally, phenetic classifications may be developed simply to provide a convenient and coherent basis for the storage of artifacts and the filing of artifact records (see Chapter 13).

As we noted briefly in Chapter 1, basic data descriptions play a much larger role in archaeological publications than they do in other fields of social science. At least in prehistoric archaeology it has long been considered obligatory to publish all finds, at least in classificatory form. For this reason, and also because they can serve so many other purposes, phenetic typologies are undoubtedly the most common of all archaeological classifications. They have been developed at one time or another for all of the different kinds of things that archaeologists uncover – tools, pottery, houses, graves, and "cultures" – though they are not of course the only way of classifying any of these things. They are probably used most consistently in the classification of stone tools, simply because there is often no other obvious basis for the classification of these artifacts.

Phenetic types may or may not be taxonomically ordered. As a general rule, the more types that are designated, the more probable it is that they will be taxonomically grouped, for mnemonic purposes if for nothing else. Taxonomic ordering is consequently very common in bead typologies, somewhat less so in pottery typologies, still less so in tool typologies, and rare in house and grave typologies.

The taxonomic grouping of phenetic types may be based either on phenetic or on other criteria. When tool types are grouped according to the material employed (stone, bone, wood, etc.) in published reports, this represents a particular kind of phenetic taxonomy. However, phenetic types can also be grouped on the basis of functional or historical criteria, as we will see in later paragraphs.

Stylistic typologies

Stylistic typologies represent a particular kind of phenetic classification: one in which it is not entities but only certain of their attributes that are classified. We will see presently that artifacts themselves are sometimes classified primarily on stylistic grounds, but there is a difference between classifying artifacts on stylistic grounds and classifying styles themselves. In the latter case no other attributes except those of style are considered. The artifacts are treated as mere background, like the canvas on which a painting is executed.

Of the various artifacts recovered in prehistoric archaeology, pottery is by far the most consistently and elaborately decorated, and therefore classifications of pottery styles are the most common stylistic typologies made by archaeologists. However, there are also stylistic classifications of architecture (especially monumental architecture) (Judd 1927; Hawley 1934: 13–30; Satterthwaite 1944; WYA 1965a), of mural art (Joralemon 1971; Quirarte 1973; V. Smith 1984), and of rock art (Steward 1929; C. Turner 1963: 5–9; Schaafsma 1971; 1975: 72, 96), among other things.

Stylistic classifications are often made by art historians simply to learn about or to describe the processes of artistic evolution. Among prehistorians their purpose is much more often ancillary. Pottery styles and architectural styles often serve as the main criteria on which we base judgments of ethnic identity; that is, we equate pottery types with peoples (cf. WYA 1968a: 197–202; 1973a: 24). This propensity is common in many areas, but is especially prevalent in the study of Andean culture history (cf. Rowe 1962; Bennett and Bird 1964: 78–182). In addition, stylistic classifications often serve as the basis for the chronological seriation of artifacts and other remains, as described in Chapter 17.

In the recent past, some interesting stylistic studies have been undertaken in the hope of reconstructing patterns of prehistoric social organization, although the results obtained were not entirely convincing. The pioneer example was Deetz' (1965) analysis of prehistoric Arikara Indian pottery, in which he was able to infer from the spatial distribution of certain stylistic features that the Arikara had followed a matrilocal rule of residence. Somewhat comparable are the stylistic analyses and interpretations undertaken by Longacre (1964; 1970), Hill (1966; 1970), and Plog (1980) in the Southwest, and McPherron (1967b) in the Northeast.

Stylistic typologies very commonly have a taxonomic dimension, simply because the number of individual styles that can be recognized is often so large as to require second-level ordering (see, e.g., Plog 1980: 40–53).

Chronological and spatial classifications
In chronological and spatial classifications, types are defined by a combination of intrinsic and contextual (i.e. distributional) features (see Chapter 14). The types that are designated are those that have discoverable and significant distributions in time and/or space, as well as intrinsic criteria of identity. The intrinsic attributes that define these types are, therefore, those that themselves show consistent chronological or spatial patterning. In practice this usually means that chronological/spatial classifications give more attention to stylistic than to functional attributes, since these are the features that are most likely to vary from time to time and from place to place. It is noteworthy in fact that the artifact types most commonly accepted as "index fossils" (cf. Chapter 14) for the identification of prehistoric "cultures" are precisely those with the highest degree of stylistic loading: projectile points in the earlier horizons, and pottery types in the later ones.

The purposes of chronological and spatial classification are essentially historical: to learn about the variation of particular materials or types in time and space. In basic typologies this is an end in itself; in ancillary typologies it is a means to the ultimate goal of dating or identifying sites or objects found in association with the things that are actually classified. The largest number of historical typologies are probably ancillary; their number would include nearly all pottery typologies and many projectile point typologies, as well as some typologies of houses and graves. As we saw in Chapter 1, these typologies provide the basis for the time and space grids by which we order prehistory itself (J. A. Ford 1954b: 52; Deetz 1967: 51–2). Because of the overriding and necessary concern for chronology in prehistoric archaeology, all of the different things found by the archaeologist – tools, containers, houses, pictographs, sites, and whole "cultures" – may at times be classified historically. Moreover, this is the most common way of classifying those things that are regularly used to define "cultures" (see below), especially pottery, projectile points, houses, and graves.

Chronological and spatial typologies are often but not necessarily taxonomic. When taxonomic ordering is present, it may be based either on extrinsic, historical criteria or on intrinsic, non-historical criteria, or both. In a purely historical taxonomy, objects are grouped together simply because they regularly occur together, regardless of whether they have any intrinsic features in common (cf. Gardin 1980: 87–8). This kind of purely chronological grouping is not common in archaeology, although it may be adopted as a way of organizing material in published descriptions (e.g. Hawley 1936).

In some pottery typologies, types are grouped into larger taxa (often called series) partly on the basis of morphological similarities and partly because they regularly occur together (see Colton and Hargrave 1937: 1–5). In the case of Nubian pottery this is exemplified by the grouping of wares into ware groups, as described in Chapter 10. Such groupings are in effect partially historical taxonomies. There are, finally, taxonomies in which historically defined types are grouped together purely on the basis of morphological similarities, and without reference to chronological information, as in the grouping of Nubian wares into families. (It is important to recall that types that were formulated for one purpose may be taxonomically ordered for quite another, as we saw in Chapter 17.)

Except in the case of "culture" classifications (see below), historical taxonomies are usually not entirely genetic, but they may have a genetic component. That is, some but not all of the relationships between types are interpreted as genetic. (Relationships between cultural types are said to be genetic when one type appears to have evolved from another.) In the subclassification of Nubian pottery styles (WYA 1986a: 213–392), many of the relationships between styles are regarded as genetic.

Chronological and spatial types may be seriated instead of, or in addition to, being ordered taxonomically. In the Nubian Pottery Typology, the ware groups into which individual wares are grouped are historical taxa, but the arrangement of the ware groups in each family into a chronological sequence represents a seriation of those taxa (see Figure 4).

Functional classifications

A functional classification is one in which artifacts or other cultural remains are differentiated on the basis of their presumed purpose, or functions. In theory, then, a functional type is defined by a combination of intrinsic and inferential attributes. In practice this is tautologous, because in prehistoric archaeology function is nearly always an inference by the archaeologist, based on observable morphological (intrinsic) features. It would therefore be more nearly correct to say that a functional type is one defined by a limited set of intrinsic variables – specifically those that give evidence of the use or intended use for which the artifacts were made.

A purely functional classification of pottery, for example, would be based mainly on vessel shapes (cups, bowls, jars, etc.), with possible consideration also for a few aspects of fabric, color, or decoration. However, pottery and many other kinds of artifacts usually exhibit attributes that cannot be related to specific functions, but that are too conspicuous and too variable to be ignored. They may be stylistic attributes that are independent of function, as in the case of most pottery decoration, or they may be attributes that presumably served some function, but we cannot be sure what it was, as in the case of many projectile point attributes. Because we are usually disinclined to ignore conspicuous but seemingly non-functional variables, the making of purely functional artifact typologies is really very rare, at least in prehistoric archaeology. The usual practice is, rather, to attempt a functional interpretation, *a posteriori*, to types that have been defined phenetically. This was done in the case of the various vessel form classes (bowls, jugs, storage jars, etc.) in the Nubian Pottery Typology (WYA 1986a: 101–83). However, this should not be mistaken for a genuinely functional classification.

Truly functional classification of artifacts really occurs almost entirely at higher taxonomic levels rather than at the level of basic typology. That is, types that were defined initially on phenetic grounds are clustered together into more inclusive taxa on the assumption that the various included types served a common purpose or purposes. This descriptive strategy is frequently employed in archaeological site reports, when artifacts are described under such headings as "agricultural tools," "weapons," "household implements," "clothing," etc., rather than as "objects of stone," "objects of bone," "objects of shell," etc. Obviously, however, the main purpose of functional classifications is interpretive; to help in reconstructing prehistoric activity patterns and activity sets (cf. Hodder 1982: 190–3; Kent 1984: 156–63). By clustering together all of the different kinds of paraphernalia that we infer were used in spinning and weaving (as we have done in Nubia), we can learn far more about ancient textile production than we could learn by the contemplation of any single artifact type.

Functional classifications can also aid in the recognition of activity areas; that is, different parts of a site where different activities were carried out, or different sites that were used for different purposes (Kent 1984). A concentration of spindles, shuttles, and loom weights in a particular area would presumably identify the ancient weavers' quarter. This technique of analysis has been used very extensively and successfully at Teotihuacán in Mexico (Millon 1973: 23, 45–6; Cowgill, Altschul, and Sload 1984). There are cases however when identification works the other way; when the use of artifacts is suggested by the areas in which they are regularly found, or by their regular association with other artifacts. Finally, functional classification is the usual way of categorizing archaeological sites. That is, they are most commonly characterized as habitation sites, workshops, religious sites, cemeteries, and so on.

Emic classifications

There is some inconsistency in the use of the term "emic" by archaeologists, as we will see in Chapter 24. As we define the term here, an emic classification is one in which the types designated by the archaeologist can be presumed to reflect some intention on the part of the makers (cf. Spaulding 1953: 305). That is, they are different from other types because the makers intended them to be different. The objective of the classifier is then to group things together in more or less the same way as the makers and users would presumably have done. This is an approach to classification that received considerable attention in the middle years of the twentieth century. The term "emic" was not then in general use; archaeologists usually talked about types as being representative of the intentions or of the "mental templates" of their makers (Deetz 1967: 45–9; cf. also Watson, LeBlanc, and Redman 1984: 208–10).

At least in prehistoric archaeology emic classification represents more an ideal than a realistic possibility. It is a byproduct of the configurationist era (see Chapter 22), when many anthropologists felt that their appropriate mission was to see and to represent the world as nearly as possible through the eyes of their subjects (cf. Kluckhohn 1939). In archaeology, this meant (among other things) the designation of types that prehistoric peoples would have recognized as such. There was not, however, any general consensus as to how this was to be done (cf. Klejn 1982: 81–2), and a later generation of archaeologists became increasingly skeptical of its practical attainability (Chang 1967: 6–17; Hodder 1982: 1–12; Watson, LeBlanc, and Redman 1984: 208–10). Nevertheless, emic classification continues to have its adherents (especially Dunnell 1971b; Read 1982).

"Culture" classifications

Some of the most familiar and most discussed archaeological classifications do not involve pottery, artifact, house, or grave types individually, but recurring combinations of those types. In the usage of archaeologists, these combinations are often called "cultures." It is necessary to use the term "culture" in quotation marks, because its meaning is substantially different from the meaning of culture to the ethnologist. A "culture" to the archaeologist is a distinctive material assemblage, which is assumed to have been produced and used by a distinct ethnic group. For prehistoric archaeologists a "culture" stands for a people.

"Culture" classification is often discussed in the archaeological literature together with artifact classification, as though the problems and procedures were the same in the two cases (e.g. Brew 1946: 44–66; Taylor 1948: 130–51; Clarke 1968: 188; Rouse 1972: 122–9). However, some terminological ambiguity is evident here. When archaeologists talk about artifact classification they are talking about classifying artifacts into types. When they talk about "culture" classification, however, they are usually not talking about classifying "cultures" into still more inclusive taxonomic units. What they are actually discussing is the process that we have called formulation (Chapter 15); that is, the clustering of pottery, tool, house, and grave types to form "culture" concepts, which themselves may or may not be classified. (For extended discussion see Klejn 1982: 145–248.)

Archaeological "cultures," then, are synthetic taxa formed by the grouping together of more specific type concepts. Often, though not always, they represent the highest level of clustering in a historical taxonomy (cf. especially Clarke 1968: 188; Klejn 1982: 251–61; also Willey and Phillips 1958: 11–43). "Cultures" have some of the properties of types, in that they are commonly used for the sorting of archaeological sites or site components on a mutually exclusive basis. However, they cannot be likened to types in the full sense of the term unless they are combined into still more comprehensive classificatory schemes. As we saw in Chapter 4, one of the essential characteristics of classes and types is that of membership in a contrasting set.

There are, in this sense, a number of true "culture" classifications in existence; that is, systems in which "cultures" themselves are classified. The most prevalent of these combine intrinsic and chronological determinants. That is, regionally distinct "cultures" are grouped under such comprehensive headings as Neolithic or Archaic, partly on the basis of intrinsic features (presence or absence of pottery, etc.) and partly on the basis of known distributions in time (but not usually in space). An anomaly in this respect is the McKern Midwest Taxonomic System (McKern 1939), whose basis is primarily spatial rather than chronological. However, the McKern system is properly speaking a method of classifying rather than an actual, comprehensive classification.

Another and more common procedure which is often referred to as "culture classification" involves the chronological seriation of a series of cultural phases which followed each other in the same area. Traditionally the phases are regarded as forming, collectively, a single "culture"; they are usually designated by a collective name but by different Roman numerals, such as Pueblo I, II, III, IV, and V in the well-known Pecos Chronology (see Kidder 1927). Here we can observe two problems of terminological ambiguity. First, the different phases in these chronological schemes are not properly classified but seriated, according to the distinction that we made in Chapter 17. Second, it is the individual phases, not the aggregation of them, that have the usual attributes of archaeological "cultures"; that is, each phase has been defined by a recurring combination of artifact, house, and grave types. When a series of different phases, defined by different artifact, house, and grave types, is designated as forming, collectively, a single "culture," it is often the case that none of the defining artifact or house types in the earliest phase of the sequence are still present in the last one. The only defining criterion for the group as a whole may be that it shows a sequence of development different from that of other such "cultures." "Culture" in this sense obviously has a dynamic aspect that is lacking in other archaeological usages. A less ambiguous term for a "culture" which involves a succession of distinct phases would be a "cultural sequence" or "cultural tradition" (cf. Willey and Phillips 1958: 34–43).

There are many areas of the world where multiple "cultures" have been recognized, but where they have not been systematically classified into larger groupings. The Anasazi, Mogollon, Hohokam, and Hakataya "cultures" of the American Southwest represent an instance of this kind (cf. Lipe 1978: 344–89). What we have here is simply a congeries of "cultures," not a classification. Each of the individual "cultures" represents the top level of a separate taxonomic clustering or seriation process (cf. Willey and Phillips 1958: 11–43). The archaeologist has the choice of assigning any particular site to one of them, to more than one of them, or to none of them, which means that they do not really have the status of taxa in an organized system. (For fuller discussion of the procedures and problems involved in "culture" classification see Willey and Phillips 1958: 11–43; and Klejn 1982: 145–291.)

OTHER SOURCES OF CLASSIFICATORY VARIATION

In addition to the factors of purpose that have so far been considered, there are also certain pragmatic considerations, having little or nothing to do with purpose, that may affect the shape that classifications and typologies take. Because these factors are practical rather than theoretical, they have not generally received much attention in the archaeological literature. Nevertheless, a number of them seem important enough to merit discussion before we conclude our review of variation in archaeological typologies.

Monothetic and polythetic classifications

A monothetic classification is one in which an entity must exhibit a certain, fixed set of attributes in order to be assigned to a type; these attributes are both necessary and sufficient conditions for type membership. A polythetic classification is one in which an entity must exhibit most but not all of a specified set of attributes in order to be assigned to a type, but no single attribute is either a necessary or a sufficient condition for type membership (cf. Beckner 1959: 22–4; Clarke 1968: 189–90; R. Needham 1975).

In the literature on artifact typologies there is a good deal of discussion of monothetic vs. polythetic classification (Clarke 1968: 189–91; Whallon 1972; Watson, LeBlanc, and Redman 1984: 202). The issue is, however, very largely one of theory vs. practice. Most of the recent programmatic literature refers specifically to monothetic classifications, since these systems conform closely to the principles of abstract logic. On the other hand most of the practical artifact typologies in use are polythetic, and do not follow absolutely rigid rules of type determination. As we suggested earlier (Chapter 6), the reasons for this lie partly in the comprehensive nature of artifact typologies, and partly in their instrumental function.

Open and closed typologies

An important distinction can be made between typologies that are, and are not, designed to access new material, above and beyond what is already in hand. We will refer to these respectively as open and closed typologies. The most immediate practical difference lies in the fact that in closed typologies classifying and sorting are the same thing. In open typologies classifying and sorting are separate operations involving separate problems, as we saw in Chapters 15 and 16.

There can be many legitimate kinds of closed typologies. They may be developed for purely descriptive purposes, to allow the publication of a varied mass of material in a limited number of pages (cf. Krieger 1944: 273; Everitt 1974: 4). In the Nile Valley most bead typologies fall into this category (e.g. Steindorff 1935: 46–58; Emery 1938: pls. 43–4), as do some pottery typologies (e.g. Reisner 1923a: 41–6; Shinnie 1955: 28–50; Shinnie and Chittick 1961: 28–67). A closed typology may also be a mnemonic aid for the filing or storage of material. The question of purpose remains highly relevant in these circumstances, as we suggested in Chapter 13, but questions of practicality and cost-effectiveness may not arise. A closed typology need not have any built-in potential for growth and change, nor is it necessary in many cases to specify what variables or organizing principles are involved.

An open typology must have a generative potential, since it is designed primarily for the typing and sorting of material not yet in hand. It must accommodate the possibility of new variables, and hence necessarily of new types, as well as the elimination of old ones. It should in theory have the potential for all kinds of expansion and revision, including the basic redefinition of existing types and type criteria. Flexibility is essential, and so in most cases are practicality and cost-effectiveness. That is, type descriptions must translate into feasible and affordable sorting procedures (see Chapter 19).

Most artifact typologies in the pre-computer era were open typologies, generated by and for active field archaeologists who were more concerned with achieving practical goals than with methodological rigor. This is not true in the case of many computer-generated typologies developed in the last twenty years (Benfer 1967; Whallon 1972; Read 1974; Vierra 1982; etc.), in which rigor is the principal concern. These systems have a certain potential for expansion, but none for internal modifications or the redefinition of types.

As in the case of other distinctions that we have discussed, the line between open and closed typologies is not absolutely rigid. In practice, there are different degrees and also different kinds of mutability. Many typologies have the capacity for adding new types but no capacity for redefining existing ones; they may be described as extendable without being otherwise mutable. There are also archaeological typologies that are meant primarily to classify material already in hand, but that have in addition a limited potential for revision on the basis of new finds. The typology of Nubian church architecture developed by WYA (1965a) is in this category. On the other hand there are pottery typologies that are relatively inflexible (e.g. Shinnie and Chittick 1961: 28–67; McPherron

1967a: 63–123), presumably because their makers did not envision that future excavations would turn up any new or different types.

Differences in material

Even when classificatory purposes are the same, different bodies of material may require quite different approaches to classification (cf. especially Brown 1982: 186–7; Hodson 1982: 21; Read 1982: 68–9; Whallon 1982). In fact, a good deal of the Typological Debate (see Chapter 22) appears to have arisen between individuals working with different kinds of material. They may or may not have been pursuing the same goals of cultural or chronological or functional reconstruction, but in any case the materials they studied have called for distinct approaches. This becomes very evident when we consider the different ways in which stone tools and potsherds have been classified.

Between lithics and ceramics there are at least two important differences to be noted. First, in the case of ceramics the number of potential variables is far larger, so that some selection among variables is essential (cf. Dunnell 1971a: 117; Hill and Evans 1972: 245–52). With lithics, on the other hand, it may be not only possible but even necessary to consider nearly all of the dimensions of variability that can be recognized.

A much more important difference arises from the fact that the great bulk of ceramic material recovered by the archaeologist is fragmentary, while a much higher proportion of lithic material is intact. As a result, form (that is, overall shape) is nearly always a basic consideration in determining lithic types, whereas in the formulation of pottery types, at least in the New World, it is usually a descriptive variable but not a diagnostic variable (see Chapter 14). This has two important consequences. First, it means that lithic specimens must usually be complete, or nearly so, to be classifiable, while with ceramic material this is emphatically not the case. Nearly all of our pottery typologies are designed specifically for the typing and sorting of small fragments.

A second consequence, which has been little remarked up to now, is that many pottery classifications are of limited value for functional analysis (but see Keighley 1973). In archaeology we infer the function of artifacts almost entirely from their form, but the great majority of potsherds give us no information about the original vessel form. Most New World pottery types (as well as those from Nubia) include under one heading the fragments of many different vessels made in different shapes, and presumably for different purposes. Therefore pottery types are not consistently distinct, or distinguishable, from one another on functional grounds, and counting or weighing all of the sherds of different types that were found in different sites or areas will not necessarily tell us anything about the activities that were performed in those places. On the other hand stone tool types, since they are defined primarily to form criteria, can usually be equated with functional types, and can be used to reconstruct prehistoric cultural activity patterns. (However, see Clay 1976 for evidence that this is not universally the case.)

We should note, finally, that some kinds of material are inherently more classifiable than others (cf. Jevons 1874, II: 325). This will become clear if we consider the different approaches to pottery classification that have developed respectively in the American Northeast and Southwest. Northeastern pottery is a singularly amorphous body of material, and it is no surprise that some of the most complex and sophisticated attempts at statistical and computer-generated typology have come out of this area (Spaulding 1953; 1960; Fitting 1965; Whallon 1972), while one archaeologist (Wright 1967) has despaired of the typological approach altogether. It is also no surprise that archaeologists in the Southwest have shown little interest in applying the methods of their Northeastern colleagues, at least for the same purposes. There is simply no demand for them, when old-fashioned intuitive methods will still yield types that nearly everyone can agree on, and whose significant distributions in time and space are consistently verified through excavation (cf. Wheat, Gifford, and Wasley 1958).

A similar difference obtains between the elaborately decorated pottery wares of Nubia, nearly all made from Nile mud, and the mass-produced factory wares of Egypt, which exhibit a bewildering variety of clays but almost no decoration. Although both Nubian and Egyptian wares are included in the Medieval Nubian Pottery Typology (because both are found in medieval Nubian sites), it has been found necessary to classify them according to somewhat different principles (see WYA 1986a: 561). In the case of the early medieval Egyptian glazed wares, their highly abstract decorative patterns have so far defied any precise classification (*ibid.*: 585; see also Jevons 1874, II: 325).

Differences of scale
The number of variables and the volume of material to be classified or sorted are additional factors that can, in practice, affect the construction and use of typologies. This is true in several different respects. There is,

first of all, the question of how many variables and attributes are to be considered significant. The number is usually far larger in pottery classifications than in lithic classifications, and in textiles (at least in Nubian textiles) it appears to be larger still. Obviously, each additional variable multiplies algebraically the number of potentially significant combinations. The more potential combinations there are, the more necessary it becomes to have a clearly defined basis for deciding which ones we will and will not consider in the determination of types.

Computers were once seen as a way out of this dilemma. In theory, computerized clustering programs should enable us to deal with far more variables than we can keep straight in our heads. In practice, however, the reverse has proved to be true. All of the computer-generated artifact typologies for which any success is claimed have involved a conspicuously small number of variables, preselected from a much larger spectrum of possibilities (cf. Read 1982: 60–1). When a large number of variables is coded, the computer will find a great many more statistically significant attribute clusters than will our intuition, but it will provide us with no rational basis for choosing among them. Choices can only be dictated by utility or non-utility for specific purposes, and this only the typologist can judge (cf. Shepard 1965: xii).

Another scale variable is the ratio of material in hand to material yet to come, insofar as we can estimate the latter. Obviously this will, or should, affect the degree of openness in a classification, as discussed earlier in this chapter. The greater is the proportion of unstudied to studied material, the greater the likelihood that not all of the significant attributes and types have yet been identified. In these circumstances a high degree of flexibility is essential. A common mistake, somewhat exacerbated since the advent of computer-coding, has been to freeze typologies in an incipient stage of development, thereby robbing them of a degree of flexibility (cf. Kaplan 1984: 31). Most coding systems can of course generate new types from existing variables, but they cannot redefine types, or add new ones on the basis of new variables, without calling the whole clustering algorithm into question.

There is, finally, the sheer volume of material to be sorted in a finite period of time. In this respect there is a quantum difference between ceramics and most other archaeological materials, except perhaps for lithic debitage and plant remains. Whatever the material, however, typologies designed for high-volume sorting must always involve practicable and rapid sorting procedures; there is simply no time to agonize over individual decisions (see Chapter 19).

Differences in information sufficiency

In an earlier section we noted that a disproportionately large share of the Typological Debate has been generated by scholars working, or attempting to work, with eastern North American ceramics. They have debated whether there are or are not "natural" types (J. A. Ford 1954a vs. Spaulding 1953), whether "natural" types are emic types (Ford 1954b vs. Krieger 1944 and Spaulding 1953), what are the best ways to discover "natural" or emic types (Ritchie and MacNeish 1949; Spaulding 1953; 1960; Fitting 1965; Whallon 1972), and even whether the typological method is valid at all (Wright 1967). Almost none of these issues have troubled the archaeologists in the Southwest. The explanation, as we suggested earlier, lies partly in the nature of the pottery being studied, but it may also lie partly in the different sufficiency of our cultural information about these respective regions.

It is an evident truth that the poorer is the material record, the more we must hope to learn from each individual artifact recovered (Clark 1957: 74–106; Fagan 1978: 29–31). In the Southwest, thanks in part to environmental conditions, the material record is incredibly rich and varied, and our understanding of prehistoric cultures is correspondingly full. Pottery, for all its abundance and decorative variety, has contributed surprisingly little to that understanding in any direct way, because it comprises so small a part of the total archaeological record. Had the Anasazi made and used nothing but Lino Grey Ware from beginning to end, we would still know almost as much about their ancient technology, society, and religion as we currently do. A great deal has been learned from the non-classificatory analysis of Southwestern pottery, but classification itself, at least until the recent past, has provided only a basis for the identification of times and peoples. Its contribution has been strictly ancillary.

In the East, and particularly in the Northeast, the situation is obviously different. In the absence of basketry, leather, textiles, wood, and standing structures, pottery comprises a far larger share of the total recovered inventory than it does in the Southwest, and we must hope to learn proportionately more from it. Here we may perhaps recognize the source of a prevalent error: the belief that the more we hope to learn from the study of any particular material, the more we may hope to learn by classifying it.

Archaeologists use pottery types, as well as projectile point types, as basic identity markers for times and peoples. In this role as "index fossils," they often assume an ancillary importance that is out of all proportion to their interpretive or historical importance. But because we use pottery and projectile point types to identify times and peoples, there may be a tendency to assume that the pottery and the points can also tell us something *about* the times and peoples; that because they can identify they can also characterize. There is clearly no logical justification for this equation of identification with characterization, but it may help to explain the belief among many archaeologists that any types which can be consistently recognized must also have had functional and/or emic significance.

We conclude, then, that the poorer is the archaeological record, the more we may be tempted to expect from typologies. There may even be a hope that typologies made for strictly ancillary purposes will at the same time yield basic cultural information. Unfortunately this expectation has no rational basis, and, at least in the case of pottery typologies, it is not likely to be realized in practice (cf. WYA 1979).

Tradition

Most archaeologists acknowledge the importance of tradition as a source of cultural variation, and this holds true for their own practices no less than for the material they study. The prevalence of different classificatory procedures in different parts of the world and in different fields of archaeology may at times reflect simply the influence of local or disciplinary tradition (cf. Trigger and Glover 1981; 1982). The importance of tradition appears to be especially marked in fields like Egyptology and Biblical archaeology, where there must in any case be a certain acceptance of received wisdom. The great methodological innovators in Egyptian archaeology were Flinders Petrie and George A. Reisner, both of whom worked more than three-quarters of a century ago. Nevertheless, many of their classificatory and other procedures remain in use, virtually without modification, down to the present day, because of the veneration that still attaches to their innovators.

19

THE BOTTOM LINE: PRACTICALITY

In the affluent 1960s and 1970s, archaeological procedures were not always closely scrutinized for their practicality or utility. However, this was an exceptional era in archaeology, one that gave researchers the unaccustomed luxury of experimenting with field and laboratory techniques whose practical value was often undetermined. In more normal times, archaeological research is usually carried out under conditions of severe financial and resource constraint. Considerations of practicality and cost-effectiveness can rarely be ignored, and must sometimes be paramount. We (or our funding agencies) are usually obliged to ask: Do our analytical procedures really tell us more than is intuitively obvious? Does increased rigor lead to measurably more useful or meaningful results? Could the same results be obtained by cheaper or less time-consuming means? Can we justify our procedures not only in terms of what we want to know, but why we want to know it? Above all, is our work likely to diminish the unknown, or merely (perhaps for the nth time), to reconfirm what is already known (see WYA 1960: 19)?

In this chapter we will be considering the issue of practical utility with specific reference to archaeological classifications and their use. In theory, two separate issues are involved here: those of practicality and of utility. Practicality refers to whether a procedure is inherently doable (feasible) and/or affordable. Utility refers to whether the results are of any use. Taken together, "practical utility" refers to whether the cost of any procedure, in time and money, is justified by the results. Broadly speaking, this is equivalent to cost-effectiveness. For economy of expression we will here use the term practicality to mean practical utility and cost-effectiveness.

Obviously, there can be no fixed rules in regard to practicality. As Foucault (1973: 140) reminds us, "the system is relative: it is able to function according to a desired degree of precision." Every archaeologist has to judge for himself how much his time is worth, what else he could be using his money for, and how badly he wants to learn whatever it is he hopes to learn from the classificatory exercise. We can however note as a general principle that practicality is likely to be more important in open classifications than in closed ones, and more important in sorting than in classifying. It is also very much a matter of scale. The larger the volume of material to be classified and/or sorted, the more important it is to develop affordable and efficient procedures. Nevertheless, there are probably no circumstances in which practicality can be altogether disregarded in the making and use of classifications. In this chapter we will consider practicality first in relation to classificatory purposes, then in relation to classificatory procedures, and finally in relation to sorting procedures. For reasons that have just been suggested, these issues are better discussed in terms of examples than of abstract precepts.

To classify or not to classify

For any given purpose, we ought to consider first of all whether classifying and sorting activities are really the easiest and cheapest way of learning what we want to know. For purposes of chronological determination, for example, there are many ways of obtaining dates besides sorting and counting potsherds. At the Nubian site of Qasr Ibrim two or three expedition members are engaged each day in the examination of potsherds, and much of this analysis is carried on solely for the purpose of calculating dates. (That is, most other kinds of ceramic analysis could be carried on with a much smaller sample of sherds.) It might therefore legitimately be asked whether there is not some more efficient way of obtaining chronological information. If, for example, the site yielded large numbers of coins or dated inscriptions, these would presumably save hundreds of man-hours spent on the sherd deck. A great many inscribed papers, papyri, and ostraca are indeed found at Qasr Ibrim, but the vast majority of them are undated. Consequently, they are dated by the potsherds found in association with them rather than vice versa.

Radiocarbon dating is now capable of yielding (for the Middle Ages) determinations at least as accurate as those obtained from potsherds, and at Qasr Ibrim the fairly considerable cost of these dates might in theory be offset by the saving in labor time. This would be a legitimate consideration if only a few dates were required, as is often true in dating prehistoric sites that were occupied only for short periods. Qasr Ibrim, however, was occupied for something like 3,500 years, and for an accurate chronological ordering of rooms and levels it is necessary to obtain a separate age determination for each deposit on the site, or a total of several hundred determinations each season (see Chapter 11). The cost of so many ^{14}C

dates would exceed the expedition's entire labor budget for a typical season. To achieve the necessary purpose of dating each deposit the excavators have found no way of eliminating the onerous task of sorting and counting hundreds of potsherds every afternoon, but they have done everything possible to eliminate unnecessary refinements from the sorting process itself.

Practicality and purpose

The question of relative practicality is inseparable from that of purpose. Procedures that are worthwhile for some purposes may not be worthwhile for others. Few archaeologists, presumably, would want to spend a great deal of time in developing a typology just for mnemonic or storage purposes, but a major expenditure of time and money might be considered worthwhile in developing a typology that would serve as a basis for dating sites.

The practice of weighing batches of potsherds, instead of or in addition to counting them (cf. Solheim 1960; McPherron 1967a: 45–6; B. Smith 1973; Johnson 1982), provides a good example of variable practicality in relation to different purposes. If sherds are classified and sorted for the purpose of determining how many pots of different kinds were originally present, then weighing obviously provides a more accurate measure than does counting. (That is, since pots break up into a great many different sherds of different sizes, it is easier to equate a certain weight of sherds with an original whole pot than it is to equate any given number of sherds.) If on the other hand the sherd counts are to be used primarily for dating, as described in Chapters 11 and 18, then the extra effort of weighing (which can be substantial where large numbers of sherds are involved) may not be justified. The index clusters used in dating Nubian sites (Chapter 11), like the pottery seriations of J. A. Ford (1962) and many others, are based on relative numbers of different sherd types, not of pots, and for these calculations it is not necessary to know how many original pots were present.

Practicality in classifying

Classification is so basic to the archaeological enterprise (see especially Chang 1967: 4–5, 71) that archaeologists have seldom questioned its validity in the abstract. They have often debated which of several alternatives is the "right" way to classify a given body of material for a given purpose (cf. Whallon 1972; Christenson and Read 1977; Hodson 1982; Klejn 1982: 118–20; Spaulding 1982), but they have not often asked whether classification itself is the best way, or even a possible way, of achieving their objectives (but see Wright 1967; Keighley 1973; Clay 1976). These are nevertheless highly appropriate questions, and we will return to them at the end of the present chapter.

With enough experimentation, most material will be found to be classifiable in some way and for some purpose. However, the archaeologist must still decide if the classification is likely to work well enough for that purpose – i.e. to yield enough previously unknown information – to justify the time spent on it. He may also want to ask if the same information could possibly be obtained in other and easier ways.

In practical situations, the question of cost-effectiveness probably arises most often in connection with efforts at objectivity or precision. These usually involve the precise identification of diagnostic attributes or attribute clusters for particular types, an effort that can be both expensive and time-consuming. A case in point is the common practice of subjecting potsherds to neutron activation and other methods of chemical or petrographic analysis (cf. Peacock 1970; Olin and Franklin 1982: 65–163). Despite their very substantial cost, these procedures will often justify themselves if they lead us to the places of origin for pottery wares (cf. Butzer 1974), or if they help us to decide whether two or more wares could or could not have been made in the same place. On the other hand, merely knowing the chemical constituency of a pottery ware is of no practical value if the knowledge itself does not lead us any further. It is obviously not a useful aid in typing and sorting, since we cannot subject each sherd to neutron activation.

None of the Nubian pottery wares was subjected to neutron activation or other chemical analyses by WYA, who considered it unlikely that they would reveal anything useful to him that was not already known. (Both the places of origin and the nature of the pottery constituents were known from the finding and excavation of the actual pottery manufacturing sites; see WYA 1986a: 13–25.) It must be admitted, however, that WYA invested several hundred hours in other would-be "objective" procedures whose practical value is equally questionable. One of these was the determination of typical Munsell color signatures for the paste, slip, and decorative colors exhibited by each Nubian ware (see *ibid.*: 203–6), a procedure that required the matching of hundreds of individual sherds against Munsell color chips. Another procedure was the determination of hardness, on the Mohs' scale, for each ware, which was discovered by scratching a large sample of sherds with testing instruments. These analyses were a concession to the demand for rigor and objectivity that has been conspicuous in the field of archaeological classification in the recent past. In practice, neither WYA nor any other sorter of Nubian sherds has ever been able to make practical use of the Munsell color values or of the Mohs' hardness values in the actual sorting operation.

The most extreme example of misplaced effort in classification is perhaps to be found in the practice, widespread especially in the Old World, of drawing hundreds of vessel rim profiles, sometimes illustrating only the most minor nuances of variation (e.g. Griffin 1943: 351–65; Shinnie 1955: 38–41; Whitcomb and Johnson 1982: 73–115). It is usually not clear whether this procedure represents an effort at classification or at seriation, since quantitative data are almost never given. That is, we are not told whether each drawing represents a single sherd or the norm for an unspecified number of sherds. The rim profiles are evidently regarded as forming part of a type description, but how they are meant to be used in practice has never been made clear. The present authors are not aware of a single case in which these drawings have been cited for reference or comparison in any work except the one in which they are published. Their only justification seems to be that they allow the archaeologist to feel that he has "done his duty by the pottery," by following a recording convention that is hallowed by tradition (cf. Chapter 18) if not justified by its utility.

Practicality in sorting

Questions of practicality and cost-effectiveness are most likely to arise not with reference to classifying *per se*, but to the application of classifications; that is, to sorting. It is hardly necessary to repeat here what has already been observed more than once: that the larger is the scale of sorting operations, the more important it is that typological distinctions should be readily observable in the sorting process. Ideally, every type should have at least one readily recognizable feature, whether or not that feature is actually basic to its definition (see Chapter 15). For the experienced sorter, at least all of the major types should in time become recognizable in the form of gestalts (see Chapter 5).

In large-scale sorting operations it is usually necessary to eliminate both expensive procedures and time-consuming ones. In the sorting of pottery, neutron activation and similar analyses will be eliminated on the ground of expense, while sherd weighing, Munsell color determination, hardness testing, and many other procedures will probably be eliminated because they are too time-consuming, unless we can be certain that they produce useful results. The practice of weighing potsherd batches has been eliminated by some archaeologists because it was not found to yield results significantly different from those obtained by counting (King 1949: 109–14; Colton 1953: 59–60).

The justification that is usually given for all of the procedures just discussed is that they ensure the highest degree of consistency in the sorting process, both by the same sorter and by different sorters (cf. Fish 1978). It is worth stressing, however, that intersubjective agreement is not an end in itself (cf. EWA and WYA 1987: 8), and for some purposes a high degree of sorting consistency may not be required. In the use of the Nubian Pottery Typology, it has been found that a 90 per cent level of agreement between sorters is sufficient for the dating methods currently employed. A higher degree of consistency could be achieved either by sorting more slowly or by applying various identification techniques such as Munsell color determination, but neither of these would lead to the calculation of more accurate dates. (See Margolis 1987: 27–8, for the practical consequences of jumping too soon and of waiting too long in decisions involving pattern recognition.)

20

PRINCIPLES OF PRACTICAL TYPOLOGY

Before concluding the practical section of our work, it seems desirable to synthesize the main ideas that have been expressed in earlier chapters into a set of general principles, which we will call "principles of practical typology." For convenience they will be subdivided into basic principles, principles of type formulation, principles of practicality, and principles of utility.

Basic principles

1. A type, as defined in this work, is at once a group of entities, our ideas about those entities, and the words and/or pictures in which we represent our ideas. In other words a type in the fullest sense has material, mental, and representational dimensions (Chapter 3).

2. The relationship between the material, mental, and representational dimensions of typehood is mutable. Either the objects, our ideas about them, or the ways in which we represent the ideas may change, without necessarily effecting change in the other dimensions (Chapter 3).

3. Types have the two essential properties of identity and meaning. That is, to be useful they have to be consistently identifiable, and they have in addition to tell us something that we want to know (Chapter 3).

4. Individual type concepts can originate in various ways, by intuition or by some process of conscious analysis. Once they have come into being, type concepts generally evolve as we apply them to actual entities, through a continuous feedback between our observations of the objects and our ideas about them. This dialectic will probably continue as long as we continue to sort new objects (Chapter 5).

5. Most practical types are neither wholly natural nor wholly artificial. In general, nature or culture creates modalities, but the typologist is forced to draw boundaries between them where there may be no such boundaries in nature. Types are therefore formulated by a combination of discovery and invention (Chapter 6).

239

6. Types are defined by their modalities or central tendencies and not by fixed boundaries. Every type modality exhibits, and is defined by, a unique combination of attributes, but some types also have clearly apparent boundaries while others do not. In the case of historically successive types there is frequently no sharp dividing line between a type and its successor (Chapter 6).

7. A classification is a matched set of contrasting categories, which are collectively meant to characterize most or all of the entities in a specified body of material. A typology is a particular kind of classification designed for sorting. That is, a typology is designed to segregate all of the entities in a particular body of material into mutually exclusive categories (Chapters 4, 7).

8. A typology is a kind of formal language. Like every other language it must be learned through experience and use. Memorizing type descriptions is helpful but not sufficient; hands-on experience in the application of type concepts to particular objects is also essential (Chapters 5, 16).

9. Typologies are developed with reference to a specific purpose or purposes, and it is those purposes that give meaning to the individual types in the system. Archaeological typologies can legitimately serve many different purposes, and these will affect the way in which types are formulated and used (Chapters 13, 18).

10. Every typology is capable, in theory, of generating far more identifiable types than are useful for any particular purpose. Typologies are therefore developed through the two processes of formulation and selection. The archaeologist first formulates provisional types on the basis of criteria of identity; from these he then selects the types that are useful for his purposes on the basis of criteria of meaning (Chapter 15).

11. The making and use of typologies involves separate processes of classifying (creating categories) and sorting (putting things into them). The problems and procedures are different in the two cases, and precision in the definition of types will not necessarily eliminate the need for arbitrary decisions in sorting (Chapters 15, 16).

Principles of type formulation

12. Types can be formulated in a variety of ways, involving varying combinations of intuition and rational analysis. No method of formulation is inherently right or wrong. The test of validity for any type is not how it was formulated but whether or not it works for its intended purpose (Chapters 5, 15).

13. Archaeological types are usually though not always defined by a combination of intrinsic and extrinsic (contextual or inferential) attributes. Intrinsic attributes provide criteria of identity, and extrinsic attributes provide criteria of meaning (Chapter 14).

14. Types are differentiated from each other by the possession of unique attribute clusters. The attribute cluster which serves to define any type must have three characteristics: statistical significance, variability of association, and meaningfulness for the purposes of the typology (Chapter 14).

15. Although every type is capable of formal definition, in terms of its unique attribute cluster, the definitions of archaeological types are rarely explicitly stated. For purposes of utility, type concepts are communicated in the form of extended descriptions (overdetermination) rather than of formal definitions (Chapter 15).

16. The purpose of type descriptions is to facilitate the typing and sorting of actual specimens; to ensure a reasonable degree of consistency among different sorters and/or on different occasions. Type descriptions should include all features that might be useful in sorting, whether or not these features are actually diagnostic of the type (Chapter 15).

17. Once they have been formulated, types can be ordered in various ways through the techniques of seriation and/or taxonomic clustering. These procedures serve to express relationships between types, which cannot be indicated in a basic (one-level) typology. Seriation and taxonomic clustering are normally procedures independent of, and subsequent to, the process of type formulation itself (Chapter 17).

18. Since they do not affect the basic definition of types, seriation and taxonomic ordering can be carried out for purposes independent of the main purpose of the typology, without detriment to its effectiveness for its main purpose. These procedures usually represent the best way of introducing secondary purposes into a classificatory scheme (Chapter 17).

Principles of practicality

19. A practical typology is one that allows for reasonably accurate and rapid sorting. That is, the type descriptions must correspond to the observable attributes of the material being sorted sufficiently closely that most entities can be unambiguously identified with one or another of the types (Chapter 16).

20. Practical type descriptions should list all features that might

be useful in sorting: that is, all of the features that may distinguish a type from some other types, not merely those that distinguish it from all other types (Chapter 15).

21. In practical typologies the most common types should have readily visible criteria of identity, so that experienced sorters can make immediate type attributions without recourse to expensive or time-consuming analytical procedures. Experienced sorters should be able to acquire a gestalt for each of the most common types (Chapters 16, 19).

22. Accuracy in sorting is a matter of intrasubjective and inter-subjective consistency: the consistency with which the same objects are identified with the same types by different persons, and/or on different occasions. It is not a question of whether one sorter perceives "reality" more accurately than another (Chapter 16).

23. A high degree of consistency in sorting may not be required for all purposes. The level of consistency required for any purpose should if possible be determined experimentally. If time or resources are limited, sorting procedures should not aim for greater accuracy than is needed for the purposes indicated (Chapter 19).

Principles of utility

24. A useful typology is one in which all of the types serve some clearly defined purpose. The types may serve additional purposes as well, but their utility for their main purpose will not necessarily be an indication of their utility for any other purpose (Chapters 13, 18).

25. A useful typology is generally an open typology; it is designed to classify new finds as well as material already in hand (Chapter 18).

26. Useful typologies may be either basic or instrumental. Basic typologies are designed to learn something about the material being classified; instrumental typologies use the material classified as a means to some other end, such as the dating of archaeological deposits. In instrumental typologies the influence of purpose is especially salient (Chapters 13, 18).

27. In useful typologies, type definitions are necessarily mutable. They are susceptible to change when experience shows that some variables and attributes are not significantly patterned, and also when new finds exhibit new variables and attributes that need to be considered (Chapters 5, 6).

28. In useful archaeological typologies, type definitions are often polythetic. That is, various combinations of attributes may serve to define a type, and the criteria of "typehood" are thus not absolutely uniform from one type to another (Chapters 6, 18).

2I

INFORMATION-THEORETIC
FORMULATIONS

In recent years there has been a trend toward employing mathematical information theory to formulate ideas about information in the fields of classification (Duncan and Estabrook 1976; Voss, Estabrook, and Voss 1983), philosophy of science (Rosenkrantz 1977), and even in the theory of knowledge (Dretske 1981). A similar application could be especially appropriate here, where we are concerned with informative typologies, because the concise expression that it gives to otherwise vague intuitions may allow us to see implications and connections between them that are not otherwise apparent.

Perhaps the most important intuition, to begin with, is that typologies like the Nubian Pottery Typology are developed primarily so that they will yield data that are useful for estimation, which means that the typologies are informative about those things that they are designed to estimate. Related theses are that the attributes, in terms of which the types are described, are informative about the types (with diagnostic attributes being the most informative), and that objectivity is useful to the extent that estimates based on objective data are better than estimates that are subjectively based.

The present chapter will sketch a way of formulating the above and other, related ideas information-theoretically. Our approach adapts to the typological case, and to the Nubian Pottery Typology in particular, certain methods that were earlier applied by EWA (1966) to quantitative measurement. This involves the application of information-theoretic concepts to typological propositions, expressed in the language of formal logic. After briefly explaining the formalism itself, we will discuss its application to the following: (1) the informativeness of attributes about types (wares in the Nubian system), and of wares about provenience-eras; (2) the structure of type descriptions; (3) multiple uses for typological data; (4) type centers (central tendencies) and boundaries; (5) typological spaces, classification, and measurement; (6) the value of objectivity; and (7) the larger picture, including questions of practicality and utility as well as of information. Our aim here is to illustrate the application of information-theoretical ideas to this broad range of topics, not to pursue any of them at length.

The language of formalism

As stated, our approach involves the application of concepts of mathematical information theory to formulas and systems of formulas of logical theory that express classificatory facts, as well as things that they may give information about. Two principal domains of "things" are involved: sherds and proveniences, which are ranged over by two kinds of thing-variables, here designated as s and p for sherds and proveniences respectively. These are to be distinguished from random variables, to be described below. Sherds have various properties, the chief ones we are concerned with being their types (wares), and the attributes in terms of which they are described. For instance, if a sherd has the property of belonging to Terminal Christian white ware (see Appendix B), this might be expressed by writing Ws, while if it has the attribute of wheel-made construction this could be expressed by Cs. Given that there are 101 mutually exclusive and exhaustive ware types in the Nubian system (see Chapter 10), the fact that a sherd s is of these types can be symbolized $W_1s, W_2s, \ldots W_{101}s$; the set of all of these symbolizations defines what in set theory is called a partition (Suppes 1957: 83). This can also be construed as a random variable in the statistician's sense (Savage 1954: 45), which we will here call simply a variable whose values are W_1s–$W_{101}s$. These variables are particularly important in relation to information, which typically has to do with their values: i.e., with which of W_1s–$W_{101}s$ is the case.

Attributes can also be regarded as values of variables, so that the method of construction variable may have the values C_1s and C_2s, the former designating wheel-made construction and the latter hand-made construction. The density variable (one of the subsets of the pottery fabric variable) has the values porous, medium, fairly dense, dense, and very dense, which may be symbolized D_1s, D_2s, D_3s, D_4s, and D_5s. In general, attributes will be symbolized by subscripted capital letters like D_1s (except that W_1s–$W_{101}s$ is a special case symbolizing ware values rather than attribute values), and the variables of which they are values will be symbolized by underlined letters. For instance, $\underline{D}s$ will symbolize the density variable with values $D_1s \ldots D_5s$, and $\underline{W}s$ will symbolize the ware variable. In general, any typology or classification system defines variables of this kind.

It is also important that we can form logical compounds of attributes.

For instance C_1s & D_2s symbolizes the combined attributes of a sherd s being wheel-made and having medium density. This in turn allows us to define the variable-product operation that is very important in connection with information. For instance $\underline{C}s \times \underline{D}s$ is the "construction and density" variable with values C_1s & D_1s, C_2s & D_1s, C_1s & D_2s, C_2s & D_2s, and so on, with $2 \times 5 = 10$ values in all. Adding further variables like surface finish, symbolized by $\underline{F}s$, with values of F_1s, F_2s, etc., allows us to define products of products like $\underline{C}s \times \underline{D}s \times \underline{F}s$, which represents the "construction-density-finish" variable. Obviously this process of compounding can go on indefinitely, and by this means we can compile the information about a sherd that is obtained by determining any number of its attributes, and we can relate this information both to the ware variable $\underline{W}s$ and to the provenience era in which the sherd is found.

The properties of proveniences that mainly interest us are their dates, which can be represented by eras of different duration. For instance, $Y_{150}p$ might express the fact that provenience p dates from the year A.D. 150, while C_2p could indicate that p derives from the second century A.D. (Possible confusion between the sherd attribute C_2s and the provenience attribute C_2p is avoided because s and p show that the first refers to sherds and the second to proveniences.) Generalizing, we will write date values as E_1p, E_2p, etc., which symbolize that p dates from Era 1, Era 2, etc., the actual durations of the eras being left unspecified. Later we will comment on appropriate choices of eras corresponding to different date-estimation methods. For now we will assume only that they form another variable, $\underline{E}p$, with values E_1p, E_2p, and so on.

There is of course an important relationship between sherds and proveniences, namely that of a sherd s being found in a provenience p, which will be symbolized by writing sFp. These are the sherds whose attributes and ware types provide the means for estimating the era of p, a procedure to which we now turn.

Proportions, uncertainties, and information

We will suppose that among all sherds there are definite proportions having each of the properties or attributes we are concerned with, and these will be symbolized by prefixing the corresponding formulas with P. Thus, $P(C_1s)$ is the proportion of all possible sherds that are wheel-made, and $P(E_1p)$ is the proportion of all possible proveniences that date from Era 1. This symbolism extends to formulas with more than one thing-variable, and to compound formulas. Thus, $P(sFp)$ is the proportion of all sherd-provenience combinations in which sherd s is found in provenience p, and

$P(sFp \& C_1s)$ is the proportion of those combinations in which sherd s is wheel-made. Technically, proportions can be regarded as probabilities since they satisfy the laws of mathematical probability. That proportions are formal probabilities allows us to define conditional proportions in the standard way, as ratios of unconditional ones. For example, the proportion of wheel-made sherds found in provenience p is given by the ratio: $P(C_1s$ given $sFp) = P(sFp \& C_1s) / P(sFp)$. These kinds of proportions, which we have elsewhere called type frequencies (Chapter 17), are the basic data from which provenience eras are estimated in the Nubian Typology, and we now take a step in that direction by defining probabilistic uncertainty.

The standard measure of probabilistic uncertainty is the so-called Shannon-Hartley measure (Shannon and Weaver 1949) which applies to variables like $\underline{W}s$:

(1) $\qquad U(\underline{W}s) = -[P(W_1s) \log P(W_1s) + \ldots + P(W_{101}s) \log P(W_{101}s)].$

(The logarithms in this formula can have different bases, depending on the unit of uncertainty measurement.) This measure has a number of important properties that justify its use, and some of them may be noted here (see also Ash 1965, Sec. 1.4). If the value of a variable is known for certain, say $P(W_{25}s) = 1$, then $U(\underline{W}s)$ is $\emptyset$; i.e. there is no uncertainty as to the value of $\underline{W}s$. On the other hand, when all the values are equally probable there is maximum uncertainty concerning $\underline{W}s$, and it equals the logarithm of the number of possible values. This would happen if $P(W_1s) = \ldots P(W_{101}s) = 1/101$, which would imply that $U(\underline{W}s) = \log 101$. All other possible uncertainties in this case lie between $\emptyset$ and $\log 101$.

The uncertainties of products relate to the uncertainties of their components in systematic ways. In particular, we can write:

(2) $\qquad U(\underline{C}s) + U(\underline{D}s) \geq U(\underline{C}s \times \underline{D}s) = U(\underline{D}s \times \underline{C}s) \geq U(\underline{C}s).$

This implies that: (1) the uncertainty of a product is independent of the order of its components; (2) it is at least as great as those of the individual components; and (3) it is no greater than their sum. The two extreme cases are important because of their connection with information. When $U(\underline{C}s \times \underline{D}s)$ is equal to either $U(\underline{C}s)$ or $U(\underline{D}s)$, say $U(\underline{C}s \times \underline{D}s) = U(\underline{D}s)$, this means that $\underline{D}s$ contains all the information in $\underline{C}s$ in the sense that the value of $\underline{D}s$ determines that of $\underline{C}s$. This, if true, would mean that the construction of a sherd could be uniquely inferred from its density. The other extreme is that at which the two variables are statistically uncorrelated so that neither gives any information about the other, where $U(\underline{C}s \times \underline{D}s) = U(\underline{C}s) + U(\underline{D}s)$.

247

To make more precise the idea of one variable giving information about another, we introduce here the definition of transmitted information, symbolized as Tr (Ash 1965: Sec. 1.5). The information that $\underline{D}$s gives about the value of $\underline{C}$s can be written:

(3) $Tr(\underline{C}s/\underline{D}s) = U(\underline{C}s) + U(\underline{D}s) - U(\underline{C}s \times \underline{D}s).$

What is most important about $Tr(\underline{C}s/\underline{D}s)$ is that it equals the expected amount by which the uncertainty of $\underline{C}$s is reduced as a result of learning the value of $\underline{D}$s. $Tr(\underline{C}s/\underline{D}s)$ satisfies the following:

(4) $U(\underline{C}s) \geq Tr(\underline{C}s/\underline{D}s) = Tr(\underline{D}s/\underline{C}s) \geq \emptyset.$

The middle equation shows that Tr is symmetric, which means that the amount of information that a first variable transmits about a second equals the amount the second transmits about the first. This will prove important in discussing the relationship between attribute and ware variables. The maximum and minimum values of $Tr(\underline{C}s/\underline{D}s)$ are also significant. When $Tr(\underline{C}s/\underline{D}s)$ has its maximum value it equals $U(\underline{C}s)$; hence learning the value of $\underline{D}$s reduces $U(\underline{C}s)$ by the amount $U(\underline{C}s)$, i.e., it reduces it to $\emptyset$. When $Tr(\underline{C}s/\underline{D}s)$ has its minimum value it equals $\emptyset$, hence learning the value of $\underline{D}$s makes no reduction in the uncertainty of $U(\underline{C}s)$.

The most important information we are concerned with is that which is provided about the value of the era variable $\underline{E}$p by knowledge of the value of the ware variable $\underline{W}$s, for any sherd s found in provenience p. If there were only one sherd s found in p, this information would be described in terms of conditional uncertainty, as in equation (1), but with ordinary probabilities replaced by conditional probabilities:

(1') $U(\underline{W}s \text{ given } sFp) = -[P(W_1s \text{ given } sFp) \log P(W_1s \text{ given } sFp)$
          $+ \ldots + P(W_{101}s \text{ given } sFp) \log P(W_{101}s \text{ given } sFp)].$

However, there is actually a series of sherds, $\underline{s} = s_1, s_2, \ldots$, found in provenience p, and we must consider uncertainties relating to all of them. Letting $\underline{s}Fp$ be the conjunction of s_1Fp, s_2Fp, etc., expressing the fact that $s_1, s_2, \ldots$ are all found in p, and setting $\underline{W}s = \underline{W}s_1 \times \underline{W}s_2 \times \ldots$, where $\underline{W}s_1$, $\underline{W}s_2 \ldots$ are the logically distinct ware variables corresponding to $s_1, s_2, \ldots$, we are interested in the three conditional uncertainties $U(\underline{E}p$ given $\underline{s}Fp)$, $U(\underline{W}s$ given $\underline{s}Fp)$ and $U(\underline{W}s \times \underline{E}p$ given $\underline{s}Fp)$. These are defined by simple variants of formula (1'), which combine to define the conditional transmitted information:

(5) $Tr(\underline{E}p/\underline{W}s \text{ given } \underline{s}Fp) = U(\underline{E}p \text{ given } \underline{s}Fp) + U(\underline{W}s \text{ given } \underline{s}Fp)$
          $- U(\underline{W}s \times \underline{E}p \text{ given } \underline{s}Fp).$

Tr($\underline{Ep}$/$\underline{W}$s given $\underline{s}$Fp) measures the amount by which the uncertainty as to the era of provenience p is reduced as a result of determining the ware types of the sherds found in it. This is the most important measure we are concerned with, and we will formulate several hypotheses about it below. As noted, the maximum value that Tr($\underline{Ep}$/$\underline{W}$s given $\underline{s}$Fp) can have is U($\underline{Ep}$), where determining the value of $\underline{W}$s would reduce uncertainty about $\underline{Ep}$ to zero, and the minimum value it can have is Ø, where determining these values would not reduce the uncertainty of $\underline{Ep}$ at all.

Ware significance and denotation

Significance. Our fundamental hypothesis is that the Nubian Pottery Typology maximizes Tr($\underline{Ep}$/$\underline{W}$s given $\underline{s}$Fp) (within the limits of practicality, to be discussed below). This means that determining the ware types of the sherds found in p reduces uncertainty as to the era of this provenience by the maximum amount possible on the basis of sherd data alone – something which was of course one of the main original purposes of the typology, as discussed in Chapters 9–11. This is not to claim literally that the typology was designed with the conscious objective of maximizing a function defined in terms of logarithms of sherd frequencies, but only that it was constructed as though that were the aim. In other words, the logarithmic formula gives a good measure of what the sherd typology was designed to maximize. Of course this is a highly conjectural hypothesis, but at least it is objective and testable. Thus, Tr($\underline{Ep}$/$\underline{W}$s given $\underline{s}$Fp) should be greater than the value of Tr($\underline{Ep}$/$\underline{W}$'s given $\underline{s}$Fp) for other practical sherd classification system $\underline{W}$'s.

Typological evolution: splitting and lumping. Given that the construction of a typology involves successive approximations, Tr($\underline{Ep}$/$\underline{W}$s given $\underline{s}$Fp) should be greater than Tr($\underline{Ep}$/$\underline{W}$'s given $\underline{s}$Fp) when $\underline{W}$'s is a ware variable corresponding to one of the earlier typologies constructed by WYA (e.g., 1962d; 1964a). In other words, we can expect typological evolution to result in progress in the sense that the more evolved typology will be more informative about that which the typology was designed to estimate than were its predecessors (see also Chapter 26).

The splitting and lumping processes described in Chapter 5 (and further discussed in Chapter 23) are often involved in the evolution of typologies, and are easily accounted for in information-theoretic terms. Splitting occurs when one type, say W_{25}s, is divided into two or more mutually exclusive types, say $W_{25a}s$ and $W_{25b}s$, so that the typology as a whole now involves more types than before. This is justified if the new typology is more informative than the old; i.e., if $Tr(\underline{Ep}/\underline{W's}$ given $\underline{s}Fp) > Tr(\underline{Ep}/\underline{Ws}$ given $\underline{s}Fp)$, where $\underline{W's}$ and $\underline{Ws}$ are the ware variables corresponding to the split and the unsplit typologies respectively. It is easily shown, incidentally, that $Tr(\underline{Ep}/\underline{W's}$ given $\underline{s}Fp)$ can never be *less* than $Tr(\underline{Ep}/\underline{Ws}$ given $\underline{s}Fp)$; hence splitting can never reduce a typology's theoretical informativeness. The reasons for avoiding it can only be pragmatic ones of cost-effectiveness and utility, which will be further discussed in the final section of this chapter.

Lumping is the exact reverse of splitting, in which two or more previously distinguished types are combined into one, thereby reducing the number of types overall. If $\underline{Ws}$ and $\underline{W's}$ are respectively the original and the lumped (combined) type variables, it is easy to see that $Tr(\underline{Ep}/\underline{Ws}$ given $\underline{s}Fp) \geq Tr(\underline{Ep}/\underline{W's}$ given $\underline{s}Fp)$, hence the lumped variable can never be more informative than were the two or more variables prior to their lumping. On the other hand the lumped variable may be nearly as informative as its two or more antecedents, and the practical saving that results from having to distinguish fewer types may offset the slight loss of information. (For further discussion see Chapter 19.)

Provenience-era durations. Relating to the foregoing, something may be said here about the choice of an era variable. As we noted earlier, eras could in theory be defined in terms of individual years, decades, centuries, etc., but in the Nubian Typology the eras that have been calculated for individual pottery wares and groups of wares vary from fifty to 200 years in duration. These choices cannot be justified on the ground that they maximize $Tr(\underline{Ep}/\underline{Ws}$ given $\underline{s}Fp)$ for any particular $\underline{Ep}$, since it is easy to see that maximizing this quantity for any given $\underline{Ep}$ would also maximize it for any other era variable. To explain the choice of a particular era variable we must take into account the fact that we do not wish merely to reduce the uncertainty of $U(\underline{Ep})$; we wish to reduce it to an acceptable level. This requires that observing the ware values of the sherds found in a provenience p will pinpoint the era of p by making $\underline{Ep}$ highly probable *a posteriori* for some particular $\underline{Ep}$, and this is only possible if the eras are of sufficient duration. Thus, while determining ware values in the Nubian Typology does somewhat reduce uncertainties about, for example, the decades of occupation for a certain provenience, it does not provide enough information to make any individual decade highly probable *a posteriori*. This is only possible with eras of greater duration, as explained in Chapter 11.

Denotation: relationships between wares and attributes. Wares are described in terms of attributes, and the ware descriptions can themselves be partially described in informational terms, as we will suggest in this section. We have symbolized the construction and density variables by $\underline{C}$s and $\underline{D}$s, respectively, and we can symbolize other variables and attributes in the same way, say as $\underline{E}$s, $\underline{F}$s, . . . , with attribute values of E_1s, E_2s, F_1s, F_2s, and so on. Let $\underline{A}$s be the composite attribute variable formed by the product of all the individual attribute variables; i.e., $\underline{A}$s = $\underline{C}$s $\times$ $\underline{D}$s $\times$ $\underline{E}$s $\times$ $\underline{F}$s $\times$ . . . That the ware variable is describable in terms of the attribute variables implies that the values of $\underline{C}$s, $\underline{D}$s, $\underline{E}$s, $\underline{F}$s, . . . determine those of $\underline{W}$s, which can be expressed information-theoretically by saying that $Tr(\underline{W}s/\underline{A}s)$ is a maximum; i.e. that $Tr(\underline{W}s/\underline{A}s) = U(\underline{A}s)$. Of course this is only an approximation, because, as we have pointed out in Chapter 16, sorters neither do nor should always go by the book in determining the ware types of sherds. When we consider objectivity in attribute and ware-type determinations we will return to this subject.

Another relation between $\underline{W}$s and $\underline{C}$s, $\underline{D}$s, etc., is that $\underline{W}$s should summarize all of the information contained in the attribute variables that is useful for determining provenience eras. This means that if we know the value of $\underline{W}$s for all of the sherds found in a provenience p, then learning the value of any particular attribute variable, say $\underline{C}$s, should not contribute any further useful information about the era of p. Stated information-theoretically, it should be the case that $Tr(\underline{E}p/\underline{W}s \times \underline{C}s$ given $\underline{s}Fp)$ = $Tr(\underline{E}p/\underline{W}s$ given $\underline{s}Fp)$.

Selection of variables. In Chapter 17 we criticized methods of Numerical Taxonomy on the ground that they provide no guidance to the selection of the relevant variables in terms of which types are described (see also Chapter 23). Given the ancillary purpose of many typological classifications for estimation, the relevant variables are clearly those that are informative about the things to be estimated, which in the case of the Nubian Pottery Typology are provenience dates. The most informative variable, which in Nubia might be painted decoration ($\underline{P}$s), must be such that $Tr(\underline{E}p/\underline{P}s$ given $\underline{s}Fp)$ is a maximum, which would mean that painted decoration is most informative about the era of a provenience. Having factored out the most important variable, the next most important, for example vessel shape ($\underline{V}$s), is that which provides the most additional information; i.e., for which the difference $Tr(\underline{E}p/\underline{P}s \times \underline{V}s$ given $\underline{s}Fp)$ − $Tr(\underline{E}p/\underline{P}s$ given $\underline{s}Fp)$ is a maximum. Proceeding in this way we arrive at a series of variables $\underline{P}$s, $\underline{V}$s, ... in descending order of value for age estimation, in terms of which the wares can be described.

The priority of attribute variables. Why bother to describe the wares in terms of attribute variables at all? Here we will comment on one of the ways in which these sorts of variables can be said to be prior to the "constructed" ware variable.

From a purely formal point of view the ware variables and the attribute variables are alike. They are simply variables, and we may ask: What sets $\underline{W}$s apart from the others? Part of our answer relates to the usually greater degree of objectivity of judgments about attributes in comparison to judgments about ware types (to be considered later); another part relates to the fact that attributes often serve as premises from which ware values are inferred. Thus, while sorters employing a typology may follow any procedures they choose, they can and do generally use attribute determinations to guide them in the identification of wares because, as we have seen, the attributes are informative about the wares. To the extent that they do this, the attributes define the types, and the type descriptions serve *de facto* as type definitions, though it is not essential that they should do so (see Chapters 1 and 12).

The foregoing sheds a certain light on the role of diagnostic attributes. Very simply, these are the attributes that identify a ware with virtual certainty (Chapters 14 and 15), in the sense that the posterior probability of a sherd being of the given ware type is very close to 1 when it has the attributes that are diagnostic of the ware.

The form of ware descriptions

It is generally very difficult to relate the content of a description, as measured by the information it transmits, to its form. Thus it is a long step from knowing that the area of a triangle can be described in terms of its sides to knowing how this is done. However, in the case of the Nubian Pottery Typology it can be shown that if the ware values can be described in terms of attribute values, then these descriptions can be given in a special form. To illustrate, suppose that painted decoration and vessel form alone determined ware values. Then any decoration–form combination, say P_1s & V_2s, would have to determine a unique ware value, say W_{25}s. It would follow that W_{25}s could be defined simply as P_1s & V_1s or ..., where the blank is filled in with all other decoration–form combinations that are comparable with W_{25}s.

The interesting point is that while the mode of description illustrated above is completely general, it does not reflect typological practice because the attribute combinations entering into practical descriptions are usually of a special, restricted form in which "either/or's" (disjunctions) only occur between different values of the same variables, and not between combinations of different variables. For instance, the description C_1s or C_2s, and D_1s or D_2s would be in restricted form, but C_2s or D_1s or C_1s or D_2s would not be, and cannot even be restated in restricted form. It seems to us that the practice of framing statements in restricted form is significant, and may even be a requirement of "typological naturalness." That is to say, if a type really corresponds to something in nature (cf. Chapters 6 and 23), it should be capable of expression in restricted form. If so, this must have important implications, one of which has to do with "non-natural" or artificial classifications that might be constructed so as to be simultaneously informative about several disparate phenomena – an issue that we will now consider.

Pluralities of purpose

We have stated in Chapter 13 that while a typology such as the Nubian Pottery Typology may be designed with one primary use in mind, the typologist will often envisage a wider range of possible secondary uses. Some of these are obvious because they are necessarily associated with the primary purpose. For instance, eras are closely associated with differing aspects of culture, and therefore whatever is informative about the former is indirectly informative about the latter. Example: Did the people who occupied such-and-such a Nubian community practice Christianity? The probabilities are that they did so if the proveniences associated with the site can be dated between A.D. 550 and 1500 – the era of Christianity in Nubia.

Related to the foregoing, it is important to note that transmitted information is symmetric, in the sense that attribute variables that transmit information about ware variables also have information about them transmitted by the latter; in other words the ware types are informative about the attributes in terms of which they are described. For instance, because wares are described partly in terms of vessel construction, they must be informative about vessel construction and anything connected with it or implied by it. In the latter category would be such things as trade relations, since in Nubia wheel-made wares were apt to be traded over very long distances, whereas hand-made wares were nearly always used in the locales where they were made.

The foregoing applies to classification for intrinsic purposes, and in particular to classification as a means of summarizing and systematizing what would otherwise be unmanageable quantities of descriptive data (cf. Chapter 13). Suppose that the typologist is given the attribute variables in the domain he wants to classify, say $\underline{C}$s, $\underline{D}$s, $\underline{E}$s, . . . Then an intrinsically informative classification should yield a type variable which maximizes $Tr(\underline{A}s/\underline{W}s)$, where $\underline{A}$s is the composite attribute variable described earlier. That is essentially the point of view expressed by classification theorists like Duncan and Estabrook (1976) and Voss, Estabrook, and Voss (1983). The only question is: How informative can a classification be about possibly quite disparate attribute variables? We can only comment on this very briefly in the present work.

If no constraints of "naturalness" are placed upon it, a classification could be constructed that necessarily gives maximum possible information about any arbitrary number of variables, $\underline{C}$s, $\underline{D}$s, . . . , no matter how many and how disparate. This is because their product, $\underline{A}$s, is itself a kind of classification, and trivially it gives complete information about all of its components. But this is classification in name only, since not only will it not ordinarily be describable in the restricted form noted above, but it will merely restate and will not summarize the data in the component variables. In fact, every individual entity classified is likely to end up as a separate type. If the classification is required to be of the restricted form, then it is subject to very tight constraints which may preclude its being informative about disparate variables. Thus, we would conjecture that there is no natural typology which is informative about both painted decoration and sherd weight. An artificial one might be constructed to encompass these two variables, but it would necessarily be excessively polythetic; something like a "height-and-profession" typology that includes the type "six-foot archaeologist." Natural typologies cannot be expected to be universally informative, and an unsolved problem, which we cannot address here, is to ascertain how informative they can be.

Classification based on perceived similarities

Similarity. Heretofore we have been assuming that classification is done in terms of attributes, and possibly for the purpose of summarizing them. This is not universally the case, as we will see in the present section. Rather than starting with previously given attributes (attribute clustering), intrinsic classification can also start with judgments of similarity (object clustering). These judgments may or may not be analyzable into dimensions of similarity that have the form of attribute variables, somewhat as in factor analysis. But it is possible to arrive directly at a classification without going through the intermediate step of attribute factor analysis. The basic idea is simple: the classification system is designed to maximize information about similarity judgments, as in the following example.

The entities to be classified might be sherds, and they might still be classified into ware types by the ware variable $\underline{W}$s. However, instead of constructing $\underline{W}$s so as to maximize information about provenience eras, the aim could be to maximize information about a relation sSs', which expresses the fact that sherd s is judged similar to sherd s'. Put information-theoretically, the aim would not be to maximize the quantity $\mathrm{Tr}(\underline{Ep}/\underline{W}$s given $\underline{s}Fp)$, but rather $\mathrm{Tr}(s\underline{Ss'}/\underline{W}s \times \underline{W}s')$, where $s\underline{Ss'}$ is the relation variable with values sS_1s' and sS_2s' (s is not similar to s'). This formulation suggests classification in terms of prototypes.

Prototypic classification: centers and boundaries. Ware types may themselves be defined in terms of similarities, as $W_1s \ldots, W_{101}s$ for sSs_1, $\ldots, sWs_{101}$, where $s_1, \ldots, s_{101}$ are prototype sherds. This means that each prototype s_i (where s_i could be a sherd of any ware from 1 to 101) is the center (i.e. represents the central tendency) of Type W_is, and sherd s is of that type if it is similar to s_i – or rather, if it is more similar to s_i than to other prototypes (cf. Torgerson 1958: 395–405).

If prototypic classification is to be maximally informative about the relation sSs', then knowing which prototypes s and s' are similar to should determine whether they are similar to each other. There are various ways in which this determination might be made, but the simplest is that sSs' should hold if and only if s and s' are similar to the same prototype. This in turn presupposes two things: (1) that every sherd should be similar to *some* prototype, and (2) that two sherds are similar to the same prototype if and only if they are similar to each other. The first of these presuppositions is a special case of the general requirement that every sherd must fit into some pigeonhole in the typology (cf. Chapter 7), which will be further considered below. The second holds true if no one sherd is similar to two different (dissimilar) prototypes, a condition that can only be met if there are distinct gaps between the prototypes, so that there are few borderline cases. Obviously this expresses the idea that the types defined in a system should be bounded.

These reflections cannot, unfortunately, be pursued further here, and we now turn to the issue of typological spaces and their connection with quantitative measurement.

255

Typological spaces and measurement

Similarity spaces. Similarity suggests nearness, and there is a natural probabilistic measure of this which in turn defines a "space" in which it is measured. The matter may be stated as follows: The proportion of possible sherds that are similar to s_i but not to s_j or similar to s_j but not to s_i is given by $d(s_i, s_j) = P(sS_1s_i \leftrightarrow sS_2s_j)$. It is well known (cf. EWA 1966) that $d(s_i, s_j)$ is necessarily pseudometric because it is symmetric, i.e. $d(s_i, s_j) = d(s_j, s_i)$, $d(s_i, s_i) = \emptyset$, and it satisfies the triangle inequality, i.e., $d(s_i, s_k) \leq d(s_i, s_j) + d(s_j, s_k)$. It therefore defines a topological space of sherds (cf. Kelley 1955), in which distances are measured by $d(s_i, s_j)$. Note that this space can be defined independently of metric presuppositions, such as that $d(s_i, s_j)$ should be a Euclidian measure on a finite-dimensional attribute space. Analyzing the properties of the space is obviously a complicated matter, which lies beyond the scope of the present discussion, but a word should be said about connections with numerical measurement.

Quality and quantity. Classification has many parallels with measurement (cf. also Chapters 7 and 12), the most obvious being in the relationship between typological variables like $\underline{W}s$ and the attributes or similarities in terms of which they are described, and numerical variables like weights of sherds, $w(s)$, and the physical operations that are used to determine them. That $\underline{W}s$ is qualitative and $w(s)$ is quantitative does not obscure the fact that they both have values that partition the domain of sherds, and we can even write w_1s, w_2s for "s has weight 1" (in some units), "s has weight 2," and so on. Given this, we can consider the amount of desired information that is yielded by knowing the value of $w(s)$, and the amount of desired information about $w(s)$ that is yielded by certain kinds of operations. For instance, we can ask how much information about the era of a provenience p is yielded by knowledge of the weights of the sherds found in it, which would be measured by $Tr(Ep/w(\underline{s})$ given $\underline{s}Fp)$. (We would expect in this case a low yield of information; otherwise $w(s)$ would be among the attribute variables in terms of which $\underline{W}s$ is described.) Or, we can ask how much information about the value of $w(s)$ is yielded by knowing the similarity of the different s's to weight standards $s_1, s_2, \ldots,$ which would be measured by $Tr(w(s)/s\underline{S}s_1 \times s\underline{S}s_2 \times \ldots)$. In this case the yield of information is presumably very high if the standards are well chosen and similarity is appropriately defined. This is the way quantitative measurement is represented in EWA 1966 (see especially Appendix therein), and it illustrates the fact that these measures are artificially constructed for more or less well-defined purposes; mostly to yield information about phenomena that are considered important.

The information-theoretic representation of measurement given here obviously downplays the specifically numerical character of measurement, making it seem that there is no essential difference between quantitative variables like w(s) and typological variables like $\underline{W}$s. However, there are differences of detail that partly explain why numbers play a more important role in measurement than they do in classification, and two of these differences will be noted here. One is the matter of accuracy, which is important in most measurements but not in many classifications. For instance, while it makes sense to say that giving the weight of a sherd as 25.5 gm is more accurate than giving it as 25 gm, it does not make sense to say that the ware value $W_{25.5}$s is more accurate than W_{25}s. Without going into detail we suggest that this can be explained on the ground that more accurate quantitative measurements yield more information about important phenomena than do less accurate ones, but there is nothing closely analogous in the case of types in a classification. (There are of course partial analogues in the case of hierarchic taxonomies such as those in the biological sciences, where in a sense it is more accurate to describe an animal as a member of the species *Canis familiaris* than just as a member of the order of mammals.)

The second feature that is special to certain kinds of quantitative measurement, and in particular to additive measurement (cf. Krantz, Luce, Suppes, and Tversky 1971: 71–132), has to do with the fact that while the numbering of types in a typology, e.g. as W_1s, W_2s, ..., is a purely arbitrary matter, it is not arbitrary that the weights of these things should be numbered, e.g. as w_1s, w_2s, ... In the currently fashionable idiom of "meaningfulness" (cf. Adams, Fagot, and Robinson 1965; Roberts 1979) it is "meaningful" to say that one sherd has twice the weight of another, but not to say that one has twice the ware value of another. The explanation is to be found in the different standards employed, on the one hand in measurement and on the other in prototypic classification. While weight standards can be physically combined so that a 2-gm weight can be formed by combining two 1-gm weights, one cannot construct a W_2s prototype by combining two W_1s prototypes. Adding numbers "represents" something in the case of weight values but not in the case of ware values.

These observations relate to our earlier comments on ware spaces constructed on the basis of similarity judgments. The ware spaces were generated by pseudometrics $d(s_i, s_j)$, measuring distances between prototypes and s_i and s_j (a type of measure which, of course, gives distances between non-prototypes as well). However, while these are distances in the formal sense we feel that they are not meaningful in the same way as are distances on the ground, for example. In particular it does not appear meaningful to say that $d(s_1, s_3) = 2d(s_1, s_2)$ – that one typological distance is twice another – and this is partly because typological distances can never be greater than 1. Again the reason is obvious: measuring real distances involves adding them, like adding the distance from s_2 to s_3 to that from s_1 to s_2, but there is no operation for adding dissimilarities. This leads us to a final observation on the "realism" issue that was originally raised in Chapter 12.

Reality and utility

Objectivity and its value. There are two kinds of objectivity that the judgments of observers may be said to have. One is a kind of realist objectivity, namely that the judgments should agree with the facts, and the other is the requirement of intersubjective agreement: that the judgments of different observers agree with each other (see also Chapters 5 and 15). Of course the former implies the latter, but it is a truism that realist objectivity is seldom attainable in practical affairs, including in the making and application of typologies. We have argued in any case (Chapter 19) that objectivity is not an end in itself in typological applications; it is only useful to the extent that it contributes to the purpose for which the classification was made. We want now to discuss this issue from the information-theoretic point of view. As with previous topics, the present discussion is intended only to sketch basic ideas.

In order to place the observer explicitly within our formulation we need to introduce another thing-variable, o, to stand for him or her. To express the idea that o judges that a sherd has some attribute, say C_1s, we will write oC_1s, and similarly we will write oW_{25}s to express the fact that o judges that s is of type W_{25}. W_{25}s will continue to symbolize that s is of type W_{25}, and of course perfect objectivity would require oW_{25}s to hold only if W_{25}s holds: i.e., o should judge that s is of type W_{25} only if it *is* of that type. However, we will later suggest that from the information-theoretic point of view this kind of objective realism is inessential.

The observer-relative symbolism oC_1s and oW_{25}s can be extended to variables having these values. Thus, $o\underline{C}$s and $o\underline{W}$s are the construction-judgment and the ware-judgment variables, respectively, with values oC_1s, oC_2s, and oW_1s . . . oW_{101}s. We can then modify our earlier definitions of products, proportions, uncertainties, and transmitted information to apply to these judgment variables and formulate information-theoretic hypotheses and conjectures concerning them and their objectivity.

One conjecture has already been stated informally: namely that attribute judgments are more objective than ware judgments. The "realist" objectivity of attribute judgments like $o\underline{C}s$ may be measured information-theoretically by the degree to which they reduce uncertainty about $\underline{C}s$ to zero: i.e., by the difference $U(\underline{C}s) - Tr(\underline{C}s/o\underline{C}s)$. What we conjecture, then, is that while both differences $U(\underline{C}s) - Tr(\underline{C}s/o\underline{C}s)$ and $U(\underline{W}s) - Tr(\underline{W}s/o\underline{W}s)$ are small (that is, judgments of both attributes and wares are fairly objective), the former is smaller than the latter. If so, this would partly explain the priority of the attributes, since judgments concerning them generally constitute firmer data.

But we suggest that objective realism is inessential, as least as far as concerns ware values; for practical purposes it is enough that there should be sufficient agreement among the subjective values $o\underline{W}s$ that represent the judgments of different observers (see Chapters 5 and 15). Information-theoretically, what is required is only that the difference $U(e\underline{W}s) - Tr(e\underline{W}s/o\underline{W}s)$ should be sufficiently small, where o and e are different observer-variables. More accurately, what is required is that this difference should be sufficiently small when e is an expert. Experts are persons whose ware judgments sufficiently agree with each other and whose judgments are more informative about provenience-eras, and the test of proficiency for learners is that their judgments should sufficiently agree with those of the experts.

But what is "sufficient agreement"? Answering this question requires that we take into account the purpose for which the value determinations are made; it is these that help us to calculate the value and the limits of objectivity.

Ware-value judgments in the Nubian Typology are data for provenience-era estimates, and they are useful to the extent that they are informative about those eras. Thus, $Tr(\underline{E}p/o\underline{W}s \text{ given } \underline{s}Fp)$ should be a maximum since that would reduce $U(\underline{E}p)$ to a minimum; therefore objectivity in the judgment $o\underline{W}s$ is useful only to the extent that it contributes to that use. Now, assuming that the experts' judgments are most informative about provenience-eras, it is clear that $Tr(\underline{E}p/o\underline{W}s \text{ given } \underline{s}Fp)$ will be high only if $U(e\underline{W}s) - Tr(e\underline{W}s/o\underline{W}s)$ is low; i.e., that $Tr(\underline{E}p/o\underline{W}s \text{ given } \underline{s}Fp)$ will be maximized if the judgments $o\underline{W}s$ agree with those of the experts, $e\underline{W}s$. But this does not mean that the judgments $o\underline{W}s$ should agree perfectly, either with one another or with those of the experts, because there are limits to the experts' own agreement. In applications of the Nubian Typology, 95 percent agreement is about the best that is likely to be obtained among the experts themselves, and it has been shown (Chapter

19) that this is all that is useful since greater agreement would not increase $Tr(\underline{Ep}/o\underline{W}s$ given $\underline{s}Fp)$.

Information, feasibility, and utility. Here we will comment on two matters that are essential to the information-theoretic picture, though they are extrinsic to information itself: namely the utility or value of the information, and the feasibility of obtaining it (see also Chapter 19). Their importance is evident in the fact that information about provenience dates is clearly of value, but it cannot be obtained by direct observation, and therefore must be estimated by indirect means. If dating information were of no value, or if it were obtainable by direct means, the main purpose of the Nubian Typology would in either case be lost. The system would certainly not justify the time and effort that were invested in its development.

Let us make some general observations about how information, utility and feasibility are interconnected. As to feasibility (elsewhere called practicality), we may say that $Tr(\underline{Ep}/\underline{W}s$ given $\underline{s}Fp)$ is of practical concern because it is feasible to determine the values of the ware variable $\underline{W}s$. In other words we are interested in information that is transmitted from feasibly determined data, but not from unobtainable data. But this example shows that obtainability itself is partly a matter of immediacy and partly of cost.

As concerns immediacy, we know that the values of $\underline{W}s$ may themselves not be immediately given, but rather inferred from firmer data comprising the values of the attribute variables in terms of which $\underline{W}s$ is described, which is why we are also interested in $Tr(\underline{W}s/\underline{C}s \times \underline{D}s \times \ldots)$. This is a complicated matter of empirical psychology or naturalized epistemology (Kornblith 1987), which we cannot further pursue here. As far as cost is concerned, it is to be noted that what is feasible to determine is what can be determined at reasonable cost, where cost includes time and effort as well as money. One such cost factor entered into our discussion of splitting and lumping, where we noted that lumping usually somewhat decreases the informativeness of a classification, but this may be justified by a decrease in the difficulty of applying the simpler classification.

The interesting point here is that cost and utility can themselves be fitted into the mathematical picture, in that the uncertainties that are reduced by transmitted information are in fact negative utilities. The key idea is that utility is a matter of mathematical expectation (cf. Raiffa and Schlaifer 1961), and it applies to variables like $\underline{C}s$ according to the following formula:

(6) $V(\underline{C}s) = P(C_1s) V(C_1s) + P(C_2s) V(C_2s).$

In effect, the expected value of sherd construction (or, more properly, vessel construction) is equal to the probability of being wheel-made times the informational value transmitted by this method of construction, plus the probability of being hand-made times the informational value transmitted by this method of construction. Replace $V(C_1s)$ and $V(C_2s)$ by $\log P(C_1s)$ and $\log P(C_2s)$ respectively, and we have $-U(\underline{C}s)$ (equation 1), which shows that uncertainty is a kind of disutility or negative utility that one hopes to reduce by gathering information.

The foregoing suggests that transmitted information generalizes to define transmitted utility. Thus, replacing U everywhere with $-V$ in equation (3) yields:

(7) $Tr_V(\underline{C}s/\underline{D}s) = V(\underline{C}s \times \underline{D}s) - V(\underline{C}s) - V(\underline{D}s).$

$Tr_V(\underline{C}s/\underline{D}s)$ is the expected amount by which the value of $\underline{C}s$ is increased as a result of learning the value of $\underline{D}s$, and it reduces to $Tr(\underline{C}s/\underline{D}s)$ when $V = -U$. It cannot be negative and is generally positive in cases where pure information is the only value in question, but it can become negative when costs are factored in. This consideration explains why lumping can have a positive value when costs are included, even though it cannot increase information. Rosenkrantz (1977) and Raiffa and Schlaifer (1961) give details about related phenomena, which cannot be entered into here, but we will conclude by drawing attention to a famous theorem by Good (1967), showing that when V measures the practical value of information, and costs are negligible, then $Tr_V(\underline{C}s/\underline{D}s)$ must also be non-negative. This obviously applies to the value of determining provenience dates, which we have so far taken as given and have not tried to justify.

One of the reasons for estimating provenience dates is that the estimates influence practical decisions, and in particular where to dig next in archaeological excavations (see especially Chapter 11). Now, expected utility also applies to actions like excavating, and one can calculate the expected utility of acting prior to obtaining information as against that of waiting for information before deciding where to dig. The thrust of Good's Theorem (Good 1967) is just this: provided it costs nothing to obtain information, the expected value of acting in the light of information can never be less than that of acting blindly, and it will naturally be greater if there is some chance that the information could lead the actor to change his decision, for example about where to dig next. However, this must be carefully qualified, as shown by Adams and Rosenkrantz (1980).

PART V

CLASSIFICATION, EXPLANATION, AND THEORY

The danger of premature closure of a conceptual structure is illustrated again and again in the history of science. Absolutely fixed concepts are always premature. Precision is not an end in itself but a means for the construction of mathematical models and the application of computer technology. Tolerance of ambiguity is as much a mark of scientific maturity as of emotional maturity.

Abraham Kaplan (1984: 31)

22

THE TYPOLOGICAL DEBATE

In the nineteenth century, prehistorians in the Old World were already much concerned with issues of cultural chronology. Inspired by the success of paleontologists and geologists in their use of the "index fossil" concept (Daniel 1964: 33–4), prehistorians began to make use of certain stone tool types and pottery types to indicate the age of deposits in the same way (see Childe 1956: 59; Rouse 1972: 126; Brown 1982: 181). The use of type concepts therefore has a long history in the Old World (cf. Gorodzov 1933; Clark 1957: 134–8; Chang 1967: 8; Klejn 1982: 38–50). In the New World, however, it was generally supposed that the native inhabitants were fairly recent immigrants from Asia, and hence that there was no significant time depth in American culture history. Consequently, there was more interest in the spatial than in the temporal variations of culture, and for this kind of ordering type concepts were not particularly important. N. C. Nelson in the Galisteo Basin was probably the first archaeologist in North America to make systematic use of type concepts for dating purposes (Nelson 1916), and the practice did not become general until a decade later.

Once they had become aware of the possibilities, however, Americans soon made up for the deficiency in their earlier use of type concepts. The late 1920s and the 1930s witnessed an enormous proliferation of arrowhead, pottery, and other typologies; indeed, more than half of the typologies in use today were probably formulated originally during that period. This outburst of activity set the stage for what has come to be called the Typological Debate (Hill and Evans 1972: 231–2; Hayden 1984: 81) – a continuing dispute between the adherents of "natural" and "artificial" classification, of lumping and splitting, of object clustering and attribute clustering, of induction and deduction, and other issues and non-issues that we will consider in the next chapter. Before doing so, however, we need first to contextualize those issues by looking at the historical circumstances in which they arose.

Dunnell (1986) has recently published a very comprehensive review and analysis of the Typological Debate, which makes it unnecessary for us to do the same here. We will confine ourselves in this chapter to a brief and summary consideration of four successive theoretical and methodological phases in the history of American archaeology, showing how each one influenced the theory if not the practice of artifact classification in its own time. In the next chapter we will consider a number of the specific issues that were raised, and how they relate to our own perspectives on artifact classification.

It is important to notice that the Typological Debate has raged almost entirely at the level of theory. In many areas and for many purposes the actual practice of artifact classification continues to function today much as it did fifty years ago. But the study of prehistory, especially in North America, has become increasingly theory-driven over the years. Prehistorians have come to insist that it is not enough for typologies to work in practice; they should also be consistent with currently prevalent theoretical paradigms. In this chapter, therefore, we will review the succession of four paradigms, or orientations, that have influenced the theory of artifact classification: the classificatory, the configurational/functional, the nomothetic, and the electronic. We must reiterate that our discussion relates specifically to the literature on archaeological classification, which may or may not bear much relation to what was concurrently going on in practice. (It should be noted that our periodization of American archaeological development does not exactly correspond with that of other authors, such as Willey and Sabloff 1974. For a critique of all such periodizations see Schuyler 1971.)

The debate that will concern us here has been conducted largely though not exclusively by Americans, who in general have been more theory-oriented than their European colleagues. There may, however, be other typological debates in French, German, and other languages, that we have overlooked, because of our unfamiliarity with the literature in those languages. (See, however, Gardin 1980 and Klejn 1982, and their respective bibliographic references.)

The classificatory phase

Fairly early in the history of every discipline, there comes a point where the unsystematic accumulation of raw data demands a major effort at systematization, before any further progress can be made. In the field of American ethnology, this was the challenge that faced John Wesley Powell when he launched the fledgling Bureau of American Ethnology in 1879 (cf.

Stegner 1982: 258–63). Powell had been trained in natural science, and from that perspective he correctly perceived that the most immediate need in ethnology was to sort out the tangle of North American Indian tribes, bands, confederations, and whatnot that were known in the literature under a truly bewildering variety of names. The first job was simply to discover who was who. For more than thirty years Powell and his successor W. H. Holmes directed the energies of the Bureau into what was in effect a vast classificatory exercise, identifying the basic units for later and more detailed studies (cf. Hallowell 1960: 56–8; Hinsley 1981: 145–89). The results were the monumental Handbooks (Powell 1891; Hodge 1907; 1910; Boas 1911a; 1922; Holmes 1919; Kroeber 1925; Steward 1946–1959) that are still appearing today in the form of the *Handbook of North American Indians*. This enormous classificatory effort laid the necessary foundations for all subsequent work in North American ethnology, whether historical, functionalist, configurationist, or ethnoscientific.

American archaeologists did not arrive at the same point until about forty years later. Early archaeological studies in North America were either minutely particularized or sweepingly general; there was seemingly no middle ground. Archaeologists dug and reported on individual sites without being able to contextualize the data in any meaningful way, other than with reference to a highly generalized picture of "prehistoric Indian life." It was not until well into the twentieth century that they began systematically to sort out the tangle of prehistoric cultures and horizons, as Powell and his cohorts had earlier sorted out the tangle of living and recently extinct peoples.

The period from the 1920s until the 1950s was devoted very largely to long overdue classificatory efforts (Willey and Sabloff 1974: 88–130). The 1930s were particularly active, and must surely be acknowledged as one of the most productive eras in the history of American prehistoric archaeology. During that decade a very large part of the basic time and space grid was erected, which has been essential to the contextualization of archaeological data ever since (see especially Bennett 1943: 208–9).

To measure how much was accomplished in a decade, we need only compare Edgar L. Hewett writing about prehistoric Southwesterners in 1930 with John McGregor writing about the same peoples in 1941. Hewett had spent a lifetime digging in Anasazi ruins, yet in his one major work of synthesis, *Ancient Life in the American Southwest* (1930), he was able to present only a generalized portrait of ancient pueblo life. By the time of McGregor's *Southwestern Archaeology* (1941), however, we already have the Hohokam, the Mogollon, and the Anasazi, the subdivision of the latter into Kayenta, Mesa Verde, Chaco, and Little Colorado regional variants, and the variously named chronological subdivisions of each of the cultures. All over the continent the same thing was happening in the same decade, thanks to the McKern Midwest Taxonomic Method (McKern 1939) and other systematics. In one way or another a large part of the archaeological enterprise of the 1920s and 1930s was devoted to classification; first of artifacts, houses, and burials individually, and then of combinations of those things into "cultures."

It has sometimes been suggested that the dominant orientation in American archaeology before 1940 was purely historical (Flannery 1967; Martin 1971; Leone 1972), but this is not entirely accurate. Archaeologists of the early twentieth century were interested first and foremost simply in the definition of cultural units, and secondly in discovering their distributions both in time and in space (cf. Willey and Sabloff 1974: 42–130). What they primarily sought was to bring order out of the chaotic tangle of prehistoric remains that their field investigations were bringing to light. According to Thomas Kuhn's (1962) formulation this phase in the development of any science is pre-paradigmatic; we should therefore technically refer to the classificatory period as a phase rather than as a paradigm.

During this formative era in American prehistoric archaeology it may be said that there were dozens of typological debates, but no Typological Debate. That is, field workers argued heatedly over the "reality" and the characteristics of particular types (cf. Gladwin 1943: 49–54; Brew 1946: viii). At the same time no one questioned the validity or value of the typological enterprise itself, when it was so evidently serving what were then the basic goals of archaeology. If we can say that prehistoric archaeology is always, figuratively speaking, a dog that is wagged by some kind of theoretical or methodological tail (see Chapter 23), then in the early twentieth century the tail that wagged the dog was classification.

The configurational/functional paradigm
In the mid-twentieth century two rival paradigms emerged in the field of ethnology: those of functionalism and of configurationism. The former was wholly predominant in the British Isles, but had its adherents in North America as well. Configurationism was, however, a somewhat stronger intellectual current among the Americans. It was a logical outgrowth of Boasian ethnology, and had its roots ultimately in nineteenth-century German *Geisteswissenschaft* (see especially Harris 1968: 267–71, 316–18; Service 1985: 290–1; Kuper 1988: 149–51).

At least in theory, the functionalist and configurationist approaches were markedly distinct. The functionalists in general took society rather than culture as their unit of analysis, their outlook was generally though not universally materialist, and they were proportionately more interested in what people did than in what they thought or said. Insofar as they were interested in culture, they thought of it mainly in terms of behavior patterns. The configurationists on the other hand took culture as their unit of analysis, they were strongly mentalistic, and they were more interested in what people thought and said than in what they did. Insofar as they were interested in collective behavior, it was mainly as an expression of underlying thought patterns. A later generation would say that the functionalists were interested in etic and the configurationists in emic explanations (see Chapter 23), although these terms did not come into general use until the 1960s. (For fuller discussion see Service 1985: 229–319.)

The most popular and widely read advocates of configurationism were Ruth Benedict and Margaret Mead, but its leading theoretician was undoubtedly Clyde Kluckhohn (cf. Kluckhohn 1939; 1950; 1951; Kluckhohn and Mowrer 1944; Kluckhohn and Kelly 1945; also Parsons and Vogt 1962). As it happened, Kluckhohn was also one of the few configurationists who had some training in archaeology (see Kluckhohn and Reiter 1939), though he soon turned his back on it. Throughout the late 1930s and 1940s he became increasingly critical of his archaeological colleagues because they did not seem to be doing what he and other configurationists were doing in ethnology: finding the behavioral significance and/or the cultural meaning of the phenomena that were actually observed (cf. Kluckhohn 1939 and 1940). Kluckhohn may be said to have launched the Typological Debate among archaeologists when he wrote in 1939 (338) that "typologies are proliferated without apparent concern for what the concepts involved are likely to mean when reduced to concrete human behaviors."

Whether or not archaeologists in the mid-century era were stimulated specifically by Kluckhohn's criticisms, they were certainly influenced by the broader theoretical currents of configurationism and functionalism that were then prevalent. As Bennett (1943: 210) observed, "The currents of American anthropology in general have shaped the interests of archaeologists." Many typologists now began to insist that they really were finding the inner cultural meanings or the behavioral significance in their data; that is, they were defining types that would somehow have been meaningful within the context of the cultures being studied. In one way or another this view was expressed by nearly all the earliest contributors to the Typological Debate: Rouse (1939 and 1960), Krieger (1944), Spaulding

(1953), Steward (1954), and Chang (1967). The most vocal exponent of the new viewpoint was however W. W. Taylor (1948), who had been a student of Kluckhohn's.

In archaeology, unlike ethnology, no clear distinction between configurationism and functionalism ever emerged, because the archaeologists tended to lump together the three different aspects of cultural phenomena that Linton (1936: 401–21) had called "function," "use," and "meaning." Put more simply, they believed that the way things were made, and the uses to which they were put, gave *a priori* evidence of the intent of the makers; thus a behavioral function was, *a priori*, evidence of a configuration of thought. The ultimate goal in artifact classification, then, was to discover the intent, or cultural preference, of the artifact makers through the study of their products. As Spaulding (1953: 305) put it, "classification into types is a process of discovery of combinations of attributes favored by the makers of the artifacts."

Similar reasoning is reflected in Taylor's assertion that "There is a most definite and important distinction to be made between empirical and cultural categories. The former include such rubrics as *Stone, Bone, Objects of Copper, Environment.* The latter include *Food, Dress, Hunting, Textile Industry, Utilization of Environment, Containers, Transportation*" (Taylor 1948: 114; emphasis in original). The use of the term "cultural categories" suggests that Taylor thought he was describing what today we would call emic categories; that is, categories that would have been meaningful within the cultures being studied. In reality, as J. A. Ford (1954b) pointed out a little later, he was simply expressing the archaeologist's own conception of functional categories. Whether or not the makers and users of the items would have categorized them in the same way is problematical (cf. Hayden 1984). The tendency to equate functional with emic categories is observable also in Rouse (1939; 1960) and Krieger (1944). Thus Willey and Sabloff (1974: 131–77) have chosen to characterize the mid-century archaeological paradigm as functionalist, while we think of it as having at the same time a strong configurationist component, reflecting the influence of contemporary American ethnology. (For further evidence of the conflation of function and configuration see Steward and Setzler 1938; Bennett 1943.)

The two principal voices raised against the configurationists-cum-functionalists were those of J. O. Brew and James A. Ford. Brew (1946: 44–66) recognized clearly that typologies are made by typologists for specific purposes; indeed he wrote that "we need more rather than fewer classifications, different classifications, always new classifications, to meet new needs" (*ibid.*: 65). Brew also denied that there is a legitimate analogy between biological and archaeological classification (*ibid.*: 44–66). The principal deficiency in his work was his failure to distinguish between artifact typologies and "culture" classifications, which he apparently viewed only as a difference of scale (see our discussion in Chapter 18).

Closely similar views were expressed by J. A. Ford (1954a; 1954b; 1962: 11–17). Like Brew he insisted that types are made by typologists, not by nature or by God. It was Ford who first pointed out the prevailing confusion between functional and emic significance, not only among archaeologists but among ethnologists as well (J. A. Ford 1954b; see also Chang 1967: 5–15). That is, the typical chapter categories in an ethnography do not really represent people's own way of thinking about their cultures; they represent the functional categories of the ethnologist himself.

Ford was unhesitating in his assertion that the primary purpose of artifact types was what it had always been: to help in the temporal and spatial ordering of data: "This tool is designed for the reconstruction of culture history in time and space. This is the beginning and not the end of the archaeologist's responsibility" (J. A. Ford 1954b: 52).

The nomothetic paradigm

In the 1960s, a number of circumstances combined to turn archaeology in a new and avowedly a more scientific direction. One factor was simply the youth revolution of that era, which encouraged a generation of young archaeologists to question and often to reject the goals of their predecessors. Another was the enormous prestige that natural science had enjoyed during and after World War II. Finally and perhaps most importantly there was the creation of the National Science Foundation, which within a decade became the principal funder of prehistoric research in North America (Patterson 1986: 16; WYA n.d.2).

Under these influences, a whole generation of archaeologists became self-consciously scientific. They went to great lengths to insist that archaeology must be scientific or it must be nothing; Lewis Binford (1968: 27) even hinted darkly at the "enforced obsolescence of . . . traditional theory and method." Moreover, they insisted that every individual procedure in archaeology, including classification, must be scientific. There was, as Levin (1973: 387) put it, a "supposition that inadequacies in the current state of archaeology, which are in reality matters of factual ignorance, can be remedied by methodological techniques." This self-proclaimed "revolution in archaeology" (Martin 1971) ushered in what we have called the nomothetic paradigm (see also Willey and Sabloff 1974: 178–211).

The self-styled New Archaeologists drew their notions of what is and is not scientific largely from the philosopher C. G. Hempel (especially 1965; 1966). Above all, in their view, science involved causal propositions, to be formulated and tested in the form of deductive hypotheses (cf. Binford 1965; Fritz and Plog 1970; Leone 1972). This basic touchstone of legitimacy was applied to classification and typology along with all other archaeological procedures. (For criticism of this approach see Salmon 1982: 39–42; Renfrew 1984: 14–19; Kelley and Hanen 1988: 167–224; WYA n.d.2.) But while the New Archaeologists were unanimous in the view that the classification ought to be scientific, they were less clear about what was needed to make it scientific. The Typological Debate in the 1960s revolved largely around this question.

Lewis Binford, the foremost champion of New Archaeology in America, has been insistent in his condemnation of all forms of traditional theory and method, including classificatory method (Binford 1965; 1968; 1972). Stripped of its rhetoric, however, his essentially functionalist approach to artifact classification (see especially 1972: 187–326) is not very different from that of Taylor and other would-be configurationists or functionalists in the previous generation. Indeed, Edmund Leach (1973: 761–2) pointed out that it is not very different from the functionalism of Malinowski in the 1930s. Other New Archaeologists, however, were more imaginative in their contributions to the Typological Debate. Hill and Evans (1972) and Read (1974) suggested that typologies themselves should be specifically designed for the testing of deductive hypotheses (see Chapter 23), while Fritz and Plog (1970: 407–8) went to the length of asserting categorically that functional classification is, *a priori*, a form of explanation, and therefore satisfies the canons of science laid down by Hempel. (For a rebuttal see Levin 1973.)

The most detailed and insightful discussion of classification by a New Archaeologist was not by an American but by the British David Clarke (1968: 187–229; 1978: 205–44). His views, however, were not entirely consistent, for Clarke had one foot in each of two paradigms: the nomothetic and the electronic (to be discussed in the next section). This ambiguous position led him to propound theoretical views that he did not follow in practice. Like many of the earlier Americans (e.g. Rouse 1939; Krieger 1944; Spaulding 1953) Clarke was a believer in types that were simultaneously "natural" and "functional" (cf. 1968: 138, 196); that is, he believed that types discovered through purely empirical procedures would automatically have functional significance. His position on this issue was essentially the same as that of Spaulding (1953; 1960). He did not, however, follow Spaulding (see especially 1982) and other Americans in equating "naturalness" with boundedness; on the contrary he wrote that "an artifact type has a reality which resides in a highly correlated inner core of attributes within an outer cloud or halo of attributes of decreasing levels of correlation" (*ibid.*: 196). Clarke was also one of the first archaeologists to recognize that most artifact types are polythetic (*ibid.*: 189–90).

At the same time Clarke was one of the earliest devotees of computerized classification, which in his time was more or less synonymous with Numerical Taxonomy (see *ibid.*: 512–634). He failed to recognize that Numerical Taxonomy programs generally do not yield types as he conceived of them; indeed they often do not yield types at all in a traditional sense (cf. Dunnell 1971b: 98–102; Klejn 1982: 65–6). The use and abuse of Numerical Taxonomy will occupy us further in the next section.

Among New Archaeologists, the principal voice raised against a nomothetic approach to classification was that of Robert Dunnell (1971a; 1971b; cf. also Deetz 1967: 45–52; Rouse 1970). It was not, unfortunately, what could be called a clarion voice. *Systematics in Prehistory* (Dunnell 1971b) is arguably the most important book on archaeological classification written up to its time, but it is certainly not the most readable. It is written in jargon so dense as to be in places almost impenetrable. Dunnell's five main theses however are clear enough: that classification is arbitrary, that qualification is more important than quantification, that classification specifies relationships only between units in the same system, that classes are not defined by the labels attached to them, and that classificatory units must be defined before they can be manipulated (*ibid.*: 46–59). He stresses also the importance of purpose in classifications (*ibid.*: 60–4), and recognizes that every approach to classification has its own strengths and weaknesses (*ibid.*: 70–110). Obviously, these are all points on which the present authors are in substantial agreement.

On the negative side, *Systematics in Prehistory* is so theoretically rarefied that it has only limited relevance to the real world. Thus it is possible to agree in principle with most of Dunnell's conceptions, while at the same time suggesting that in real life things are rarely that straightforward. The main point of difference between ourselves and Dunnell is that he does not recognize the dialectic factor: the continual feedback between objects and our conceptions of them that we see as a basic feature of typological concept formation (see Chapter 5). (For more extended critiques of Dunnell see Salmon 1982: 150–5, and Watson 1986: 444–6.)

The nomothetic paradigm in artifact classification had not proceeded very far when it was overtaken by the onrush of computer technology. In most areas of archaeology this was not an occasion for a radical paradigm shift, for theory in archaeology, as in most of social science, is largely independent of method. Computers for the most part were effectively adapted to the previously defined needs of nomothetic research design (but see WYA n.d.2). One field in which this did not hold true, however, was that of classification, which by its nature is methodological rather than theoretical.

The electronic paradigm

For the probabilistic social sciences, including economics, sociology, political science, and experimental psychology, the advent of computers came as a godsend. Scientific "proof" in these disciplines is necessarily statistical proof, and computers permit the use of far more and better statistics than were dreamed of in the pre-electronic age. On the other hand traditional anthropology has always been normative rather than probabilistic, and here statistics have played a much more limited role. Anthropologists nevertheless rushed to embrace the new electronic technology as readily as did sociologists and economists, perhaps in part because the inclusion of a computer application gives to any research project an aura of instant scientific respectability (cf. Thomas 1986: vi–vii).

At least in theory, computer applications are recognized as a means to an end rather than as ends in themselves. As long as this principle is adhered to, the introduction of computers is not likely to result in paradigmatic revolutions; the machines merely provide better and infinitely faster ways of achieving old goals. In general this has been true in archaeology, where all kinds of good and bad computer applications have been tried without significantly undermining existing paradigms. In the field of classification, however, computers have wrought such a fundamental change of direction that we are obliged to recognize a new, electronic paradigm beginning in the early 1970s. Unlike the three earlier paradigms, therefore, the electronic paradigm that we will discuss here is limited to the field of classification, and does not embrace other dimensions of archaeology. We have to reiterate that we are speaking only about developments in the programmatic literature, which since about 1970 has been devoted almost exclusively to the discussion of computerized clustering programs. The number of archaeologists who actually tried to use such programs in the field was probably never very large.

The special appeal of computer classification programs is that they are in theory "automatic" (cf. Doran and Hodson 1975: 158–86; Brown 1982:

183–5), eliminating finally the uncertainty and the indecision of human judgment. All variables are coded, none is weighted, and it is then left to the machine to discover which are the statistically strongest attribute clusters (cf. Voorrips 1982: 111). Computers seemed at last to bring within reach the long-elusive goal of objectivity in classification. Where earlier phases of the Typological Debate had concerned the legitimacy of individual types, or of particular uses of the type concept, the debate now became one over the legitimacy or utility of particular computer algorithms.

Archaeologists did not initially experiment with algorithms of their own. As they had done previously in the case of Hempel's philosophy and of General Systems Theory, they simply borrowed a set of established models from the biologists (see WYA n.d.2). These were the various programs of Numerical Taxonomy (Sneath 1962; Sokal and Sneath 1963; Sokal 1966; Sneath and Sokal 1973). All of the earliest computer applications by archaeologists involved Numerical Taxonomy in one form or another (e.g. Benfer 1967). David Clarke was also one of its early champions, and was the first to provide a detailed analysis of the new methodology in print (Clarke 1968: 512–634). (For a review of these and other archaeological applications see Doran and Hodson 1975: 173–85.)

Before long, however, some classifiers began to notice that many of the groupings produced by Numerical Taxonomy had no obvious meaning and no utility for any specifiable purpose (see Dunnell 1971b: 98–102). They then began to experiment with other clustering programs. As a result the Typological Debate reemerged in a wholly new form: as a debate between the continuing adherents of Numerical Taxonomy (Doran and Hodson 1975; Aldenderfer and Blashfield 1978) and those who had come to doubt its validity or utility and to experiment with other programs (Thomas 1972; Whallon 1972; Christenson and Read 1977).

At the present time there appears to be general though not universal disillusionment with Numerical Taxonomy (cf. Kronenfeld 1985), though no one for the moment has come up with a conspicuously more successful algorithm. But for better or worse the advocates of electronic classification remain wedded to their computers, even if they are less and less sure what to do with the results (cf. Whallon and Brown 1982: xv–xvi). Computerized classification as a result has become far more nearly an end in itself than was true of any earlier classificatory efforts. Kluckhohn's (1939: 338) admonition that "typologies are proliferated without apparent concern for what the concepts involved are likely to mean" is more apposite today than it was when the words were written half a century ago.

275

A French perspective

Standing rather apart from all of the paradigms heretofore discussed is the work of Jean-Claude Gardin, a French historical archaeologist. Over a quarter of a century he has published an extraordinary volume of writings on archaeological method and theory (see Gardin 1980: 188–90), of which the best known in English is *Archaeological Constructs* (1980). Here Gardin expresses a highly original and in some respects an offbeat view of the classificatory process, reflecting the fact that he comes from an intellectual tradition quite different from that of British and American prehistorians.

With reference to the purposes of archaeological classification, Gardin aligns himself with the American prehistorians of fifty years ago. He takes it for granted that the fundamental purpose of classifications is to aid in the reconstruction of culture history, and does not really consider other possibilities. His ideas, however, are expressed in the technical jargon and with the terminological formality of the nomothetic school. At the same time Gardin has been one of the earliest to introduce computer applications in French archaeology (Gardin 1962), without however overstating their importance. Unlike many American archaeologists he is not a computer addict; indeed computerized classification plays only a small part in his discussion (Gardin 1980: 38–40, 82–4).

Gardin's overall perspective on classification resembles our own, and differs from most other recent discussion, in that it focuses on field practice rather than on programmatic debates. Among many other things Gardin has recognized the roles played by foreknowledge (*ibid.*: 82), purpose (*ibid.*: 26), gestalts (*ibid.*: 11), representation (*ibid.*: 31–6), and extrinsic attributes (*ibid.*: 65–8). Above all he has been almost alone in recognizing the dialectical dimension in type-concept formation: the continual feedback between objects and our conception of them (*ibid.*: 62–90).

The principal limitation of Gardin's work is its failure to recognize other than historical reasons for classifying artifacts. As a result he is somewhat ambiguous as to the relationship between classification and explanation (*ibid.*: 76–80). Also, like most American commentators, he fails to distinguish between artifact typologies and "culture" classifications, moving back and forth between them as though the difference were purely one of scale (see Chapter 18). It remains to add that some of Gardin's conceptual terms (e.g. "construct") are not familiarly used by anglophones, and their meaning for us is not always precisely clear.

A Russian overview

The Russian archaeologist Leo Klejn is well known to British and American readers for a series of magisterial overviews (Klejn 1973a; 1973b; 1973c; 1977; 1982) in which he has surveyed the development of archaeological theory on both sides of the Atlantic and on both sides of the Iron Curtain. The most recent of his surveys is *Archaeological Typology*, of which the English translation was published in 1982 (Klejn 1982). One of the main virtues of this work, as of its various predecessors, is in putting Western readers in touch with a good deal of work, especially by Soviet archaeologists, that might otherwise escape their notice.

Archaeological Typology shares certain features and certain perspectives with the present work. It is, like our book, the work of a field archaeologist who is attempting to develop a theory of classification consistent with his own years of field experience. Klejn, too, recognizes that there is no general agreement on the definition of type or typology (*ibid.*: 18–19); that purpose plays a critical role in the formulation of types (*ibid.*: 51–3); that the belief that there is any one "best typology" is illusory (*ibid.*: 118–20); that polythetic types cannot be defined by their boundaries (*ibid.*: 58–64); that there is an important distinction between basic and instrumental types (which he calls respectively "empirical" and "conditional"; *ibid.*: 95–6); and that Numerical Taxonomy has serious deficiencies as a classificatory tool (*ibid.*: 64–6).

It must be acknowledged, however, that most of the aforementioned issues are not pursued at any great length, for *Archaeological Typology* is concerned much more with the classification of "cultures" than it is with the classification of artifacts. The author is concerned above all with developing a theory of "culture" classification as something fundamentally different from artifact classification, and something that cannot be arrived at simply by the pyramiding of artifact, grave, and house types (*ibid.*: 251–61; *contra* Willey and Phillips 1958: 40–3; Clarke 1968: 188). While we have made the same point in earlier pages (Chapter 19), Klejn has pursued the idea at much greater length than have we or any other authors (1982: 145–291), and this is by far the most original feature of his work.

23

ISSUES AND NON-ISSUES IN
THE TYPOLOGICAL DEBATE

In this chapter we want to identify some of the most important issues that have emerged in the course of the Typological Debate, and to discuss them in relation to our own point of view. Some of these are genuine issues that have been around as long as classification itself, and are certainly incapable of resolution. Others from our perspective are non-issues that have arisen through conceptual misunderstandings, or as a result of the intrusion of inappropriate theoretical considerations. The issues that are discussed here are obviously not all of equal importance, nor is the list comprehensive. In general we have selected for discussion those issues that are particularly relevant to our own interests.

Natural vs. artificial classification

This issue dominated the Typological Debate during its configurational/functional phase, but its origins are much older. In fact, it is surely the oldest and the most persistent of all classificatory controversies, tracing back in a certain sense to the age-old debate between "fixists," who believe in a settled order of things, and "fluxists," who do not. This question troubled both the Greek and the Chinese philosophers of ancient times (cf. Foucault 1973: 127–8).

The debate over natural vs. artificial classification was evidently flourishing in 1874, when W. S. Jevons published his path-breaking *Principles of Science*. Jevons wrote then that

> In approaching the question of how any group of objects may best be classified, let it be remarked that there must generally be an unlimited number of modes of classifying any group of objects. Misled . . . by the problem of classification in the natural sciences, philosophers often seem to think that in each subject there must be one essential natural classification which is to be selected, to the exclusion of all others. We shall naturally . . . select that classification which appears to be most convenient and instructive for our principal purpose.

278

But it does not follow that this system of classification possesses any exclusive excellence, and there will usually be many other possible arrangements, each valuable in its own way. (Jevons 1874, II: 348–9)

Three-quarters of a century later, G. G. Simpson (1945: 13) said much the same thing about biological classification: "If there were no disagreement as to the phylogeny of mammals . . . it would still be possible to base on that phylogeny a variety of classifications . . . certainly running into many millions, all different and all valid and natural in the sense of being consistent with phylogeny." (See also Lakoff 1984: 22–6.)

From our perspective all classifications are to a degree natural and to a degree artificial (cf. also Willey and Phillips 1958: 13). As Holland and Quinn (1987: 3) observe, "Undeniably, a great deal of order exists in the natural world we experience. However, much of the order we perceive in the world is there only because we put it there." By and large it is nature (or culture) that creates modalities, but it is the typologist who selects among them for his particular purposes. Every typological system is capable of generating a great many more phenetically recognizable types than are useful for any particular purpose (cf. Chapters 14 and 15). It is also very frequently, at least in the study of culture, the typologist who draws boundaries between the modalities, where culture has not created them.

Modalities, and even boundaries, are much more clearly apparent in some fields of classification than they are in others. Recognizing that "naturalness" is a matter of degree rather than an absolute (cf. also Ellen 1979: 8–12), we can go on to observe that some typologies are more nearly "natural" than others. But there can also be a great deal of variation in the degree of "naturalness" from one type to another in the same system. This is well exemplified in the Medieval Nubian Pottery Typology. Some of its types are so sharply distinct that the makers' intent seems clearly evident. Others are differentiated by such subtle criteria that the makers themselves may well have been unaware of them. But all the types have proved useful for dating purposes, and the degree of their "naturalness" is irrelevant to that purpose. As James Deetz (1967: 51) put it, "It may well be that some types are almost perfect descriptions of the templates responsible for them; whether this is true or not in no way interferes with the main aim of typology, that of classification which permits comparison."

The problem of typological boundaries

Closely associated with the issue, or non-issue, of natural classification is that of boundedness (cf. Rosch 1973; 1975; Klejn 1982: 58–64). The most natural type, it is often suggested, is the most sharply bounded one – hence the assertion that the typologist's job is to "find the seams in nature" (cf. Nelson, quoted in Krieger 1944: 273; Taylor 1948: 130; Spaulding 1982: 11). Almost certainly this reflects the "halo effect" of mammalian biology. The mammalian species is probably the closest thing there is to a true natural type, at least among living organisms (but see Diver 1940: 303; Simpson 1945: 22–4; Holsinger 1984), and for that reason it seems to be everyone's ideal model for what a type should be (cf. Colton and Hargrave 1937; J. A. Ford 1954a: 391; Krieger 1960: 141; Foucault 1973: 132). But the boundaries between species are the result of genetic inheritance and sexual reproduction, neither of which has any relevance to cultural phenomena.

Given the tendency of cultural phenomena to intergrade without sharp boundaries (cf. Kroeber 1964: 234; Clarke 1968: 191–2; R. Needham 1975: 364), it may often be that the most sharply bounded type is the most artificial one, not the most natural one. In the paradigmatic method of classification (see Dunnell 1971b: 70–6), it is easy for the classifier to group attributes *a priori*, and to specify in advance that any artifact exhibiting attributes A, B, and C belongs to Type ABC, while anything without those attributes does not. Such a type has clearly defined boundaries, but it would be hard to imagine anything more artificial.

As we have observed several times previously, boundaries are a practical need in the sorting process, not a theoretical need in classifying.

Lumpers and splitters

The division of typologists into general camps of lumpers and splitters has long been recognized (Kidder and Shepard 1936: xxv, 626; Judd 1940: 430; Simpson 1945: 22–4; Brew 1946: 55; Taylor 1948: 126–7), though it is of course a difference of degree and not of kind. However, it is not a difference that gives rise to fundamentally different schools, or approaches, to the formulation of basic typologies. It is rather a matter of individual variation among typologists, both in their perceptions and in their value orientations. Recognizing that types are defined by a combination of "internal cohesion and external isolation" (Cormack 1971: 329), we may suggest that splitters are proportionately more impressed by the appearance of internal cohesion, and lumpers by external isolation. It may also be that splitters have simply a sharper eye for differences than have lumpers, or they may have a lower tolerance for diversity. The result is that, given the same body of material to classify in the same way and for the same purposes, some typologists will always come up with more types than will others. (For a discussion of this problem in the fields of biology see especially Simpson 1945: 22–4.)

The issue of lumping vs. splitting becomes methodologically relevant when we talk about the taxonomic ordering of types, rather than their formulation (see Chapter 17). Taxonomies can be generated either entirely by lumping or entirely by splitting, or both (see Dunnell 1971b: 70–84; Everitt 1974: 8–24). We suggested in Chapter 17 that most practical taxonomies, which are formulated with reference to a specific purpose, are made by lumping (see also Mayr 1942: 11–17), while computer-generated taxonomies, which are formulated without reference to a purpose (see Dunnell 1971b: 97–8; Voorrips 1982: 111), are often made by a splitting process. The end results are entirely different in the two cases, since in lumping (agglomerative) taxonomies types are the beginning point, while in splitting (divisive) taxonomies they are the end point. This essential difference furnishes one more reason why the recent theoretical literature on computerized classification bears so little relation to actual practice (Dunnell 1986: 150).

Induction vs. deduction

W. S. Jevons (1874, II: 346) described the process of classifying as one of "perfect induction." At the opposite extreme, some New Archaeologists insisted that, to be scientifically valid, types should be formulated and used deductively (Fritz and Plog 1970: 407–8; Hill and Evans 1972: 252–68; Read 1974). However, the use of these two terms by archaeologists, and indeed by scientists in general, tends to be very loose and imprecise (e.g. Binford 1972: 89–91; Voorrips 1982: 98; for discussion see Salmon 1976). They refer properly to logical operations, not to methodological or scientific ones (cf. Levin 1973: 388). Hempel (1966: 14–15) argued that "pure" induction is a practical impossibility, but he could have said the same in regard to "pure" deduction. There can be no concept that is not ultimately based in someone's sensory experience, but there can also be no concept that does not relate to a purpose (cf. Vygotsky 1962: 54; Salmon 1976; Watson 1986: 451).

Types, as we have noted several times previously, have the necessary properties of identity and meaning. For the most part identity is arrived at through induction, and meaning through deduction. In the actual processes of classifying and sorting, as in practically all other human cognition, there is a continual feedback between the two reasoning processes, as we observed in Chapter 6 (see also Vygotsky 1962: 80; Gardin 1980: 88–9). Even Marvin Harris, one of the most insistent advocates of "pure" science, has acknowledged that "Science has always consisted of an interplay between induction and deduction, between empiricism and rationalism; any attempt to draw the line on one side or the other conflicts with actual scientific practice" (Harris 1980: 8). (For much more extended discussion of the complex and often misunderstood relationship between induction and deduction see Kelley and Hanen 1988: 44–59.)

Emic vs. etic classification

Would the artifact types designated by the archaeologist have been recognized as types by the people who made and used them? That is, do the types differ from each other because they were meant to be different? Should it be the main objective of the typologist to "discover" such differences? These were major issues during the configurational/functional phase of the Typological Debate. A later generation of archaeologists would refer to types that reflect the intent of their makers as emic types, in contrast to etic types which are designated purely for the heuristic convenience of the typologist. However, the terms "emic" and "etic" (originally coined by Kenneth Pike in 1954) did not come into general use until the 1960s; earlier archaeologists had been wont to speak of types as reflecting the mental templates of the makers (Deetz 1967: 45; see also Read 1982: 60–4; Watson, LeBlanc, and Redman 1984: 208–10).

Many contributors to the Typological Debate of the 1940s and 1950s suggested, or at least implied, that the typologist's proper task should be to discover what today we would call emic types (e.g. Rouse 1939: 11–12; 1960: 317–21; Krieger 1944: 278–9; 1960: 141; Taylor 1948: 113–51; Spaulding 1953: 305). The outlook of these authors clearly reflected the dominant influence of configurationism in the mid-century era. Spaulding (1953: 305) put the matter simply: "classification into types is a process of discovery of combinations of attributes favored by the makers of the artifacts, not an arbitrary procedure of the classifier." At the same time, the would-be configurationists were frequently critical of earlier archaeological typologies because the types did not necessarily relate to any intention or any consistent behavioral practices on the part of the makers. As Kluckhohn (1939: 338) had written, "typologies are proliferated without apparent concern for what the concepts involved are likely to mean when reduced to concrete human behaviors."

(We will not here pursue the somewhat vexed issue of whether the mid-century archaeologists were really interested in the mind-sets or in the habitual behaviors of artifact makers. They tended to speak mostly in behavioral terms, but it is clear also that they thought of habitual behavior as resulting from pre-existing mental norms, or templates. See especially Read 1982: 60–4.)

An obvious problem for the prehistoric archaeologist was to be sure that he had correctly divined the intentions of long-dead artifact makers. The solution proposed by Rouse (1939; 1960), Krieger (1944: 273), and Spaulding (1953) lay in the selection of variables and attributes to be included in the classification: they should be variables that were clearly referable to the influence of culture, or at least of individual habit. To quote again from Spaulding (1953: 305): "a properly established type is the result of sound inferences concerning the customary behavior of the makers of the artifacts and cannot fail to have historical meaning." Nevertheless, later archaeologists became increasingly doubtful about the possibility of discovering emic types (cf. Chang 1967: 6–17; Hodder 1982: 1–12; Read 1982: 60–1; Watson, LeBlanc, and Redman 1984: 208–10), and with the general decline of configurationism in the 1960s the emphasis on discovering emic types also declined (but see Dunnell 1971b; Read 1982).

Quite separate from the question of whether emic types are really discoverable, and much more relevant to our concerns, is the question of what purpose is served by such a classification. Interestingly, this issue was hardly raised during the 1940s and 1950s. It is evident that Rouse, Krieger, and Spaulding all continued, at least in the beginning, to think of classification primarily in historical terms – the dominant orientation of the preceding, classificatory era. But they now began to argue that the most useful types (indeed, the only legitimate types) for historical classification were what today we would call emic types: those that clearly reflected the intentions of the makers (Krieger 1944: 273; Spaulding 1953: 305). Such types, according to Spaulding (*ibid.*), "cannot fail to have historical meaning."

From our perspective, the advocates of emic typology in the midcentury era were confounding two quite separate purposes in artifact classification, one basic and the other instrumental (see Chapter 13). They wanted to designate types that would reflect the mind-sets or the behavioral practices of artifact makers, but at the same time would be useful in the reconstruction of culture history. Their mistake was in assuming that what is useful for one purpose must necessarily be useful for the other, and that what will not serve one purpose will not serve the other. It may be true that emic types must necessarily have historical meaning, but this is true also of many purely etic types (cf. Deetz 1967: 51). The Nubian Pottery Typology includes many types that clearly were meant to be distinctive by their creators, and many others that probably resulted from accidental and unconscious factors, but the historical significance of all of them is demonstrated by their predictable distributions in time and space.

From our viewpoint the practice of emic classification (that is, the construction of typologies composed entirely of emic types) is clearly relevant to the broader goal of reconstructing the mind-sets of extinct peoples – though whether this is really attainable in practice remains debatable (cf. Chang 1967: 6–17; Hodder 1982: 1–12; Watson, LeBlanc, and Redman 1984: 208–10). On the other hand it is not necessarily relevant to any other goal. The utility of supposedly emic types for other than emic purposes cannot be assumed *a priori*; it can only be established experimentally (cf. Read 1982). In reality it will probably be found that most archaeological typologies, like the Nubian Pottery Typology, include types of widely varying emic significance.

This brings us to the final observation that "emicness," or emic significance, is really a matter of degree. Presumably any consistent difference between artifact groups which can be recognized by archaeologists could also have been recognized by the makers and users of the artifacts, but there is nothing to indicate how important those differences would have been considered. Probably some of them would have been regarded as vital, and others as trivial (cf. Hayden 1984: 86).

Formal vs. functional classification

Are the artifact types designated by the archaeologist indicative of different intended or actual uses of the artifacts? Should it be the goal of the archaeologist to "discover" types that were meant for different purposes (that is, functional types), rather than to distinguish them purely on the basis of form attributes (cf. Taylor 1948: 122–3; Chang 1967: 7–17; Deetz 1967: 79–80)? In the mid-century era these questions were closely bound up with the issue of emic classification; indeed, some archaeologists seem to have confused functional with emic classification. This is clearly implicit in Taylor's (1948: 114) assertion that "cultural categories . . . include *Food, Dress, Hunting, Textile Industry, Utilization of Environment, Containers, Transportation*" (emphasis in the original) and his further assertion (*ibid.*: 122) that cultural categories "relate to the world of bygone peoples." As J. A. Ford (1954b) pointed out a little later, Taylor's "cultural categories" are really functional categories in the archaeologist's own culture; they might or might not have been considered significant by the artifact makers and users.

There are nevertheless good reasons for making a purely functional classification, if our interest in artifacts is primarily for what they can tell us about prehistoric activity patterns. It must at the same time be recognized that function is an inferential variable (see Chapter 14); that is, it is an inference made by the archaeologist himself, mostly on the basis of the observable form of the artifact. Consequently there is no real dichotomy between functional and formal classification (*contra* Taylor 1948: 122–3); functional classification merely involves the consideration of certain specific attributes of form and not others.

A practical difficulty arises from the fact that there is often no reliable way of inferring the function of prehistoric artifacts. Potsherds are often too small to permit an identification of the original vessel form (cf. Keighley 1973), while in the case of many stone tool types we simply do not know precisely what function they performed. Categories such as "scraper," "chopper," and "graver" have been given names indicative of a presumed function, but in reality these tool types are differentiated on the basis of form attributes, not on the basis of any secure knowledge of their use. For these and other reasons it is rare to find basic artifact typologies that are genuinely and exclusively functional. Most typologies probably include some types that performed clearly distinct functions, and others that did not.

Functional classification in archaeology is much more often encountered at higher taxonomic levels than at the level of basic typology. That is, types that were differentiated at least partly on morphological grounds are grouped, for descriptive or interpretive purposes, into larger taxa on the basis of a presumed affinity of function. Thus in published archaeological reports it is common to find chapters on hunting equipment, agricultural implements, and so on, in place of a purely morphological arrangement of chapters on objects of stone, objects of bone, etc. In practice, therefore, function in archaeological classifications is mainly a taxonomic issue, not a typological one.

Object clustering vs. attribute clustering

This seems to have been the most commonly debated issue of the electronic era; that is, since about 1970 (cf. Whallon and Brown 1982: xvi–xvii). Should types be formulated empirically by clustering objects (Doran and Hodson 1975: 102–3; Hodson 1982) or *a priori* by clustering attributes (Dunnell 1971b: 70–6; Spaulding 1982)? Or are they simply alternative means to the same end (Cowgill 1982; Read 1982; Voorrips 1982)?

In some respects the debate over object clustering vs. attribute clustering is only a new phrasing of a much older and more fundamental question: Are type concepts to be regarded as prescriptive or descriptive? If we make a cluster of attributes A, B, and C, and then say that any object possessing those attributes is an exemplar of Type ABC, then obviously the type concept is prescriptive. If we bring together a group of objects of similar appearance, find that they all possess attributes A, B, and C, and then say that other objects that appear similar will probably also possess attributes A, B, and C, then the concept is descriptive.

It should be obvious from the discussion in Chapters 6 and 15 that the present authors are not in agreement with the proponents either of exclusive object clustering or of exclusive attribute clustering. We see the making and use of practical typologies as involving a continual feedback between things and our ideas about them; that is to say between entities and concepts. Object clustering and attribute clustering are therefore not separate means to the same end; they are both part and parcel of the same process. Every type concept must be communicated in the form of a list of descriptive attributes, but the concept has no utility unless and until it has been applied to a group of objects. When that happens, the attributes exhibited by the objects themselves will modify our understanding of the definition of the type. Vygotsky (1962: 52–81) and Margolis (1987: 91, 115) have argued that this is an essential feature of all human concept formation. (For a parallel argument in regard to biological classification see Gilmour 1951: 402.)

As long as the dialectic between concepts and entities takes place, it does not matter in theory whether it begins with a conscious act of object clustering or with an act of attribute clustering. We have suggested however (Chapter 5) that it is usually necessary to have at least a collection of material to start with; otherwise the typologist is not likely to know what attributes are available to be clustered. And if the collection exhibits some intuitively obvious types, it is more than probable that these will be differentiated before any attempt at conscious attribute analysis is made. In this sense we are suggesting that the making of typologies most commonly starts with object clustering.

Many of the earlier practical typologists seem to have agreed, at least implicitly, with our dialectical approach to object clustering and attribute clustering (e.g. J. A. Ford 1962: 13–15; Shepard 1965: 306). It is noteworthy that the difference between the two approaches has become polarized only in the last fifteen years; that is to say, in the computer era. When types are to be generated by a computer clustering program, there must obviously be an *a priori* choice as to what data units are to be coded. This is one of several reasons why, as we will suggest later, useful typologies can rarely be generated by any of the currently available computer programs.

Paradigmatic and taxonomic classification

In his influential 1971 book, *Systematics in Prehistory*, Robert Dunnell presents what he calls a "classification of classifications" (Dunnell 1971b: 69–86). In fact only two kinds of classifications are included, which the author calls paradigmatic (*ibid.*: 70–6) and taxonomic (*ibid.*: 76–84). Paradigmatic classification is tantamount to attribute clustering, which we have discussed in the preceding section. Taxonomic classification, in Dunnell's usage, refers to any classificatory system in which types are generated by the subdivision of larger clusterings, either of objects or of attributes.

Like much of the discussion in *Systematics in Prehistory*, the distinction between paradigmatic and taxonomic classification seems more relevant at the level of theory than at the level of practice. It is evident to us that no very useful typology could be generated exclusively by either process. Both systems would be likely to generate far more types than would be manageable or useful for any purpose, and in addition the constituent types would be entirely lacking in flexibility.

Even at the theoretical level, it seems to us that Dunnell has lumped together and dichotomized what are in reality a number of different and rather complex issues. Taxonomic classification is necessarily hierarchical, whereas paradigmatic classification may or may not be. Paradigmatic types are formulated exclusively by attribute clustering, while taxonomic types may be formulated by subdividing either object groups or attribute groups. The most consistent basis of distinction seems to be that paradigmatic types are defined entirely by internal cohesion, while taxonomic types are defined entirely by external isolation. But we believe, following Cormack (1971: 329) and many others, that all useful types have a measure of both.

"Empiricist" and "positivist" approaches

This was a distinction proposed by Hill and Evans in "A model for classification and typology" (1972). Their choice of terms was perhaps ill-advised, since both "empiricist" and "positivist" may have more than one meaning.

As defined by the authors, "empiricism" and "positivism" were to some extent new names for the old doctrines of "natural" and "artificial" classification, which we discussed earlier. The "empiricist" school "holds to the metaphysical notion that all phenomena (including artefacts) have meanings or significance inherent in some sense within themselves" (*ibid.*: 233). "The positivist view is that phenomena do *not* have inherent or primary meanings to be discovered. Rather, any phenomenon, or set of phenomena, is assigned meaning by the human mind, and it may be assigned as many different meanings as the investigator chooses to give it" (*ibid.*: 252). The authors did acknowledge at another point that artifacts could have both inherent meanings and additional meanings assigned to them by the investigator (*ibid.*: 246). Like many archaeologists at the time, however, they failed to distinguish between the meaning of artifacts as entities and their meaning as types (see Chapter 24).

In theory, then, "positivist" classifications are all those formulated in relation to some purpose. "The positivist *begins* his work with his problems, tentative inferences or hypotheses about the materials he is observing or has observed, and then proceeds to select the kinds of attributes he feels will lead to typologies that will be useful for his particular analysis" (*ibid.*: 253). In practice, however, "positivist" classification as advocated by Hill and Evans referred exclusively to classifications that had been made in order to test hypotheses (e.g. Longacre 1964; 1970; Deetz 1965; Hill 1966; 1970). A hypothesis was stated, and types were then formulated for the purpose of testing it. If the hypothesis was not confirmed, however, it was never made entirely clear whether this reflected on the validity of the hypothesis, or on the validity of the proposed types.

"Empiricism," in the usage of Hill and Evans, really became a residual catchall for all classifications that had not been designed to test hypotheses, whether they were "natural" or "artificial," emic or etic, formal or functional. In one way or another the "empirical" category seemed to include just about all of the classifications then in existence, except their own.

Obviously we are not in disagreement with the main thesis of Hill and Evans, that typologies should be developed with reference to some clearly understood purpose. We would, however, contend that most of them are, at least to some degree, and that the distinction between "positivist" and "empiricist" approaches is more apparent than real. All typologies are "positivist" to the extent that they are developed for some recognized or unrecognized purpose which affects the choice of variables and/or types for inclusion (see Chapter 13). All of them are also "empiricist" insofar as their types work for their intended purpose, which indicates that they must possess some degree of inherent "reality" (see Chapter 6). The distinction made by Hill and Evans applies more legitimately to archaeologists' perceptions of what they are doing than to what they are actually doing. (For further criticism see Klejn 1982: 120–5.)

Our main disagreement with Hill and Evans is, however, at the level of practice. There can be no possible justification, either theoretical or practical, for asserting that the only legitimate "positivist" classifications are those designed to test a hypothesis. This is tantamount to saying that hypothesis-testing is the only purpose for which classifications can legitimately be made. Type concepts, like all concepts, are formulated in reference to some problem (cf. Vygotsky 1962: 54), but there are many problems that cannot be stated in the form of a testable hypothesis (cf. Renfrew 1984: 16–18). Hill and Evans, however, were bowing to the prevalent belief in the 1970s that all archaeology must be scientific, and that scientific archaeology must involve hypothesis-testing (see Chapter 22). In Chapter 25 we will argue, on the contrary, that causal propositions *cannot* be unambiguously confirmed by any classificatory process.

Free, guided and imposed constructions

These terms, unfamiliar to most English-speaking archaeologists, were introduced by the French archaeologist J.-C. Gardin in his 1980 book, *Archaeological Constructs* (Gardin 1980: 81–9). "Free constructions" in Gardin's usage are "objective" classifications (primarily those generated by computer) that are unrelated to any purpose. The author shares our view that types formulated in this fashion have little practical value (*ibid.*: 84).

Much more interesting is Gardin's distinction between what he calls "guided constructions: induced typologies" and "imposed constructions: deduced typologies" (*ibid.*: 84–9). At issue here are the respective roles of intrinsic and extrinsic attributes in the definition of types (see Chapter 14). In "guided constructions," according to Gardin, we designate classes of like objects which, because of their morphological similarities, we assume to have been made at the same time and/or in the same area. We then have to determine empirically, through distribution studies, whether or not this is true. In other words intrinsic attributes are the initial basis of type designation, while extrinsic attributes have to be discovered empirically. Although Gardin does not pursue the point, we may infer that, if a common distribution in time and/or space is not found, the "induced types" are no longer to be considered as types.

In "imposed constructions: deduced typologies" the facts of time and space distribution are known in advance. The archaeologist's task is then to discover if artifacts having a common distribution also have morphological features in common. In other words extrinsic attributes come first, and intrinsic attributes must be sought. (Incidentally, Gardin takes it for granted that all archaeological typologies are made in the broadest sense for purposes of historical reconstruction; hence the meaning of types is equated with distributional significance.)

From a theoretical perspective, the interesting feature of Gardin's "induced–deduced" dichotomy is that it relates to the relative importance of what we have called identity and of meaning (Chapter 3) as criteria of type definition. "Induced" types (we will continue to use Gardin's terms, although we are not entirely happy with them) have clear morphological indices of identity, while meaning must be sought in the form of their temporal and/or spatial distributions. "Deduced" types have clear criteria of meaning in their known distributions, while morphological criteria of identity must be sought. At least by implication, therefore, it seems that "induced" types are defined more by identity than by meaning, while with "deduced" types the reverse is true. Gardin clearly believes, as we do, that types must necessarily have both identity and meaning, but so far as we know he is alone in raising the question of which comes first.

Gardin makes a sharp conceptual distinction between his "inductive" and "deductive" approaches, and suggests that the classificatory strategies are markedly different in the two cases (*ibid.*: 84–9). Elsewhere in his work, however, he has stressed, as we have, that classification really involves a continual feedback between induction and deduction (*ibid.*: 88). Following the same reasoning, we have to suggest that the distinction between "guided" and "imposed" constructions is of more interest theoretically than practically. In the actual formulation of provisional types (see Chapter 15) we will certainly make simultaneous use of both morphological and distributional evidence, to the extent that we have it available. Within the same typology, moreover, some types may be relatively more "guided" and others more "imposed." In the Medieval Nubian Typology, for example, the Ware Groups N.IV, N.V, and N.VI are defined more by morphological than by distributional criteria, while the wares in Groups N.II and N.VII are grouped together under one heading primarily because they were made at the same time and always occur together, though they do share some common morphological features as well.

Typology and statistics

In discussing this rather complex subject we must first reemphasize our distinction between basic typologies and taxonomies (see Chapter 17). There is a great deal of literature on the role of statistics in the development of classifications (see especially Doran and Hodson 1975; Orton 1982), but usually no distinction is made between typological and taxonomic classifications (cf. especiaily Dunnell 1971b: 65–86). In our view, and especially with reference to this particular issue, the difference is fundamental. We hold that the role of statistics in the making of basic, practical typologies is generally small, while in the making of taxonomies it may be much larger. Most of our concern in the present discussion will be with basic typologies, because it is primarily here that the role of statistical procedures appears to have been misunderstood.

Archaeologists have made use of relatively crude statistics, mostly of their own devising, at least since the beginning of the twentieth century (see, e.g., Petrie 1899). However, Albert Spaulding was apparently the first archaeologist to learn something of the methods of the professional statistician; that is, to acquire what today we would call "statistical literacy." With singular constancy he has argued, from 1953 onward (see, e.g., Spaulding 1982), that statistical procedures hold the answer to many of the problems of classification that we have discussed throughout this book. Since the advent of computers, his outlook has come to be shared by many other archaeological typologists as well (see especially Whallon and Brown 1982).

The statistical approach to classification generally involves three premises. First, types are defined by clusters of attributes. Second, before any attribute cluster can be accepted as definitive of a type, it must first be established that the attributes occur together with a certain degree of predictability (nonrandomly). Third, any nonrandom attribute cluster must be accepted as definitive of a type. (It is clear at least by implication that attributes may be selected by the typologist prior to the clustering process. Once the attributes have been selected, however, recurrent clusters of attributes cannot also be selected by the typologist. On the contrary, any consistent attribute cluster must be accepted as a type.)

It is important to notice that most advocates of statistical classification have not claimed complete objectivity for this approach. The initial choice of variables to be examined and attributes to be selected is left to the typologist (cf. Brainerd 1951: 117; Spaulding 1953; Shepard 1965: 332), and there is no suggestion that all attributes must be considered (*contra* Clarke 1968: 520–5; Sabloff and Smith 1969: 278). Statistical methods are thus seen as an addition and a corrective to traditional classificatory practice rather than as heralding a radically new methodology. There are, nevertheless, practical as well as theoretical difficulties involved in the statistical approach.

First, statistical significance is a matter of degree. Thomas (1978: 233; 1986: 463–4) reminds us that "confusing statistical significance with strength of association" is one of the archaeologist's most pervasive logical errors. As it happens, most of the statistical tests applied to attribute clusters by archaeologists (especially chi-square) are relatively weak measures of association (cf. Voorrips 1982: 123). Even when typologists are consciously aware of different strengths of association between different attribute clusters, moreover, they usually have no way of evaluating or interpreting the differences. An attribute cluster occurring in 97 percent of cases and one occurring in 37 percent of cases may be treated as equally nonrandom, and therefore equally definitive of types, while a cluster occurring in 17 percent of cases is random and therefore nondefinitive.

A second important consideration is that statistical tests do not reveal the *causes* of nonrandomness, the reasons why certain clusters of attributes regularly occur together. Thus, they indicate that a type is significant without suggesting why it is significant (cf. Thomas 1986: 460–1). In terms of the distinction that we made in Chapter 3, we may say that types defined solely on the basis of nonrandom attribute clusters have significance but no known meaning (cf. Sackett 1966).

A third point, which follows directly from the preceding, is that statistical significance is a necessary but not a sufficient condition for "typehood." In terms of the two essential properties of types, statistics provide (or more often verify) criteria of identity, but not of meaning. On the basis of statistical significance alone, most artifact typologies could generate literally thousands of types; that is, thousands of different and statistically significant attribute clusters (cf. Chang 1967: 81; Watson, LeBlanc, and Redman 1984: 204–7). But in any practical typology there will be a selection of those nonrandom types that are also readily distinguishable and/or are useful for the typologist's purpose.

So far as the formulation of basic types is concerned, we would conclude with the general observation that while statistical *principles* are important, statistical *procedures* usually are not. On the one hand, any type that the archaeologist can consistently recognize, and that is also found useful for his purpose, can be assumed *a priori* to be statistically significant (see especially Watson, LeBlanc, and Redman 1971: 127; 1984: 203, 212; Thomas 1978: 236). On the other hand any type for which no meaning can be discovered will not be retained in a practical typology, regardless of its statistical significance.

What has been said above applies only to the formulation of basic types. It obviously does not apply to the ordering of types, either by taxonomy or by seriation (see Chapter 17). These orderings are undertaken precisely to discover or to indicate the relationships between types, which cannot be indicated in a basic (one-level) typology. Since many typological relationships are quantitative, or capable of expression in quantitative terms, statistics have a large and legitimate role to play, as we saw in Chapter 17. From our perspective the uses of statistics in taxonomy and seriation are not controversial, and therefore do not require further discussion in the present chapter.

Typology and the computer

With the advent of computers, a whole generation of archaeologists became instant converts to statistical methodology, whether they realized it or not. In the field of classification, they rushed to embrace the new machines in the hope and expectation that they would solve age-old classificatory problems, and above all the problem of subjectivity (cf. Clarke 1968: 512–634; Doran and Hodson 1975: 158–86). The first archaeological publications involving computerized classification programs appeared in the late 1960s (Benfer 1967; Clarke 1968: 512–634); within five years the new methodology had come completely to dominate the literature on artifact classification.

Most of the earliest computer applications involved one or another of the programs of Numerical Taxonomy, which were borrowed *in toto* from the natural sciences (Sneath 1962; Sokal and Sneath 1963; Sokal 1966; Sneath and Sokal 1973). Later it became apparent that Numerical Taxonomy was not yielding very meaningful results, and archaeologists began experimenting with various other algorithms (e.g. Whallon 1972; Christenson and Read 1977). In general, however, these also have failed to live up to expectations. Archaeologists in the present day appear to be somewhat disillusioned with computerized classifications, but are by no means ready to give up on them. There is a continuing hope that computers can still overcome the age-old problem of subjectivity, if only the right algorithm can be found (cf. Brown 1982: 183–4).

Recent typological literature gives the impression that computers have simply become the tail wagging the dog of artifact classification. The would-be classifiers often understand their computers, mechanically and operationally, much better than they understand statistical theory, with the result that they are often using good tools for bad purposes (see especially Thomas 1978). As Thomas (1986: vi) has observed, "computers are seductive devices which tend to lure the unwary down the endless trail toward numerical obscurity." Numerical Taxonomy, for example, is an approach in which degrees of relationship between units are measured by the number of traits they share, without regard for what the traits are. This kind of purely numerical measurement is potentially appropriate to genetic classification, but has no relevance at all to non-genetic classification (see Chapter 17; also WYA n.d.2). To say that artifact Type A shares more traits with Type B than it does with Type C is a statement that is rarely if ever susceptible of any meaningful interpretation, yet it took archaeologists a decade of experimentation to find this out. (Even in the biological sciences, Simpson observed as long ago as 1945 [p. 8] that "simple tabulation of 'characters in common' is not a practical means of classification.")

A detailed critique of computer classification programs and their results would require discussion of each of the various algorithms that have been tried, for each has its own strengths and weaknesses (cf. Cormack 1971; Everitt 1974; Aldenderfer and Blashfield 1978: 503–4). Obviously such detailed consideration is beyond the scope of the present book, not to mention the expertise of its authors. At a more general level there is not much to be said about computerized classification that has not already been said, in the previous section, about statistical procedures in general. Like other statistical operations, computer programs cannot select attributes (cf. Shepard 1965: xii); they generally produce far more types than are useful for any purpose; and the types frequently have no specifiable meaning (cf. Dunnell 1971b: 97–8).

Above all, it is evident that computerized classification has failed to deliver the promised "objectivity" which in the beginning was its main attraction (see especially Clarke 1968: 512–634; Doran and Hodson 1975: 158–86). As Brown (1982: 183–4) acknowledged, "the automatic aspect of practical typological analysis seems to be receding rapidly . . . it is still necessary to introduce informed judgment at critical stages in the analysis to avoid pitfalls in the *data* that prevent satisfactory results" (emphasis added). (Nothing could better exemplify how the computer tail wags the classificatory dog than Brown's assumption that the pitfalls are in the *data* rather than in the method.)

Computers and statistics have not solved the most basic and immemorial problems of classification because these are, in the last analysis, problems of judgment and not of information or measurement (see Chapters 15 and 16). Decision-making of a complex order may be possible with the fifth-generation computers that are now under development, but it is beyond the capability of any machine or program currently in use. As Margolis (1987: 3) observes, "the most elaborate computerized character recognizer cannot yet match a bright six-year-old in recognizing letters of the alphabet from many different fonts. No computer, in fact, can yet match a well-trained pigeon in distinguishing pictures that contain some person from pictures that don't (Herrnstein *et al.* 1976; Abu-Mustafa and Psaltis 1987)." On this note it seems appropriate to close with a quotation from Cormack (1971: 346): "how in practice does one tailor statistical methods to the real needs of the user, when the real need of the user is to be forced to sit and think?"

24

CONCEPTUAL PROBLEMS

In its early days the Typological Debate was somewhat beclouded by the lack of an adequate conceptual vocabulary, a problem that has been common to all sciences in their formative stages. Commentators like Rouse (1939; 1960), Krieger (1944), Brew (1946: 44–66) and Taylor (1948: 113–51) had to use too few words to mean too many things, and it is not surprising that their ideas were not always expressed very precisely. They rarely distinguished between entities and concepts, between variables and attributes, between classifying and sorting, or between typology and taxonomy.

Lack of an adequate vocabulary is no longer the problem that it once was. In some respects we now have more conceptual terminology than we can reasonably use. Many typologists in the last thirty years have attempted to solve the stubborn problems of artifact classification, or to reduce the gap between theory and practice, by offering new conceptual formulations. Unfortunately these have often been expressed in the form of false dichotomies, as we will see later in the chapter, and their effect has at times been to further becloud the Typological Debate rather than to clarify it.

The problem today is not so much one of inadequate conceptual tools, as of tools unused or unsystematically used. In this chapter we will consider a number of persistent problems with regard to classification and typology whose basis is at least partly conceptual. We will take up first some problems that arise purely and simply from a failure to make conceptual distinctions; we will then turn to problems whose basis is partly conceptual and partly due to the misapplication of theory. In conclusion we will consider two general propensities of human thought – overgeneralization and dichotomization – that have further complicated the Typological Debate.

Failure to distinguish between classification, typology, and taxonomy

Some participants in the Typological Debate prefer to talk about classification (Linton 1936: 382–400; Rouse 1960; Dunnell 1986), some about typology (Krieger 1944; 1960; J. A. Ford 1954b; Kluckhohn 1960), and some about taxonomy (Brew 1946: 44–66), but to a large extent these terms have been used interchangeably. In the usage of different authors, and in different contexts, all three of the terms can designate any of the three kinds of classificatory systems that we have here called classifications, typologies, and taxonomies.

Our definitions of classification, typology, and taxonomy have been given in Chapter 4 and in Appendix A. We do not insist on the use of this particular set of terms by others; only that the different kinds of systems that they designate should be recognized as different. Here we will be concerned specifically with those differences, and how they are expressed in theory and in practice.

Classification and typology. A classification, according to our definition (Chapter 4), is any matched set of contrasting categories. A typology is a particular kind of classification designed for the sorting of entities into mutually exclusive pigeonholes. A typology in other words is designed to be used for some purpose in addition to simple communication. As such it introduces practical problems of judgment that are not necessarily present in other classifications, and that cannot be eliminated at the theoretical level. While the classes in a classification need only be theoretically distinct, and the distinction between them may even require cumbersome verification, the types in a typology must be practically distinguishable. Practically usable types have to be formulated with this in mind. While in other kinds of classifications criteria of identity are often less important than are criteria of meaning, in practical typologies the reverse is mostly true. Finally, and again because of practical considerations, the classes in a non-typological classification often need only be defined, but the types in a typology must be extensively described (overdetermined), as we saw in Chapter 15.

The consequences of failing to distinguish between non-typological classifications and typologies are evident at two points in the Typological Debate. Early discussants rather consistently lumped artifact classification and "culture" classification together, as though the problems and procedures were the same in the two cases (Brew 1946: 44–66; Taylor 1948: 113–51; Clarke 1968: 187–91). What they failed to observe is that artifact classifications (at least in the pre-computer era) are nearly always typologies, while "culture" classifications are not. The problems of class formulation (that is, of deciding what is and is not a "culture") are wholly theoretical in the case of "culture" classifications, while in the case of artifact types they are at least as much practical as theoretical.

In artifact classification itself, the electronic era has witnessed the development of that conspicuous gap between theory and practice that was noted by Hill and Evans (1972: 231), Dunnell (1986: 150), and others (e.g. Rodrigues de Areia 1985). The gap, in reality, is very largely a gap between the *theory* of classification and the *practice* of typology. The computerized artifact classifications that have dominated the recent theoretical literature are mostly not typologies, and cannot be used as such, as we saw in Chapter 23. As a result the computer archaeologists who are concerned with classifications and the field archaeologists who are concerned with typologies are often talking past each other.

Typology and taxonomy. The distinction between typology and taxonomy is no less important than the distinction between typology and classification, but it too has often been ignored. Put in the simplest terms, typology, according to our definition, involves the making of types (Chapter 15), while taxonomy involves the ordering or grouping of types once they have been made (Chapter 17). These latter processes normally do not affect the actual definition or the membership of the types.

The issue that is involved here concerns the role of quantification, respectively in typologies and in taxonomies. As we saw in Chapter 6, artifact types are mostly "apples and oranges": the differences between them are fundamentally qualitative (Lévi-Strauss 1953: 528; Dunnell 1971b: 52–6). Usually, no type can be differentiated from other types in the same system by any purely quantitative procedure. On the other hand taxonomies are concerned specifically with relationships between types, which are often quantitative, or capable of expression in quantitative terms. The result is that quantification and measurement play relatively minor roles in the formulation of typologies, but are much more important in the formulation of taxonomies. However, this does not seem to be generally recognized in the extensive literature on the use of mathematics and computers in archaeological classification.

Failure to distinguish between classifying and sorting
Basic to the distinction that we made earlier, between non-typological classifications and typologies, is the distinction between classifying (creating categories) and sorting (putting things into them). Non-

typological classifications are not used for sorting, while typologies necessarily are. Only a few commentators seem to have noted that classifying and sorting are separate processes (cf. Dunnell 1971b: 44–5; Vierra 1982: 162–3; Voorrips 1982: 116–17), and fewer still have recognized that the problems involved are different in the two cases (see Chapters 15 and 16). There seems to have been, rather, a feeling that if we could only define our categories precisely enough, all of our objects would fall neatly into them (cf. Doran and Hodson 1975: 158–86). As a result nearly all of the recent literature on archaeological classification refers to the theoretical problems involved in classifying, while ignoring the practical problems involved in sorting.

Sorting problems could really be forestalled at the classification stage only if types were defined by their boundaries. In archaeology this is rarely if ever the case, as we have observed in Chapter 6 and elsewhere. Types are defined by central tendencies, from which most actual specimens deviate in some characteristics and in some degree. Ideal type definitions, no matter how precisely they are formulated, can never solve the problem of where to put borderline specimens (Shepard 1965: 317; Klejn 1982: 58–64).

Classifying involves a certain amount of judgment, as we saw in Chapter 15, but sorting is a process of continual judgment. Various objectification procedures can be introduced to reduce the judgment factor in classifying, but none of them can eliminate or even significantly reduce the role of judgment in sorting. In our view, the judgmental aspects of both classifying and sorting have received too little attention in the typological literature.

Failure to distinguish between genetic and non-genetic taxonomies

As we defined them in Chapter 17, taxonomies are classificatory systems designed to indicate various kinds of relationships between types. However, the relationships involved in genetic and non-genetic taxonomies are fundamentally different. In genetic taxonomies the lower taxa are descendants of a common ancestor, which usually existed at an earlier point in time and is now extinct. In non-genetic taxonomies the lower taxa are grouped on the basis of various shared characteristics that have nothing to do with a common origin.

There is, in this respect, a basic though sometimes unrecognized difference between taxonomic "culture" classifications, which are usually genetic, and taxonomic artifact typologies, which are not. The bases of taxonomic grouping are quite different in the two cases, and a "culture" taxonomy is not simply the sum of a group of artifact typologies (see especially Klejn 1982: 145-261).

The failure of archaeologists to distinguish between genetic and non-genetic taxonomies is perhaps most conspicuous in their numerous attempts to apply the methods of Numerical Taxonomy to the classification of artifacts (see Chapter 17). The algorithms of Numerical Taxonomy were developed by biological scientists specifically for purposes of genetic classification: to determine closeness or distance from a common ancestor by the number of traits shared by two species, genera, or orders. This kind of measurement continues to be useful for biologists, linguists, and other practitioners of genetic classification (but see Simpson 1945: 8). On the other hand it has clearly no relevance for the making of non-genetic (morphological, functional, or historical) taxonomies such as are usually applied to artifacts.

Confusion of natural and social science

The notion that archaeology (or at least prehistoric archaeology) is a natural science is very dear to its practitioners, and it has led them again and again to look for inspiration to the methods and concepts of the so-called "hard" sciences. From physics and from biology they have borrowed the hypothetico-deductive research philosophy of C. G. Hempel (1965; 1966), the Open Systems Theory of Ludwig von Bertalanffy (1950; 1951; 1962), the Numerical Taxonomy algorithms of Sokal and Sneath (1963; Sneath and Sokal 1973), and a variety of other methods and procedures (see WYA n.d.2). It should be noted by the way that in no case did the original developers of these procedures suggest that they were appropriate for the study of human society and culture.

We have already made reference to the inappropriate use of Numerical Taxonomy in artifact classification. Much older and more pervasive, however, has been the adoption of a Linnean approach to artifact classification, and particularly the equation of artifact type with biological species (cf. Brew 1946: 47; Ford 1954a: 391; Krieger 1960: 141-2). It is this equation which results in the assumption that artifact classification is a matter of "finding the joints in nature" (Spaulding 1982: 11), and that the most "natural" types are, like mammalian species, the most clearly bounded ones. As we suggested in Chapter 6, culture does not usually create sharp boundaries, and there is no justification for equating boundedness with naturalness. In fact, the most sharply bounded types formulated by archaeologists are generally the most artificial ones (cf. Chapter 23).

Confusion of entity and concept

Artifacts were made by prehistoric craftsmen and women, usually for some reasonably specific purpose, and their meaning *as artifacts* derives from that purpose, plus whatever other associations they may have had for their makers and users. This is what we have elsewhere called individual meaning (Chapter 3). Types are made by typologists, for some purpose which may or may not have anything to do with the artifact maker's purpose, and their meaning *as types* derives from the purpose for which the typology was made. This is what we have called typological meaning (Chapter 3). The individual meaning of an object and its typological meaning are often quite different.

To cite a specific but hypothetical example: a bowl of red, orange, and black polychrome pottery was made by a prehistoric Indian woman living in Tsegi Canyon between A.D. 1225 and 1300; it was meant primarily for the mixing and serving of corn meal mush. Its meaning for the maker and owner was "holder and server of corn meal mush"; secondarily, perhaps, "this is our Tsegi style," or "I have beautiful things," or "I am a skilled potter." The pottery type Tsegi polychrome, of which this particular bowl is an exemplar, was created by Colton and Hargrave in 1937 (p. 96), as part of a typology designed primarily for the dating of archaeological sites in northern Arizona. The meaning of the bowl for the typologists was "identifier of archaeological sites dating between 1225 and 1300" and "identifier of prehistoric trade contacts with Tsegi Canyon."

Failure to distinguish between the individual meanings of artifacts and their typological meanings has been fairly pervasive; it was the fundamental error of such would-be configurationists as Krieger (1944; 1960) and Taylor (1948: 113–51). They thought that types should be devised to reflect the inherent or emic meanings of artifacts, but the meanings that they sought were really the meanings of the artifacts as individual objects, not their meanings as type exemplars. To the extent that emic meanings were discoverable, their discovery was not necessarily aided by the imposition of a classificatory scheme.

Confusion of classification and explanation

This is another conceptual error with a long history, but one which was especially prevalent at one particular phase of the Typological Debate. It was the prevailing error of the nomothetic phase, when there was a general belief that archaeology must be explanatory or it must be nothing. Since the nomothetic archaeologists were no better able to get along without typologies than were their predecessors, they did what they could to make classification itself seem like an explanatory procedure (cf. Fritz and Plog 1970: 407–8; Hill and Evans 1972; Read 1974). This misconception will occupy us in the next chapter, and we therefore need not pursue it further here.

Confusion of means and ends

The issue of means and ends brings us back once again to the distinction between classifications in general and typologies in particular. In a non-typological classification it may often be true that the means are synonymous with the ends; that is, the purpose of the classification is simply to construct a set of verbal categories to facilitate communication. This obviously does not apply to typologies as we have defined them. A typology is made for the immediate purpose of sorting entities into discrete groups, which itself is ancillary to some more fundamental purpose such as statistical comparison or taxonomy-making. In the case of typologies, therefore, the distinction between means and ends should in theory be quite clear. The typology is a communicative means toward some end other than communication itself.

Archaeologists have nevertheless accused each other from time to time of "making typologies for their own sake" (Kluckhohn 1939: 338; Bennett 1943: 208; Clark 1952: 1). If this were true, it would certainly indicate a confusion of means and ends. However, the problem for a long time was more apparent than real. Typologists may have mistakenly thought that they were merely discovering natural order or emic significance in their data, but because they followed what were basically sound instincts (cf. Watson, LeBlanc, and Redman 1971: 127; Watson 1986: 450–1) their typologies usually served some useful purpose – descriptive, comparative, or historical. The problem was not that the typologies had no purpose, but that it was not clearly stated or understood.

Confusion of means and ends has become genuinely prevalent only since the advent of computer classifications. A few archaeologists have developed their own algorithms with reference to particular problems (Whallon 1972; Hill and Evans 1972; Read 1974); a much larger number have simply adopted one or another of the many available software packages that are essentially purpose-free (cf. Cormack 1971: 329; Voorrips 1982: 111). As Voorrips (1982: 111) has nicely put it,

> . . . we see the modern archaeologist . . . performing the painstaking labor of measuring an almost endless number of variables on an almost equally endless number of artifacts, keypunching an almost endless number of cards, and finally

running some kind of cluster analysis which happens to be popular at the local computer center, after which it is proudly announced that now the objective or natural order of things has been revealed.

The choice of programs, as Voorrips correctly noted, is dictated not by any particular problem but by the current popularity of the program itself.

Overgeneralization

Scientific understanding, like all human understanding, grows through processes of abstraction and generalization. Scientists discover limited or situational truths through their individual experiences, decide that these truths may be applicable in other situations as well, and proceed through experimentation or application to see how far they will hold true (cf. Margolis 1987: 91). Usually their limits are discovered only when they have been exceeded. To that extent overgeneralization is a necessary feature in the growth of science; it is part of the scientific dialectic.

Overgeneralization, or the mistaking of situational truths for general truths, becomes a problem when limits are reached but are not recognized. There are plentiful examples of this in the history of artifact classification. Classificatory procedures that have been found useful in particular areas and for particular purposes are forthwith proclaimed as the "right" methods of classification, and are recommended to the use of all archaeologists everywhere. Examples include the type-variety system of pottery classification (Wheat, Gifford, and Wasley 1958; Sabloff and Smith 1969), which works in the American Southwest but not in the Northeast (see Wright 1967), and a number of computer programs that at one time or another were proclaimed as offering the long-sought solution to the problem of objective classification (e.g. Clarke 1968: 512–47; Christenson and Read 1977; Read 1982: 64–79).

Readers of this book may well conclude that its authors have themselves been guilty of overgeneralization, in laying too much stress on certain kinds of practical problems that are peculiar to the classification and sorting of Nubian pottery. Because practicing field archaeologists have contributed so little to the recent literature on artifact classification, it is difficult for us to know how many of them have experienced the same kinds of classificatory problems that are described here. We suspect, based largely on informal conversations, that there may be a silent majority, or at least a sizable minority, of field archaeologists whose experiences and perspectives are similar to our own (cf., at least, Gardin 1980 and Klejn 1982).

Dichotomization

If there is one factor that has caused more confusion than any other throughout the years of the Typological Debate, it is probably the pervasive tendency (at least among Western scholars) toward dichotomous thinking (cf. Lévi-Strauss 1966: 135–60). Of the twelve issues and non-issues that were discussed in the previous chapter, no fewer than nine have been expressed at one time or another in the form of binary oppositions. These include the issues of "natural" vs. "artificial" classification, lumping vs. splitting, induction vs. deduction, emic vs. etic classification, formal vs. functional classification, object clustering vs. attribute clustering, paradigmatic vs. taxonomic classification, "empiricist" vs. "positivist" approaches, and "guided" vs. "imposed" constructions.

We regard all of these as false dichotomies. We would argue that all typologies are simultaneously "empiricist" and "positivist"; all types are to a degree natural and to a degree artificial; all are formulated through a feedback between object clustering and attribute clustering, and therefore between induction and deduction; all types probably have some measure of emic significance and some measure of functional significance, in addition to other meanings which they may have for the typologist; and all archaeologists are lumpers on some occasions and splitters on others. As we tried to suggest in Chapter 6, type concepts are not simple, and neither are the minds that can make and use them effectively. We are inclined to agree with Amitai Etzioni (1988: 203) that "Dichotomies are the curse of intellectual and scholarly discourse."

25

THE USE AND ABUSE OF THEORY

One of the most insightful early discussions of archaeological typology and its problems was "The use and abuse of taxonomy," by J. O. Brew (1946: 44–66). (In most contexts "taxonomy" was to Brew what "typology" is to us.) Brew was not the first to recognize the theoretical problems involved in archaeological classification (cf. Kluckhohn 1939: 338; Rouse 1939: 9–35), but he was one of the first who correctly understood their nature. It was not (as Kluckhohn had implied) that artifact types had no theoretical significance, but that their significance was widely misinterpreted. Brew saw this as evidence that typological practice was being used in ways inappropriate to theory-building – hence the title of his chapter. Here we will argue, conversely, that theory has often been used in ways inappropriate to typology-building.

We have suggested at many points in this book that there really was not, and is not, anything seriously wrong with the practice of artifact classification. By the time that Brew wrote, however, it had largely achieved its original goal of erecting a basic time/space grid for the contextualization of North American archaeological materials. Precisely because this edifice was now largely complete, archaeologists were beginning to look around for new questions to ask. As they did so, they began to criticize the old typologies because they were not answering the new questions. As we will see a little later, this is one of the frequent consequences of paradigm shifts in the social sciences.

We are going to suggest, then, that if a gap has developed between the theory and the practice of artifact classification (cf. Hill and Evans 1972: 231–2; Dunnell 1986: 150), it is not because the practice has been misused but because the theory has been misused. As we see it there are three factors involved: a misunderstanding of the basic nature of social science theory, a misunderstanding of the appropriate relationship between theory and method, and a misunderstanding of the nature of classification itself.

The last of these issues has been sufficiently dealt with in earlier chapters (especially Part II); the other two will occupy us here.

The nature of social science theory

In *The Structure of Scientific Revolutions*, Thomas Kuhn (1962) has given us the very useful concept of the scientific paradigm. Kuhn postulated that natural science does not advance in an orderly and systematic fashion, but through a kind of cladistic progression from one steady state, or paradigm, to another. Each paradigm has its own particular research interests and orientations, involving a tacit agreement that certain kinds of questions are to be asked and not to be asked, and certain kinds of "proofs" are to be accepted and not to be accepted. However, narrowly focused and limited research objectives cannot prevent the discovery of new and unexpected facts, resulting in a widening gap between the observed and the expected. Eventually theory can no longer sustain the burden of unexplained fact, and it is likely to give way quite abruptly to new theoretical formulations that are more congruent with the latest facts. There is, consequently, a kind of Hegelian dialectic between new discoveries and old ideas, leading periodically to revolutionary shifts of interest and new paradigms.

The history of American archaeology in the twentieth century, as outlined in Chapter 22, suggests at least superficially that this same path of development may occur in the social sciences. On the other hand, Kuhn's explanation for paradigm shifts in terms of new technologies and unexpected discoveries appears to have little relevance to social science, where there usually is not a close interrelationship between theory, method, and data. The social sciences are still only one step removed from their origins in social philosophy, and they continue to be much more theory-driven than method-driven or data-driven. Most social science methodology has been developed *post hoc* to provide support for some previously conceived theory, and it has seldom failed to deliver what was required of it. Consequently, it is questionable if the term "discovery" has much relevance in the fields of social science (cf. WYA n.d.2). "Invention" would be more appropriate, for the progress of social science can be measured mainly by the development of new and better conceptual tools (cf. Lowie 1937: 281).

At bottom, social science theory consists of mankind's self-comprehension. As we see it, that comprehension has at least three dimensions, which we will here call prediction, explanation, and understanding. It is necessary briefly to explain our usage of these terms, which is not always the same as that of other authors (e.g. Kelley and Hanen 1988:

355–6). In our view, prediction, explanation, and understanding each involves a different kind of reasoning.

Prediction is a matter involving implicative statements: if A happens then B will also happen; if and only if A and B happen, then C will happen, and so on. This is not in any sense tantamount to explanation; we can often demonstrate experimentally that where there is A there must always be B, without knowing why this is so. The whole methodology of probabilistic social science is based on the principles of population statistics, which, with sufficient aggregation, can predict without explaining.

Explanation is a more complex matter than prediction; its exact nature has long been a subject of debate among philosophers of science (cf. especially Scriven 1958). Everyone agrees, however, that it is something other than prediction. Explanation is generally regarded as involving causal reasoning: the ability to state that condition B happened because factor A was present, and why this was so. But the problem lies in deciding what legitimately constitutes a "cause," when many factors besides A could explain the presence of condition B (see Waldrop 1987). Archaeologists nevertheless make extensive use of causal explanation, relying mostly on common-sense notions of causality that are accepted by most of their colleagues, if not necessarily by logicians.

In the physical sciences explanation often implies prediction (but cf. Hempel 1966: 58–69), since causality in these sciences is frequently invariant (that is, it involves true laws). In the social sciences on the other hand explanation is tantamount to prediction only in a statistical sense, and not in every individual case. This means that general theories in social science usually cannot be falsified by any single deductive experiment, a fact that has been widely ignored by the archaeologist followers of Hempel (see WYA n.d.2).

Understanding is the most complex of the three components of human self-knowledge; so much so that it is not reducible to formal or rigorous analysis. In our usage it corresponds more or less to the *Verstehen* of Dilthey (1976: 186–95) and Weber (1947: 87, 94–6): the idea that we know others by knowing ourselves. Primarily this involves analogical reasoning, which may be expressed by the formula: A is to B as C is to D. That is, it is a matter of establishing equivalences between things, which may be either exact or approximate. Things that are outside our experience are rendered intelligible by likening them to things within our experience.

Thus it has often been suggested that the ethnologist's task is primarily one of translation: making the institutions of an unfamiliar culture intelligible by analogy with the institutions of our own (cf. Radin 1933: 183–252; Kluckhohn 1949: 168–95; Geertz 1973: 3–30). This kind of non-mathematical and non-rigorous reasoning has sometimes been dismissed as non-scientific; in fact it is basic to normative social science as well as to many of the humanities (see also Waldrop 1987: 1298–9). It is obvious that understanding depends much more on effective verbal communication than do prediction and explanation, though it may be enhanced also by classifications, diagrams, formulas, and other deliberately improvised concepts.

Ideally, a fully comprehensive social science theory would involve equal parts of prediction, explanation, and understanding. In the world of reality this ideal is never likely to be achieved, because a theory that effectively combined prediction, explanation, and understanding would be as complex and as cumbersome as the real world itself. The first requirement for sanity in a bafflingly complex world is to bring it down to a manageably simple frame of reference through some form of reductionism, and this has been the traditional role alike of mythology, of philosophy, and of social science theory. All of the most compelling social science theories – Marxist, Freudian, Durkheimian, ecological – are in fact reductionist philosophies, given an appearance of science by the use of carefully marshaled factual evidence.

In sum, the first requirement of all philosophies is to provide reasonably simple answers to complicated questions. In the realm of social science theory this has generally been achieved by emphasizing either prediction or explanation or understanding at the expense of the other two dimensions of self-knowledge. Here, we believe, is the explanation both for paradigms and for paradigm shifts in the social sciences. Theory does not change when new data require new explanations; it changes either when we have answered the old questions, or (much more commonly) when we have become frustrated by our inability to do so. The solution in either case is to find new questions to ask. In the process, there is often a shift from theories emphasizing prediction to those emphasizing explanation, or from explanation to understanding, or from understanding to prediction.

Paradigms and paradigm shifts in anthropology
Paradigmatic shifts between prediction, explanation, and understanding are clearly illustrated in the history of American anthropology, which we

have partially reviewed in Chapter 22. In the nineteenth century the dominant paradigm was that of unilinear evolutionism, which is powerful as an explanatory theory but is neither very predictive in individual cases nor very perceptive in helping us understand ourselves. In the early twentieth century the disciples of Boas began to notice how many exceptions there were to the supposed uniformity of evolutionary progress; they also protested that evolutionary doctrine as it was then understood denigrated the mentality of living primitive peoples (cf. Boas 1911b). They turned instead first to descriptive particularism and then to configurationism; both paradigms (derived ultimately from nineteenth-century *Geisteswissenschaft*) that emphasize understanding rather than prediction or explanation. But when configurationism began to seem too unscientific and humanistic, its adherents attempted to give it a predictive dimension by undertaking controlled studies of comparative values (Kluckhohn 1956; Vogt and Albert 1966: 1–33) and of personality formation processes (Leighton and Kluckhohn 1948; Joseph, Spicer, and Chesky 1949; Thompson and Joseph 1965). These, however, never achieved any genuine scientific rigor, and their failure to do so helped to hasten the demise of the configurationist paradigm.

In the 1960s, thanks in considerable part to the influence of the National Science Foundation (see WYA n.d.2 and Chapter 22), the pendulum swung back once again in the direction of explanation, this time embodied in the materialist doctrine of cultural ecology. In archaeology this was often coupled with the methodology of so-called General Systems Theory (see especially Binford 1965; Clarke 1968: 43–82). However, many ethnologists rejected these essentially mechanistic and dehumanizing doctrines as being devoid of cultural understanding. This was true particularly of ethnologists who had worked and lived for substantial periods among native peoples, and who had mastered their languages. Many of these scholars turned instead in the direction of structuralism, which for the most part involves prediction without either explanation or understanding.

This cycle of alternating reductionisms is by no means unique to anthropology. On the contrary, it is hardly more than a microcosm of the larger dialectic between materialists and mentalists, essentialists and instrumentalists, empiricists and humanists, that has been going on in the philosophical world at least since ancient Greek times, and that is not likely to end at any time in the foreseeable future.

The consequences for archaeological classification

In the natural sciences, if we can believe Kuhn (1962), new theories are forced by new discoveries and methodologies. In social science the opposite is more commonly true: new methods are developed to give support to new theories. In Chapter 22 we saw this clearly illustrated in the case of American archaeology and American artifact classification. Throughout the twentieth century archaeological theory has generally followed the lead of anthropological theory (or occasionally biological theory), and archaeological practice, including classificatory practice, has attempted to follow in turn (Bennett 1943: 210; Willey and Phillips 1958: 1–7). It is that inverted relationship – the dominance of theory over practice – that is responsible for much of the Typological Debate that we discussed in the three preceding chapters, and in particular for the recurring disparity between theory and practice.

Systematic artifact classification in the Americas only goes back about seventy years, and the gap between theory and practice did not really develop until a generation after that. There was no gap during what we have called the classificatory era (*c.* 1920–1940) for the simple but fundamental reason that classification itself was then the dominant concern of American archaeologists, and it was developed for wholly pragmatic ends. As long as that remained true, there could not be any significant disparity between the theory and the practice of classification. A good classification in theory was one that worked in practice, and any classification that did not yield practical results was eventually discarded.

The primary function of archaeological classification in those early days was predictive (or, to be more technically accurate, retrodictive). The finding of a particular pottery or arrowhead type in a particular site predicted that the site dated from a particular period in time; the finding of unique combinations of pottery, arrowhead, and other artifact types in particular sites predicted that those sites had belonged to particular peoples, or "cultures." In practical field tests these predictions were repeatedly confirmed, and in the process the legitimacy of the types themselves seemed to be confirmed. It was in these circumstances that artifact types became firmly established among the archaeologist's most basic tools.

When, around 1940, the classificatory paradigm gave way to the configurational/functional, archaeologists simultaneously turned their main focus of interest from prediction to understanding, as we defined those terms earlier. When they did so, they demanded that classificatory practice should follow along. It was not enough that artifact types should predict what sites belonged to what periods and what peoples; they should now also help us to understand the belief and behavior systems of those peoples.

The practical difficulty was that artifact classifications were still needed for their old job of contextualizing archaeological remains in time and space. While archaeologists might no longer look upon this activity as an end in itself, it was still a necessary beginning before they could turn their attention to more distant and lofty goals. "[Typologies are] designed for the reconstruction of culture history in time and space. This is the beginning and not the end of the archaeologist's responsibility," as J. A. Ford (1954b: 52) had succinctly put it. As a result, archaeologists could not really dispense with the old typologies developed in the old ways and for the old purposes. They could only hope that the old typologies would also work for new purposes, as Krieger (1944) had insisted, or develop new typologies adapted to their new purposes, as recommended by Rouse (1939), Taylor (1948: 113–51) and Spaulding (1953). However, the attempts to advance cultural understanding through emic and/or functional typologies were never very successful, partly because the archaeologists did not clearly separate these two different objectives in classification (cf. Chapter 22).

When the nomothetic paradigm succeeded the configurationist, archaeologists turned in effect from understanding to explanation as the main focus of their interest. Once again it was expected that classificatory practice would follow along. There was now an insistence that archaeological classifications must lend themselves to hypothesis-testing and to theory-building, in the rather narrow sense in which theory was then defined. But the old problem persisted: classifications still had to go on performing their traditional function of providing time and space contexts.

This time there was no very widespread expectation that the old typologies could be adapted to new purposes. There was, instead, a movement to experiment with new classificatory schemes, a process that was shortly overtaken by the electronic revolution of computerized classification. But the difficulty with computerized systems is that they were not, for the most part, made for any specified purpose. The result has been to widen the already substantial gap between theory and practice to the point where, as Dunnell (1986: 150) observes, "the two are now unrelated."

The Typological Debate has developed, then, because theory has led where practice could not follow. Archaeological theory has continually moved, or tried to move, in step with the twists and turns of anthropological theory more generally; typological practice has largely stood still because the old questions of time and space context, for which the practice is so well adapted, have still to be answered first.

Classification, theory, and science

The gap between archaeological theory and typological practice obviously does not constitute an indictment of archaeological theory *per se*. The successive theoretical paradigms that have dominated American archaeology in the twentieth century have all been scientifically legitimate in one way or another, depending on whether one saw prediction, understanding, or explanation as the primary goal of science. The problem lies, rather, with a faulty perception of the relationship between classification and theory. For half a century there has been a continuing insistence that classificatory practice must be congruent with, and subservient to, the current canons of theory, as though classification were itself an aspect of theory.

This is a fundamental error. Salmon (1982: 154) has correctly observed that "Concept formation . . . and theory formation can only proceed in a highly interactive way," but this does not mean that concepts and theory are equivalent. On the contrary, the dialectic between them clearly demonstrates that they are not. Moreover, the dialectic can proceed only when neither concept nor theory is made wholly subservient to the other.

Unlike genuine theories, classificatory concepts and schemes *per se* are neither predictive nor explanatory, nor do they involve intrinsic understanding. The theoretical claims that have been made for them at each stage of the Typological Debate are illusory, for under close scrutiny their supposed theoretical contributions can be seen as tautologous. Archaeological types in the classificatory era were thought to predict cultural affinities which in fact they defined *a priori*; in the configurational/functional era they were declared to be emically or functionally significant when in fact their function was an inference of the archaeologist himself; in the nomothetic era their "typehood" was sometimes determined by whether or not they verified hypotheses. In each of these circumstances, whatever truth they contained was truth by definition.

Here, then, lies the crux of the matter. Classification and other conceptual and measurement devices do not constitute theory because definition is not explanation (cf. Scriven 1958; Levin 1973: 391–2). They are, in Dunnell's (1986: 152) words, "instrumentalities of the investigator without empirical import." As with all tools, they have to be judged by their utility, not their validity. The ultimate test is not whether they are true or false, but whether they work for any particular purpose.

In Chapter 4, and at various subsequent points, we have spoken of typologies as a kind of restricted, formal language. They stand in relation to theory-building in the same way as do all other languages. That is, they are a necessary starting point for the development of theory, and they themselves evolve through a dialectical relationship with theory, but in and of themselves they are not theory. Their role might be described as pre-theoretical, in that they must often be in place before theory-building can begin.

Wallace Stegner, speaking of the pioneering classificatory efforts of John Wesley Powell (cf. Chapter 22), wrote "Before starting to write the science of American ethnology, create its alphabet" (Stegner 1982: 263). This, in our view, precisely characterizes the work of the archaeological typologists. They created the alphabet, or better the language, in which prehistoric archaeology is still very largely written.

26

PARADIGMS AND PROGRESS

In the last chapter we applied certain general considerations abut theory and its use to the understanding of how archaeological typologies are developed and used. Here we will reverse the procedure, bringing our findings about archaeological typologies to bear on general issues of scientific theory and method. In particular we will consider their relevance to the currently controversial issue of scientific progress. This issue arises because the "official" or orthodox epistemology of most of the sciences is a vague empiricism, and it is associated with a special conception of scientific progress against which Thomas Kuhn (1962; 1970) and his followers have launched a powerful attack. The empiricist paradigm will be explained in more detail in the next section, following which we will bring some of our own typological considerations to bear in criticizing Kuhn's critique, as well as in commenting on some related issues, and most particularly on the "problem of pseudoproblems" (Carnap 1927). In a short chapter we can hardly offer definitive resolutions to these very general and very fundamental questions, but we feel that insights drawn from our study of archaeological typologies are suggestive enough to warrant remark. We will start with a sketch of "orthodox empiricism" and the conceptions of scientific progress, and of scientific concept formation, that are implicit in it.

The empiricist paradigm

Since the time of Bacon and Galileo it has been scientific orthodoxy to hold that: (1) the aim of research in the natural sciences is to attain knowledge and understanding of nature, and (2) the primary mode of access to nature is sense observation. Thus, the first Aphorism of the *Novum Organon* reads: "Man, being the servant and interpreter of Nature, can do and understand so much and so much only as he has observed in fact or in thought in the course of Nature. Beyond this he neither knows anything nor can do anything" (Bacon 1620). Replacing "Nature" by "surroundings," we find the same message in the opening sentence of a contemporary college physics text: "In the study of physics we are interested in studying our surroundings and the only contacts we have with these surroundings are through our senses, by which we see, hear, taste, and smell" (Freier 1965: 1).

Although theses (1) and (2) are the central theses of sense empiricism, they are supplemented by another of hardly less importance. That is: (3) that the most sought-after knowledge about nature is general; that is, it extends beyond the facts thus far determined by sense observation in a way that permits us to anticipate, to explain, and to some extent to control, phenomena not yet observed. This explains the emphasis that empiricism places on laws and theories (or hypotheses) as the proper goals of scientific inquiry, and it also explains why these hypotheses are necessarily provisional and subject to revision when they are found to conflict with observationally determined facts. In these terms it becomes possible to give a simple definition of scientific progress: it involves the continual replacement of laws or theories that have been found to conflict with observational facts, by new laws or theories that do not conflict with the facts, and that account for all of the facts that the replaced hypothesis had accounted for. In other words, we seek accurate and comprehensive descriptions of nature, and scientific progress consists in replacing one theory or hypothesis by another which is more accurate and at least as comprehensive as its predecessor. Note that data and theory play asymmetrical roles in the empiricist picture of scientific progress, because when they conflict it is always theory that must give way. Theory depends on data, but data are independent of theory. This involves what we may call conceptual independence.

Concepts enter the picture with language – the vehicle in which data, theory, and laws must all be expressed. The concepts stand in relation to data, theory, and laws much as words stand in relation to the sentences and paragraphs which are formed from them (cf. Chapter 23). For instance, the sentence "Force equals mass times acceleration" states a law (Newton's second law of motion). The words "force," "mass," and "acceleration" stand for the concepts involved in the law, and the concepts stand to the law much as the words stand to the sentence. The theory is complicated, and may sound absurd when baldly stated, but it postulates a triple correspondence between explicit words like "force," the possibly subjective concepts or ideas they express, like the idea of force, and the possibly objective physical things they name or stand for, like physical forces. Moreover, as the words hang together to form sentences like "Force equals mass times acceleration," so the corresponding ideas combine to form a thought, and the corresponding things combine to form a fact. This philosophy of language is associated with the names of Gottlob Frege (1892; 1977) and Bertrand Russell (1924), and was perhaps most fully articulated by Ludwig Wittgenstein in the so-called "picture theory of meaning" in his *Tractatus Logico-Philosophicus* (Wittgenstein 1922).

The same theory strongly influenced the views on philosophy of science expressed by the logical empiricists Schlick, Feigl, Hempel, and others, and allies of theirs such as Popper and Carnap. As Hempel put it, "Broadly speaking, the vocabulary of science has two basic functions: first, to permit an adequate *description* of things and events that are the objects of scientific investigation; second, to permit the establishment of general laws or theories by means of which particular events may be *explained* and *understood*" (Hempel 1965: 139; italics in the original).

Given this outlook, scientific concept formation has a clearly defined objective, namely to seek words and concepts that will make it possible to formulate progressively more accurate and comprehensive laws and theories. To quote Hempel again: "In order to attain theories of great precision, wide scope, and high empirical confirmation, science has therefore evolved, in its different branches, comprehensive systems of special concepts, referred to by technical terms" (Hempel 1952: 21). In one way Hempel's view subordinates concepts to theories, in that they are like the parts of a machine, which have no intrinsic value independent of the machine. But in another way the part is necessarily prior to the machine.

Orthodox empiricism insists that scientific tests should be independent of the theories tested, and logical empiricism translates this into the requirement of conceptual independence that was mentioned earlier. The empirical test of a theory is assumed to consist in determining its consistency with observational data, and both theory and data are presumed to be expressable in sentences formed from terms in the language of the theory. But the test must be unbiased, and this can only be the case if the terms are neutral and not "theory-loaded," in the sense of presupposing the correctness of the theory in their very definitions. Thus, it would not be legitimate to choose between geocentric and heliocentric theories on the basis of "data" like "The sun rises in the east," because "rises," by its very definition, presupposes motion on the part of the sun. To avoid such problems, the logical empiricists have insisted that the data against which theories are tested must be expressed in pure observation languages that do not involve theoretical presuppositions, and efforts were made to characterize such languages rigorously (cf. Carnap 1956). But these efforts were recognized as unsatisfactory by the empiricists themselves, and this weak point in empiricist theory became the focal point for Kuhn's attack on it.

Kuhn's challenge

Kuhn's attack on empiricism begins with the undeniable observation that the assumed priority of data over theory does not square with the way in which science has actually developed up to now. Normal science does not test fundamental theories like Newton's law of motion against observational data, and when facts come to light that do not seem to fit a theory (like, for example, some early data on the motion of the moon), the theory is not forthwith rejected. Instead, the most strenuous efforts are made, including reexamination of the data themselves, to reconcile data and theory, and even when they cannot be reconciled the theory is not abandoned unless another theory is found that has most of the advantages of the earlier one, and at the same time overcomes the difficulties in the earlier one.

In the real world, adherence to theory in the teeth of contrary evidence may be explained as a practical necessity. We do not abandon imperfect instruments of prediction unless and until more satisfactory instruments are found to replace them, and this in itself is not inconsistent with empiricism. Empiricism distinguishes between pure and applied science, and its ideals apply to the former even while it acknowledges the claims of the latter. But it has greater difficulty in meeting another of Kuhn's challenges, directed against the assumption that scientific theories must be tested against data which are expressible in pure observation languages.

Kuhn's fundamental thesis, based partly on the facts of history, partly on Gestalt psychology, and partly on skeptical trends in philosophy itself, is that there are no completely neutral scientific data, and moreover science has no need of them (cf. Salmon 1982: 154). There are data and there are theories, but they are not neatly separable as dependent theories tested against independent data expressed in terms of independent concepts. Instead, they are interdependent elements of something more inclusive: a paradigm of normal scientific activity that, in addition to its cognitive elements, includes also shared aims, rules of procedure, and presuppositions, not to mention rather specific notions of what constitutes scientific proof and scientific truth. Moreover, the fact that theory and data are interdependent, and both depend on a paradigm, implies that when paradigms change as a result of scientific revolutions, the old and new paradigms will not deal with precisely the same data. They will have different and incommensurable world views. As Kuhn put it, with reference to the different "schools" of science that have succeeded one another, "What differentiated these various schools was not one or another failure of method – they were all 'scientific' – but what we shall come to call their incommensurable ways of seeing the world and of practicing science in it" (Kuhn 1970: 4).

The outlook clearly calls into question the empiricists' vision of scientific progress, as we discussed it earlier. If scientific revolutions result in changes affecting not only the theories but the data as well, it is no longer clear what "the" data are, that are more accurately and comprehensively described by the new theories than by the old ones. Kuhn's view can certainly account for change, insofar as normal scientific activity includes collecting data which, if sufficiently irreconcilable with the existing paradigm, may eventually result in the overthrow of the paradigm. But it is no longer clear that this change can be equated with progress.

(For additional discussion of Kuhn's theory, and particularly of its applicability to the field of archaeology, see Meltzer 1979; Kelley and Hanen 1988: 61–97; and WYA n.d.2.)

Progress in typological paradigms

At this point the first of our considerations regarding classification may be introduced, to suggest that in spite of Kuhn's view there can be progress. However, such progress does not necessarily conform to either the empiricist or the Kuhnian perspective.

We will begin with a rather contentious suggestion: that typologies are not inappropriately regarded as microparadigms, and typological changes as microrevolutions. Thus, the earlier and later versions of the Nubian Pottery Typology have been employed by small scientific communities with shared aims, methods, assumptions, and vocabularies. Theory, in the formalized sense of the logical empiricists, has admittedly not played a significant role in the formulation of the typologies, but the gathering of data, and their description in typological vocabularies, certainly has been involved. Moreover, changing the typology and its vocabulary has led to a new microparadigm which is incommensurable with the old, at least in the sense that the old data are not always translatable into the new vocabulary. For example the original Meroitic Pottery Typology (WYA 1964a) involved some ware distinctions based on criteria of identity that are no longer recognized as significant; therefore many of the former "wares" do not appear in the new typology (WYA 1986a). But this does not mean that we cannot speak of progress.

To speak meaningfully about progress it is necessary and sufficient that there should be common objectives toward which our efforts are directed, and it is neither necessary nor sufficient for this that paradigms should share a common language. The microparadigms of the earlier and later Nubian typologies do not have a completely common language but they do have a common purpose, namely to yield data for the estimation of provenience-dates. For this purpose the newer scheme is undeniably superior to the old, and it can therefore be asserted that progress has been made, even though it may not satisfy the empiricists' criterion of attaining a more accurate and comprehensive description of nature. It is also incommensurate with Kuhn's notion of the sovereignty of paradigms, to which we now turn.

The sovereignty of paradigms

Kuhn holds that scientific paradigms are not only autonomous in their theories, concepts, and methods, but they are "sovereign" in their fundamental aims. What this means is that each paradigm defines its own goals, and there is no overarching common goal toward which all strive. Therefore scientific evolution cannot be viewed as a teleological, goal-directed process. Kuhn likens it more to biological evolution: "the entire process may have occurred, as we now suppose biological evolution did, without benefit of a set goal, a permanent fixed scientific truth, of which each stage in the development of scientific knowledge is a better exemplar" (Kuhn 1970: 172–3).

Obviously this does not describe the sort of change that led from the earlier to the later versions of the Nubian Pottery Typology, since in that case there was a fixed goal, and it was the pursuit of that goal which led to the alteration of the typology. It could be argued from this that the microparadigms represented by the earlier and later pottery typologies are not paradigms in the Kuhnian sense, but we feel that something much more fundamental is involved. It is plausible to suggest that what Kuhn is describing is something very like empiricism, but now relativized in conformity to the different world views or conceptions of nature involved in each particular paradigm. As in orthodox empiricism, normal scientists make observations, record data, and attempt to fit them to theory, but, in the Kuhnian view, the "nature" that furnishes the data varies from one paradigm to another.

Nevertheless, the fact that observation and data-recording are common to all scientific endeavor suggests a common aim as well, and that aim can at least roughly be identified. Observation and recording are tantamount to experience sought and experience reflected on, and relating them to theory amounts to comparing our experience with expectations that may be formed about it. Different paradigms may perhaps concentrate on different kinds of experience, and record it in different ways, and they may even form and use expectations about it in different ways, but we might speculate that all scientific paradigms involve experience and something like expectations related to it, and all of them strive in one way or another to minimize the difference between experience and expectation. To this extent, the various sciences are not so different in their aims as Kuhn would suggest. Lowie (1937: 281) put the matter succinctly half a century ago: "The clarification of concepts . . . directly gauges scientific progress."

It is important that our position on this point should not be misunderstood. Our views on typology, like Kuhn's, may suggest a kind of paradigm-relative empiricism, but they in no way support the idea that scientific paradigms have unlimited sovereignty. To accept such a premise would in effect grant to every group, organization, faction, or clique an equal right to call itself "scientific," and to claim the respect and privilege that scientific activity has increasingly, and properly, acquired through the centuries. Such a relativistic position is insupportable, and is very far from our own view. We consider that all science must continually justify itself by striving to explain, and to reaffirm in each generation, what it is about scientific endeavor that entitles it to respect and protection. But this is a much less easy task than the empiricists have imagined.

As we noted at the beginning of the book, we cannot hope to accomplish in these pages what in some respects has eluded our predecessors from Bacon and Galileo to Carnap and Kuhn: a precise definition of what is distinctive and universal about science. We can, however, offer a further critique of the notion of scientific relativism (or paradigmatic autonomy), based, as before, on our studies of typology.

Conceptual autonomy

The Nubian Pottery Typology is designed to yield estimates of provenience-dates, which can be regarded as "locations in the historical picture." This is consistent with the information-theoretic schema sketched in Chapter 21, but it appears to conflict with Kuhnian relativism insofar as history, like nature, may be regarded as something "out there" waiting to be discovered, and independent of paradigms. To elaborate this point a little further, we may note that archaeology and history are not the only sciences that aim to recover the happenings of the past. In fact, the

320

very physical sciences whose revolutionary developments were the stimulus for Kuhn's theories about paradigms and paradigm shifts are also concerned with a kind of world history. Thus, Book III of Newton's *Principia* (1729), titled "The System of the World," which introduces the principle of universal gravitation, can be interpreted as historical, as indeed can all other cosmological theories. If Kuhn were right about cosmological paradigms there should be no such thing as *the* history of the world, and consequently no unique historical or prehistoric record for the archaeologist to reconstruct. But again the typological example makes this doubtful.

Consider data that are obtained by potsherd typing, for instance that a given percentage of sherds found in a given provenience are representatives of Ware W14 (Terminal Christian decorated white ware). Obviously these data are partly paradigm-dependent, because the very idea of a Ware W14 is an artifact of the typology, and is not found in other typologies. But the provenience-dates that are indicated by the potsherd data are not artifacts of the typology; they are extrinsic to it. Thus, the typological microparadigm only partly creates its own world.

We would suggest that what is true of the typological microparadigm is true also of Kuhnian macroparadigms. They are far from being sovereign over all of nature, and in reality only a small number of the scientists' gestalts and concepts are likely to change as a result of a change in the paradigm. In other words, scientific concepts are frequently independent of the so-called sovereignty of paradigms, and may be autonomous in their own right. Thus, the extreme relativism implicit in the metaphor "after Copernicus, astronomers lived in a different world" (Kuhn 1970: 126) cannot be taken literally.

Readers will be aware that our own position in regard to scientific classifications is avowedly relativistic. However, ours is a fundamentally different kind of relativism from that adopted by some of the more extreme followers of Kuhn, for it relates to practical purposes rather than to theories. To argue, as we do, that the practical utility of a classification can only be judged in relation to some specific purpose is not at all the same thing as arguing that the truth of a classification, or any other scientific procedure, can only be relative to some specific theory. Indeed we have been at some pains to suggest that classifications, like other tools, have no content of truth independent of their utility. We will therefore avoid any discussion of the relativistic doctrines now becoming fashionable in archaeology and anthropology (cf. Bernstein 1983; Hodder 1983; Shanks and Tilley 1987; Wylie 1989; compare also Lakatos 1970), for they raise issues that are not relevant to our own discussion, and that lie far beyond the scope of this book.

The problem of pseudoproblems

Our final remarks concern another problem which the empiricists hoped to approach by means of ideal, theory-neutral observation languages, but which might seem to be complicated by Kuhn's critique: "As for pure observation-language, perhaps one will yet be devised. But three centuries after Descartes our hope for such an eventuality still depends exclusively upon a theory of perception and the mind" (Kuhn 1970: 126).

The problem is that of distinguishing statements of fact from definitions or conventions, a distinction which, if it is not made, can lead to what Carnap (1927) called pseudoproblems in science and philosophy. Here again our observations on typology, together with historical observations, can be brought to bear. They suggest that the problem of pseudoproblems can be expected to arise within scientific paradigms, that it is a serious one, and that it cannot be resolved by routine scientific methods. Rather, it is best approached by a combination of routine methods and the kind of non-routine philosophical analysis that we have attempted in this book.

The kind of pseudoproblem we are concerned with can be exemplified in the case of the law, "Force equals mass times acceleration." It is not *a priori* obvious whether this is a factual claim about a relation between the three independently defined quantities of force, mass, and acceleration, or whether it is really just a definition of, say, force. If the latter is true then there is no sense in testing the law for its agreement with the facts, because it is not a factual claim. To treat it as though it were factual and try to determine its truth would constitute the kind of mistake that methodologists should be on guard against, in order to save themselves and their fellow scientists from useless efforts. It is important to recognize that the problem of pseudoproblems is, or can be, a serious one, for it is by no means self-evident when scientific disputes are mere verbal disputes and when they have substantive content. Interestingly, this may first have been recognized in the cosmological sciences that were the stimulus for Kuhn's own theories. The early disputants in the controversy over Copernicanism obviously regarded the claim "The sun is at rest" as a statement of fact, to be accepted by the heliocentrists but disputed by the geocentrists. More than 300 years were to elapse before it was suggested that saying "The sun is at rest" is merely a convention, stipulating a special meaning of the term "at rest." It was not until 1893 that Ernst Mach wrote: "When quite modern authors let themselves be led astray by the Newtonian arguments

. . . to distinguish relative and absolute motion, they do not reflect that the system of the world is only given *once* to us, and the Ptolemaic and Copernican view is *our* interpretation, but both are equally actual [i.e. factual]" (Mach 1893: 279; italics in the original). In other words Mach was claiming that the dispute between geocentrists and heliocentrists was not a dispute over the factual evidence of cosmic history, but a dispute over how to interpret the evidence.

If such a profound thinker as Mach should have been at pains to argue that what others had regarded as a matter of fact was not really factual at all, then it clearly is not always obvious when a claim is factual and when it is interpretational. We may note by the way that the very insight that the supposedly incommensurable heliocentric and geocentric paradigms were only different interpretations of the same facts was quite truly the basis for a scientific revolution, though not of a kind encompassed within the Kuhnian theory of revolution. It was also an important precursor of Einstein's Relativity. In a vein similar to Mach, Henri Poincaré wrote in 1898 that "the axioms of geometry . . . are only definitions in disguise . . . One geometry cannot be more true than another, it can only be more convenient" (Poincaré 1902: 50).

It was this recognition of the importance and of the difficulty of distinguishing between factual claims and "definitions in disguise" that led philosophers of science like Bridgman (1927) and logical empiricists like Carnap (1937; 1956) to try and devise a systematic means for making such distinctions. This led in turn to attempts to identify and characterize the "purely observational components" of scientific languages, attempts that were severely criticized by Kuhn on the ground that there are no such components. But we suggest that in attacking empiricism, Kuhn was only underscoring a problem that had long been recognized by the empiricists themselves (cf. Quine 1953; Hempel 1957; Maxwell 1962). Recognition of the problem facilitated the acceptance of Kuhn's views, but it did nothing to solve the problem, and Kuhn's work as well as our own observations on typology suggest that it is likely to arise *within* the boundaries of specific paradigms. We will conclude with a few further observations on this point.

The distinction between fact and convention, like all distinctions, obviously depends on a clear characterization of the things being distinguished. But neither fact nor convention is easily characterized, partly because verbal formulations cannot be relied upon to make the distinction. As concerns conventions or definitions – things that instruct in meaning – our earlier considerations suggest that they need not always be explicitly statable in words. Laboratory instruction, when its purpose is to develop a proficiency in getting answers that agree with the answers obtained by other experts, can serve just as well as formally stated definitions. Moreover, even explicit verbal definitions are often far from satisfying the theorist's requirement of giving logically necessary and sufficient conditions for the application of terms, as for example the application of *Canis familiaris* to a particular animal. Finally, there is no reason why laws cannot themselves be used to instruct in the meanings of the terms they involve, providing that the laws have factual content. For example, even though in some instances "force," "mass," and "acceleration" may be independently characterized, in other instances the law "Force equals mass times acceleration" can be used to teach the meanings of the three terms (cf. Harré 1960: 61). This being so, it follows that there is no way of determining from the verbal forms of expressions whether or not they have factual content, even when they are explicitly labeled as definitions.

Turning to the question of what is a fact, we would suggest that it is related to the sort of natural meaning discussed in Chapter 12, meaning that is discovered *a posteriori* (such as that a falling barometer means rain) and not by reference to *a priori* ideas about human sensory capabilities (cf. Grice 1957; 1969). For example, in the Copernican case it was recognized from the beginning that real motion might be unperceivable (cf. Drake 1953: 250). However, Newton later argued that rotary motion can be inferred from its perceivable effects – that is, centrifugal forces. On the basis of James Maxwell's work (1877) it seemed for a time that the same might be true of translational motion, but the failure to detect this led directly to the Einsteinian revolution. It is significant that these disagreements about the observability of motion did not take place between scientists who "lived in different worlds" (cf. Kuhn 1970: 117), for all of them shared the Copernican-Newtonian paradigm. Moreover, their views about observability were determined by *a posteriori* scientific considerations and not primarily by *a priori* theories about sense perception. Thus, whether a claim is factual or is a mere definition in disguise may itself depend on what is found to be scientifically meaningful – something that cannot be determined *a priori*.

Finally, if the examples cited above are representative, they show that questions concerning observability and scientific meaningfulness can be both very important and very difficult. Moreover, they are questions that cannot be resolved by routine scientific methods – by procedures of observation, experiment, and theorizing such as are taught in standard scientific training programs. We suggest that if they are to be addressed at all (as indeed they must), it must be with a combination of scientific and philosophical viewpoints that transcends the narrow boundaries of paradigms and standard scientific training, even though Kuhn believes that such boundaries cannot be transcended. We think otherwise; indeed we believe that the work of Mach and other thinkers whom we have cited here has already broken free of paradigmatic limitations. In a much more modest way we hope that we have done the same in our analysis of Nubian pottery, and its implications for the theory and practice of science.

APPENDICES

APPENDIX A

GLOSSARY OF DEFINITIONS

The following definitions are employed throughout the present work as consistently as seems necessary for purposes of conceptual clarity. These definitions are different in many cases from those employed by other authors, and even from the definitions that are normatively used in philosophy and other disciplines. They should be understood as our own definitions, relative to the present work; there is no suggestion that they are or should be the only definitions. Within each definition, words appearing in bold-face type are themselves defined elsewhere in the glossary. At the end of most entries there is a reference to a particular chapter or chapters in this book where the concept under consideration is more fully discussed.

Abstraction. The mental process involved in creating a **category**, by mentally grouping things together, and thinking of them collectively, on the basis of certain shared characteristics, while ignoring other characteristics that are not shared. (See Chapter 4.)

Acquired gestalt. As used in the present book, a **gestalt** is an immediate **sensory image** which we form upon examining a particular **entity**, and which indicates to us that the entity is a **member** of a particular **type**, without any process of conscious analysis. An acquired gestalt is one which we are able to form only after we have had considerable experience in handling the type in question, in contrast to an **intuitive gestalt** which we are able to form even before types have been formally defined. (See Chapter 4.)

Agglomerative program. A **taxonomic program** in which a **taxonomy** is created by grouping an original set of **basic types** into larger and more inclusive units. The conceptual opposite of an agglomerative program is a **divisive program**. See also **Taxonomic clustering**. (See Chapter 17.)

Analytical purpose. An analytical purpose is served when a **classification** or **typology** is made in order to learn something about the **entities**

being classified. Analytical purposes in archaeological classification may be **intrinsic, interpretive,** or **historical.** (See Chapter 13.)

Analytical type. A **type** which has been **formulated** by a process of conscious analysis of **attributes** and **attribute clusters,** in contrast to an **intuitive type** which is formulated on the basis of a **gestalt.** (See Chapters 6 and 14.)

Ancillary purpose. An ancillary purpose is a particular kind of **instrumental purpose** in classification, when a **classification** or **typology** is made in order to yield information about something other than the actual **entities** being classified. The classification of pottery in order to use the **pottery types** as a basis for the dating of archaeological deposits is an example of an ancillary purpose. (See Chapter 13.)

Apriorism. See **Conceptual apriorism.**

Archaeological ceramologist. A person specializing in the study of pottery found in **archaeological sites.**

Archaeological context. Literally, a particular place in an **archaeological site.** More figuratively, an archaeological context is considered to be a spatial location as well as all of the things that can be associated with, or inferred from, that location. Thus, the context for any **artifact** may comprise the place of its finding, the kind of deposit in which it was found, the other things found in association with it, and the date of the deposit in which it was found. See also **Provenience.**

Archaeological remains. Any physical entities or objects that are known or believed to be the products of human activity in the past. Common kinds of archaeological remains include abandoned dwellings, graves, inscriptions, rock drawings, and **artifacts.** The places where archaeological remains are found *in situ* are referred to as **archaeological sites.**

Archaeological site. Any place where **archaeological remains** are found *in situ*.

Archaeological stratification. An **archaeological site** is said to be stratified when its deposits occur in layers that can be distinguished by the archaeologist. Normally it is assumed that each successive layer, from bottom to top, represents a later period of occupation than did the preceding one. (See Chapter 9.)

Artifact. As used in this book, an artifact is any portable object produced or modified by human activity, whether whole or fragmentary.

Artifact classification or **typology.** Any **classification** or **typology** of **artifacts.**

Artifact type. In archaeology, an artifact type is a grouping together of

artifacts having similar characteristics, which distinguish them from other groups of artifacts having different characteristics. See also **Type**.

Artificial classification or **typology**. In theory, a **classification** or **typology** consisting of **artificial types**; that is, types "**invented**" by the classifier for his own **purposes**. An artificial classification is conceptually opposed to a **natural classification**, which is presumed to reflect nature's ordering rather than the classifier's. In reality we hold that nearly all classifications are partly artificial and partly natural. (See Chapters 6 and 23.)

Artificial type. A **type** which is recognized as having been "**invented**" by the **typologist** for his own **purposes**, rather than representing natural or cultural order. The conceptual opposite of an artificial type is a **natural type**, although we hold that in reality nearly all types are partly artificial and partly natural. (See Chapters 6 and 23.)

Association. The mental process of attaching **meanings** to **entities**, above and beyond what is evident from examining them. (See Chapter 4.)

Associative classification or **typology**. A **classification** or **typology** in which **entities** are classified into groups on the basis of other things with which they are associated, rather than on the basis of shared **intrinsic attributes** alone. A classification of **pottery types** on the basis of the kinds of **sites** in which they are found would be an example of an associative classification. Two common kinds of associative classifications in archaeology are **chronological classifications** and **spatial classifications**. (See Chapter 18.)

Attribute. A particular characteristic or feature which is found in many **entities**, and which helps to define them as constituting a **class** or **type**. That is, all of the **members** of any class or type exhibit a common set of attributes. An attribute is a particular, fixed manifestation of a **variable**; for example, "red" is an attribute of the variable "color." (See especially Chapter 14.)

Attribute clustering. The process of making a **classification** or **typology** by deciding in advance that certain combinations, or clusters, of **attributes** will *a priori* serve to **define** particular **classes** or **types**. For example, an *a priori* decision that all pottery having a red **slip** and a polished surface will automatically constitute "Type RP" would be a case of attribute clustering. Classifying by the process of attribute clustering is often contrasted with the empirical process of classifying by **object clustering**. (See Chapter 23.)

Attribute combination or **cluster**. A combination of **attributes** which regularly occur together in particular **entities**. (See Chapter 14.)

Attribute selection. The process of selecting particular **attributes** that are to be used in **classifying entities** into **classes** or **types**; that is, the selection of attributes that distinguish one class or type from another. (See Chapter 14.)

Attributing, attribution. See **Type attribution**.

Basic purpose. A basic purpose is served when **entities** are **classified** in order to learn something about the entities themselves. A basic purpose contrasts with an **instrumental purpose**, when entities are classified for some purpose other than to learn about the entities themselves. In archaeological classification, basic purposes may be **descriptive**, **comparative**, or **analytical**. (See Chapter 13.)

Basic typology. A **typology** involving only a single **taxonomic level**; that is, a typology in which the **types** are not clustered into larger and more inclusive units, or split into smaller ones. According to our definition, a basic typology is therefore not a **taxonomy**. (See Chapter 17.)

Bimodal, bimodality. A **type** is said to be bimodal when it regularly occurs in two slightly different variants, so that there is no single **norm** or **central tendency**. (See Chapter 4.)

Boundaries. See **Type boundaries**.

Boundedness. As applied to **typologies**, boundedness refers to the fact that **typological boundaries** must be clearly specified; that is, it must be clear what **entities** are and are not to be included in the typology. (See Chapter 7.) As applied to **types**, boundedness refers to the extent to which individual types exhibit clearly defined **type boundaries**; that is, the extent to which they are sharply distinct from other types. (See Chapter 6.)

Category. A collective, abstract **concept** which brings together our mental impressions of a number of distinct things, acts, or experiences which are not identical in every detail, but which are sufficiently similar so that we can think of them collectively and can, if necessary, give them a single categorical **label**. "Tree," "ride," and "pleasure" are examples of categories. (See Chapter 4.)

Center. See **Central tendency**.

Central tendency. A statistical concept referring to the mid-point in any curve of variation, or to the most commonly occurring cluster of traits in any group of related objects or experiences. In the case of **classes** and **types**, the central tendency refers to the group of characteristics that are shared by the largest number of their **members**. In the case specifically of **artifact types**, the central tendency is presumed to represent the **norm**, or ideal, which the artifact maker was striving to achieve in each individual specimen, but did not always attain in practice. That is, some individual **artifacts** always fall closer to the norm or central tendency than do others. Central tendency is more or less synonymous with **modality**. (See Chapter 6.)

Ceramologist. See **Archaeological ceramologist.**

Chronological classification or **typology.** A **classification** or **typology** in which **entities** are assigned to **classes** or **types** at least partly on the basis of when they were made or used. A classification in which all objects made in the twelfth century were assigned to one class, all objects from the thirteenth century to another, and all objects from the fourteenth century to still another, would be an example of a purely chronological classification. (See Chapter 18.)

Chronological seriation. The arrangement of **entities** or **types** in a **linear order** based primarily on the dates of their manufacture or use. (See Chapter 17.)

Class. One of the **categories** in a **classification.**

Classes of variables. As employed in the present book, classes of variables are **intrinsic variables, contextual variables** and **inferential variables.** (See Chapter 14.)

Classification. A matched **set** of contrasting **categories** which, collectively, include all of the **entities** or phenomena within a particular field of study, or set of **boundaries.** A **typology** is a particular kind of classification made for **sorting** entities. (See especially Chapter 4.)

Classificatory dialectic. The continual **feedback** between **entities** and **concepts**; that is, between objects on the one hand and our ideas about them on the other. We argue that **type concepts** (our ideas about groups of objects) continually change as we become familiar with more and more objects, resulting in the redefinition of **types.** This in turn will determine which objects are subsequently assigned to the types. (See especially Chapter 5.)

Classificatory era. See **Classificatory paradigm.**

Classificatory hierarchy. See **Classificatory ranking** and **Taxonomy.**

Classificatory paradigm. The dominant research orientation in American archaeology before about 1940, when the main concern of archaeologists was to develop **temporal** and **spatial classifications** of prehistoric "**cultures.**" (See Chapter 22.)

Classificatory ranking or **taxonomy.** An **ordering** of **classes** or **types** into larger and more inclusive groupings, based on features of similarity among the classes or types. A **classificatory ranking** is synonymous with a **classificatory hierarchy** and with a **taxonomy**, as the term is employed in this book. (See Chapters 7 and 17.)

Classify, classifying, classified. The process of making a **classification**. Not to be confused with **sorting**, which is the assignment of **entities** to **classes** once the classification has been made. (See Chapter 15.)

Closed typology. A **typology** which is designed only for the **sorting** and/or **typing** of **entities** that are already in hand, without any consideration for additional entities that may be discovered in the future. The conceptual opposite of a closed typology is an **open typology**. (See Chapter 18.)

Cluster (noun). See **Attribute combination**.

Cluster (verb). See **Attribute clustering** and **Object clustering**.

Cluster analysis. Any of several systems of computerized classification in which the computer discovers which combinations of **attributes** most regularly occur together. These **attribute clusters** are then often **designated** as **types**. **Numerical Taxonomy** is the most common form of cluster analysis employed by archaeologists. A **dendrogram** is the visual representation of the relationship between types developed by cluster analysis. (See Chapter 23.)

Collection. Any group of **entities** that are to be **classified**. (See Chapter 5.)

Color. See **Pottery color**.

Comparative purpose. In archaeology, a comparative purpose is served when a **typology** is made in order to permit comparison of **entities** found in different **sites** or in different levels. (See Chapter 13.)

Comprehensive, comprehensiveness. One of the essential features of a **typology**, which must always have enough **types** so that every **entity** within the **typological boundaries** is assignable to one type or another within the system. (See Chapter 7.)

Concept. Any more or less fixed idea about the nature of a thing, experience, etc. In the case of material **entities**, a concept usually involves both a **sensory image** of the entity, and any **associations** that the sensory image regularly calls up. See also **Type concept**. (See Chapter 4.)

Conceptual apriorism. In philosophy of science, conceptual apriorism involves the belief that **scientific concepts** should correspond to some absolute reality, and therefore can be evaluated in absolute terms as "true" or "false" without reference to any theory, hypothesis, or purpose. In this respect conceptual apriorism stands in contrast to **conceptual instrumentalism**. (See Chapter 1.)

Conceptual instrumentalism. The doctrine that concepts are instruments that can be deliberately developed and used for specific purposes. For example, the concept of heat was deliberately developed in thermodynamics, and is used in practice and research to describe thermal phenomena. Conceptual instrumentalism is the position endorsed by the authors of the present book, in contrast to the opposite position of **conceptual apriorism**. (See Chapters 1 and 12.)

Conditional probability. When the probability of one thing is conditional on another. For example, the probability of a person's surviving to age 80 is conditional on his surviving to age 60. Conditional probability is usually defined as a ratio between **unconditional probabilities**; e.g. the ratio between the probability of surviving to age 60 and the probability of surviving to age 80. (See Chapter 21.)

Conditional uncertainty. When the probabilistic uncertainty of an event or possibility is conditional on something else being the case. An example would be the uncertainty in regard to the species of a particular animal, given that it is a mammal. (See Chapter 21.)

Configurational/functional paradigm. A research orientation in American archaeology in the 1940s and 1950s, which was influenced by the contemporary development of both **configurationism** and **functionalism** in ethnology. Archaeologists came to feel that their most important task was to discover the cultural or **emic meanings** or the behavioral significance of the things they discovered, and thereby to reconstruct the thought processes or habitual behaviors of the people who had made and used the things. (See Chapter 22.)

Configurationism. A theoretical and research orientation that was prevalent in American anthropology in the 1940s and 1950s, when it was felt that the most important task of the anthropologist was to discover and describe the enduring norms, values, and interests that were held to be the central features of each human culture. The combination of these norms, values, and interests was characterized as the configuration of each culture. (See Chapters 22 and 25.)

Congeries. A group of things brought together by accident or by design, but having no systematic relationship to one another. (See Chapter 4.)

Consistency of definition. The principle that all of the **types** in any **basic typology** must be defined on the basis of the same overall set of **variables,** so that the definition of any given type cannot wholly overlap with the definition of any other type. (See Chapter 7.)

Context. See **Archaeological context**.

Contextual variable. One of several kinds of **extrinsic variables** that may serve to define **artifact types**. Contextual variables have to do not with the physical properties of the types, but with the circumstances in which they are found. Distribution in time (i.e. the dates of deposits in which types are found), distribution in space (the areas in which types are found), and associations (other types with which the type is regularly found) are examples of contextual variables. (See Chapter 14.)

Contypical, contypicality. Two or more entities are said to be contypical when they are **members** of the same **type**.

Cultural ecology. A currently prevalent theoretical **paradigm** in anthropology and archaeology, in which human cultures are viewed as adaptive systems, and differences between cultures are attributed to their adaptation to different environmental or economic circumstances. (See Chapter 25.)

"Culture." The archaeologist's term for a combination of **artifact types**, dwelling types (when present), grave types (when present), and other cultural remains that regularly occur together in a particular area, and that can be assigned to a specific period in time. Such associations are interpreted by prehistoric archaeologists as evidence of **ethnic identity**; that is, each distinctive combination of cultural remains is attributed to the activities of a different people. (See Chapter 18.)

"Culture" classification. The arrangement of archaeological **"cultures"** in a classificatory scheme, based on their perceived resemblance or presumed relationship to one another. "Culture" classifications are often **genetic taxonomies**, in which it is assumed that the later "cultures" are descended from the earlier ones. (See Chapter 18.)

Decoration. See **Pottery decoration**.

Decorative element. A particular kind of decorative **design** which is applied to a particular area of the exterior or interior of a pottery vessel. Stripes painted along the rim, friezes painted just below the rim, and radiating designs in the interior of bowls are examples of decorative elements. (See Chapter 10.)

Decorative field. A particular area of pottery vessel surfaces which, in particular **wares**, is frequently decorated. In Nubian Ware W14 (see Appendix B) the most common decorative fields are those comprising the upper two-thirds of vase exteriors, and the interior centers of bowls. (See Chapter 10.)

Decorative motif. A particular kind of **design** employed in the decoration of pottery. Common motifs employed in the decoration of medieval Nubian pottery include various kinds of cross designs, animal and bird figures, and floral wreaths. (See Chapter 10.)

Decorative program. The complete combination of **decorative elements** found on any one pottery vessel. (See Chapter 10.)

Deduction. Reasoning from general principles to specific cases. If we know that there is a law of gravity, we deduce that if we let go an object it will fall to the ground. Deduction is the conceptual opposite of **induction**, although in practice there is usually a continual **feedback** between the two reasoning processes. (See Chapters 6 and 23.)

Deductive classification. In theory, a **classification** made by **deduction**. If we knew in advance that a certain ancient people had practiced agriculture, but had also hunted and fished, we might deduce that they had used pottery, hoes, bows and arrows, and fishing gear, even if we had not actually found examples of these. Pots, hoes, arrow points, and fishhooks would therefore comprise a deductive classification of artifact types. The conceptual opposite of a deductive classification is an **inductive classification**, but in practice the great majority of archaeological classifications are partly deductive and partly inductive. (See Chapters 6 and 23.).

Define, defining, defined. The process of formulating a **definition**. In the present book this refers specifically to the process of formulating a **type definition**. (See Chapter 15.)

Definition. See **Type definition**.

Dendrogram. A diagram expressing visually the relationships, and degrees of relationship, between **types** that have been generated by a program of **cluster analysis**, or between individual **entities**. (See Chapter 17.)

Describing, description. See **Type description**.

Descriptive attribute. An **attribute** which is characteristic but not definitive, or **diagnostic**, of a **type**. Matte surface finish is a descriptive attribute of Nubian Ware W14 (see Appendix B), in that most but not all members of the ware have this characteristic. (See Chapter 15.)

Descriptive purpose. A descriptive purpose is served when a **typology** is made simply to facilitate description of the **entities** being classified; that is, to convey an accurate impression of a group of entities to other readers or hearers. (See Chapter 13.)

Descriptive type concept. A **mutable** type concept which is held to be accurately descriptive of **type members** currently in hand, but which may be modified when new type members are found. In archaeology, a descriptive type concept usually results when entities are classified by the technique of **object clustering**. Descriptive type concepts can theoretically be contrasted with **prescriptive type concepts**. (See Chapter 15.)

337

Descriptive variable. A variable feature which is included in a **typology**, and in **type descriptions**, because it frequently helps in the recognition of **type members**, even though it may not be **diagnostic** of them. In this respect a descriptive variable contrasts with a **defining variable**. (See Chapter 15.)

Design. See **Pottery design**.

Designating, designation. See **Type designation**.

Diagnostic attribute. A particular **attribute** which is essential to the **definition** of a **type**, so that any given **entity** must exhibit this attribute before it can be identified as a **member** of the type. In other words, possession of one or more diagnostic attributes is a **necessary condition** for **type attribution** in the case of any entity. A cream to light orange **slip** color is one of the diagnostic attributes of Nubian Ware W14, described in Appendix B. (See Chapters 14 and 15.)

Diagnostic attribute cluster or **combination**. A combination of **attributes** that serve to **define** a particular **type**, so that any **entity** exhibiting these attributes can automatically be identified as a **member** of the type. In other words, possession of a diagnostic attribute cluster is both a **necessary** and a **sufficient condition** for **type attribution** in the case of particular entities. The diagnostic attribute cluster for Nubian Ware W14 involves a combination of Nile mud **fabric**, cream **slip**, brown **decoration**, and decorative designs in Style N.VII (see Appendix B). (See Chapters 14 and 15.)

Dialectic. See **Classificatory dialectic**.

Differentiating, differentiation. See **Type differentiation**.

Dimensions of typehood. We say that every **type** is composed partly of a group of **entities**, partly of our ideas about those entities, and partly of the words and/or pictures in which we express our ideas. These are respectively the physical, mental, and representational dimensions of typehood. (See Chapter 3.)

Discovering, discovery. See **Type discovery**.

Divisive program. A **taxonomic program** in which a **taxonomy** is created by dividing an original group of **basic types** into finer and finer subdivisions. The conceptual opposite of a divisive program is an **agglomerative program**. See also **taxonomic splitting**. (See Chapter 17.)

Domain of variability. A complex **classification**, such as a classification of pottery, usually includes not only a great many individual **variables**, but variables of many different kinds, which we have designated as **domains of variability**. The kinds of variables included in the

Medieval Nubian Pottery Typology include **method of construction, fabric, surface treatment, vessel forms, colors, painted decoration,** and **relief decoration**. (See Chapter 14.)

Electronic paradigm. As defined in the present work, the electronic paradigm is an approach to **classification** that relies heavily or exclusively on the use of computers to generate **classes** or **types**. This has been the dominant paradigm in American **artifact classification,** at least in the theoretical literature, since about 1970. (See Chapter 22.)

Elements of typehood. The mental, physical, and representational components which together go to make up a **type**. These include **type concepts, type descriptions, type definitions, type labels, type names, type categories,** and **type members**. (See Chapter 3.)

Emic classification or **typology**. As employed in the present work, an emic typology is any **typology** composed entirely of what the archaeologist believes are **emic types**. It is not to be confused with a **folk typology,** which in the case of **artifacts** would be a classification of the artifacts made by their actual makers and users. (See Chapters 18 and 23.)

Emic meaning. The **meaning** which an **entity** or **type** is known or presumed to have had for its makers and users. (See Chapters 4 and 24.)

Emic significance. An **artifact type** is said to have emic significance if it is believed that the type would in some sense have been recognized as a type by its makers and users. That is, the type results from a deliberate attempt on the part of the makers to produce a group of artifacts similar or identical to one another, and at the same time different in some degree from other groups of artifacts. (See Chapters 18 and 23.)

Emic type. An **artifact type** which, it is believed, the makers and users would themselves have recognized as constituting a distinct type or category. That is, it is different from other types because it was meant to be different. See also **Emic classification** and **Emic meaning**. (See Chapter 18.)

Empirical significance, empirically significant. We say that a **type** or an **entity** is empirically significant when it has a known **meaning**. The conceptual opposite of empirical significance is **intuitive significance,** when we assume that a type or entity has meaning but we do not know what it is. (See Chapter 4.)

Empiricism. The doctrine that all non-deductive truths, including most scientific laws, are ultimately justified by appeal to experience. (See Chapter 26.)

"Empiricist" classification. A term introduced by Hill and Evans (1972) to describe what others have called **natural classification**. In the formulation of Hill and Evans, "empiricist" classification contrasts with **"positivist" classification**. (See Chapter 23.)

Entity. We use this term to designate whatever is **classified** and/or **sorted** in a **typology**. In **artifact typologies** the entities classified and sorted are always physical objects, i.e. **artifacts**, but this is not true in the case of typologies of house plans, grave plans, or rock drawings, where the classified entities are not physical things but incomplete representations of them. (See Chapter 4.)

Equidistance of types. The principle that all **types** in a **basic typology** are equally similar and equally dissimilar to one another. (See Chapter 7.)

Equivalence of types. The principle that all **types** in a **basic typology** are equal in importance, regardless of the number of their **members**. (See Chapter 7.)

Essential classification or **typology**. In theory, a **classification** or **typology** in which **entities** are classified on the basis of their physical characteristics and/or their known associations, but without reference to any **purpose**. The conceptual opposite of an essential classification is an **instrumental classification**; however, in practice most classifications are partly essential and partly instrumental. (See Chapter 6.)

Ethnic identification. As used in the present book, ethnic identification refers to the association of a particular **artifact type**, or types, with a particular tribe or people. Finding of the artifact type or types is therefore taken as *a priori* evidence that a particular people was formerly present. Ethnic identification establishes **ethnic identity**. (See Chapters 13 and 18.)

Ethnic identity. Any human social group having a name for itself, and exhibiting some degree of cultural difference from other social groups, is said to have ethnic identity. In the study of prehistoric archaeology, ethnic identity is often ascribed on the basis of **artifact types**. That is, particular artifact types are taken as *a priori* evidence for the presence of particular human groups. See also **Ethnic identification**. (See Chapters 13 and 18.)

Etic classification. The **classification** of **entities** into **classes** or **types** that have some **meaning** for the classifier, without any consideration for whether the classes or types would have had meaning for the makers and users of the entities (**emic meaning**). Etic classification is often contrasted with **emic classification**, in which it is assumed that the classes or types would have been recognized as such by the makers and users of the entities. (See Chapters 18 and 23.)

Etic meaning. The **meaning** which a **class** or **type** has for the **typologist**. In the case of types, etic meaning is equivalent to **typological meaning**, or **relevance**. Etic meaning is often contrasted with **emic meaning**, the meaning which an entity or type is presumed to have had for its makers and users. (See Chapters 4 and 24.)

Exemplar. Synonymous with **Type member**.

Explanation. As defined in this book, explanation refers to that kind of human cognition which involves causal reasoning: A causes B, etc. Other kinds of cognition discussed by us are **prediction** and **understanding**. (See Chapter 25.)

Explicit definition. See **Explicit type definition**.

Explicit type definition. In this book we say that a **type** has an explicit definition when its **diagnostic attributes** have been formally stated in words and/or pictures. (See Chapter 3.)

Extendable typology. A **typology** that is capable of enlargement to include new **types** as they are discovered or **designated**. An extendable typology is not necessarily synonymous with a **mutable typology**, which is also capable of the redefinition of existing types. (See Chapter 18.)

External criteria. See **Extrinsic variable**.

External isolation. One of the two essential bases of **type identity**, referring to the fact that **types** must have some kind of identifiable **type boundaries**. That is, they must be sufficiently different from other types so that their **members** can be readily distinguished. (See Chapters 3 and 6.)

Extrinsic attribute. A characteristic of any **type** which cannot be determined simply by examining **members** of the type. In the case of **artifact types**, extrinsic attributes include dates of manufacture, places of manufacture, presumed uses of the artifact, etc. The conceptual opposite of an extrinsic attribute is an **intrinsic attribute**. (See Chapter 14.)

Extrinsic feature. See **Extrinsic attribute**.

Extrinsic variable. A **variable** feature of any **type** which is not directly manifest, or visible, in the **members** of the type, but which relates to the circumstances in which the members are found (**contextual variables**), their presumed function (**inferential variables**), or some other characteristic which cannot be determined simply by examination of the type members themselves. The distribution of an **artifact type** in time (e.g. thirteenth to fifteenth century) and in space (e.g. in the Nile Valley from the First to the Second Cataract) are extrinsic variables of that type. The conceptual opposite of extrinsic variables are **intrinsic variables**. (See Chapter 14.)

Fabric. See **Pottery fabric**.

Factor analysis. The technique of estimating the weights of linear "factors" that contribute to determining the value of a **random variable**. For example, factor analysis might help to determine how many years of education, how much parents' wealth, and how much aptitudes of various kinds might contribute to determining a person's income at age 40. (See Chapter 21.)

Family. See **Pottery family**.

Feasible, feasibility. Synonymous with **Practical, practicality**.

Feedback. As applied to **artifact typologies**, feedback refers to the **dialectical** relationship between **type concepts** and **entities** (**type members**) that are **classified** according to those concepts. We argue that type concepts are originally **formulated** on the basis of an initial **collection** of **artifacts**, but they are then continually modified as we examine and **type** additional artifacts. See also **Classificatory dialectic**. (See especially Chapter 5.)

Field of decoration. See **Decorative field**.

Folk classification, typology, or **taxonomy**. In the usage of anthropologists and linguists, a folk classification usually refers to a **vernacular classification** which is in use among non-literate peoples. (See Chapters 4 and 5.)

Folk concept. A concept or abstraction occurring in popular speech, not developed or used for any scientific purpose. As employed in this work, a folk concept contrasts with a **scientific concept**; for example, "dog" is a folk concept while *Canis familiaris* is a scientific concept. See also **Vernacular type**. (See Chapter 12.)

Foreknowledge. Knowledge about the nature of certain **entities** which is possessed by the classifier prior to the act of **classifying** the entities, and which affects the way in which they are classified. (See Chapter 5.)

Form class. See **Vessel form class**.

Formulating, formulation. The process by which a **type concept** comes into being, whether by intuition, **object clustering, attribute clustering**, or any mental process. See also **Type formulation**. (See Chapter 15.)

Frequency. See **Type frequency**.

Frequency seriation. The arrangement of **type frequency** data in a chronological order. Most commonly, a series of **collections** is arranged in chronological order on the basis of the frequency with which certain **types** occur in them, relative to the frequency of other types. (See Chapter 17.)

Functional classification or **typology**. A **classification** or **typology** in which **entities** that are presumed to have performed the same function are grouped together, whether or not they are similar in shape, size, or other characteristics. Functional classification is often contrasted with **morphological** or **phenetic** classification, where objects are grouped on the basis of physical similarities alone. (See Chapter 18.)

Functionalism. A theoretical **paradigm** that was influential in British and American anthropology in the middle years of the twentieth century. Among ethnologists, functionalism involved the attempt to explain cultural beliefs or activity patterns with reference to what purpose they served, either for individuals or for social groups. Among archaeologists, functionalism involved the attempt to explain cultural remains, including **artifact types**, with reference to specific prehistoric activity patterns. See also **Functionalist paradigm**. (See Chapters 22 and 23.)

Functionalist paradigm. In the field of archaeology, the functionalist paradigm is an approach which holds that **artifacts** should be analyzed and classified in terms of what functions they performed for the makers and users. See also **Functional classification** and **Functionalism**. (See Chapter 22.)

Fuzzy set. In **fuzzy set theory**, a fuzzy set is a group of things (designated in fuzzy set theory as a class) which does not have precisely defined criteria of membership. A fuzzy set is defined by a **central tendency** but has no sharp **boundaries**; on the contrary fuzzy sets overlap with one another at the boundaries. The conceptual opposite of a fuzzy set is an **ordinary set**. See also **Fuzzy set theory**. (See Chapter 6.)

Fuzzy set theory. An approach to classification in which things are grouped into **fuzzy sets** which have no precisely defined criteria of membership. The distinctive feature of fuzzy set theory, in contrast to the systems of classification discussed in this book, is that **entities** have variable and measurable degrees of membership in a fuzzy set, whereas in the classifications discussed by us an entity is either a **member** of a **type** or it is not. Fuzzy set theory is not employed by archaeologists and is only briefly considered in the present book. (See Chapter 6.)

Generative typology. Essentially the same as an **open typology**; that is, a typology in which it is possible to generate new types on the basis of the same criteria used in defining existing types. (See Chapter 19.)

Genetic classification. The practice of **classifying** things in such a way as to show their genetic relationships to one another; that is, to show which **entities** or **types** are believed to be derived or descended from

343

which other entities or types. The end product of genetic classification is a **genetic taxonomy**. (See Chapter 17.)

Genetic taxonomy. A **taxonomy** in which the **entities** in each **taxon** are grouped together on the assumption that they are all descended from a common ancestor, which may itself comprise a taxon at a higher **taxonomic level**. The conceptual opposite of a genetic taxonomy is a **non-genetic taxonomy**. (See Chapter 17.)

Gestalt. As employed in the present book, a gestalt refers to an immediate **sensory image**, derived from the examination of an **entity**, which leads us to conclude that the entity is representative of a **type**, even though no process of conscious analysis is involved. We say that gestalts are either **intuitive** or **acquired**. Our usage of this term does not correspond precisely with that of Gestalt psychologists or of some philosophers. (See Chapters 4 and 5.)

Hand-made wares. Pottery wares produced without the aid of the potter's wheel. The conceptual opposite of hand-made wares are **wheel-made wares**. (See Chapters 9 and 10.)

Hierarchic ordering. See **Taxonomic classification**.

Hierarchy. See **Classificatory ranking** and **Social ranking**.

Historical classification or **typology**. A **classification** or **typology** in which **entities** are grouped together on the basis of historical relationship to one another; that is, because they were all made at the same time and/or in the same area, or are otherwise related historically. (See Chapter 18.)

Historical purpose. One of several kinds of **analytical purposes** which a **classification** or **typology** may serve. A historical purpose is served when a classification or typology is made in order to aid in the reconstruction of history or culture history. Many **ancillary typologies** are made for historical purposes. (See Chapter 13.)

"Ideal type." A **type** in which the **ideal type specimen** is considered to be normative, but in which the majority of **members** actually deviate to some extent from the **norm**. (See Chapter 6.)

Ideal type specimen. An **entity** which exhibits in the fullest degree all of the **diagnostic** and **descriptive attributes** of the **type** to which it belongs. In many types the ideal type specimen is actually atypical; that is, the majority of **type members** do not exhibit the defining and descriptive attributes to the fullest degree. See also **"Ideal type."** (See Chapter 6).

Identifiable, identifiability. The consistency with which the **members** of a **type** can be recognized as such (i.e. can be **sorted** into the appropriate **type categories**) on the basis of their physical characteristics

344

or of the contexts in which they occur. Consistent identifiability is one of the necessary **properties** of **useful types**. (See Chapter 3.)

Identifiable type. A **type** possessing the property of **identifiability**; that is, one whose **members** can be fairly consistently recognized as such on the basis either of physical characteristics or of the contexts in which they occur. The conceptual opposite of an identifiable type is an **occult type**. (See Chapter 3.)

Identity. Every **entity** is said to possess an **individual identity** and a **typological identity**. (See Chapter 3.)

Implicit definition. See **Implicit type definition**.

Implicit type definition. In this book we say that a **type** has an implicit definition, rather than an **explicit definition**, when its **defining attributes** have not been formally stated in words and/or pictures. (See Chapter 3.)

Imprinting, imprintation. The process through which a **sensory perception** becomes a **sensory image**; that is, it becomes sufficiently fixed in the mind that it can be recalled when the original stimulating object or experience is no longer present. (See Chapter 4.)

Incidental purpose. A particular kind of **instrumental purpose**. We say that an incidental purpose is served when a **classification** is made for some kind of convenience, such as convenience for the storage of objects or the filing of records, rather than for any scholarly or scientific **purpose**. (See Chapter 13.)

Independence of types. The principle that the existence of no **type** in a **basic typology** depends on the pre-existence of any other type. (See Chapter 7.)

Index cluster. As employed in the dating of Nubian **archaeological sites**, an index cluster is a distinctive combination of **pottery wares** that consistently occur together in relatively constant proportions. (See Chapter 11.)

Index fossil. In geology and palaeontology, an index fossil is the fossil of a particular plant or animal species, whose presence automatically indicates that the surrounding deposit or formation is of a particular geological age. In archaeology, an **artifact type** which indicates that the surrounding archaeological deposit belongs to a particular age or "**culture**" is thought of as analogous to an index fossil. (See Chapter 13.)

Individual identity. The individual identity of any **entity** constitutes its status as a thing separate from all other things, as established by the characteristics that distinguish it from all other things. Individual identity

345

contrasts with **typological identity**, which is shared with all of the other entities in the same **type**. (See Chapter 3.)

Individual meaning. The individual meanings of any **entity** are the associations that it has for us, or that can be inferred from it, as an individual thing different from all other things. Individual meaning contrasts with **typological meaning**, which is the meaning that a thing has for us because it is a **member** of a **type**, and is shared with other members of the same type. (See Chapter 3.)

Induction. Reasoning from specific instances to general principles. If we observe a sufficient number of objects fall to the ground, we may induce that there is a law of gravity. Induction is the theoretical opposite of **deduction**, although in practice there is usually a continual feedback between the two kinds of reasoning. (See Chapters 6 and 23.)

Inductive classification. In theory, a **classification** made by **induction**; that is, one in which **type concepts** are **formulated** only after examining a large number of actual **entities**, and dividing them into groups on the basis of observed similarities. An inductive classification is the theoretical opposite of a **deductive classification**. In practice, however, the great majority of archaeological classifications are partly inductive and partly deductive. (See Chapters 6 and 23.)

Inferential variable. One of several kinds of **extrinsic variables** that may serve to define **artifact types**. Inferential variables refer not to physical or observable characteristics of the artifacts, but to inferences about what they were used for (functional significance) or about what they meant to their makers (**emic meaning**). (See Chapter 14.)

Information theory. Mathematical theory of information based on concepts of probability and entropy. (See Chapter 21.)

Informative typology. As employed in this work, an informative typology is synonymous with a **useful typology**, one that yields desired information for some specified purpose. (See Chapters 19–21.)

Instantiation. In philosophy and logic, instantiation means that there are concrete examples, or instances, corresponding to an abstract concept, or showing that something that has been imagined really exists. (See Chapter 12.)

Instrumental classification or **typology**. In theory, a **classification** or **typology** in which **classes** or **types** are **formulated** entirely with reference to a specific **purpose**; that is, no class or type is included which does not serve the purpose of the classification, no matter how morphologically distinct it may be. The conceptual opposite of an instrumental classification is an **essential classification**; however, in practice most classifications are partly essential and partly instrumental. (See Chapter 6.)

Instrumental purpose. An instrumental purpose is served when a **classification** or **typology** is not made in order to learn or express anything about the **entities** being classified, but for some other purpose, which may be either **ancillary** or **incidental**. (See Chapter 13.)

Instrumental relativism. The doctrine espoused by the authors of this book, holding that the **practical utility** of a **classification** can not be judged in the abstract, but only in relation to some specific **purpose**. Instrumental relativism is not to be confused with **theoretical relativism**. (See Chapter 1.)

Instrumentalism. See **Conceptual instrumentalism**.

Internal cohesion. One of the essential bases of **type identity**, referring to the fact that the **members** of any **type** must have a sufficient number of features in common so that the commonality among them is evident. (See Chapters 3 and 6.)

Internal criteria. See **Intrinsic variable**.

Interpersonal objectivity. A **classification** is said to have interpersonal objectivity if all persons trained in its use agree on its application in particular cases. See also **Real objectivity**. (See Chapter 21.)

Interpretive purpose. One of several kinds of **analytical purposes** which a **classification** or **typology** may serve. An interpretive purpose is served when **entities** are **classified** in such a way as to facilitate interpretation of how they were used (**functional classification**) or what they meant to the makers and users (**emic classification**), rather than to express their physical resemblances. (See Chapter 13.)

Intersubjective agreement or **consistency**. The consistency with which two or more **sorters** will make the same **type attributions**; that is, they will identify the same or closely similar **entities** as members of the same **types**. See also **Intrasubjective agreement**. (See Chapters 5 and 15.)

Interval scale. A particular kind of measurement, in which the **attributes** of a **variable** are designated as equally distributed scores along a linear scale. When the length of artifacts is designated as "short" (0–10 cm), "medium" (10–20 cm), "long" (20–30 cm), or "very long" (30–40 cm), artifact length is measured on an interval scale. While interval scales are theoretically different from **ordinal scales**, the nature of the difference between them is a subject of philosophical dispute. See also **Nominal scale**, **Ordinal scale**, and **Ratio scale**. (See Chapters 12 and 16.)

347

Interval variable. A **variable** whose **attributes** are differentiated from each other according to an **interval scale**. (See Chapter 16.)

Intrasubjective agreement or **consistency**. The consistency with which an individual **sorter** will make the same or similar **type attributions** on different occasions; that is, he will identify the same or closely similar **entities** as members of the same **types**. See also **Intersubjective agreement**. (See Chapters 5 and 15.)

Intrinsic attribute. A characteristic of any **type** which can be determined by examining **members** of the type itself, without knowing anything about where they came from, their associations, etc. The conceptual opposite of an intrinsic attribute is an **extrinsic attribute**. (See Chapter 16.)

Intrinsic feature. See **Intrinsic attribute**.

Intrinsic purpose. One of several kinds of **analytical purposes** which a **classification** or **typology** may serve. An intrinsic purpose is served when **entities** are **classified** in order to learn something about the entities themselves, e.g. whether they vary in certain morphological characteristics. (See Chapter 13.)

Intrinsic variable. A **variable** feature of any **type** which is directly manifest in the **members** of the type. That is, it can be determined by examination of the members themselves, without any knowledge about the contexts from which they came or the purpose for which they were used. An intrinsic variable is the conceptual opposite of an **extrinsic variable**. (See Chapter 14.)

Intuitive class. See **Intuitive type**.

Intuitive classification or **typology**. In theory, a **classification** or **typology** made up of **intuitive classes** or **types**; that is, types **formulated** only by the classifier's intuition. An intuitive classification is the conceptual opposite of a **rational classification**, although in practice most classifications are partly intuitive and partly rational. (See Chapters 5 and 15.)

Intuitive gestalt. As employed in the present book, an intuitive gestalt is an immediate **sensory image**, derived from the examination of an **entity** or group of entities, which causes us to conclude that the entity or entities are representatives of a **type**, even though the type may not yet have been consciously defined. See also **Acquired gestalt**. (See Chapters 4 and 5.)

Intuitive significance, intuitively significant. We say that an **entity** or **type** has intuitive significance when its **identity** is so distinctive that we intuitively conclude that it must have some **meaning** or **relevance**, even though we do not yet know what the meaning or relevance is. Intuitive significance is one of the aspects of a **gestalt**, as we use the term here. The conceptual opposite of intuitive significance is **empirical significance**. (See Chapter 3.)

Intuitive type. A **type** which is **designated** purely on the basis of the classifier's intuition, without any attempt at conscious analysis. Intuitive types usually disclose themselves through **intuitive gestalts**. The conceptual opposite of an intuitive type is an **analytical type**. (See Chapters 5 and 15.)

Invariant. An **attribute** that is common to all of the **types** in a **typology**. (See Chapter 14.)

Inventing, invention. See **Type invention**.

Irrelevant type. A **type** which is **identifiable** on the basis of its physical characteristics, but which has no **utility** for the **purposes** of the **typology** of which it is a **member**. An irrelevant type is not necessarily synonymous with a **meaningless type**, which has no utility for any purpose. (See Chapter 3.)

Label. An identifying symbol, such as a word, phrase, number, or picture, which is associated with a **concept**, so that the concept can be communicated from one person to another simply by speaking, writing, or exhibiting the label. The labels that we are concerned with in this book are **type labels**. (See Chapter 4.)

Labeling. The act of attaching a **label** to a **concept**. (See Chapter 4.)

Language. As used in this book, language is synonymous with **lexicon**. It refers only to a set of labeled **concepts** (**words**), ignoring the linguistic features of grammar and syntax. (See Chapter 4.)

Lexicon. The sum total of all the labeled **concepts** (**words**) that are regularly used and/or understood by any human individual or group. The words in a natural language constitute a lexicon; so in the broadest sense do the **types** in a **typology**. (See Chapter 4.)

Linear ordering. See **Seriation**.

Logical empiricism. A kind of **empiricism** in which scientific propositions are to be expressed in formal, logical languages. In logical empiricism, basic data are to be derived from sense experience, while laws and theories are to be justified by virtue of their formal deductive (sometimes probabilistic) relations to these data. (See Chapter 26.)

Lumper. A classifier who, in the process of making a **typology**, is prone to the practice of **lumping**. The conceptual opposite of a lumper is a **splitter**. (See Chapter 23.)

Lumping. When a **typology** is made by **object clustering**, lumping refers to the tendency on the part of classifiers to divide the classified **entities** into a limited number of rather variable **types**, rather than into a larger number of more uniform types. The conceptual opposite of lumping is **splitting**. (See Chapter 23.)

Mathematical probability. The mathematical theory of probabilities, and relations among probabilities, as applied to arbitrary classes of events or propositions. (See Chapter 21.)

Meaning. In our usage, every **entity** is said to possess **individual meanings** and **typological meanings**.

Meaningful, meaningfulness. As employed in this book, meaningfulness refers to **typological meaning**. An **entity** is said to be meaningful when it possesses **typological meaning**; a **type** is said to be meaningful when it is **relevant** to the **purpose** of the **typology** of which it is a **member**. (See Chapter 3.)

Meaningless type. A **type** which has **identity** but no **meaning**; that is, it has no **utility** for any specific **purpose**. (See Chapter 3.)

Medieval Nubian Pottery Typology. A comprehensive **typology** of **pottery wares** made and used in **Nubia** between about A.D. 200 and 1600. (See Chapters 9–11.)

Member. See **Type member.**

Mental template. An idea or ideal which is presumed to have existed in the mind of an **artifact** maker as to how particular **artifact types** should be made, and which governed the ways in which they were actually made. In **emic classifications**, **types** are always presumed to represent mental templates. (See Chapters 18 and 23.)

Method of construction. See **Method of pottery construction.**

Method of pottery construction. The way in which pottery wares are formed, or constructed: by hand, on the potter's wheel, or by molding. See also **Hand-made wares** and **Wheel-made wares.** (See Chapter 9.)

Modality. When the **members** of a **type** show a normal curve of variability, the modality of the type is synonymous with its **central tendency**. However, if the type exhibits two consistent but slightly different variants, we say that it exhibits two modalities but no central tendency. In this case it is described as **bimodal**. (See Chapter 4.)

Monothetic classification or **typology**. A **classification** or **typology** in which each **class** or **type** is **defined** by an unvarying set of **attributes**, and every **entity** must exhibit all of those attributes before it can be **identified** as a **member** of the type. The conceptual opposite of a monothetic classification is a **polythetic classification**. (See Chapter 18.)

Morphological classification or **typology**. A **classification** or

typology of **entities** based entirely on their physical, visible, or tactile properties such as size, shape, and color. Morphological classification is more or less synonymous with **phenetic classification,** a term more commonly used in the biological sciences. (See Chapter 18.)

Mutable type, mutability. A **type** whose **definition** and/or **description** can change when new **entities** are added to it, and it is thereupon decided that earlier definitions and/or descriptions were not entirely adequate. (See Chapter 5.)

Mutually exclusive, mutual exclusiveness. As employed in this book, mutual exclusiveness refers to the uniqueness of **type concepts.** That is, each **type** must be **formulated** in such a way that its definition does not overlap with that of any other type, so that each **entity** which is **sorted** can be put into one **type category** only. (See Chapter 7.)

Natural classification or **typology.** In theory, a **classification** or **typology** in which the **classes** or **types** correspond to natural or cultural order, which has merely been **discovered** by the typologist. A natural classification is the conceptual opposite of an **artificial classification,** although in practice nearly all classifications are partly natural and partly artificial. See also **Natural type.** (See Chapters 6 and 23.)

Natural kind. See **Natural type.**

Natural type. A **type** which supposedly represents natural or cultural ordering; that is, a type which is believed to have been **discovered** rather than **invented** by the typologist. A natural type is the conceptual opposite of an **artificial type,** although in practice the great majority of types are partly natural and partly artificial. (See Chapters 6 and 23.)

Necessary condition. A condition which must be met before something else can happen, or which must be present before something else can be true. In the field of **artifact classification,** a necessary condition refers to an **attribute** or group of attributes that must be present before a particular specimen can be identified as a **member** of a particular **type.** See also **Sufficient condition.**

Nominal scale. Theoretically, the kind of "measurement" that is involved when the **attributes** of a **variable** differ from each other in a purely qualitative way, so that the relationship between them cannot be quantitatively expressed. The difference between "apples" and "oranges" can only be "measured" on a nominal scale. See also **Interval scale, Ordinal scale,** and **Ratio scale.** (See Chapters 12 and 14.)

Nominal variable. A **variable** whose **attributes** are differentiated from each other according to a **nominal scale.** "Apples" and "oranges" are attributes of the nominal variable "fruit." (See Chapter 14.)

Nominalism, nominalist. In philosophy of science, a school of thought holding that abstract concepts like "red" and "dog" are not "real" in the same sense as are concrete things like individual red objects or individual dogs. The conceptual opposite of nominalism is **realism**. (See Chapter 12.)

Nomothetic paradigm. The research orientation which was dominant in American archaeology from about 1960 to 1975, when it was argued that all archaeological research should involve the testing of causal propositions. (See Chapter 22.)

Non-genetic taxonomy. A **taxonomy** in which the lower or more specific **taxa** are grouped into larger and more inclusive taxa on the basis of physical similarities, common associations, or some other factor which does not imply that the common features shared by the members of any one **taxon** are due to their descent from a common ancestor. A non-genetic taxonomy is the conceptual opposite of a **genetic taxonomy**. (See Chapter 17.)

Non-numerical variable. A qualitative variable, as for example between apples and oranges, that cannot be expressed in quantitative terms. Many non-numerical variables are **thing variables**. The conceptual opposite of a non-numerical variable is a **numerical variable**.

Nonrandom, nonrandomness. In probability theory, an event or phenomenon is said to occur nonrandomly, or to have a nonrandom distribution, when its occurrence in any given set of circumstances can be predicted at a reasonable level of probability, suggesting that its occurrence is probably due to some causal factor rather than to chance. The conceptual opposite of nonrandomness is **randomness**. (See Chapter 23.)

Norm. See **Type norm**.

Nubia. An area of the Nile Valley extending approximately from the First Cataract of the Nile, in southern Egypt, to the Fourth Cataract, in the Republic of Sudan.

Nubian Typology, Nubian Pottery Typology. See **Medieval Nubian Pottery Typology**.

Numerical Taxonomy. The name given to a group of computerized **cluster analysis** programs in which **entities** are grouped into **classes** in terms of the number of **attributes** that they share, without consideration for what the attributes are. Numerical Taxonomy includes both **agglomerative** and **divisive** clustering programs. (See Chapter 17.)

Numerical variable. A quantitative variable comprising a number or something that can be measured, as for example the unknowns in the equation $X + Y = 5$. The conceptual opposite of a numerical variable is a **non-numerical variable**.

Object attributes. The **attributes** exhibited by any individual object, or **entity**. Many of these will also be **type attributes**; that is, they will be characteristics of the **type** to which the object belongs. However, some object attributes will be peculiar to the individual object in which they are found, and will not be exhibited by other **members** of the same type. (See Chapter 14.)

Object clustering. An empirical approach to **classifying** in which **classes** or **types** are **formulated** after examining a **collection** of objects, arranging them into groups on the basis of observed similarities and differences among the objects, and **designating** these groups as classes or types. Object clustering therefore gives rise to **descriptive** rather than **prescriptive type concepts**. Object clustering is often contrasted with the *a priori* approach of **attribute clustering**. (See Chapter 23.)

Objectivity. See **Interpersonal objectivity** and **Real objectivity**. (See Chapter 21.)

Observation language. In some versions of **logical empiricism**, the basic vocabulary of the logical language is assumed to be divided into two classes of terms: *observation terms* whose applicability can be established by direct observation (e.g. "hot to the touch"), and *theoretical terms* whose application can only be established indirectly (e.g. "wave length of 10^{-5} cm"). The observation language, or observational part of the total logical language, is that part which is formed only from observation terms together with purely logical terms such as "if . . . then." (See Chapter 26.)

Occult type. A **type** which is **defined** in such a way that its **members** cannot be readily or consistently recognized through examination. A type which consisted of all the paper plates made in June 1986 would be an occult type, since there are no physical criteria by which the plates could be distinguished from other paper plates. An occult type is never a **useful type**, as defined in this book. The conceptual opposite of an occult type is an **identifiable type**. (See Chapter 3.)

One-level typology. See **Basic typology**.

Ontological commitment. A theory is ontologically committed to the existence of things of a given kind if the theory itself implies their existence. For example, an evolutionary theory that implies that new biological species have come into existence is ontologically committed to the existence of biological species. (See Chapter 12.)

Open typology. A **typology** which is designed for the **sorting** and **typing** of **entities** that have not yet been found, in addition to entities

353

currently in hand. The **types** in an open typology must be **mutable**, to allow for future discoveries that may not correspond exactly to anything that is currently known. The conceptual opposite of an open typology is a **closed typology**. (See Chapter 18.)

Ordering of types. See **Type ordering**.

Ordinal scale. A particular kind of measurement in which the **attributes** of a **variable** are ranged along some kind of a lineal scale, e.g. from the largest to the smallest or from the oldest to the newest. The differences between the various attributes are capable of measurement, but there is no standard increment of difference as in the case of **interval scales**. There is nevertheless dispute among philosophers as to the true nature of the differences between ordinal scales, interval scales, and **ratio scales**. (See Chapters 12 and 14.)

Ordinal variable. A **variable** whose **attributes** are differentiated from each other according to an **ordinal scale**. (See Chapter 14.)

Ordinary set. In **fuzzy set theory,** an ordinary set is a group of things (designated in fuzzy set theory as a *class*) having precisely defined criteria of membership, so that there is never any doubt as to whether a particular **entity** does or does not belong to a particular class. The conceptual opposite of an ordinary set is a **fuzzy set**. However, fuzzy set theory is not employed in the present book. (See Chapter 6.)

Orthodox empiricism. See **Empiricism**.

Overdetermination. The practice of **describing** a **type** far more fully than is necessary for purposes of formal **definition**, in order to facilitate the **recognition** of objects that may be **attributed** to the type. (See Chapter 16.)

Painted decoration. Any **decoration** that is applied to pottery vessels by the use of **color**. (See Chapters 9 and 10.)

Paradigm. See **Scientific paradigm**.

Paradigm shift. The replacement of any dominant **scientific paradigm** by another paradigm, in any field of science. (See Chapter 25.)

Paradigmatic classification. A particular kind of *a priori* **classification** based on **attribute clustering**, in which it is decided in advance that certain combinations of **attributes** will automatically constitute a separate **type**. A paradigmatic classification is therefore a fully comprehensive **attribute clustering** classification. (See Chapter 23.)

Partition. A **set** is partitioned when it is subdivided into mutually exclusive and exhaustive subsets. For example, the set of all whole numbers can be partitioned into subsets of even numbers and odd numbers. (See Chapter 21.)

Partitioning. Synonymous with **Segregation**.

Pattern recognition. The conscious or unconscious recognition, in any human mind, that certain things occur in regularly recurring combinations, or patterns. (See Chapter 4.)

Permissible transformation. A concept developed by the psychologist S. S. Stevens (1959), designating a **transformation** that changes numerical values without changing their sense. For example, multiplying a linear measure by 12 is a permissible transformation when it changes length in feet to length in inches, but adding 12 to the measure of length in feet is not. (See Chapter 12.)

Phenetic classification. In biological classification, a phenetic classification is one based entirely on **intrinsic variables**. That is, **entities** are grouped into **classes** purely on the basis of physical similarities, without consideration for whether they had a common ancestor, common environment, etc. The equivalent term which is more widely used in archaeology is **morphological classification**. (See Chapter 18.)

Phylogenetic classification. In the biological sciences, phylogenetic classification is more or less equivalent to what in archaeology is called **genetic classification**.

Polythetic classification or **typology**. A **classification** or **typology** in which no single **attribute** or **attribute cluster** is a **necessary** or a **sufficient condition** for **membership** in any **type**. That is, an **entity** may be assigned to a type if it exhibits a large number, but not all, of the **defining attributes** of the type. The conceptual opposite of a polythetic classification is a **monothetic classification**. (See Chapters 6 and 18.)

"Positivist" classification. A term introduced by Hill and Evans (1972) to describe a **classification** made specifically in order to test a hypothesis. The **classes** or **types** in a "positivist" classification are not presumed to have any intrinsic **meaning**, except with reference to whether they confirm or disconfirm the hypothesis. In the formulation of Hill and Evans, "positivist" classification is contrasted with **"empiricist" classification**. (See Chapter 23.)

Potential type. Synonymous with **Unrealized type**.

Potsherd. Any fragment of broken pottery. As employed by archaeologists, the term always refers to fragments of ancient pottery, that is, to fragments which are **archaeological remains**.

Pottery color. Any color which is applied decoratively to a pottery vessel surface. Included in this category are **slips**, which are all-over colorings, and any colors applied as **painted decoration**. (See Chapter 9.)

355

Pottery decoration. Any alteration or adornment of a pottery vessel surface for aesthetic purposes, whether by the use of **color** (**painted decoration**) or by manipulating the surface contours (**relief decoration**). (See Chapters 9 and 10.)

Pottery design. A specific decorative pattern applied to the surface of a pottery vessel, either by the use of **color** (**painted decoration**) or by manipulating the surface contours (**relief decoration**). (See Chapter 10.)

Pottery fabric. A collective term for the internal constituents used in making pottery. These include the basic clay, marl, or mud which is the primary constituent, and any other material (temper, levigation, etc.) which is mixed into the clay, marl, or mud to facilitate firing or to impart hardness, porosity, or other characteristics to the vessel walls. (See Chapter 9.)

Pottery family. In the **Medieval Nubian Pottery Typology**, a pottery family is made up of **pottery wares** having the same **method of construction** and **fabric**. It is assumed that the wares in any one family were all made by the same people in the same area, but possibly over a long period of time. When pottery families were made over a long period of time, they can usually be subdivided into **ware groups**, which succeeded each other in time. (See Chapters 9 and 10.)

Pottery slip. A decorative **color** which covers the whole surface of a pottery vessel. (See Chapters 9 and 10.)

Pottery style. In the **Medieval Nubian Pottery Typology**, a pottery style is composed of a group of similar **pottery designs** which were regularly used to decorate a particular **pottery ware** or **ware group**. (See Chapter 10.)

Pottery sub-family. In the **Medieval Nubian Pottery Typology**, a sub-family is a classificatory subdivision of a **pottery family**, which is distinguished from other sub-families mainly by differences in **fabric**. (See Chapter 10.)

Pottery surface treatment. Any kind of manipulation or alteration of the surface of a pottery vessel after it has been formed. Some common kinds of surface treatment are polishing, glazing, and scoring. (See Chapter 10.)

Pottery type. In archaeology, a pottery type is a particular kind of **artifact type** made up of ancient pottery vessels or their fragments (**potsherds**). In the **Medieval Nubian Pottery Typology**, pottery types are referred to as **pottery wares**.

Pottery vessel forms. The different shapes in which a **pottery ware** is or was more or less regularly made. (See Chapters 9 and 10.)

Pottery ware. In the **Medieval Nubian Pottery Typology,** a pottery ware comprises vessels having the same **method of construction,** the same **fabric,** the same **surface treatment,** the same group of **vessel forms,** the same combination of **colors,** and the same **decoration.** A pottery ware in this classification is equivalent to what in other classifications is called a **pottery type;** it has all the properties of "**typehood**" that are discussed in this book. (See Chapters 9 and 10.)

Pottery ware group. In the **Medieval Nubian Pottery Typology,** a pottery ware group comprises a group of **wares** that exhibit the same **method of construction,** the same **fabric,** the same group of **vessel forms,** and the same decorative **style.** It is assumed that all of the wares in a given ware group were made at more or less the same time, by the same people, in the same area. (See Chapters 9 and 10.)

Practical description. See **Practical type description.**

Practical type description. A **type description** that is framed in such a way that it is useful to **sorters** in the processes of **typing** and **sorting.** That is, the type description contains the necessary information on which sorting decisions can be based. (See Chapters 16 and 21.)

Practical typology. A **typology** possessing the qualities of **practicality** and **utility.** In archaeology this usually means a typology that can be used in the field or in the laboratory for the **sorting** of newly recovered **artifacts,** without an expenditure of effort or resources that is greater than is justified by the importance of the results. (See Chapters 19 and 20.)

Practical utility. As applied to **typologies,** practical utility refers to a combination of the qualities of **practicality** and **utility.** (See Chapter 19.)

Practicality. As applied to **typologies,** practicality refers to whether or not the member **types** can be readily and consistently **recognized** in the **sorting** process, without an expenditure of time and effort that is not justified by the importance of the results. (See Chapters 19 and 20.)

Praxis. As employed in the present book, praxis refers to what has also been called the **classificatory dialectic,** the continual **feedback** between the theory and the practice of **artifact classification.** In this process, **type concepts** are continually modified as they are applied to the **typing** of newly acquired **artifacts.** (See Chapter 5.)

Prediction. As defined in this book, prediction is a particular aspect of human cognition, involving implicative reasoning: if A then B. Other aspects of cognition which we discuss are **explanation** and **understanding**. (See Chapter 25.)

Prescriptive attribute. Synonymous with **Diagnostic attribute**.

Prescriptive type concept. A mental conception about the nature and characteristics of a **type** which serves *a priori* to **define** the type, so that **entities** must conform to this conception in order to be considered **members** of the type. The formal expression of a prescriptive type concept is a **type definition**, although in practice many types are never given formal definition. Prescriptive type concepts can theoretically be contrasted with **descriptive type concepts**. (See Chapter 15.)

Probabilistic uncertainty. A basic concept of **information theory**. Applied to sets of mutually exclusive and exhaustive possibilities, it is defined in terms of the logarithms of their probabilities. It equals 0 when one of them is certain and all the others are certainly false, and it is at a maximum when all the possibilities have the same probability. (See Chapter 21.)

Properties of types. See **Type properties**.

Provenience. A specific locality within an **archaeological site**, which is used as a reference when recording the place of finding for **artifacts**, **potsherds**, and other finds. In Nubian sites, a provenience may be a numbered grid square within a grid system, or a room within a house, or a grave in a cemetery. Normally, all of the deposit within any designated provenience is assumed to be of the same age, i.e. to have the same **provenience-date**. See also **Archaeological context** and **Archaeological site**.

Provenience-date. The date or dates that can be assigned to a particular archaeological **provenience**. This term is likely to be used, in preference to **provenience-era**, when a provenience can be dated with a considerable degree of precision. (See Chapters 21 and 26.)

Provenience-era. The time period to which a particular **provenience** can be assigned. This term will be used, in preference to **provenience-date**, when a provenience can be assigned to a general era, but not to any very specific span of years. (See Chapters 21 and 26.)

Provisional type. A **type** that has been **formulated** but not yet **designated**. That is, a decision has not yet been made that the type should be included in a **typology**. Normally, a provisional type is one which has an evident **identity**, but does not yet have a known **meaning**. (See Chapter 15.)

Pseudoproblem. A concept introduced by Rudolf Carnap (1927). Roughly speaking, it designates an apparently scientific problem that analysis shows to arise from verbal misunderstandings. For example, if we assume that lengths are defined by comparison with the standard meter-bar, it is a pseudoproblem to debate whether the standard meter ever changes in length. Carnap argued that many of the enduring controversies in philosophy and science are partly unsolvable pseudoproblems, and that philosophy of science should aim to distinguish between the "real" and the "pseudo" parts of problems so that time would not be wasted on the latter. (See Chapter 26.)

Purpose. As employed in this book, **purpose** refers to the ends which a **typology** is meant to serve. We contend that all typologies are designed for some purpose or purposes, and these determine the choice of **variables** and **attributes** that will be considered. (See Chapter 13.)

Random, randomness. In probability theory, an event or phenomenon is said to occur randomly, or to have a random distribution, when its occurrence in any given set of circumstances cannot be predicted, and the possibility therefore exists that any particular occurrence is due to chance. The conceptual opposite of randomness is **nonrandomness**. (See Chapter 23.)

Random variable. A value that varies depending on the things that are measured, as for example the heights of persons or the species of animals. A random variable is a variable in a statistical rather than in a mathematical sense. (See Chapter 21.)

Ratio scale. A particular kind of measurement in which the **attributes** of a **variable** stand in different ratio relationships to a constant value, as in the case of "atmospheres" in physics and "light-years" in astronomy. Ratio scales are theoretically distinct both from **interval scales** and from **ordinal scales,** but the precise nature of the differences is a subject of philosophical dispute. (See Chapters 12 and 14.)

Ratio variable. A **variable** whose **attributes** are differentiated from each other according to a **ratio scale**. (See Chapter 14.)

Rational classification or **typology.** In theory, a **classification** or **typology** composed entirely of **analytical types**; that is, **types** that have been **formulated** entirely by a conscious process of **attribute** analysis, without any element of intuition. The conceptual opposite of a rational classification is an **intuitive classification,** although in practice most classifications are partly rational and partly intuitive. (See Chapters 5 and 15.)

Real objectivity. A **classification** is said to have real objectivity if it classifies things "as they really are." For example, a biological species classification has real objectivity if it classifies things as belonging to the same species if and only if they really do belong to the same species. The present authors do not believe that most classifications should, or can, have real objectivity. See also **Interpersonal objectivity**. (See Chapter 21.)

Realism, realist. In philosophy of science, a school of thought holding that abstract concepts like "red" and "dog" are not "real" in the same sense as are concrete entities like red objects or individual dogs. The conceptual opposite of realism is **nominalism**. (See Chapter 12.)

Realized type. When a **type** is formulated by **attribute clustering**, it exists in the beginning only as a mental **concept**. We say that it is realized when actual exemplars, or **type members**, have been found which correspond to the type concept. Thus in our usage a realized type is more or less synonymous with a **type**, since we consider that a type which has no members is not a type in the fullest sense of the word. The conceptual opposite of a realized type is an **unrealized type**. (See Chapters 3 and 8.)

Recognizing, recognition. See **Type recognition**.

Reified, reification. The mental process through which we come to believe that **types** correspond to natural reality (i.e. are part of nature's ordering) rather than being constructs of the **typologist**. (See Chapter 16.)

Relevant, relevance. The relevance of a **type** refers to its **meaningfulness** or **utility** for the **purposes** of the **typology** of which it is a member. The relevance of a type as a whole is more or less equivalent to the **typological meaning** of the individual **type members**. See also **Relevant type**. (See Chapter 3.)

Relevant type. A **type** which possesses the quality of **relevance**; that is, one which serves the **purposes** of the **typology** of which it is a member. If a pottery typology has been developed for the purpose of dating archaeological deposits, a **pottery type** which can be accurately dated is a relevant type; a type which cannot be dated is an **irrelevant type**. (See Chapter 3.)

Relief decoration. Any **decoration** applied to the surface of pottery vessels by altering the contours of the surface, for example by incising, punching, or stamping. (See Chapter 9.)

Representing, representation. See **Type representation**.

Scale type. This term refers to the different kinds of measurement scales that, among other things, may distinguish the **attributes** of particular **variables**, e.g. **interval**, **nominal**, **ordinal**, and **ratio scales**. (See Chapters 12 and 14.)

Scientific classification or **typology**. A **classification** or **typology** which has been developed for scientific **purposes**, and which works effectively for those purposes. Scientific classifications are distinguished from many other kinds of classifications by the absence of any evaluative ranking of the **classes**. (See Chapters 3 and 7.)

Scientific concept. A concept developed and used for scientific purposes, such as the **type concepts** in a **scientific typology**. A scientific concept contrasts with a **folk concept**, which is employed in everyday speech but not in scientific parlance or for scientific purposes. (See Chapter 12.)

Scientific paradigm. A specific theoretical and/or research orientation within any science, involving an interest in certain questions but not in others, and the acceptance of certain canons of proof but not others. (See Chapter 25.)

Segmentary classification or **system**. In the usage of social anthropologists, a segmentary classification is one in which a particular population is subdivided into groups, such as families, lineages, or clans, that are generally similar to one another in structure, and that are theoretically equal in importance. (See Chapter 7.)

Segregating, **segregation**. The process of dividing a particular field of **entities** into **types** that are **mutually exclusive**, such that each entity can be a **member** of only one type. (See Chapter 4.)

Sense empiricism. A version of **empiricism** holding that the experience justifying non-deductive truths must be sensory. (See Chapter 26.)

Sensory image. A lasting sensory impression which the encounter with any object, act, or experience **imprints** on the human memory, so that the image can be recalled even when the stimulating object, act, or experience is not present. Visual sensory images are basic to the formation of many **type concepts** in archaeology. (See Chapter 4.)

Sensory perception. The mental process which involves separating out an object or act from the undifferentiated stream of experience, and focusing on it independently of its surroundings. A lasting sensory perception which can be recalled at a later time is referred to as a **sensory image**. (See Chapter 4.)

Sequence dating. A procedure in which **archaeological sites** are arranged in chronological order by a **seriation** of the artifacts that are found in them. (See Chapter 17.)

Seriating, **seriation**. The linear **ordering** of **entities** or **types** into a **series**, according to one particular **variable** feature, such as size or age. Thus, a group of **artifacts** may be arranged in a series from the largest to the smallest, or a group of **artifact types** may be arranged in a series from the oldest type to the most recent. In archaeology it is usually **type frequencies** rather than types themselves that are seriated; see **Frequency seriation**. (See Chapter 17.)

Series. The end product of the process of **seriation**; that is, an arrangement of **entities** or **types** in a linear order according to one particular **variable** feature such as size or age. (See Chapter 17.)

Set. As employed in this book, a set is a group of matched, partly contrasting **categories** which collectively make up a **classification**. See also **Fuzzy set** and **Ordinary set**. (See Chapter 4.)

Set theory. A branch of pure mathematics concerned with properties and relations among **ordinary sets**. Set theory is now commonly regarded as fundamental to all mathematics. (See Chapter 21.)

Sherd. See **Potsherd**.

Shifting criteria. A **typology** is said to involve shifting criteria of **typehood** when **types** are not always **differentiated** on the basis of the same **variables** and **attributes**; when, for example, **pottery types** are differentiated from each other sometimes on the basis of **fabric** and sometimes on the basis of **style**. (See Chapter 14.)

Significance. See **Significant type**.

Significant attribute. In any given **typology**, significant attributes are those **attributes** of a particular **variable** that are regularly used to differentiate one **type** from another. In some pottery typologies, for example, the variable **color** is subdivided only into the attributes white, red, and black, meaning that these are the only colors used to differentiate one type from another, even though other shades of color may occur. White, red, and black are therefore significant attributes of the variable "color," while pink, grey, and brown are not. (See Chapter 14.)

Significant type. In the present book a **type** is said to be significant when we are certain that it has **typological meaning**, whether or not we know what the meaning is. (See Chapter 3.)

Significant variable. A **variable** which is always taken into account in distinguishing one **type** from another in any given **typology**. **Surface color** is usually a significant variable in pottery typologies, but not in typologies of stone tools. That is, pottery types are differentiated from each other on the basis of surface color, but tool types are not. (See Chapter 14.)

Similarity space. The "distance" between two things in the same class, when distance is measured inversely to similarity. According to this concept, relationships or resemblances which may be qualitative are expressed in quantitative terms, as varying degrees of distance or closeness. (See Chapter 21.)

Site. See **Archaeological site**.

Slip. See **Pottery slip**.

Social ranking. The ordering of persons or groups of persons into a hierarchy according to some principle of evaluation. (See Chapter 7.)

Sorter. A person who engages in the activity of **sorting**.

Sorting. A comprehensive series of **type attributions**, in which all of the **entities** in a particular **collection** are assigned to one **type category** or another. Sorting is the collective dimension of **typing**. (See Chapter 16.)

Sorting category. Synonymous with **Type category**.

Spatial classification or **typology**. A **classification** or **typology** in which **classes** or **types** are **defined** at least partially on the basis of where the classified **entities** were made and used. A classification in which all of the entities made in prehistoric North America were assigned to one class, those made in prehistoric Europe to another class, and those made in prehistoric Africa to a third class, would be an example of a purely spatial classification. (See Chapter 18.)

Splitter. A classifier who, in the process of making a **typology**, is prone to the process of **splitting**. The conceptual opposite of a splitter is a **lumper**. (See Chapter 23.)

Splitting. When a **typology** is made by the process of **object clustering**, splitting refers to the tendency on the part of classifiers to divide the objects into a large number of highly uniform **types**, rather than into a smaller number of more variable types. The conceptual opposite of splitting is **lumping**. (See Chapter 23.)

Statistical significance, statistically significant. The association or co-occurrence of any group of **attributes, entities,** or **types** is said to be statistically significant when they occur together with a frequency greater than can be attributed to chance. In practice there are a number of different measures of statistical significance which yield somewhat different estimates of what is and is not due to chance. As employed in the present book, statistical significance is equal to **nonrandomness**. (See Chapters 14 and 23.)

Stratified, stratification. See **Archaeological stratification**.

Stylistic classification or **typology**. A **classification** or **typology** in which the **classes** or **types** are **defined** at least partly in terms of stylistic features. A pottery classification in which all pots decorated with parallel stripes were assigned to one class, all pots with vertical stripes to another class, and all pots with cross-hatched decoration to a third class, would be an example of a purely stylistic classification. (See Chapter 18.)

Sub-family. See **Pottery sub-family.**

Sufficient condition. A condition which, when present, is sufficient to insure that something else will happen, or that something else will be true. In the field of **artifact classification**, the possession of a particular **attribute** or group of attributes may be a sufficient condition for **membership** in a particular **type**, if any **artifact** possessing those attributes is identified automatically as a member of that type. See also **Necessary condition.**

Surface treatment. See **Pottery surface treatment.**

Symbolizing, symbolization. As employed in the present book, symbolization refers to the process of devising a verbal, numerical, or pictorial **label** for each **type concept**, so that all of the ideas associated with the concept can be communicated by one person to another simply by speaking, writing, or exhibiting the label. Thus, symbolization in our usage is synonymous with **labeling**. (See Chapter 4.)

Taxa. The plural form of **taxon.**

Taxon. One of the classificatory units in a **taxonomy**; that is, a **class** or **type** which has been included in a hierarchically ordered system. (See Chapter 17.)

Taxonomic category. Synonymous with **Taxon.**

Taxonomic classification. The process of formulating a **taxonomy**, either by **taxonomic clustering** or by **taxonomic splitting**. (See Chapter 17.)

Taxonomic clustering. The process of formulating a **taxonomy** specifically by grouping smaller and more specific **taxa** into larger and more inclusive ones; in effect, a **classification** of **classes**. Taxonomic clustering is synonymous with **taxonomic ordering**. The conceptual opposite of taxonomic clustering is **taxonomic splitting**. See also **Agglomerative program**. (See Chapter 17.)

Taxonomic level. One of the different hierarchic levels in a **taxonomy**, made up of two or more **taxa** that are considered to be conceptually equivalent. In biological classification, species, genus, and order are different taxonomic levels. In the **Type-variety system** of pottery classification, type and variety are different taxonomic levels. (See Chapter 17.)

Taxonomic ordering. Synonymous with **Taxonomic clustering.**

Taxonomic program. A method (usually a computer program) for creating a **taxonomy**, either by clustering an original group of **basic types**

into larger units (**agglomerative program**), or by splitting them into smaller units (**divisive program**). (See Chapter 17.)

Taxonomic splitting. The process of formulating a **taxonomy** by dividing an original field of **entities** into subdivisions, and these in turn into finer subdivisions. The most common taxonomic splitting program employed by archaeologists is that of **Numerical Taxonomy**. Taxonomic splitting is the conceptual opposite of **taxonomic clustering**. See also **Divisive program**. (See Chapter 17.)

Taxonomy. In our usage, a taxonomy is a particular kind of **classification** having a specifically hierarchic feature; that is, a classification in which smaller and more specific classes, or **taxa**, are grouped into larger and more general ones. A taxonomy can be formulated either by **taxonomic clustering** or by **taxonomic splitting**, but the former is by far the more common procedure both in archaeology and in biology. (See Chapter 17.)

Terminus ante quem. Literally, "date before which." As applied to **artifact types**, this usually means the latest date at which the type is known to have occurred.

Terminus post quem. Literally, "date after which." As applied to **artifact types**, this usually means the earliest date at which the type is known to have occurred.

Theoretical relativism. A doctrine holding that the truth of any scientific observation or procedure can only be relative to some specific theory. Theoretical relativism is not to be confused with **instrumental relativism**. (See Chapter 26.)

Thing variable. When individual things are treated as **variables**, as in the statement "The pot is to the left of the kettle," they are said to be thing variables. (See Chapter 21.)

Transfinite, transfinitely. A **set** or collection of things is said to be transfinite when it has an infinite number of members, as for example in the case of the set of all whole numbers. (See Chapter 12.)

Transformation. As applied to scales of measurement, a transformation is any mathematical operation that changes measures on one scale into measures on another scale that measures the same thing. For example, multiplying by 12 is a transformation that changes lengths in feet into lengths in inches. (See Chapter 12.)

Transmitted information. A term employed in **information theory**. It is defined as the amount to which uncertainty about which of a set of possibilities is correct can be expected to be reduced as a result of gaining certain information. This amount is never negative, since new information can never be expected to increase uncertainty, and it will always be positive unless the new information is statistically independent of the possibilities in question. (See Chapter 21.)

Type. In our usage, a type is a particular kind of **class** which is a member of a **typology.** Types differ from classes more generally in that they must always be **mutually exclusive,** because they are used as **sorting categories.** That is, a **collection** of **entities** is **sorted** into types in such a way that each **entity** can be a **member** of one and only one type. According to our usage a fully defined type involves a **type concept,** a stated or unstated **type definition,** a **type description,** a **type label,** a **type category,** and one or more **type members.** (See Chapters 3–6.)

Type attributes. The series of **attributes** that are characteristic of a **type** collectively; that is, they are part of the **type concept.** They are observable in most but not necessarily all of the individual **members** of the type. Type attributes are mostly but not entirely the same as the **object attributes** exhibited by the individual type members. (See Chapter 14.)

Type attribution. The process of recognizing, or deciding, that particular **entities** are **members** of particular **types,** and **sorting** them into **type categories** accordingly. Type attribution is essentially synonymous with **type recognition.** A single instance of type attribution is referred to as the **typing** of a particular entity. (See Chapter 16.)

Type boundaries. The outer limits of variability that can be exhibited by the **members** of any **type. Entities** that deviate from the **type norms** to such an extent that they fall outside the type boundaries are not considered to be members of the type in question. However, most archaeological types do not have precisely defined boundaries. (See Chapter 6.)

Type category. A type category is, figuratively speaking, the sorting pigeonhole corresponding to each **type concept.** That is, when an **entity** has been **typed,** we say that it has been put into a type category. (See Chapters 3 and 16.)

Type concept. A body of ideas about the nature and characteristics of a **type**; that is, about the distinguishing characteristics of a group of **entities** that are thought of collectively. In archaeology, a type concept will usually include ideas about what the **type members** look like (**intrinsic features**), and also ideas about where they may be found and/or what they were used for (**extrinsic features**). (See Chapters 3–5.)

Type counting. Synonymous with **Sorting.**

Type definition. In theory, a type definition would be a minimum statement of the **diagnostic attributes** of any given **type**; that is, it would furnish the minimum amount of information about any type which would be sufficient to distinguish it from all other types. In archaeology, most types are not given **explicit definitions**; they are **represented** in the form of **type descriptions** rather than of definitions. (See Chapters 3 and 15.)

Type description. A verbal and/or pictorial **representation** of a **type concept** which is designed to communicate the concept as fully as possible from one person to another, and to facilitate the **recognition** of **type members** in practice. Type descriptions differ from **type definitions** in that they normally include all of the characteristics of the type, and not just the **diagnostic** ones. In archaeology type descriptions are usually both verbal and pictorial. (See Chapters 3 and 15.)

Type designation. A **type** is said to have been designated when it has been given a formal **type description** and a **type label**, and when a decision has been made to include it in a **typology**. Prior to that time it may constitute a **provisional type**. (See Chapter 15.)

Type differentiation. One of the processes of **type formulation**, in which **types** are formulated by **object clustering** in a stepwise process. That is, groups of obviously similar objects are removed from an unclassified **collection** of material, and **designated** as types; then other groups are removed and designated, and so on in a stepwise progression, the original collection being further reduced at each step. (See Chapters 5 and 6.)

Type discovery. In theory, type discovery refers to the finding of **natural types**; that is, **types** that are presumed to represent "nature's order" rather than order imposed by the **typologist**. Type discovery is the conceptual opposite of **type invention**, although in practice most types are partly discovered and partly invented. (See Chapters 3 and 6.)

Type formulation. The process of creating a **type**. It usually begins with the formation of a **type concept**, either by intuition or by rational analysis, followed by the **description** and **labeling** of the type. (See Chapters 5 and 15.)

Type frequency. In archaeology, type frequency refers to the relative frequency with which **members** of particular **types** occur in any given **context** (e.g. in a site or a stratigraphic level), in proportion to the frequency of other types. (See Chapter 17.)

Type identification. See **Typing**.

Type identity. As employed in the present book, identity refers to the **identifiability** of a **type**; the extent to which its **members** can consistently be recognized as such, and can be distinguished from the members of other types. (See Chapter 3.)

Type invention. Type invention refers to the **formulation** of **artificial types**; that is, types that are devised by the **typologist** for his own **purposes**, and are not presumed to represent natural or cultural order. Type invention is the conceptual opposite of **type discovery**, although in practice most types are partly invented and partly discovered. (See Chapters 3 and 6.)

Type label. An identifying number, letter, word, or words attached to a **type concept**, which make possible the communication of the concept from one person to another merely by speaking, writing, or exhibiting the label. A type label differs from a **type name** in that it is a purely arbitrary designation, and does not involve any element of description. (See Chapter 3.)

Type meaning. The mental associations that any **type** has for us, above and beyond the denotata of its **identity**; in other words, anything we know about a type which cannot be discovered simply by looking at its **members**. When a type meaning is specifically relevant to the **purposes** of the **typology** to which the type belongs, we refer to it as the **relevance** of the type. (See Chapter 3.)

Type member. An **entity** which has been identified as exemplifying the characteristics of a particular **type**, and has been assigned to that **type category**. (See Chapter 3.)

Type name. An identifying word or, usually, a combination of words attached to a **type concept**, which makes it possible to communicate the concept from one person to another merely by speaking or writing the name. A type name differs from a **type label** in that it is usually to some extent descriptive of the type. (See Chapter 3.)

Type norm. The "ideal" or "perfect" expression of a **type concept**, exemplifying to the fullest degree all of the **defining attributes** and **descriptive attributes** of the **type**. A type norm usually represents the **central tendency** in a continuum of variation, meaning that many individual **type members** deviate to a greater or lesser degree from the norm. In **artifact typologies**, norms are usually thought to represent the ideal that the artifact maker was trying to achieve, but frequently did not fully attain. As applied to **artifact types**, norm is essentially synonymous with **modality**. (See Chapter 6.)

Type ordering. The arrangement of **types** in some kind of formal order, after they have been **designated**. The two kinds of ordering that are discussed in this book are **taxonomy** and **seriation**. (See Chapter 17.)

Type properties. Properties that must be possessed by every **useful type**, namely **identity** and **meaning**. (See Chapter 3.)

Type recognition. The act of recognizing, or deciding, that a particular **entity** is a **member** of a particular **type**, and assigning it to a **type category** accordingly. Type recognition is essentially synonymous with **typing** and with **type attribution**. (See Chapter 16.)

Type representation. The process of formulating a **type description**; that is, of making a **type concept** communicable from one person to another by representing it in words, pictures, diagrams, or some combination of those things. (See Chapter 5.)

Type specimen. See **Ideal type specimen**.

Type-variety system. A two-level **taxonomy** of pottery developed by archaeologists in the American Southwest and Mesoamerica, in which the basic classificatory units are called types, but these are further subdivided into varieties. (See Wheat, Gifford, and Wasley 1958; Gifford 1960.)

Typehood. The status of being or constituting a **type**. It is a status involving mental, physical, and representational components, which we refer to as **elements of typehood**: a **type concept**, a **type definition**, a **type description**, a **type name** and/or **label**, a **type category**, and **type members**. (See Chapters 3 and 15.)

Typing. As used in the present book, typing refers to any single act of **type attribution**; that is, to the **recognition** or decision that a particular **entity** is a **member** of a particular **type**. (See Chapter 16.)

Typological boundaries. The limits of inclusion for all the **entities** that are to be **classified** in a **typology**. That is, all entities falling within the specified boundaries are to be classified, while entries falling outside the boundaries are to be excluded. For example, an archaeological pottery classification will usually include all ceramic vessels, but will exclude ceramic figurines and implements. (See Chapters 4 and 7.)

Typological Debate. A name that has been given to the continuing discussion among archaeologists, particularly in North America, as to what **types** are, how they should be **formulated**, and what they mean. (See Chapter 22.)

Typological identity. The membership of any **entity** in a **type** constitutes its typological identity. Most entities also have **individual identities** that are not connected with their type membership. (See Chapter 3.)

Typological meaning. Typological meanings are the meanings or associations that attach to an **entity** by virtue of its membership in a **type**. Many entities also have **individual meanings** that are not connected with their type membership. (See Chapter 3.)

Typological space. Equivalent to the class of all **types** that fall under a given **typology**. For example, the typological space of biological species comprises the class of all biological species. (See Chapter 21.)

Typologist. A person who creates a **typology**.

Typology. As employed in this book, a typology is a particular kind of **classification**, one made specifically for the **sorting** of **entities** into **mutually exclusive** categories which we call **types**. (See Chapters 4 and 7.)

Typology construction. The process of making or developing a **typology**.

Unconditional probability. The condition which exists when one probability is not dependent on another; that is, when the probability of something being true does not depend on whether or not something else is true. The conceptual opposite of an unconditional probability is a **conditional probability**. (See Chapter 21.)

Understanding. As defined in this book, understanding is a particular aspect of human cognition involving analogical reasoning: A is to B as C is to D. Other aspects of cognition which we discuss are **explanation** and **prediction**. (See Chapter 25.)

Unilinear evolutionism. The dominant theoretical **paradigm** in anthropology in the later nineteenth century, when it was held that all human cultures progress through a fixed series of developmental stages, regardless of environmental differences. Each stage is marked by distinctive modes of subsistence, social organization, and other cultural institutions. (See Chapter 25.)

Universe of variability. See **Domain of variability**.

Unrealized type. A mental conception of a **type**, for which no actual physical exemplars, or **type members,** have been found. An unrealized type is the conceptual opposite of a **realized type**. (See Chapters 3 and 7.)

Useful, usefulness. See **Relevance**.

Useful type. See **Relevant type**.

Useful typology. A **typology** which serves some clearly recognized **purpose**. (See Chapters 19 and 20.)

Utility. As applied to **typologies,** utility refers to whether or not the results obtained when a typology is applied to the **sorting** of **entities** are of any practical value for the purposes of the **sorter**. See also **Practicality**. (See Chapters 19 and 20.)

Variable. A feature or characteristic, such as color, which varies from one **entity** to another, and which is taken into account in the **definition** and/or **description** of **types**. Particular manifestations, or variations, of a variable are referred to as **attributes**. Red, black, and white are attributes of the variable "color," and serve as the basis for the differentiation of **pottery wares** in the **Medieval Nubian Pottery Typology**. Variables may be either **numerical** or **non-numerical**, a class that includes **thing variables**. (See Chapter 14.)

Variable association of attributes. As employed in this book, variable association refers to any **association** or **clustering** of **attributes** that is not constant, so that the attribute clusters in question are present in some **types** but not in others. (See Chapter 14.)

Variable product. A combination of two or more **random variables**. For example, the product of the species variable and the sex variable of an animal is the one that gives both its species and its sex. (See Chapter 21.)

Variable selection. The process of selecting particular **variables** that are to be used in **classifying**; that is, variables such as color and shape that are to be considered significant in distinguishing one group of **entities** from another, and in **designating** them as **classes** or **types**. (See Chapter 14.)

Vernacular classification. A **classification** which is part of everyday **language**, and is regularly used by non-scientists as well as by scientists. A vernacular classification is conceptually distinct from a **scientific classification**. The **types** in a vernacular classification are referred to as **vernacular types**. (See Chapter 3.)

Vernacular type. Any of the classificatory categories in a **vernacular classification**. A vernacular type is one kind of **folk concept**. (See Chapter 3.)

Vessel form class. In the **Medieval Nubian Pottery Typology**, a vessel form class is made up of recurring vessel forms that have been grouped together and given a common class designation because of **morphological** similarities. (See Chapter 10.)

Vessel forms. See **Pottery vessel forms**.

Ware. See **Pottery ware**.

Ware description. Synonymous with **type description**, as applied to a **pottery ware**. (See especially Chapter 10 and Appendix B.)

Ware group. See **Pottery ware group**.

Ware space. Equivalent to **typological space** in a **pottery typology** that includes the category of **wares**. The class of all wares in the **Nubian Pottery Typology** is its ware space. (See Chapter 21.)

Wheel-made wares. **Pottery wares** produced with the aid of the potter's wheel, in contrast to **hand-made wares** which are made without the wheel. The production of pottery on the wheel is sometimes referred to as "throwing," and the resulting vessels are called "wheel-thrown." (See Chapters 9 and 10.)

Word. In natural **language**, a word is the verbal (spoken or written) symbol which **labels** a **concept**, so that the concept can be communicated from one person to another merely by speaking or writing the word. (See Chapter 4.)

APPENDIX B

SPECIMEN POTTERY WARE DESCRIPTION

Family N   Group N.VII
Ware W14. Terminal Christian decorated white ware

A rather heavy matte white ware decorated in Style N.VII; the most distinctive ware of the Terminal Chrjstian period. It is presumably evolved from Wares W15 and W16 in Group N.VI, but is distinguished from them by its bolder and simpler decorative style and a distinctive, rather heavy group of vessel forms.

CONSTRUCTION: Wheel-made.

FABRIC: *Paste*: Nile mud. *Density*: Medium. *Texture*: Medium. *Color*: Tan, light brown or red-brown shading to darker, often purplish core (typical Munsell signatures 2.5YR 4/5, 2.5YR 6/6). *Carbon streak*: Occasional; seldom dark. *Hardness*: Generally medium soft (Mohs' value 2.5 to 4.5, av. 3.0). *Solid temper*: Fairly abundant fine sand, black and red fragments. *Organic temper*: None seen. *Variability*: Apparently low. *Remarks*: Same fabric as Ware R28.

SURFACES: *Covering*: Medium thick, soft slip. *Finish*: Matte or sometimes lightly polished. *Texture*: Usually rather chalky or gritty. *Configuration*: Level; rotation marks not prominent on interiors. *Variability*: Surfaces may be matte or lightly polished; never glossy.

VESSEL FORMS: *Most common forms*: Cups, plain bowls, vases (Fig. 11). *Less common forms*: Goblets, footed bowls, lids, jars (Fig. 11). *Forms not illustrated*: A9, A20, A23, D44, D47, F27A, Q6. *Doubtful forms*: C12, C34, C42, F16. *Vessel sizes*: Mostly medium. *Rims*: Rounded, frequently thickened. *Bases*: Ring almost completely absent; a few examples of very low, solid ring base on footed vessels. *Wall thickness*: Generally notably thick, especially in larger vessels (7–13 mm, av. 9.6 mm). *Execution*: Generally fairly precise. *Variability*: Apparently low.

COLORS: *Natural color*: Tan, light brown, or red-brown (typical Munsell signatures 2.5YR 4/5, 2.5YR 6/6). *Slip*: Shades from cream to pale pink, yellow tan, or orange (typical Munsell signatures 7.5YR 7/8, 5YR 6/8). Interior usually cream or white, exterior often darker. *Primary decoration*: Very dark brown or dense black (typical Munsell signatures 10R 3/1, 10R 3/2). *Secondary decoration*: Medium to dark red (typical Munsell signatures 2.5YR 4/6, 10R 4/6); common only as rim stripe and spacer stripes on larger vessels. *Rim stripe*: Usually broad red; occasionally narrow black. *Variability*: High variability in slip color, but slip usually fairly uniform on any given vessel.

PAINTED DECORATION: *Frequency*: Usual. *Principal style*: N.VII. *Other styles*: II, V. *Most common elements*: Rim stripes, borders, friezes. *Other elements*: Plain body stripes, radial designs. *Exterior program*: Most commonly a single broad frieze; less often a single narrow border; very occasionally a frieze with narrow border above it. *Interior program*: Not common; most often a simple radial design extending to the vessel rim, without surrounding border or frieze. *Execution*: Fairly precise. *Delineation*: Bold. *Variability*: Apparently low.

RELIEF DECORATION: None.

APPRAISAL: *Material*: Not common, but numerous whole vessels collected from Diffinarti. *Adequacy of description*: Probably incomplete. *Variability*: Apparently low, except in regard to slip color. *Temporal variation*: Not known. *Geographic variation*: Probably none; all made at one place. *Intergradation*: Possibly with predecessor wares W15 and W16 in Group N.VI, and with companion wares W18 and R28. *Diagnostics*: Matte white ware decorated in Style N.VII; distinctive group of vessel forms (shared with Ware R28). *Problems*: Material insufficient for full description. Geographic range and center of production not determined.

SIGNIFICANCE: *Earliest appearance*: A.D. 1250. *Main period of production*: A.D. 1300–1500. *Continued use*: To A.D. 1600. *Persistence of sherds*: Not determined. *Archaeological contexts*: Domestic refuse. *Area of distribution*: Identified from Qasr Ibrim through Batn el-Hajar; wider distribution uncertain. *Production centers*: Not determined; presumably same

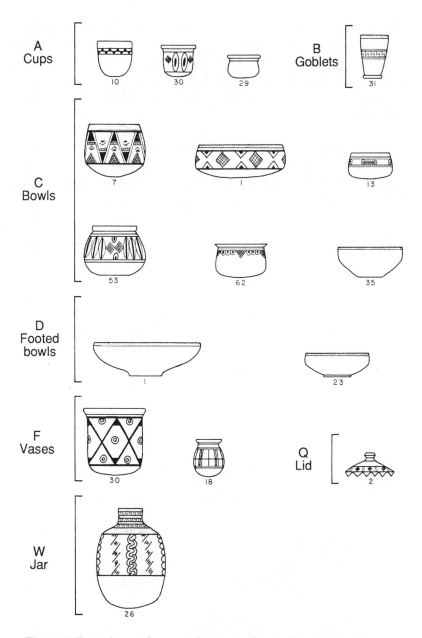

Figure 11 Typical vessel form and decoration illustrations to accompany description of Nubian Ware W14.

375

as for Ware R28. *Frequency*: Not common. *Relationships*: Presumably an outgrowth of Wares W15 and W16 in Group N.VI. Companion Ware R28 is a red-slipped counterpart. There is no successor ware. *Associations*: Utility Wares U5 and U10; domestic Group D.III; imported utility Wares U6, U12, and U13; glazed ware Groups G.II and G.IV. *Index clusters*: LC2 (2%), TC (2%).

REFERENCES: *Vessel photos*: WYA 1970a, pl. 64; Monneret de Villard 1957, vol. 4, pl. CCII, B, D; pl. CCIII; Schneider 1970, pl. 35; Van Moorsel *et al.* 1975, pl. 35; Villa Hügel 1963, kat. 486. *Sherd drawings*: Monneret de Villard 1957, vol. 4, pl. CXCII, 71; pl. CXCVI, 94.

APPENDIX C

ESTIMATED DATES FOR POTTERY WARES FOUND IN NUBIA

Group/Ware	Earliest appearance	Main manufacture	Persistence Vessels	Persistence Sherds
Group D.I	100 B.C.	100–1000	—[b]	1100
H1	100 B.C.	100–1000	—	1100
H9	?	200–350	—	—
H11	100 B.C.	100–350	—	—
H12	?	200–350	—	—
Group D.II	350	350–1000	?[a]	1100
H1		(see Group D.I)		
H13	500	550–650	?	700
H18	?	350?–650?	?	—
H2	550	550–1000	?	1100
H3	550	550–1000	?	1100
Group D.III	950	1000–1600+	?	?
H4	950	1000–1600+	?	?
H5	950	1000–1600+	?	?
H6	1150	1350–1600	?	?
H7	1150	1350–1600	?	?
H8	?	1000–1300	1500	?
H14	1150	1350–1600	?	?
Group D.IV	?	1550–?	?	?
H4		(see Group D.III)		
H5		(see Group D.III)		
H15	?	1550–?	?	?
H16	?	1550–?	?	?

Group/Ware	Earliest appearance	Main manufacture	Persistence Vessels	Sherds
Family M	100	200–550	650	—
R35	100	200–350	?	?
W26	100	200–350	?	?
W27	?	?	?	?
W30	?	400–550	650	750
Group N.I	100	100–350	425	500
R32	100	100–350	425	500
R33	100?	100?–350	425	?
R34	?	?–350	425	?
W25	100	100–350	425	500
Group N.II	300	350–650	750	800
R25	300	350–600	650	—
R1	400	450–650	750	800
R2	550	550–650	750	—
R10		(see Group N.III)		
W11	450?	450?–550	600	650
W29	400	450–550	600	650
Group N.III	550	650–975	1025	1100
R10	550	600–975	1025	1100
R3	?	650–975	1025	1100
R5	550	650–975	1025	1100
W1	550	650–975	1025	1100
W2	550	650–975	1025	1100
W9	550	650–975	1025	1100
Group N.IV	800	850–1100	1150	1250
R7	900?	950–1100	?	?
R23	900?	?	?	?
W5	800	850–1000	1100	1250
W6	800	850–1100	1150	1250
W10	800	850–1100	1150	1250
W7	850	850–1250	?	?

| Group/Ware | Earliest appearance | Main manufacture | Persistence | |
			Vessels	Sherds
Group N.V	900	1000–1200	1300	—
R21	900	1000–1200	1300	—
R22	900	1000–1200	1300	—
R36	?	?	?	?
W20	900?	1000–1200	1300	—
W23	?	1000–1200?	1300?	—
W21	?	?	?	?
W7		(see Group N.IV)		
Group N.VI	1100	1150–1500	1600	?
R11	1100	1150–1500	1600	?
R17	1100	1150–1500	1600	?
R19	1100	1150–1500	1600	?
W15	1100	1150–1500	1600	?
W16	1100	1150–1500	1600	?
Group N.VII	1250	1300–1500	1600	?
R20	?	?	?	?
R26	1250	1300–1500	1600	?
R27	?	1300–1500?	?	?
R28	?	1300–1500?	?	?
W14	1250	1300–1500	1600	?
W18	?	?	?	?
W31	?	?	?	?
Group NU	100	100–1600+	?	?
U1	100	100–650	800	850
U5	100	550–1600+	?	?
U10	850	1000–1500	1600	?
U14	850	1000–1400	1500	?
U23	?	1050–1200?	?	?
U24	?	1050–1200?	?	?
Group A.I	100 B.C.	100–475	550	650
R30	100 B.C.	100–475	550	650
R31	400	450–550	?	?
R37	?	350–475	550	?
W24	?	200?–400?	550?	?
W32	?	400?–500?	?	?

Group/Ware	Earliest appearance	Main manufacture	Persistence Vessels	Persistence Sherds
Group A.II	400	400–850	950	1100
R4	400	550–850	950	1000
R14	?	650?–750?	?	—
W3	650	650–850	—	—
U2 plain	400	400–750	850	1100
U2 ribbed	450	550–850	1000	1100
Group A.III	750	850–1100	1200	1250
R12	?	850?–950?	?	?
R13	750	850–1250	1300	1500
W22	?	850?–950?	?	?
U8	850	850—1100	1250	—
Group A.IV	700	950–1500	1600	?
R13		(see Group A.III)		
R24	?	950–1300?	?	?
W12	750	950–1300	1400	1500
U6	700	950–1500	1600	?
G.V	1300	1350–1450	1500	?
Family T	100	350–850	1000	1100
R25	300	350–600	650	—
W11	450?	450?—550?	600	?
W28	350	400–550	600?	750
U4	100	350–850	1000	1100
Family E				
U20	?	1400–1500?	?	?
U21	1350	1400–1500	?	?
Sub-family LB				
U16	300?	400?–500?	?	?
U9	?	700?–800?	?	?
U12	400	1100–1500	1600	?
Sub-family LF				
U13	350	1300–1500	1600	?
U19	?	1000–1150	?	?
Sub-family LG				
U17	?	1050–1300?	?	?

| Group/Ware | Earliest appearance | Main manufacture | Persistence | |
			Vessels	Sherds
Sub-family LS				
U3	200	400–650	—	850
U15	?	1300–1400?	?	?
Unclassified				
U18	350	350–650	—	—
Family G				
Group G.I	900	950–1100	1250	—
Group G.II	950	1100–1500	1550	?
Group G.III	1000	1100–1500	1550	?
Group G.IV	1200	1300–1500	1550	?
Ware G.V	1300	1350–1450	1500	?

[a] Insufficient data for estimation
[b] Apparently no significant persistence

APPENDIX D

EXAMPLES OF POTTERY WARE DISTRIBUTION DATA FROM QASR IBRIM

1 Ware distribution in excavation units of the XC2 period (c. A.D. 600–650)[a]

Excavation unit			Total sherds	Family D			Family N				Gp. NU			Family A					Family L	
House	Room	Level		Total	D.II	D.III	Total	N.III	N.IV	N.V	Total	U5	U10	Total	A.II	A.III	A.IV	U12	Others	Glazed wares
211	1	4	476	8	4	3	73	10	5	1	42	25	16	18	1	1	16	3	3	
	2	1	288	6	2	4	83	2	3		45	36	7	10	2		8			1
		2	296	7	4	3	75	3	3		40	31	8	16	3	1	12			
		3	101	5	4	1	76		12		49	35	12	13		1	12			
	3	1	150	7		7	66	1	1	1	39	30	9	16	4	1	8	5	11	
		2	34	18	18		68	6	9		33	15	8	9	9		9	6	12	

1 Ware distribution in excavation units of the XC2 period (c. A.D. 600–650) (cont.)

House	Room	Level	Total sherds	Family D Total	D.II	D.III	Family N Total	N.III	N.IV	N.V	Gp. NU Total	U5	U10	Family A Total	A.II	A.III	A.IV	Family L U12	Others	Glazed wares
763	1–2	3	190	6	3	3	68	1	7		45	32	12	22	2		20			3
		4	127	8	6	1	78	15	3		46	33	10	9	5		5		2	3
	3	3	56	4	4		59	2			18	16		36	5	2	29			2
		4	39	13	13		62		1		36	26	10	26	5		20	1	1	1
		5	141	3	2	1	74	1			21	10	10	21	2		17	1	1	1
	5	3	401	2	2		71				47	35	11	24	1	3	20	1	1	
	7	4	249	2	2		73	1	4		55	33	22	23	3		20		2	
	8	3	117	3	3		78	2	15		25	13	12	15	1	1	14	1	1	2
		4	155	1	1		74	1	5		48	40	8	23	3	12	6	1		
		5	110	4	1	3	79		1	1	32	17	14	14	4		10		1	2
764	*	3	1381	5	1	4	77	1	1	1	11	7	4	15	3	1	11	1	1	1
781	1	4	186	10	9	1	74	32	3	1	19	13	3	14	3	6	5	1	1	
	2	2	192	7	3	5	83	2	3		61	38	18	6	3		3		1	

		Total															
848	2C	255	7	7		80	12		33	25	6	11	3	8			1
3	2E	606	3	2	1	70	1	2	55	32	22	23	2	17	2	2	
	2W	131	4	4		76	2	6	50	31	13	17	4	12	1	3	
	3P	150	29	29		47	2	3	18	6	9	19	2	15	1	1	
	3W	161	4	4	2	76	2	7	57	44	12	17	4	9	1	1	
	4	56				43		4	21	14	7	34		20		2	
4	1	63	6	3	3	73		5	56	44	10	17	3	13	2	2	
	2	154	6	5	1	75	3	4	47	27	15	16	1	8	2		
5	5	76	5	5		55	1	8	39	14	25	39	1	16	1	1	
Mean		230	7	5	2	71	4	4	39	26	11	19	3	13	1	2	1
SD			6	6	2	10	7	4	14	11	6	8	2	6	1	3	1

a All figures have been rounded to the nearest whole number. Therefore, figures in the "Total" columns do not always equal the sum of figures in the adjoining columns. Also, in Family N, the "Total" includes certain ware groups in addition to those listed in the adjoining columns. All figures are percentages, except for "Total sherds."

2 Ware distribution in excavation units of the CC2 period (c. A.D. 1000–1100)

House	Room	Level	Total sherds	Family D	Family N — Family total	Group N.II — Group total	R25	R1	R2	Gp. N.III	Group NU — Group total	U1	U5	Family A — Family total	R4	U2 plain	U2 ribbed	U3	U4
189	1–3	2	42	10	88	59	14	40	5	12	2	2	2	2		2			
194	2	2	131	4	66	15	2	8	4	1	6	5	2	18		11	7	2	3
	16	Cr	66	3	65	36	14	21		3				23		17	6	2	6
196	3	3	224	1	73	32	14	15	1	8	9	6	3	16		6	2	2	5
207	3	6	62	11	61	15	8	3	2	2	21	2	15	18	3	5	8		2
210	1	2	23		83	13	4	9		9	13	13		17		4	9		
	6	1	613	16	71	31	23	5	2	1	2	2		7		1	4	1	2
217	3	2	340	10	74	51	37	12	1	2	23	7	16	8	1	5	2	1	3
248	1	2	374	4	75	65	6	49	9	5	5	1	4	15	6	4	4	1	1
273	1	1	130	2	66	39	17	22		8	10	3	6	8			2	2	5
	2–3	1	130	4	78	40	13	24		9	12	11	1	2					7
287	14	U	72	5	71	43	37	1	1	10	18	4	13	11		11			7
	21	2	179	2	79	20	2	14	2	3	2		2	16		5	10	2	1
	30	2	282	2	82	20	1	19	1	8	8	4	2	10		7	2	2	1
		U	263	7	78	29	3	18	8	6	5	3	2	11	1	9	1	2	3

			Total sherds																
290	1	U	121	6	64	19	2	15		4	7	7		19	1	7	8	1	1
293	2	1	343	2	77	12	3	8		4	8	4		10	1	6	2	1	6
334[a]	A	1	252	7	71	45	14	30	1	14	2	20	14	18		2		1	2
357[a]	SW	2	454	5	83	73	10	62	1	10	1	8	6	8	1	3	4	2	1
		3	895	3	79	75	26	46		26	7	3	3	7		6	1	2	6
		3x	316	4	75	34	8	22	2	8	11	4	3	12	1	8	3	4	5
358[a]	N	11	1150	3	72	23	6	16	1	6	11	1	1	17	1	11	4	1	1
	C	5	989	3	67	17	4	9	1	4	11	6	1	17	1	7	8	2	5
	SE	4	65	5	73	20	8	12		8	6	5	2	9		6	6		6
931	1	2	186	5	78	14	7	6		7	6	8	7	8		2	4	1	5
Mean			306	5	74	33	11	19	2	11	6	8	4	12	1	5	4	1	3
SD				3	6	26	10	15	2	10	4	6	4	5	1	4	3	1	2

All figures are percentages, except for "Total sherds"

[a] Street and plaza deposits

REFERENCES

Abu-Lughod, Lila 1989. Zones of theory in the anthropology of the Arab world. *Annual Review of Anthropology* 18: 267–306.

Abu-Mustafa, Y. S. and D. Psaltis 1987. Optical neural computers. *Scientific American* 256 (3): 88–95.

Ach, N. 1921. *Über die Begriffsbildung*. Bamberg: Buchner.

Adams, Ernest W. [cited in text as EWA] 1966. On the nature and purpose of measurement. *Synthèse* 16: 125–69.

Adams, Ernest W. and William Y. Adams [cited in text as EWA and WYA] 1987. Purpose and scientific concept formation. *British Journal for the Philosophy of Science* 38: 419–40.

Adams, Ernest W. and I. F. Carlstrom 1979. Representing approximate ordering and equivalence relations. *Journal of Mathematical Psychology* 19: 182–207.

Adams, Ernest W., Robert F. Fagot, and Richard E. Robinson 1965. A theory of appropriate statistics. *Psychometrika* 2: 99–127.

Adams, Ernest W. and R. D. Rosenkrantz 1980. Applying the Jeffrey Decision Model to rational betting and information acquisition. *Theory and Decision* 12: 1–20.

Adams, Robert McC. 1984. Smithsonian horizons. *Smithsonian Magazine* 15 (8): 14.

Adams, William Y. [cited in text as WYA] 1960. *Ninety Years of Glen Canyon Archaeology, 1869–1959. Museum of Northern Arizona Bulletin* 33.

1961. Archaeological survey of Sudanese Nubia: the Christian Potteries at Faras. *Kush* 9: 30–43.

1962a. Archaeological survey on the west bank of the Nile: Introduction. *Kush* 10: 10–18.

1962b. Archaeological survey on the west bank of the Nile: Pottery kiln excavations. *Kush* 10: 62–75.

1962c. A day in the life of an archaeologist. *Unesco Features* 401: 10–14.

1962d. An introductory classification of Christian Nubian pottery. *Kush* 10: 245–88.

1963. *Shonto: A Study of the Role of the Trader in a Modern Navaho Community. Smithsonian Institution, Bureau of American Ethnology Bulletin* 188.

1964a. An introductory classification of Meroitic pottery. *Kush* 12: 126–73.

1964b. Sudan Antiquities Service excavations in Nubia: fourth season, 1962–63. *Kush* 12: 216–50.

1965a. Architectural evolution of the Nubian church, 500–1400 A.D. *Journal of the American Research Center in Egypt* 4: 87–140.

1965b. Sudan Antiquities Service excavations at Meinarti, 1963–64. *Kush* 13: 148–76.

1966. Post-Pharaonic Nubia in the light of archaeology, III. *Journal of Egyptian Archaeology* 52: 147–62.

1968a. Invasion, diffusion, evolution? *Antiquity* 42: 194–215.

1968b. Organizational problems in international salvage archaeology. *Anthropological Quarterly* 41: 110–21.

1968c. Settlement pattern in microcosm: the changing aspect of a Nubian village during twelve centuries; in K.-C. Chang, ed., *Settlement Archaeology*, pp. 174–207. Palo Alto: National Press Books.

1969. Publication des poteries d'époques pharaonique, romaine, et chrétienne. *Bulletin de l'Institut Français d'Archéologie Orientale* 67: 213–27.

1970a. The evolution of Christian Nubian pottery; in Erich Dinkler, ed., *Kunst und Geschichte Nubiens in christlicher Zeit*, pp. 111–28. Recklinghausen: Aurel Bongers Verlag.

1970b. The University of Kentucky excavations at Kulubnarti, 1969; in Erich Dinkler, ed., *Kunst und Geschichte Nubiens in christlicher Zeit*, pp. 141–54. Recklinghausen: Aurel Bongers Verlag.

1973a. The archaeologist as detective; in Donald W. Lathrap and Jody Douglas, eds., *Variation in Anthropology*, pp. 17–29. Urbana: Illinois Archaeological Survey.

1973b. Pottery, society and history in Meroitic Nubia; in Fritz Hintze, ed., *Sudan in Altertum (Meroitica* 1), pp. 177–219, 227–40.

1973c. Progress report on Nubian pottery, I. The native wares. *Kush* 15: 1–50.

1973d. Strategy of archaeological salvage; in W. C. Ackermann, G. F. White, and E. B. Worthington, eds., *Man-Made Lakes, Their Problems and Environmental Effects*, pp. 826–35. *American Geophysical Union, Geophysical Monograph Series* 17.

1975. Principles and pragmatics of pottery classification: some lessons from Nubia; in J. S. Raymond *et al.*, eds., *Primitive Art and Technology*, pp. 81–91. Calgary: Archaeological Association of the University of Calgary.

1978. Varia ceramica; in *Etudes nubiennes*, pp. 1–24. *Institut Français d'Archéologie Orientale, Bibliothèque d'Etude* 77.

1979. On the argument from ceramics to history: a challenge based on evidence from medieval Nubia. *Current Anthropology* 20 (4): 727–44.

1981a. The archaeologist and the ceramologist. *Bulletin de Liaison du Groupe International d'Etude de la Céramique Egyptienne* 6: 44–5.

1981b. Comments on Nubian pottery collections at Stavanger; in Torgny Säve-

Söderbergh, ed., *Late Nubian Cemeteries*, pp. 24–7. *The Scandinavian Joint Expedition to Sudanese Nubia Publications* 6.

1981c. Medieval Nubian design elements; in William K. Simpson and Whitney Davis, eds., *Studies in Ancient Egypt, the Aegean, and the Sudan*, pp. 1–10. Boston: Museum of Fine Arts.

1984. Science and ethics in rescue archaeology. *Boreas: Uppsala Studies in Ancient Mediterranean and Near Eastern Civilizations* 13: 9–15.

1985. Ptolemaic and Roman occupation at Qasr Ibrim; in Francis Geus and Florence Thill, eds., *Mélanges offerts à Jean Vercoutter*, pp. 9–17. Paris: Editions Recherche sur les Civilisations.

1986a. *Ceramic Industries of Medieval Nubia. Memoirs of the Unesco Archaeological Survey of Sudanese Nubia*, vol. 1 (2 vols.).

1986b. From pottery to history: the dating of archaeological deposits by ceramic statistics. *Wissenschaftliche Zeitschrift der Humboldt-Universität zu Berlin. Gesellschaftswissenschaftliche Reihe* 35: 27–45.

1987. Time, types, and sites: the interrelationship of ceramic chronology and typology. *Bulletin of the Egyptology Seminar* 8: 7–46.

1988. Archaeological classification: theory vs practice. *Antiquity* 62: 40–59.

n.d.1. Ceramics and archaeological dating at Qasr Ibrim, Egypt. Paper read at the 86th annual meeting of the Archaeological Institute of America, Toronto, ON, December 29, 1984.

n.d.2. Archaeology: natural and/or social science? Paper read at the Third American–Soviet Archaeological Symposium, Washington, DC, May 7, 1986.

n.d.3. Ceramic chronology and context: the interpretation of pottery deposits from medieval Nubian sites. Paper read at the 88th annual meeting of the Archaeological Institute of America, San Antonio, TX, December 28, 1986.

MS 1. Field Manual of Christian Nubian Pottery Wares. MS distributed by the Sudan Antiquities Service.

MS 2. Pottery Wares of the Ptolemaic and Roman Periods at Qasr Ibrim: Preliminary Ware Descriptions. MS distributed by the Qasr Ibrim Expedition and the University of Kentucky.

Adams, William Y. and Nettie K. Adams [cited as WYA and Nettie K. Adams] 1959. *An Inventory of Prehistoric Sites on the Lower San Juan River, Utah. Museum of Northern Arizona Bulletin* 31.

Adams, William Y., J. A. Alexander, and R. Allen 1983. Qasr Ibrim 1980 and 1982. *Journal of Egyptian Archaeology* 69: 43–60.

Aldenderfer, Mark S. and Roger K. Blashfield 1978. Cluster analysis and archaeological classification. *American Antiquity* 43 (3): 502–6.

Alexander, John A. and Boyce N. Driskell 1985. Qasr Ibrim 1984. *Journal of Egyptian Archaeology* 71: 12–26.

Ammerman, A. J. 1971. A computer analysis of epipaleolithic assemblages; in F. R. Hodson, D. G. Kendall, and P. Tautu, eds., *Mathematics in the Archaeo-*

logical and Historical Sciences, pp. 133–7. Edinburgh: Edinburgh University Press.

Anderson, Norman H. 1961. Scales and statistics: parametric and nonparametric. *Psychological Bulletin* 58: 305–16.

Anderson, Robert D. and William Y. Adams 1979. Qasr Ibrim 1978. *Journal of Egyptian Archaeology* 65: 30–41.

Anonymous 1975. The establishment of a manual of ancient Egyptian pottery. *Bulletin de Liaison du Groupe International d'Etude de la Céramique Egyptienne* 1: 19–37.

Ash, Robert B. 1965. *Information Theory*. New York: Interscience Publishers.

Bacon, Francis 1620. *The Novum Organon*. Modern edition 1960, ed. F. H. Anderson. New York: Bobbs-Merrill.

Barnes, J. A. 1954. *Politics in a Changing Society*. London: Oxford University Press.

Barnouw, Victor 1963. *Culture and Personality*. Homewood, IL: The Dorsey Press.

Beck, Horace C. 1973. *Classification and Nomenclature of Beads and Pendants*. York, PA: Liberty Cap Books.

Beckner, Morton 1959. *The Biological Way of Thought*. New York: Columbia University Press.

Benacerraf, Paul and Hilary Putnam, eds., 1983. *Philosophy of Mathematics: Selected Readings*. New York: Cambridge University Press.

Benedict, Ruth 1930. Psychological types in the cultures of the Southwest. *Proceedings of the Twenty-Third International Congress of Americanists*, pp. 571–81.

1932. Configurations of culture in North America. *American Anthropologist* 34: 1–27.

1934. *Patterns of Culture*. Boston: Houghton Mifflin.

Benfer, Robert A. 1967. A design for the study of archaeological characteristics. *American Anthropologist* 69 (6): 719–32.

Bennett, John W. 1943. Recent developments in the functional interpretation of archaeological data. *American Antiquity* 9: 208–19.

Bennett, Wendell C. and Junius B. Bird 1964. *Andean Culture History*, 2nd edn. New York: American Museum Science Books.

Berlin, Brent 1973. Folk systematics in relation to biological classification and nomenclature. *Annual Review of Ecology and Systematics* 4: 259–71.

Berlin, Brent and Paul Kay 1969. *Basic Color Terms*. Berkeley: University of California Press.

Bernstein, Richard J. 1983. *Beyond Objectivism and Relativism: Science, Hermeneutics, and Praxis*. Philadelphia: University of Pennsylvania Press.

Binford, Lewis R. 1965. Archaeological systematics and the study of culture process. *American Antiquity* 31: 203–10.

1968. Archaeological perspectives; in Sally R. Binford and Lewis R. Binford, eds., *New Perspectives in Archaeology*, pp. 5–32. Chicago: Aldine Publishing Co.

1972. *An Archaeological Perspective.* New York: Seminar Press.

Bloch, Ned, ed. 1981. *Imagery.* Cambridge, MA: MIT Press.

Boas, Franz 1911a. *Handbook of American Indian Languages,* Part 1. *Bureau of American Ethnology Bulletin* 40.

1911b. *The Mind of Primitive Man.* New York: Macmillan & Co.

1922. *Handbook of American Indian Languages,* Part 2. *Bureau of American Ethnology Bulletin* 40.

Bock, Philip K. 1980. *Continuities in Psychological Anthropology.* San Francisco: W. H. Freeman & Co.

Bourriau, Janine 1985. Technology and typology of Egyptian ceramics; in W. D. Kingery, ed., *Ancient Technology and Modern Science,* pp. 27–42. *Ceramics and Civilization,* vol. 1.

Brainerd, George W. 1951. The use of mathematical formulations in archaeological analysis; in James B. Griffin, ed., *Essays on Archaeological Methods,* pp. 117–27. *University of Michigan Museum of Anthropology, Anthropological Papers* 8.

Brew, John Otis 1946. *Archaeology of Alkali Ridge, Southeastern Utah. Papers of the Peabody Museum of American Archaeology and Ethnology, Harvard University* 21.

Bridgman, Percy W. 1927. *The Logic of Modern Physics.* New York: Macmillan.

Brown, James A. 1982. On the structure of artifact typologies; in Robert Whallon and James A. Brown, eds., *Essays on Archaeological Typology,* pp. 176–90. Evanston, IL: Center for American Archaeology Press.

Bulmer, R. 1967. Why is the cassowary not a bird? A problem of zoological taxonomy among the Karam of the New Guinea Highlands. *Man,* new series 2 (1): 5–25.

Burma, B. H. 1949. The species concept: a semantic review. *Evolution* 3: 369–70.

Buroker, Jill 1978. *Space and Incongruence: the Origin of Kant's Idealism.* Dordrecht, Netherlands: D. Reidel Publishing Co.

Butzer, Karl W. 1974. Modern Egyptian pottery clays and Predynastic Buff Ware. *Journal of Near Eastern Studies* 33: 377–82.

Canfield, John W. 1981. *Wittgenstein, Language and World.* Amherst: University of Massachusetts Press.

Carnap, Rudolf 1927. Testability and meaning. *Philosophy of Science* 4 (1): 1–40.

1928. Scheinprobleme der Philosophie; republished in English translation in Rudolf Carnap, *The Logical Structure of the World and Pseudoproblems of Philosophy,* pp. 305–43. Berkeley: University of California Press, 1967.

1937. *Foundations of Logic and Mathematics. Encyclopedia of Unified Science,* vol. 3. Chicago: University of Chicago Press.

1956. The methodological character of theoretical concepts; in Herbert Feigl and Michael Scriven, eds., *Minnesota Studies in the Philosophy of Science* 1: 38–76. Minneapolis: University of Minnesota Press.

Ceram, C. W. 1951. *Gods, Graves, and Scholars.* New York: Alfred A. Knopf.

Chalmers, Neil 1980. *Social Behavior in Primates*. Baltimore: University Park Press.

Chang, K.-C. 1967. *Rethinking Archaeology*. New York: Random House.

Chihara, Charles S. 1973. *Ontology and the Vicious-Circle Principle*. Ithaca: Cornell University Press.

Childe, V. Gordon 1956. *Piecing Together the Past*. London: Routledge & Kegan Paul.

Christenson, Andres L. and Dwight W. Read 1977. Numerical Taxonomy, R-Mode factor analysis, and archaeological classification. *American Antiquity* 42 (2): 163–79.

Clark, J. Grahame D. 1952. *Prehistoric Europe: the Economic Basis*. New York: Philosophical Library, Inc.

1957. *Archaeology and Society*. London: University Paperbacks.

Clarke, David L. 1968. *Analytical Archaeology*. London: Methuen.

1978. *Analytical Archaeology*, 2nd edn. London: Methuen.

Clay, R. Berle 1976. Typological classification, attribute analysis, and lithic variability. *Journal of Field Archaeology* 3 (3): 303-11.

Cole, Michael and Sylvia Scribner 1974. *Culture and Thought*. New York: John Wiley & Sons.

Colton, Harold S. 1953. *Potsherds. Museum of Northern Arizona Bulletin* 25.

1955. *Pottery Types of the Southwest: Wares 8A, 8B, 9A, 9B. Museum of Northern Arizona Ceramic Series* 3a.

1956. *Pottery Types of the Southwest: Wares 5A, 5B, 6A, 6B, 7A, 7B, 7C. Museum of Northern Arizona Ceramic Series* 3c.

1958. *Pottery Types of the Southwest: Wares 14, 15, 16, 17, 18. Museum of Northern Arizona Ceramic Series* 3d.

Colton, Harold S. and Lyndon L. Hargrave 1937. *Handbook of Northern Arizona Pottery Wares. Museum of Northern Arizona Bulletin* 11.

Cormack, R. M. 1971. A review of classification. *Journal of the Royal Statistical Society*, Series A, 134: 321–53.

Cowgill, George L. 1972. Models, methods, and techniques for seriation; in David L. Clarke, ed., *Models in Archaeology*, pp. 381–424. London: Methuen.

1982. Clusters of objects and associations between variables: two approaches to archaeological classification; in Robert Whallon and James A. Brown, eds., *Essays on Archaeological Typology*, pp. 30–55. Evanston, IL: Center for American Archaeology Press.

Cowgill, George L., Jeffrey H. Altschul, and Rebecca S. Sload 1984. Spatial analysis of Teotihuacan: a Mesoamerican metropolis; in Harold J. Hietala, ed., *Intrasite Spatial Analysis in Archaeology*, pp. 154–95. Cambridge: Cambridge University Press.

Daniel, Glyn 1950. *A Hundred Years of Archaeology*. London: Gerald Duckworth.

1964. *The Idea of Prehistory*. Harmondsworth: Penguin Books.

Daugherty, J. W. D. 1978. Salience and relativity in classification. *American Ethnologist* 5: 66–80.

Deetz, James F. 1965. *The Dynamics of Stylistic Change in Arikara Ceramics. University of Illinois Series in Anthropology* 4.

1967. *Invitation to Archaeology*. Garden City: Natural History Press.

De Paor, Liam 1967. *Archaeology, an Illustrated Introduction*. Baltimore: Penguin Books.

De Saussure, Ferdinand 1940. *Course in General Linguistics*, trans. Wade Baskin. New York: McGraw Hill.

Dilthey, Wilhelm 1976. *W. Dilthey Selected Writings*, ed., trans., and introduced by H. P. Rickman. Cambridge: Cambridge University Press.

Diver, C. 1940. The problems of closely related species living in the same area; in Julian Huxley, ed., *The New Systematics*, pp. 303–28. Oxford: Oxford University Press.

Dobzhansky, Theodosius 1937. What is a species? *Scientia* 1937: 280–6.

Doran, J. E. and F. R. Hodson 1975. *Mathematics and Computers in Archaeology*. Cambridge, MA: Harvard University Press.

Douglas, Mary 1966. *Purity and Danger*. London: Routledge & Kegan Paul.

1970. *Natural Symbols*. London: Barrie & Rockliff.

ed., 1973. *Rules and Meanings*. Harmondsworth: Penguin Books.

1975. *Implicit Meanings*. London: Routledge & Kegan Paul.

Dragendorff, H. 1898. *Die Arretinischen Vasen und ihr Verhältnis zur Augusteichen Kunst. Bonn Jahrbuch* 103, pp. 87ff.

Drake, Stillman 1953. *Galileo Galilei. Dialogue Concerning the Two Chief World Systems*, trans. Stillman Drake, foreword by Albert Einstein. Berkeley: University of California Press.

Dresch, Paul 1986. The significance of the course events take in segmentary systems. *American Ethnologist* 13 (2): 309–24.

Dretske, Fred I. 1981. *Knowledge and the Flow of Information*. Cambridge, MA: MIT Press.

Dumont, Louis 1970. *Homo Hierarchicus*. Chicago: University of Chicago Press.

Duncan, T. and G. F. Estabrook 1976. An operational method for evaluating classifications. *Systematic Botany* 1: 373–82.

Dunnell, Robert C. 1970. Seriation method and its evaluation. *American Antiquity* 35: 305–19.

1971a. Sabloff and Smith's "The importance of both analytic and taxonomic classification in the Type-Variety System." *American Antiquity* 36 (1): 115–18.

1971b. *Systematics in Prehistory*. New York: Free Press.

1986. Methodological issues in Americanist artifact classification. *Advances in Archaeological Method and Theory* 9: 149–207.

Durkheim, Emile 1893. *De la Division du travail social*. Paris: Alcan.

1898. Représentations individuelles et représentations collectives. *Revue de Métaphysique et de Morale* 6: 273–303.

1912. *Les Formes élémentaires de la vie religieuse*. Paris: Alcan.

1947. *The Division of Labor in Society*, trans. George Simpson. Glencoe, IL: Free Press.

Durkheim, Emile and Marcel Mauss 1903. *De quelques formes primitives de classification. Année Sociologique* 1901–2.

Dyen, Isidore 1965. *A Lexicostatistical Classification of the Austronesian Languages. University of Indiana Publications in Anthropology and Linguistics* 19.

Ellen, Roy F. 1979. Introductory essay; in Roy F. Ellen and David Reason, eds., *Classifications in their Social Context*, pp. 1–32. New York: Academic Press.

Ellen, Roy F. and David Reason, eds., 1979. *Classifications in their Social Context*. New York: Academic Press.

Emery, W. B. 1938. *The Royal Tombs of Ballana and Qustul* (2 vols.). Cairo: Government Press.

Etzioni, Amitai 1988. *The Moral Dimension: Toward a New Economics*. New York: Free Press.

Everitt, Brian 1974. *Cluster Analysis*. New York: John Wiley & Sons.

Fagan, Brian M. 1978. *Archaeology, a Brief Introduction*. Boston: Little, Brown.

Fish, Paul R. 1978. Consistency in archaeological measurement and classification: a pilot study. *American Antiquity* 43 (1): 86–9.

Fitting, James E. 1965. *Late Woodland Cultures of Southeastern Michigan. University of Michigan Museum of Anthropology, Anthropological Papers* 24.

Flannery, Kent V. 1967. Culture history vs. culture process: a debate in American archaeology. *Scientific American* 217 (2): 119–22.

Ford, James A. 1954a. Comment on A. C. Spaulding, "Statistical techniques for the discovery of artifact types." *American Antiquity* 19 (4): 390–1.

1954b. The type concept revisited. *American Anthropologist* 56 (1): 42–54.

1962. *A Quantitative Method for Deriving Culture Chronology. Pan American Union, Technical Manual* 1.

Ford, James A. and Gordon R. Willey 1949. *Surface Survey of the Viru Valley, Peru. American Museum of Natural History, Anthropological Papers* 43 (1).

Ford, Joseph 1983. How random is a coin toss? *Physics Today* 36 (4): 40–7.

Ford, Richard I., Albert H. Schroeder, and Stewart L. Peckham 1972. Three perspectives on Puebloan prehistory; in Alfonso Ortiz, ed., *New Perspectives on the Pueblos*, pp. 19–39. Albuquerque: University of New Mexico Press.

Fortes, Meyer and E. E. Evans-Pritchard 1940. *African Political Systems*. London: Oxford University Press.

Foucault, Michel 1973. *The Order of Things*. New York: Vintage Books.

Frege, Gottlob 1892. Uber Sinn und Bedeutung. *Zeitschrift für Philosophie und philosophische Kritik* 100: 25–50. English translation, "On sense and reference," by Max Black in P. T. Geach and M. Black, eds., *Translations from the*

Philosophical Writings of Gottlob Frege, pp. 56–78. New York: Philosophical Library, 1952.

Freier, G. D. 1965. *University Physics, Experiment and Theory*. New York: Appleton-Century-Crofts.

1977. *Logical Investigations*, ed. and with preface by P. T. Geach, trans. by P. T. Geach and R. H. Stoothoff. New Haven: Yale University Press.

Friedman, Jonathan 1987. An interview with Eric Wolf. *Current Anthropology* 28 (1): 107–18.

Friedman, Michael 1983. *Foundations of Space–Time Theories: Relativistic Physics and Philosophy of Science*. Princeton: Princeton University Press.

Fritz, John M. and Fred T. Plog 1970. The nature of archaeological explanation. *American Antiquity* 35 (4): 405–12.

Gardberg, C. J. 1970. *Late Nubian Sites. The Scandinavian Joint Expedition to Sudanese Nubia Publications*. 7.

Gardin, Jean-Claude 1962. Documentation sur cartes perforées et travaux sur ordinateur dans les sciences humaines. *Revue Internationale de la Documentation* 29: 83–92.

1980. *Archaeological Constructs*. Cambridge: Cambridge University Press.

Geertz, Clifford 1966. Religion as a cultural system; in Michael Banton, ed., *Anthropological Approaches to the Study of Religion*, pp. 1–46. *Association of Social Anthropologists Monographs* 3.

1973. *The Interpretation of Cultures*. New York: Basic Books.

Gellner, Ernest 1974. *Legitimation of Belief*. Cambridge: Cambridge University Press.

Ghiselin, Michael T. 1966. On psychologism in the logic of taxonomic controversies. *Systematic Zoology* 15: 207–15.

Gifford, James C. 1960. The Type-Variety method of ceramic classification as an indicator of cultural phenomena. *American Antiquity* 25 (3): 341–7.

Gilmour, J. S. L. 1940. Taxonomy and philosophy; in Julian Huxley, ed., *The New Systematics*, pp. 461–74. Oxford: Oxford University Press.

1951. The development of taxonomic theory since 1851. *Nature* 168: 400–2.

Gladwin, Harold S. 1943. *A Review and Analysis of the Flagstaff Culture. Gila Pueblo Medallion Papers* 31.

Gladwin, Thomas and William C. Sturtevant, eds., 1962. *Anthropology and Human Behavior*. Washington, DC: Anthropological Society of Washington.

Gladwin, Winifred and Harold S. Gladwin 1930. *A Method for the Designation of Southwestern Pottery Types. Gila Pueblo Medallion Papers* 7.

Good, Isidore J. 1967. On the principle of total evidence. *British Journal for the Philosophy of Science* 17: 319–21.

Goodman, D. W. and J. E. Houston 1987. Catalysis: new perspectives from surface science. *Science* 236: 403–9.

Gorodzov, V. A. 1933. The typological method in archaeology. *American Anthropologist* 35: 95–102.

396

Greenwood, Davydd J. 1984. *The Taming of Evolution*. Ithaca: Cornell University Press.

Grice, H. P. 1957. Meaning. *Philosophical Review* 66: 377–88.

1969. Utterers' meanings and intentions. *Philosophical Review* 78 (2): 147–75.

Griffin, James B. 1943. *The Fort Ancient Aspect; Its Cultural and Chronological Position in Mississippi Valley Archaeology*. Ann Arbor: University of Michigan Press.

Hallowell, A. Irving 1960. The beginnings of anthropology in America; in Frederica De Laguna, ed., *Selected Papers from the American Anthropologist 1888–1970*, pp. 1–90. New York: Row, Peterson.

Hargrave, Lyndon L. 1932. *Guide to Forty Pottery Types from the Hopi Country and the San Francisco Mountains, Arizona. Museum of Northern Arizona Bulletin* 1.

Harré, Romano 1960. *An Introduction to the Logic of the Sciences*. London: Macmillan.

Harris, Marvin 1968. *The Rise of Anthropological Theory*. New York: Thomas Y. Crowell.

1980. *Cultural Materialism: The Struggle for a Science of Culture*. New York: Vintage Books.

Hatch, Elvin 1973. *Theories of Man and Culture*. New York: Columbia University Press.

Hawley, Florence M. 1934. The significance of the dated prehistory of Chetro Ketl, Chaco Canyon, New Mexico. *University of New Mexico Bulletin, Monograph Series* 1 (1): 13–30.

1936. *Field Manual of Prehistoric Southwestern Pottery Types. University of New Mexico Bulletin* 291; *Anthropological Series* 1 (4).

Hayden, Brian 1984. Are emic types relevant to archaeology? *Ethnohistory* 31 (2): 79–92.

Hayes, John W. 1972. *Late Roman Pottery*. London: British School at Rome.

Haymet, A. D. J. 1987. Freezing. *Science* 236: 1076–80.

Heider, Karl G. 1967. Archaeological assumptions and ethnological facts: a cautionary tale from New Guinea. *Southwestern Journal of Anthropology* 23: 52–64.

Hempel, Carl G. 1952. *Fundamentals of Concept Formation in Empirical Science*. Chicago: University of Chicago Press.

1957. The theoretician's dilemma, a study in the logic of theory construction; in H. Feigl, M. Scriven, and G. Maxwell, eds., *Minnesota Studies in the Philosophy of Science*, vol. 2, pp. 57–96. Minneapolis: University of Minnesota Press.

1965. *Aspects of Scientific Explanation and Other Essays in the Philosophy of Science*. New York: Free Press.

1966. *Philosophy of Natural Science*. Englewood Cliffs, NJ: Prentice-Hall.

1970. A logical appraisal of operationalism; in Baruch A. Brody, ed., *Readings in the Philosophy of Science*, pp. 200–10. Englewood Cliffs, NJ: Prentice-Hall.

Herrnstein, R. J., D. H. Loveland, and C. Cable 1976. Natural concepts in pigeons. *Journal of Experimental Psychology: Animal Behavior Processes* 2: 285–311.

Herskovits, Melville J. 1973. *Cultural Relativism*. New York: Vintage Books.

Hewett, Edgar L. 1930. *Ancient Life in the American Southwest*. New York: Bobbs-Merrill Co.

Hietala, Harold J., ed., 1984. *Intrasite Spatial Analysis in Archaeology*. Cambridge: Cambridge University Press.

Hill, James N. 1966. A prehistoric community in eastern Arizona. *Southwestern Journal of Anthropology* 22 (1): 9–30.

   1970. *Broken K Pueblo: Prehistoric Social Organization in the American Southwest. University of Arizona Anthropological Papers* 18.

Hill, James and R. K. Evans 1972. A model for classification and typology; in David L. Clarke, ed., *Models in Archaeology*, pp. 231–73. London: Methuen.

Hinde, R. A. 1979. The nature of social structure; in David A. Hamburg and Elizabeth R. McCown, eds., *The Great Apes*, pp. 295–315. Menlo Park, CA: Benjamin Cummings.

Hinsley, Curtis M., Jr. 1981. *Savages and Scientists*. Washington, DC: Smithsonian Institution Press.

Hodder, Ian 1982. *Symbols in Action*. Cambridge: Cambridge University Press.

   1983. Archaeology, ideology and contemporary society. *Royal Anthropological Institute News* 56: 6–7.

Hodge, Frederick W., ed., 1907. *Handbook of American Indians North of Mexico*, Part 1. *Bureau of American Ethnology Bulletin* 30.

   1910. *Handbook of American Indians North of Mexico*, Part 2. *Bureau of American Ethnology Bulletin* 30.

Hodson, F. R. 1982. Some aspects of archaeological classification; in Robert Whallon and James A. Brown, eds., *Essays on Archaeological Typology*, pp. 21–9. Evanston, IL: Center for American Archaeology Press.

Hodson, F. R., D. G. Kendall, and P. Tautu, eds., 1971. *Mathematics in the Archaeological and Historical Sciences*. Edinburgh: Edinburgh University Press.

Hole, Frank and Robert F. Heizer 1965. *An Introduction to Prehistoric Archaeology*. New York: Holt, Rinehart and Winston.

Holland, Dorothy and Naomi Quinn, eds., 1987. *Cultural Models in Language and Thought*. Cambridge: Cambridge University Press.

Holmes, William H. 1919. *Handbook of Aboriginal American Antiquities*, Part 1. *Bureau of American Ethnology Bulletin* 60.

Holsinger, Kent E. 1984. The nature of biological species. *Philosophy of Science* 51: 293–307.

Hull, David L. 1974. *Philosophy of Biological Science*. Englewood Cliffs: Prentice-Hall.

   1978. A matter of individuality. *Philosophy of Science* 45: 335–60.

398

Hunn, Eugene 1976. Toward a perceptual model of folk classification. *American Ethnologist* 3: 508–24.

Huxley, Julian, ed., 1940. *The New Systematics*. Oxford: Clarendon Press.

Jevons, W. S. 1874. *The Principles of Science* (2 vols.). New York: Macmillan & Co.

Johnson, W. C. 1982. Ceramics; in J. M. Adovasio, ed., *The Prehistory of the Paintsville Reservoir, Johnson and Morgan Counties, Kentucky*, pp. 752–826. *Ethnology Monographs* 6.

Johnson-Laird, P. N. and P. C. Wason 1977a. Introduction to conceptual thinking; in P. N. Johnson-Laird and P. N. Wason, eds., *Thinking: Readings in Cognitive Science*, pp. 169–84. Cambridge: Cambridge University Press.

eds., 1977b. *Thinking: Readings in Cognitive Science*. Cambridge: Cambridge University Press.

Joralemon, Peter D. 1971. *A Study of Olmec Iconography*. Dumbarton Oaks, *Studies in Pre-Columbian Art and Archaeology* 7.

Jorgensen, Joseph G. 1969. *Salish Language and Culture: A Statistical Analysis of Internal Relationships, History and Evolution*. Indiana University Language Science Monographs 3.

Joseph, Alice, Rosamond B. Spicer, and Jane Chesky 1949. *The Desert People*. Chicago: University of Chicago Press.

Judd, Neil M. 1927. Archaeological investigations in Chaco Canyon, New Mexico. *Smithsonian Miscellaneous Collections* 78 (7): 158–68.

1940. Progress in the Southwest; in *Essays in Historical Anthropology*, pp. 417–44. *Smithsonian Miscellaneous Collections* 100.

Kaplan, Abraham 1984. Philosophy of science in anthropology. *Annual Review of Anthropology* 13: 25–39.

Kay, Paul and Chad D. McDaniel 1978. Linguistic significance and the meaning of basic color terms. *Language* 54 (3): 610–46.

Keighley, Jennifer 1973. Some problems in the quantitative interpretation of ceramic data; in Colin Renfrew, ed., *The Explanation of Culture Change; Models in Prehistory*, pp. 131–6. London: Gerald Duckworth.

Kelley, Jane H. and Marsha P. Hanen 1988. *Archaeology and the Methodology of Science*. Albuquerque: University of New Mexico Press.

Kelley, John L. 1955. *General Topology*. New York: Springer-Verlag.

Kempton, Willett 1978. Category grading and taxonomic relations: a mug is a sort of a cup. *American Ethnologist* 5 (1): 44–65.

Kendall, D. G. 1969. Some problems and methods in statistical archaeology. *World Archaeology* 1: 68–76.

Kent, Susan 1984. *Analyzing Activity Areas*. Albuquerque: University of New Mexico Press.

Kidder, Alfred V. 1927. Southwestern archaeological conference. *Science* 66 (1716): 489–91.

Kidder, Alfred V. and Anna O. Shepard 1936. *The Pottery of Pecos*, vol. 2. *Phillips Academy, Papers of the Southwestern Expedition* 7.

King, Dale S. 1949. *Nalakihu. Museum of Northern Arizona Bulletin* 23.

Klejn, Leo S. 1973a. On major aspects of the interrelationship of archaeology and ethnology. *Current Anthropology* 14 (3): 311–20.

1973b. Marxism, the systematic approach, and archaeology; in Colin Renfrew, ed., *The Explanation of Culture Change: Models in Prehistory*, pp. 691–710. London: Gerald Duckworth.

1973c. Review of Sally R. and Lewis R. Binford, eds., *New Perspectives in Archaeology. Soviet Archaeology* 2: 303–412.

1977. A panorama of theoretical archaeology. *Current Anthropology* 18: 1–42.

1982. *Archaeological Typology*, trans. Penelope Dole. *BAR International Series* 153.

Kluckhohn, Clyde 1939. The place of theory in anthropological studies. *Philosophy of Science* 6 (3): 328–44.

1940. The conceptual structure in Middle American studies; in Clarence L. Hay *et al.*, eds., *The Maya and Their Neighbors*, pp. 41–51. New York: D. Appleton-Century Co.

1949. *Mirror for Man*. New York: Whittlesey House.

1950. Anthropology comes of age. *American Scholar* 19: 241–56.

1951. The study of culture; in Daniel Lerner and Harold Lasswell, eds., *The Policy Sciences*, pp. 86–101. Palo Alto, CA: Stanford University Press.

1956. Toward a comparison of value-emphasis in different cultures; in L. D. White, ed., *The State of the Social Sciences*, pp. 116–32. Chicago: University of Chicago Press.

1960. The use of typology in anthropological theory; in Anthony F. C. Wallace, ed., *Men and Cultures: Selected Papers of the Fifth International Congress of Anthropological and Ethnological Sciences*, pp. 134–40. Philadelphia: University of Pennsylvania Press.

Kluckhohn, Clyde and William H. Kelley 1945. The concept of culture; in Ralph Linton, ed., *The Science of Man in the World Crisis*, pp. 78–105. New York: Columbia University Press.

Kluckhohn, Clyde and Dorothea Leighton 1946. *The Navaho*. Cambridge, MA: Harvard University Press.

Kluckhohn, Clyde and O. H. Mowrer 1944. Culture and personality: a conceptual scheme. *American Anthropologist* 46: 1–29.

Kluckhohn, Clyde and Paul Reiter 1939. *Preliminary Report on the 1937 Excavations, Bc50-51, Chaco Canyon, New Mexico. University of New Mexico Bulletin, Anthropological Series* 3 (2).

Köhler, Wolfgang 1940. *Dynamics in Psychology*. New York: Liveright Publishing Co.

1947. *Gestalt Psychology*. New York: Liveright Publishing Co.

Kolata, Gina 1986. What does it mean to be random? *Science* 231: 1068–70.

Krantz, David H., R. D. Luce, P. Suppes, and A. Tversky 1971. *Foundations of Measurement, Volume 1*. New York: Academic Press.

Krieger, Alex D. 1944. The typological concept. *American Antiquity* 9 (3): 271–88.

1960. Archaeological typology in theory and practice; in Anthony F. C. Wallace, ed., *Men and Cultures: Selected Papers of the Fifth International Congress of Anthropological and Ethnological Sciences*, pp. 141–51. Philadelphia: University of Pennsylvania Press.

Kroeber, A. L. 1925. *Handbook of the Indians of California. Bureau of American Ethnology Bulletin* 78.

1964. *Anthropology: Culture Patterns and Processes*. New York: Harcourt, Brace.

Kronenfeld, David B. 1985. Numerical Taxonomy: old techniques and new assumptions. *Current Anthropology* 26 (1): 21–41.

Kuhn, Thomas S. 1962. *The Structure of Scientific Revolutions*. Chicago: University of Chicago Press.

1970. *The Structure of Scientific Revolutions*; 2nd edn. Chicago: University of Chicago Press.

Kuper, Adam 1988. *The Invention of Primitive Society*. London: Routledge.

Lakatos, Imre 1970. Falsification of the methodology of scientific research programmes; in Imre Lakatos and Alan Musgrave, eds., *Criticism and the Growth of Knowledge*, pp. 91–197. Cambridge: Cambridge University Press.

Lakoff, George 1984. *Classifiers as a Reflection of Mind: A Cognitive Model Approach to Prototype Theory. Berkeley Cognitive Science Report* 19.

Leach, Edmund 1972. The structure of symbolism; in J. S. LaFontaine, ed., *The Interpretation of Ritual*, pp. 239–75, London: Tavistock.

1973. Concluding address; in Colin Renfrew, ed., *The Explanation of Culture Change: Models in Prehistory*, pp. 761–71. London: Gerald Duckworth.

1976. *Culture and Communication*. Cambridge: Cambridge University Press.

Leighton, Dorothea and Clyde Kluckhohn 1948. *Children of the People*. Cambridge, MA: Harvard University Press.

Leone, Mark P. 1972. Issues in anthropological archaeology; in Mark P. Leone, ed., *Contemporary Archaeology*, pp. 14–27. Carbondale, IL: Southern Illinois University Press.

Lévi-Strauss, Claude 1953. Social structure; in A. L. Kroeber, ed., *Anthropology Today*, pp. 524–53. Chicago: University of Chicago Press.

1966. *The Savage Mind*. Chicago: University of Chicago Press.

Levin, Michael E. 1973. On explanation in archaeology: a rebuttal to Fritz and Plog. *American Antiquity* 38: 387–95.

Lévy-Bruhl, Lucien 1985. *How Natives Think*. Princeton: Princeton University Press.

Linnaeus, Carolus 1735. *Systema Naturae*. Leyden: Theodorus Haak.

Linton, Ralph 1936. *The Study of Man*. New York: Appleton-Century-Crofts.

Lipe, William D. 1978. The Southwest; in Jesse D. Jennings, ed., *Ancient Native Americans*, pp. 327–401. San Francisco: W. H. Freeman & Co.

Longacre, William A. 1964. Archaeology as anthropology: a case study. *Science* 144: 1454–5.

1970. *Archaeology as Anthropology: A Case Study. University of Arizona Anthropological Papers* 17.

Lord, Frederick M. 1953. On the statistical treatment of football numbers. *American Psychologist* 8: 750–1.

Loux, Michael J. 1970. *Universals and Particulars: Readings in Ontology.* Garden City: Anchor Books.

Lowie, Robert H. 1924. *Primitive Religion.* New York: Liveright Publishing Co.

1937. *The History of Ethnological Theory.* New York: Farrar & Rinehart, Inc.

Mach, Ernst 1893. *The Science of Mechanics: A Critical and Historical Account of its Development,* trans. T. J. McCormick, LaSalle, IL: Open Court, 1960.

Malinowski, Bronislaw 1948. *Magic, Science and Religion, and Other Essays.* New York: Anchor Books.

1960. *A Scientific Theory of Culture.* New York: Oxford University Press.

Margolis, Howard 1987. *Patterns, Thinking, and Cognition.* Chicago: University of Chicago Press.

Marks, Anthony E. and Robin Robertson 1986. Shaqadud Cave: the organization of the 3rd mil. B.C. ceramics seen through seriation. *Wissenschaftliche Zeitschrift der Humboldt-Universität zu Berlin. Gesellschaftswissenschaftliche Reihe* 35 (1): 70–6.

Marquardt, William H. 1978. Advances in archaeological seriation. *Advances in Archaeological Method and Theory* 1: 257–314.

Martin, Paul S. 1971. The revolution in archaeology. *American Antiquity* 36 (1): 1–8.

Maxwell, Grover 1962. On the ontological status of theoretical entities; in Herbert Feigl and Michael Scriven, eds., *Minnesota Studies in the Philosophy of Science,* vol. 3, pp. 3–27. Minneapolis: University of Minnesota Press.

Maxwell, James C. 1877. *Matter and Motion.* Cambridge: Cambridge University Press.

Mayr, Ernst 1942. *Systematics and the Origin of Species. Columbia Biological Series, Columbia University* 13.

1949. The species concept: systematics versus semantics. *Evolution* 3: 371–2.

1981. Biological classification: toward a synthesis of opposing methodologies. *Science* 214: 510–16.

1982. *The Growth of Biological Thought.* Cambridge, MA: Belknap Press.

McGregor, John C. 1941. *Southwestern Archaeology.* New York: John Wiley & Sons.

McKern, W. C. 1939. The Midwestern Taxonomic Method as an aid to archaeological culture study. *American Antiquity* 4 (4): 301–13.

McPherron, Alan 1967a. *The Juntunen Site and the Late Woodland Prehistory of the Upper Great Lakes Area. University of Michigan Museum of Anthropology, Anthropological Papers* 30.

1967b. On the sociology of ceramics: pottery style clustering, marital residence, and cultural adaptations of an Algonkian–Iroquoian border; in E. Tooker, ed.,

Iroquois Culture, History, and Prehistory, pp. 101–7. *Proceedings of the 1965 Conference on Iroquois Research, New York State Museum and Science Service.*

Meltzer, David J. 1979. Paradigms and the nature of change in American archaeology. *American Antiquity* 44 (4): 644–57.

Middleton, John and David Tait, eds., 1958. *Tribes Without Rulers.* London: Routledge & Kegan Paul.

Miller, George 1956. The magical number seven, plus or minus two: some limits on our capacity for processing information. *Psychological Review* 63: 81–97.

Miller, Wick R. 1984. The classification of the Uto–Aztecan languages based on lexical evidence. *International Journal of American Linguistics* 50 (1): 1–24.

Millon, René 1973. *Urbanization at Teotihuacán, Mexico, Volume 1: The Teotihuacán Map*, Part 1. Austin: University of Texas Press.

Mond, Robert and Oliver H. Myers 1934. *The Bucheum. Egypt Exploration Society, Memoir* 43 (3 vols.).

Monneret de Villard, Ugo 1957. *La Nubia Medioevale*, vols. 3–4. Cairo: Imprimerie de l'Institut Français d'Archéologie Orientale.

Moody, Ernest A. 1967. William of Occam; in P. Edwards, editor-in-chief, *The Encyclopedia of Philosophy* 5, pp. 533–4.

Nagel, Ernest 1961. *The Structure of Science: Problems in the Logic of Scientific Explanation.* New York: Harcourt, Brace & Co.

Narens, Louis 1985. *Abstract Measurement Theory.* Cambridge, MA: MIT Press.

Needham, Joseph 1969. *The Grand Titration.* London: George Allen & Unwin, Ltd.

Needham, Rodney 1975. Polythetic classification: convergence and consequences. *Man,* new series 10 (3): 349–69.

Nelson, Alan 1986. New foundations for individualistic economics. *Noûs* 20: 469–690.

Nelson, N. C. 1916. Chronology of the Tano Ruins, New Mexico. *American Anthropologist* 18 (2): 159–80.

Newton, Isaac 1729. *Mathematical Principles of Natural Philosophy and His System of the World*, trans. A. Motte, revised F. Cajori. Berkeley: University of California Press, 1946.

Norman, Colin 1981. Snail Darter's status threatened. *Science* 212: 761.

Olin, Jacqueline S. and Alan D. Franklin, eds., 1982. *Archaeological Ceramics.* Washington, DC: Smithsonian Institution Press.

Orton, Clive 1982. *Mathematics in Archaeology.* Cambridge: Cambridge University Press.

Palm, Robert 1979. Deep sixing the Snail Darter. *Politics Today* 6: 58–9.

Parsons, Talcott and Evon Z. Vogt 1962. Clyde Kay Maben Kluckhohn. *American Anthropologist* 64: 140–61.

Patterson, Thomas C. 1986. The last sixty years: toward a social history of Americanist archaeology in the United States. *American Anthropologist* 88 (1): 7–26.

Peacock, D. P. S. 1970. The scientific analysis of ancient ceramics: a review. *World Archaeology* 1: 375–89.

Petrie, W. M. Flinders 1899. Sequences in prehistoric remains. *Journal of the Anthropological Institute of Great Britain and Ireland* 29 (3–4): 295–301.

1905. *Ehnasya. Egypt Exploration Fund, Memoir* 26.

Piaget, Jean 1926. *The Language and Thought of the Child*, trans. Marjorie Worden. New York: Harcourt, Brace & World.

1928. *Judgment and Reasoning in the Child*, trans. Marjorie Worden. New York: Harcourt, Brace & World.

1929. *The Child's Conception of the World*, trans. Joan and Andrew Tomlinson. New York: Harcourt, Brace & World.

Pike, Kenneth 1954. *Language in Relation to a Unified Theory of the Structure of Human Behavior*, Part 1. Glendale, CA: Summer Institute of Linguistics.

Plog, Stephen 1980. *Stylistic Variation in Prehistoric Ceramics*. Cambridge: Cambridge University Press.

Plumley, J. Martin 1966. Qasr Ibrim 1966. *Journal of Egyptian Archaeology* 52: 9–12.

1975. Qasr Ibrim 1974. *Journal of Egyptian Archaeology* 61: 5–27.

Plumley, J. Martin and William Y. Adams 1974. Qasr Ibrim, 1972. *Journal of Egyptian Archaeology* 60: 212–38.

Plumley, J. Martin, W. Y. Adams, and Elisabeth Crowfoot 1977. Qasr Ibrim 1976. *Journal of Egyptian Archaeology* 63: 29–47.

Poincaré, Henri 1902. *Science and Hypothesis*. Original English translation 1905. New York: Dover Edition, 1952.

Popper, Karl 1935. *Logik der Forschung*. Vienna: Springer. English translation *The Logic of Scientific Discovery* published by Hutchinson, London, 1959.

1963. *Conjectures and Refutations: the Growth of Scientific Knowledge*. New York: Basic Books.

Porter, Theodore M. 1986. *The Rise of Statistical Thinking, 1820–1900*. Princeton: Princeton University Press.

Powell, John Wesley 1891. Indian linguistic families north of Mexico. *Bureau of American Ethnology, 7th Annual Report*, pp. 1–142.

Quine, Willard V. 1953. *From a Logical Point of View*. Cambridge, MA: Harvard University Press.

1969. *Ontological Relativity and Other Essays*. New York: Columbia University Press.

Quirarte, Jacinto 1973. *Izapan-Style Art, a Study of its Form and Meaning. Dumbarton Oaks, Studies in Pre-Columbian Art and Archaeology* 10.

Radcliffe-Brown, A. R. and Daryll Forde, eds., 1950. *African Systems of Kinship and Marriage*. London: Oxford University Press.

Radin, Paul 1933. *The Method and Theory of Ethnology*. New York: McGraw-Hill Book Co.

Raiffa, Howard and Robert Schlaifer 1961. *Applied Statistical Decision Theory*.

Boston: Division of Research, Graduate School of Business Administration, Harvard University.

Rathje, William J. and Michael B. Schiffer 1982. *Archaeology*. New York: Harcourt Brace Jovanovitch.

Read, Dwight W. 1974. Some comments on typologies in archaeology and an outline of a methodology. *American Antiquity* 39 (2): 216–42.

1982. Toward a theory of archaeological classification; in Robert Whallon and James A. Brown, eds., *Essays on Archaeological Typology*, pp. 56–92. Evanston, IL: Center for American Archaeology Press.

Reisner, George A. 1923a. *Excavations at Kerma, I–III. Harvard African Studies* 5. 1923b. *Excavations at Kerma, IV–V. Harvard African Studies* 6.

Renfrew, Colin 1984. *Approaches to Social Archaeology*. Cambridge, MA: Harvard University Press.

Richard, A. F. and A. R. Schulman 1982. Sociobiology: primate field studies. *Annual Review of Anthropology* 11: 231–55.

Riedl, Rupert 1983. The role of morphology in the theory of evolution; in Marjorie Grene, ed., *Dimensions of Darwinism*, pp. 205–38. Cambridge: Cambridge University Press.

Ritchie, William A. and Richard S. MacNeish 1949. The pre-Iroquoian pottery of New York state. *American Antiquity* 15: 97–124.

Roberts, Fred S. 1979. *Measurement Theory*. Reading, MA: Addison-Wesley.

Robinson, W. S. 1951. A method for chronologically ordering archaeological deposits. *American Antiquity* 16: 293–301.

Rodrigues de Areia, M. L. 1985. On Numerical Taxonomy. *Current Anthropology* 26 (3): 404.

Rosch, Eleanor 1973. On the internal structure of perceptual and semantic categories; in T. Moore, ed., *Cognitive Development and the Acquisition of Language*, pp. 513–18. New York: Academic Press.

1975. Universals and cultural specifics in human categorization; in R. Brislin, S. Bochner, and W. Lonner, eds., *Cross-Cultural Perspectives on Learning*, pp. 218–19. New York: Sage Publications.

Rosch, Eleanor, *et al.* 1976. Basic objects in natural categories. *Cognitive Psychology* 8: 382–439.

Rosenkrantz, Roger D. 1977. *Inference, Method and Decision*. Dordrecht: D. Reidl.

Rouse, Irving 1939. *Prehistory in Haiti, a Study in Method. Yale University Publications in Anthropology* 21.

1960. The classification of artifacts in archaeology. *American Antiquity* 25 (3): 313–23.

1965. The place of 'peoples' in prehistoric research. *Journal of the Royal Anthropological Institute* 95: 1–15.

1967. Seriation in archaeology; in Carroll L. Riley and Walter W. Taylor, eds., *American Historical Anthropology*, pp. 153–96. Carbondale, IL: Southern Illinois University Press.

1970. Classification for what? Comments on *Analytical Archaeology*, by D. L. Clarke. *Norwegian Archaeological Review* 3: 9–12.

1972. *Introduction to Prehistory*. New York: McGraw-Hill.

Rowe, John H. 1962. Stages and periods in archaeological interpretation. *Southwestern Journal of Anthropology* 18 (1): 40–54.

Rowell, T. E. 1967. Variability in the social organization of primates; in Desmond Morris, ed., *Primate Ethology*, pp. 219–35. Chicago: Aldine Publishing Co.

Russell, Bertrand 1919. The relation of sense data to physics; in Bertrand Russell, *Mysticism and Logic*, pp. 139–70. London: George Allen and Unwin.

1924. Logical atomism; reprinted in Robert C. Marsh, ed., *Bertrand Russell. Logic and Knowledge, Essays 1901–1950*, pp. 321–43. London: George Allen and Unwin, 1956.

Sabloff, Jeremy A. and Robert E. Smith 1969. The importance of both analytic and taxonomic classification in the Type-Variety System. *American Antiquity* 34 (3): 278–85.

Sackett, James R. 1966. Quantitative analysis of Upper Paleolithic stone tools; in J. Desmond Clark and F. Clark Howell, eds., *Recent Studies in Paleoanthropology. American Anthropologist* 68 (2), part 2: 356–94.

Salmon, Merrilee H. 1976. "Deduction" vs. "induction" in archaeology. *American Antiquity* 41 (3): 376–81.

1982. *Philosophy and Archaeology*. New York: Academic Press.

Sapir, Edward 1921. *Language*. New York: Harcourt, Brace.

Satterthwaite, Linton 1944. *Piedras Negras Archaeology: Architecture*, Part 4, no. 1. *Ball Court Terminology*. Philadelphia: University Museum of the University of Pennsylvania.

Sauneron, Serge 1975. Présentation. *Bulletin de Liaison du Groupe Internationale d'Etude de la Céramique Egyptienne* 1: i–ii.

Savage, Leonard J. 1954. *The Foundations of Statistics*. New York: John Wiley and Sons.

Säve-Söderbergh, Torgny 1987. *Temples and Tombs of Ancient Nubia*. New York: Thames and Hudson.

ed., 1981. *Late Nubian Cemeteries. The Scandinavian Joint Expedition to Sudanese Nubia Publications* 6.

Scanlon, George T. 1970. Excavations at Kasr el-Wizz: a preliminary report. *Journal of Egyptian Archaeology* 56: 29–57.

Schaafsma, Polly 1971. *The Rock Art of Utah. Papers of the Peabody Museum of Archaeology and Ethnology, Harvard University* 65.

1975. *Rock Art in New Mexico*. Albuquerque: University of New Mexico Press.

Schneider, Hans D. 1970. Abdallah Nirqi: description and chronology of the central church; in Erich Dinkler, ed., *Kunst und Geschichte Nubiens in christlicher Zeit*, pp. 87–102. Recklinghausen: Aurel Bongers Verlag.

1975. The pottery; in Paul Van Moorsel, Jean Jacquet, and Hans Schneider, *The Central Church of Abdallah Nirqi*, pp. 37–53. Leiden: E. J. Brill.

Schuyler, Robert L. 1971. The history of American archaeology: an examination of procedure. *American Antiquity* 36 (4): 383–409.

Scriven, Michael 1958. Definitions, explanations, and theories; in Herbert Feigl, Michael Scriven, and Grover Maxwell, eds., *Minnesota Studies in the Philosophy of Science* 2: 99–195. Minneapolis: University of Minnesota Press.

Sears, Paul B. 1950. *Charles Darwin, the Naturalist as a Cultural Force*. New York: Charles Scribner's Sons.

Service, Elman R. 1985. *A Century of Controversy*. New York: Academic Press.

Shanks, Michael and Christopher Tilley 1987. *Social Theory and Archaeology*. Cambridge: Polity Press.

Shannon, Claude E. and W. Weaver 1949. *The Mathematical Theory of Communication*. Urbana: University of Illinois Press.

Shepard, Anna O. 1965. *Ceramics for the Archaeologist*, 5th printing. *Carnegie Institution of Washington, Publication* 609.

Shinnie, P. L. 1955. *Excavations at Soba. Sudan Antiquities Service, Occasional Papers* 3.

Shinnie, P. L. and H. N. Chittick 1961. *Ghazali – a Monastery in the Northern Sudan. Sudan Antiquities Service, Occasional Papers* 5.

Shinnie, P. L. and Margaret Shinnie 1978. *Debeira West, a Medieval Nubian Town*. Warminster: Aris & Phillips.

Simpson, George Gaylord 1945. *The Principles of Classification and a Classification of Mammals. Bulletin of the American Museum of Natural History* 85.

Smith, Bruce D. 1973. *Prehistoric Patterns of Human Behavior*. New York: Academic Press.

Smith, R. E., G. R. Willey, and J. C. Gifford 1960. The Type-Variety concept as a basis for the analysis of Maya pottery. *American Antiquity* 25 (3): 330–40.

Smith, Virginia G. 1984. *Izapa Relief Carving: Form, Content, Rules for Design, and Role in Mesoamerican Art History. Dumbarton Oaks, Studies in Pre-Columbian Art and Archaeology* 27.

Smoke, K. L. 1932. *An Objective Study of Concept Formation. Psychological Monographs* 191.

Sneath, P. H. A. 1962. The construction of taxonomic groups; in G. C. Ainsworth and P. H. A. Sneath, eds., *Microbial Classification*, pp. 289–322. Cambridge: Cambridge University Press.

Sneath, P. H. A. and Robert R. Sokal 1973. *Numerical Taxonomy*. San Francisco: W. H. Freeman & Co.

Sokal, Robert R. 1966. Numerical Taxonomy. *Scientific American* 215 (6): 107–17.

    1977. Classification: purposes, principles, progress, prospects; in P. N. Johnson-Laird and P. C. Wason, eds., *Thinking: Readings in Cognitive Science*, pp. 185–98. Cambridge: Cambridge University Press.

Sokal, Robert R. and P. H. A. Sneath 1963. *Principles of Numerical Taxonomy*. San Francisco: W. H. Freeman & Co.

Solheim, Wilhelm G. 1960. The use of sherd weights and counts in the handling of archaeological data. *Current Anthropology* 1 (4): 325–9.

Spaulding, Albert C. 1953. Statistical techniques for the discovery of artifact types. *American Antiquity* 18 (4): 305–13.

1960. Statistical description and comparison in artifact assemblages; in R. F. Heizer and S. F. Cook, eds., *The Application of Quantitative Methods in Archaeology*, pp. 60–83. *Viking Fund Publications in Anthropology* 28.

1982. Structure in archaeological data: nominal variables; in Robert Whallon and James A. Brown, eds., *Essays on Archaeological Typology*, pp. 1–20. Evanston, IL: Center for American Archaeology Press.

Stegner, Wallace 1982. *Beyond the Hundredth Meridian*. Lincoln: University of Nebraska Press.

Steindorff, Georg 1935. *Aniba*, vol. 1. Glückstadt and Hamburg: J. J. Augustin.

Stevens, Stanley S. 1946. On the theory of scales of measurement. *Science* 103: 667–80.

1959. Measurement, psychophysics, and utility; in Charles W. Churchman and Philburn Ratoosh, eds., *Measurement: Definitions and Theories*, pp. 18–63. New York: John Wiley & Sons.

Steward, Julian H. 1929. *Petroglyphs of California and Adjoining States. University of California Publications in American Archaeology and Ethnology* 24 (2).

1954. Types of Types. *American Anthropologist* 56: 54–7.

Steward, Julian H., ed., 1946–1959. *Handbook of South American Indians* (7 vols.). *Bureau of American Ethnology Bulletin* 146.

Steward, Julian H. and Frank M. Setzler 1938. Function and configuration in archaeology. *American Antiquity* 4 (1): 4–10.

Stitch, Stephen 1983. *From Folk Psychology to Cognitive Science: The Case Against Belief*. Cambridge, MA: MIT Press.

Stone, Lyle M. 1970. Formal classification and the analysis of historical artifacts. *Historical Archaeology* 4: 90–102.

Sturtevant, William C. 1964. Studies in ethnoscience; in A. Kimball Romney and Roy D'Andrade, eds., *Transcultural Studies in Cognition*, pp. 99–131. *American Anthropologist* 66 (3), Part 2.

Suppes, Patrick 1957. *Introduction to Logic*. Princeton: D. Van Nostrand Co.

Taylor, Walter W. 1948. *A Study of Archaeology. American Anthropological Association, Memoir* 69.

Thomas, David Hurst 1972. The use and abuse of numerical taxonomy in archaeology. *Archaeology and Physical Anthropology in Oceania* 7: 31–49.

1978. The awful truth about statistics in archaeology. *American Antiquity* 43 (2): 231–44.

1986. *Refiguring Anthropology*. Prospect Heights, IL: Waveland Press.

Thompson, Laura and Alice Joseph 1965. *The Hopi Way*. New York: Russell & Russell.

Torgerson, Warren 1958. *Theory and Methods of Scaling.* New York: John Wiley & Sons.

Trigger, Bruce G. and Ian Glover, eds., 1981. *Regional Traditions of Archaeological Research, I. World Archaeology* 13 (2).

1982. *Regional Traditions of Archaeological Research, II. World Archaeology* 13 (3).

Turner, Christy G., II 1963. *Petroglyphs of the Glen Canyon Region. Museum of Northern Arizona Bulletin* 38.

Turner, Victor 1967. *The Forest of Symbols.* Ithaca, NY: Cornell University Press.

1969. *The Ritual Process: Structure and Anti-Structure.* Chicago: Aldine Publishing Co.

Tyler, Stephen A., ed., 1969. *Cognitive Anthropology.* New York: Holt, Rinehart and Winston.

Tylor, Edward B. 1958. *The Origins of Culture.* New York: Harper Torchbooks.

Van Moorsel, Paul, Jean Jacquet and Hans Schneider 1975. *The Central Church at Abdallah Nirqi.* Leiden: National Museum of Antiquities at Leiden.

Vierra, Robert K. 1982. Typology, classification, and theory building; in Robert Whallon and James A. Brown, eds., *Essays on Archaeological Typology,* pp. 162–75. Evanston, IL: Center for American Archaeology Press.

Villa Hügel 1963. *Koptische Kunst: Christentum am Nil.* Catalogue of an exhibition held at the Villa Hügel, Essen, May 3–August 15, 1963.

Vlastos, Gregory 1975. *Plato's Universe.* Seattle: University of Washington Press.

Vogt, Evon Z. and Ethel M. Albert 1966. *People of Rimrock.* Cambridge, MA: Harvard University Press.

Von Bertalanffy, Ludwig 1950. The theory of open systems in physics and biology. *Science* 111: 23–9.

1951. Problems of General System Theory. *Human Biology* 23: 302–12.

1962. General System Theory – a critical review. *General Systems* 7: 1–20.

Voorrips, A. 1982. Mambrino's helmet: a framework for structuring archaeological data; in Robert Whallon and James A. Brown, eds., *Essays on Archaeological Typology,* pp. 93–126. Evanston, IL: Center for American Archaeology Press.

Voss, R. S., G. F. Estabrook, and N. A. Voss 1983. A comparison of information-theoretically optimal classifications with estimates of phylogenetic relations in the squid family Cranchiidae (Cephalopoda: Oegopsida). *Zeitschrift für Zoologische Systematik und Evolutionsforschung* 21 (2): 81–95.

Vygotsky, L. S. 1962. *Thought and Language,* trans. Eugenia Hanfmann and Gertrude Walker. New York: John Wiley & Sons.

Waldrop, M. Mitchell 1987. Causality, structure, and common sense. *Science* 237: 1297–9.

Wallace, Anthony F. C. 1961. On being just complicated enough. *Proceedings of the National Academy of Sciences* 47: 458–64.

Watson, Patty Jo 1986. Archaeological interpretation, 1985; in David A. Meltzer,

Don D. Fowler, and Jeremy A. Sabloff, eds., *American Archaeology Past and Future*, pp. 439–57. Washington, DC: Smithsonian Institution Press.

Watson, Patty Jo, Steven A. LeBlanc, and Charles L. Redman 1971. *Explanation in Archaeology, an Explicitly Scientific Approach*. New York: Columbia University Press.

1984. *Archaeological Explanation*. New York: Columbia University Press.

Waugh, Linda R. 1976. *Roman Jakobson's Science of Language*. Lisse: Peter de Ridder Press.

Weber, Max 1947. *The Theory of Social and Economic Organization*, trans. A. M. Henderson and Talcott Parsons. New York: Oxford University Press.

Weston, T. S. 1987. Approximate truth. *Journal of Philosophical Logic* 16: 203–27.

Whallon, Robert, Jr. 1972. A new approach to pottery typology. *American Antiquity* 37 (1): 13–34.

1973. Spatial analysis of Paleolithic occupation areas; in Colin Renfrew, ed., *The Explanation of Culture Change: Models in Prehistory*, pp. 115–30. London: Gerald Duckworth.

1974. Spatial analysis of occupation floors II: analysis of variance and nearest neighbor. *American Antiquity* 39 (1): 16–34.

1982. Variables and dimensions: the critical step in quantitative typology; in Robert Whallon and James A. Brown, eds., *Essays on Archaeological Typology*, pp. 127–61. Evanston, IL: Center for American Archaeology Press.

Whallon, Robert and James A. Brown, eds., 1982. *Essays on Archaeological Typology*. Evanston, IL: Center for American Archaeology Press.

Wheat, J. B., J. C. Gifford, and W. Wasley 1958. Ceramic variety, type cluster, and ceramic system in Southwestern pottery analysis. *American Antiquity* 24 (1): 34–47.

Whitcomb, Donald S. and Janet H. Johnson 1982. *Quseir el-Qadim 1980. American Research Center in Egypt Reports* 7.

White, Leslie A. 1949. *The Science of Culture*. New York: Grove Press.

Willey, Gordon R. and Philip Phillips 1958. *Method and Theory in American Archaeology*. Chicago: University of Chicago Press.

Willey, Gordon R. and Jeremy Sabloff 1974. *A History of American Archaeology*. San Francisco: W. H. Freeman & Co.

Wilson, Mark 1982. Predicate meets property. *The Philosophy Review* 91 (4): 549–89.

Wittgenstein, Ludwig 1922. *Tractatus Logico-Philosophicus*, trans. C. K. Ogden. London: Routledge & Kegan Paul.

Woozley, Anthony D. 1949. *Theory of Knowledge, an Introduction*. London: Hutchinson's University Library.

Wrangham, Richard W. 1979. On the evolution of ape social systems. *Social Science Information* 18 (3): 335–68.

Wright, J. V. 1967. Type and attribute analysis: their application to Iroquois culture history; in E. Tooker, ed., *Iroquois Culture, History, and Prehistory*, pp. 99–100. *Proceedings of the 1965 Conference on Iroquois Research, New York State Museum and Science Service.*

Wylie, Alison 1989. Archaeological cables and tacking: the implications of Bernstein's "Options beyond objectivism and relativism." *Philosophy of Social Science* 19: 1–18.

Zadeh, L. A. 1965. Fuzzy sets. *Information and Control* 8: 338–53.

1971. Quantitative fuzzy semantics. *Information Sciences* 3: 159–76.

Ziman, John 1978. *Reliable Knowledge.* Cambridge: Cambridge University Press.

INDEX

abstraction, 41, 44–6, 48
Abu-Lughod, Janet, 81
acquired gestalts, 42, 54, 138–9, 198, 242, 329; *see also* gestalts
activity patterns, 92, 222, 229, 285, 343
Adams, Robert M., 10
agglomerative programs, 206, 281, 329; *see also* lumping
ambiguity, 296–304; conceptual, 169, 300–3; in Linnean classification, 58; in programmatic statements, 65; in sorting, 77; in type recognition, 45–6; in typologies, 76, 83; of purpose, 166, 301–3; of terminology, 16–17, 25, 88, 224–5, 296–300, 303–4
American Indians, xx, 6, 267, 301; *see also* Anasazi
American Northeast, 220, 229, 231, 303
American Southwest: archaeological record, 231; architectural typologies in, 9; classification methods in, 103–4, 110, 220, 231, 303; "culture" groups in, 164, 196, 225, 231, 267–8; grave types in, 9; pottery in, 29, 31, 51, 196, 231, 301; type nomenclature in, 31; WYA excavations in, 51, 101
analogical reasoning, 307–8
analytical purposes, 160–3, 329
Anasazi, 164, 196, 225, 231, 267
ancillary purpose, 5, 21, 163–4, 166, 167, 215, 232, 251, 302, 330
ancillary typologies, 164, 215–16, 219, 220
Andean culture history, 219
animal ethology, *see* ethology
anthropology, 83–8, 308–9; classification in, 4–8, 70, 266–70; definition of, 46; paradigms in, 308–9; philosophy in, 13, 321; theory in, 6–8, 81–2, 83–8, 268–9,

274, 308–9, 311–12, 321; *see also* ethnology
anti-representationalists, 148
apriorism, 13, 334
Archaeological Constructs, 276, 289
architectural classifications, xx, 9, 162, 219, 227
Arikara Indian pottery, 162, 220
arrowhead typologies, *see* projectile point typologies
art historians, 160–1, 219
artificial classification, 20, 67–8, 253–4, 278–80, 331; artificial types, 15, 66–8, 215, 279–80, 331; vs. natural classification, 25, 67–8, 93, 217, 239, 265, 278–9, 287–8, 304
artificial intelligence, 4, 42
artificial types, *see* artificial classification
associative classifications, 179, 331
Aswan pottery, 117, 121, 130, 139; *see also* Egyptian pottery
attribute clustering, 177–9, 331; and type definition, 185, 236, 241, 288; meaning of, 178; paradigmatic, 95, 287, 354; significance of, 22, 52, 67, 177, 185, 191, 230, 291–2; vs. object clustering, 25, 60, 63, 182, 192, 254, 265, 285–6, 304, 353
attribute differentiation, 173–5
attribute selection, 160–1, 168, 174, 190–1, 332
attribute-space, 256
attribution, *see* type attribution
automatic classification, xvi, 274, 294

Bacon, Francis, 314, 320
baseball umpire, 200–1
basic purposes, 158–63, 166, 167, 332

basic typologies, 78–9, 215–17, 220, 332; formulation of, 274, 284; vs. instrumental typologies, 78–9, 80, 211, 219, 282, 287–8

"battleship graphs", 209, 211

bead typologies, 157, 159, 218, 227

Benedict, Ruth, 269

Bennett, John W., 269

Biblical archaeology, 232

bimodality, 71, 332; see also modality

binary division, 174, 206, 304

Binford, Lewis, 9–10, 271–2

biological classification, 122, 152, 154, 206, 271, 279, 286; see also species

biological evolution, 319

biological sciences, 186, 202, 257, 294, 300; see also biologists, biology

biological species, see species

biologists, 46, 64, 147, 187, 204, 205, 275; see also biology

biology, 4, 7, 13, 69, 146, 195, 203, 280, 281, 300; see also biologists

Boas, Franz, 309

Boasian ethnology, 268

Bohr, Nils, 8

boundaries, 71–2, 85–8, 279–80, 366; of classes, 46, 85–8; of types, 20, 47, 68, 71–2, 77, 143–4, 187, 195, 239–40, 255, 277, 279–80, 299, 300, 366; of typologies, 45, 47, 65, 76, 332; see also boundedness

boundedness, 49, 76, 83, 273, 279, 332; see also boundaries

Brew, J. O., 167, 270–1, 296, 305

Bridgman, Percy, 323

Bureau of American Ethnology, 266

Carnap, Rudolf, xxii, 11, 12, 316, 320, 322, 323

causation, xxii, 35, 74, 177, 191, 272, 289, 307

centers, 143–4, 244, 255, 332; see also central tendencies, modalities

central tendencies, 255, 332–3; and type definition, 20, 46, 71–2, 77–8, 240, 255, 299; lack of, 71; of ideal types, 240, 299; vs. boundaries, 20, 195, 240; see also centers, modalities

ceramic index clusters, 134, 136–7, 235, 345

Ceramic Industries of Medieval Nubia, 109

ceramic recording procedures, 128, 129–30, 131–5, 139–41

ceramologists, 101, 140, 330, 333

chance, 35, 53, 79, 177–8, 191; see also randomness, nonrandomness

Chang, K.-C., 8, 270

chi-square test, 292

Childe, V. Gordon, 178

Christenson, Andres, 8

chronological classifications, 23, 36, 161, 162–3, 216, 220–1, 333

chronological seriation, 9, 23, 59, 101, 137, 208–12, 219, 225, 333

church architecture, xx, 227

Clarke, David L., 70, 272, 275

classes of variables, 175–6, 333

classificatory era, see classificatory paradigm

classificatory paradigm, 266–8, 310, 312, 333

classificatory ranking, see taxonomic ranking

closed typologies, 149, 159, 226–8, 234, 334

cluster analysis, 33, 149, 206–7, 303, 334; see also agglomerative programs, computerized classifications, Numerical Taxonomy

cognitive psychology, xix, 7, 57, 86; see also psychology

cognitive science, 39; see also cognitive psychology

collections, 52–3, 57, 61, 72, 160, 209–10, 286, 334

colors, see pottery colors

Colton, Harold S., 60, 101, 301

comparative classifications, 159–60

comparative purposes, 21, 48, 81, 89, 158–60, 197, 202, 218, 279, 302, 334

comprehensiveness, 76; of recording procedures, 136–7; of sorting activity, 197; of taxonomies, 203; of theories, 314–20; of type descriptions, 171, 187–8; of typologies, 47, 65, 70, 76, 80, 83, 91–2, 153, 226

computer programs, 276, 286, 287, 293, 303; see also cluster analysis, computerized classifications, Numerical Taxonomy

computer technology, 273

computerized classifications, xvii–xviii, xix, 206–9, 212–13, 230, 271–2, 290, 293–4,

computerized classifications (*cont.*)
298, 339; closed typologies, xviii, 227;
clustering programs, 283–4, 302–3, 334;
differentiation programs, 23, 55, 92, 278;
in French archaeology, 276; meaningless
types, 42, 270, 272, 286, 294, 302–3,
311; "objectivity", 171, 188, 230, 272,
294, 303; seriation programs, 213–14;
taxonomic programs, 206–7, 364;
unrealized types, 33; *see also*
agglomerative programs, cluster analysis,
divisive programs, Numerical Taxonomy
computers, xvii, 124, 210, 212, 274, 291,
293–6, 301; *see also* computer programs,
computer technology, computerized
classifications
conceptual apriorism, 334
conceptual independence, 315–17
conceptual instrumentalism, 21, 143–54,
335
conceptual problems, xvi, 16–17, 25, 277,
296–304
conceptual systems, 5, 20, 29, 75–90, 91–2
conceptual vocabulary, 16–17, 25, 296
conditional probabilities, 248, 335
conditional proportions, 247
conditional uncertainty, 248, 335
configurational/functional era, *see*
configurational/functional paradigm
configurational/functional paradigm,
268–71, 282, 301, 310–12, 335
configurationism, 267, 268–9, 270, 282–3,
309, 311, 335; *see also* configurationist
paradigm
configurationist era in ethnology, *see*
configurationist paradigm
configurationist paradigm, 167, 223, 309
congeries, 44, 45, 54, 335
consistency among sorters, *see* intersubjective agreement
consistency of definition, 78, 335
container spaces, 153
contextual attributes, 22, 58, 161, 176,
178–9, 180, 191–2, 218, 241; *see also*
contextual variables
contextual evidence, 199–200; *see also*
contextual features, contextual variables,
extrinsic evidence
contextual features, 170, 176, 192, 220; *see*
also contextual evidence, contextual
variables

contextual variables, 119, 161, 176, 335–6
continuum of variation, *see* intergradation
contypicality, 151–2, 336
Copernican theory, 322–4
Copernicus, 321, 322
Cormack, R. M., 71, 94, 287, 295
cost-effectiveness, xvii, xx, 23–4, 138, 227,
233–4, 236–7, 250, 260
Cowgill, George, xxi
criteria of identity, 45; concrete properties,
34; external, 45; in "induced" typologies,
290; in practical typologies, 242, 297; in
taxonomies, 204, 219; intrinsic, 45, 204,
220–1, 241; mental images of, 32; of
"cultures", 40; or provisional types, 168,
185–6, 240; qualitative, 81; related to
purposes, 92; revision of, 227; role of
attributes as, 172, 178, 241; role of
statistics as, 292; unknown, 36;
variability of, 65–6, 70, 152, 179; *see also*
diagnostic attributes
criteria of meaning, 45–6; in "deduced"
typologies, 290; in practical typologies,
297; in selection of types, 186, 240; in
taxonomies, 204; known associations,
34–5; related to purposes, 45–6; role of
extrinsic attributes as, 178, 241; role of
variables as, 174; *see also* meaning
criteria of typehood, 64–6, 71–2, 124,
143–4, 151–2, 179, 207, 243, 292, 312;
see also dimensions of typehood, elements
of typehood
"cultural" categories, 270, 284
"cultural" classifications, 23, 214, 224–5,
277, 336; contrast with artifact
classifications, 203, 211, 212, 214,
224–5, 271, 276, 297–8, 299–300;
formulation of, 224, 277, 297–8; genetic
component in, 215, 221, 225
cultural ecology, 309, 336
"cultural" sequences, 225
"cultures", 162, 214, 224, 265, 336;
defined, 224, 336; identification of, 40,
220–1, 310; reconstruction of, 215, 216;
temporal sequences of, 208, 216, 225; *see*
also "cultural" classifications

Daniel, Glyn, 85
Darwin, Charles, 58
dating procedures, 74, 79, 89, 99, 131,
135–42, 180, 209–10, 234–5; *see also*

frequency seriation, radiocarbon dating, sequence dating

dating purposes, 162–4, 215, 220–1; attributes useful for, 14, 111, 139; pottery used for, 79, 128–9, 131, 136, 163–4, 233–4, 235; selection of variables for, 189–90; type frequencies used for, 209–12; types used for, 40, 58, 69, 74, 100, 122, 131, 204, 265, 279; typologies made for, 38, 100–3, 129, 163–4, 166–7, 215, 220–1, 235, 301

de Saussure, Ferdinand, 50

decision-making, 188–93; in attribute selection, 173–4, 190–1; in excavation, 130, 261; in sorting, 22–3, 56, 193, 197–201, 230, 238, 240; in type differentiation, 71–2, 77; in type formulation, 22, 275; in type selection, 69, 93, 191–3; in variable selection, 171–2, 189–90; see also judgment, type selection

decision theory, xxii

decoration, see pottery decoration

"deduced" typologies, 180, 289–90

deduction, 12, 60–1, 67, 281–2, 290, 304, 307, 337; see also deductive classifications

deductive classifications, 66, 182, 337

deductive hypotheses, 272

Deetz, James F., 162, 220, 279

defining variables, 107; see also significant variables

definiteness, 143–6

definition, see type definition

degrees of membership, 73; see also fuzzy sets

degrees of relationship, 80

dendrochronology, 180

dendrogram, 206, 207, 337

denotata of identity, see criteria of identity

Descartes, René, 13, 322

description, see type description

descriptive attributes, 72, 182, 186–8, 286, 337

descriptive labels, 31, 44, 59, 196, 222

descriptive particularism, 309

descriptive purposes, 21, 158–9, 160, 227, 253–4, 285, 302, 337

descriptive type concepts, 286, 337

descriptive typologies, 159, 160

descriptive variables, 228, 338

designation, see type designation

determinants of typehood, see criteria of typehood

development of classificatory systems, 61, 149, 159, 192, 214, 239

diagnostic attribute clusters, 177–9, 338; basis of type definition, 30, 63, 177, 185; basis of type identity, 37; identification of, 236; meaningfulness of, 178–9; statistical significance of, 177, 212; variability of association in, 177–8; see also diagnostic attributes, criteria of identity

diagnostic attributes, 147, 186–8, 195–6, 338; basis of type definition, 30, 63, 174; basis of type identification, 252; identification of, 195, 236; in ideal type specimens, 72; in individual specimens, 195–6; informational value of, 244, 252; kinds of, 22; vs. descriptive attributes, 147, 182, 186–8; see also criteria of identity, diagnostic attribute clusters

diagnostic variables, 228

dialectics, 17, 19, 50–62, 309, 333; between aspects of typehood, 50, 60–1, 239, 273, 276, 286, 312; between learning and communication, 61–2; method and theory, xxiii, 286, 303, 306, 309, 313; of scientific paradigms, xxii, xxiii; of type formulation, 19, 50–62; see also feedback

dichotomies, 285, 287–90, 296, 304

differentiation, see type differentiation

dimensions of typehood, xvi, 18–19, 29–38, 73, 239, 338; see also typehood

discovery of types, see type discovery

divisive programs, 206, 281, 338; see also splitting

domains of variability, 79, 104–5, 169, 176, 178, 188, 254, 256, 338–9

Dumont, Louis, 83–4

Duncan, T., 254

Dunnell, Robert, xvii, xviii, 266, 273, 287, 298, 311, 312

Durkheim, Emile, 81–2, 85, 86, 308

Durkheimian sociology, 308

Eastern North America, see American Northeast

eclecticism, xvii, xviii, 6–7

economic studies, 103, 136, 139; see also economics

economics, 13, 136, 139, 162, 274; *see also* economic studies
Egyptian pottery, 51, 52, 107, 118–19, 122, 130, 139, 165–6, 180–1, 229
Egyptology, 129, 232
Einstein, Albert, 323, 324
Einsteinian theory, 323, 324
electronic era, *see* electronic paradigm
electronic paradigm, 274, 298, 339
elements of typehood, 18, 30–2, 339; *see also* dimensions of typehood
emic categories, 270
emic classifications, 23, 162, 179, 222, 269, 270, 282–4, 304, 311, 339; *see also* emic types
emic explanations, 269
emic meaning, *see* emic significance
emic significance, 167, 176, 179, 232, 271, 284, 301, 302, 304, 339
emic types, 4, 231, 282–4, 339; *see also* emic classifications
empirical categories, 270
empirical significance, 35, 312, 339
empiricism, xxiii, 6–7, 11–15, 21, 60, 260, 282, 287–8, 314–25, 339; *see also* empiricists
"empiricist" classification, 287–8, 304, 339
empiricists, 11–13, 144, 309, 317–25; *see also* empiricism
environmentalism, 79_80
epistemology, 8, 11–13
equidistance of types, 80, 81, 83, 340
equivalence of types, 78–84, 340
essential classification, 66, 68–9, 340
esentialists, 309
Estabrook, G. F., 254
ethnic identification, 164, 219, 224, 231–2, 340
ethnography, 271
ethnologists, xxi, 224, 271, 308–9; *see also* ethnology
ethnology, xx, 9–10, 266–71, 313; *see also* ethnologists
ethnoscience, xix, 79, 267
ethology, 82–3
etic classification, 4, 269, 282–4, 304, 340; *see also* natural classification
etic meaning, 341
Etzioni, Amitai, 304
evaluative ranking, 83–5
Evans, R. K., 272, 287–9, 298

evolution of typologies, *see* development of classificatory systems
exclusivity of attributes, 172
experimental psychology, 274; *see also* psychology
experts, 145–6, 259, 323
explanation in science, 9, 24–5, 272, 276, 301–2, 307–8, 311–12, 315, 341; *see also* scientific thought
explicit type definitions, 30, 63, 341; *see also* type definitions
extendable typologies, 227, 341; *see also* open typologies
external criteria, *see* extrinsic evidence
external isolation, 46, 58, 71–2, 94, 143–4, 280–1, 287, 341
extrinsic attributes, 58, 69, 178–9, 188, 191–2, 199, 218, 241, 276, 289–90, 341
extrinsic evidence, 45, 69, 76, 102–4, 175, 192, 199–200, 212, 221, 341; *see also* extrinsic attributes, extrinsic variables
extrinsic variables, 102, 119–20, 175–6, 341

fabric, *see* pottery fabric
factor analysis, 254, 255, 342
families, *see* pottery families
Faras Potteries, 100–1, 102, 104, 105, 129
feasibility, 260–1, 342; *see also* practicality
features of typehood, *see* criteria of typehood
feedback, 342; between induction and deduction, 60, 67, 281, 290, 337; between learning and communication, 62; between object clustering and attribute clustering, 304; between objects and ideas, 19, 50, 60, 239, 273, 276, 286, 333; between structure and performance, 50; *see also* dialectics
Feigl, Herbert, 316
fixists, 278
flexibility, 230, 287
fluxists, 278
folk classifications, 40–1, 54, 84–5, 177, 342; *see also* vernacular classifications
folk concepts, 148, 342
Ford, James A., 9, 59, 235, 270–1, 284, 311
foreknowledge, 51–2, 183–4, 185, 189, 276, 342

formal classifications, 4, 25, 46–7, 104, 110–11, 285, 288, 304

formal definitions, 18, 29, 30–1, 43, 62–6, 72, 184–5, 186–7, 198, 241; *see also* type definitions

formal language, 44, 240, 245–6, 313

formal logic, 70, 74, 244

formulation, *see* type formulation

Foucault, Michel, 169, 233

"free constructions", 289–90

Frege, Gottlob, 316

frequency seriation, xviii, 89, 137, 209–12, 342; *see also* seriation

Freudian theory, 308

Fritz, John M., 272

functional analyses, 129, 139, 140, 179, 228; *see also* functional inferences, functional interpretation

functional attributes, 58, 179, 220

functional categories, 270–1, 284

functional change, 209

functional classes, 110; *see also* functional classifications

functional classifications, 221–3, 270–1, 284–5, 343; as explanation, 272; attributes of, 179; genetic component in, 80; of pottery, 36, 161, 222; purpose of, 23, 222–3, 270, 311; taxonomies, 203–5, 300; vs. formal classifications, 4, 25, 284–5, 304

functional inferences, 128, 285; *see also* functional interpretation

functional interpretation, 129, 163, 167, 222, 228; *see also* functional analyses, functional inferences

functional purposes, 218

functional relationships, 58, 89, 200, 201, 202, 203, 204, 205

functional significance, 93, 190, 192, 232, 271, 312

functional taxonomies, 219, 222, 285, 300

functional types, 192, 221–2, 229, 272, 284, 285; *see also* functional classification

functional variables, 222

functionalism, 7, 267, 268–9, 272, 343

fuzzy sets, 72–3, 343

Galileo, 314, 320

Gardin, Jean-Claude, 179–80, 276, 289–90

Geertz, Clifford, 91

Geisteswissenschaft, 268, 309

genera, 46, 71, 84, 203, 204, 300; *see also* biological classification

General Systems Theory, 275, 300, 309

generative rules, 46; *see also* generative typologies

generative typologies, 159, 343

genetic classifications, 205–6, 215, 299–300, 343–4; biological, 58–9, 205–6; computerized programs, 212, 294, 300; contrast with non-genetic classifications, 47, 203, 205–6, 207, 215, 294, 299–300; hierarchic character, 47, 80; historical, 221; linguistic, 211; Medieval Nubian Pottery Typology, 108, 121; taxonomies, 58–9, 203, 205–6

genetic inheritance, 280

genetic relationships, 58, 208, 224

geneticists, 74

geocentric paradigm, 323

geocentrists, 322

geologists, 265

German morphological school of biology, 54

gestalt acquisition, *see* acquired gestalts

Gestalt psychology, 42, 54

gestalts, 42–3, 54–6, 147, 150, 276, 321, 344, 348; and type differentiation, 54–6; and type recognition, 45, 54–6, 147, 189, 198, 237; definition of, 17, 19, 35, 41, 42–3, 49; formation of, 42–3; intuitive and acquired gestalts contrasted, 42; *see also* acquired gestalts, intuitive gestalts

glazed pottery, 111–22, 123, 126, 130, 165, 203, 229, 375

Good, Isidore J., 261

Good's Theorem, 261

grave types, 32, 208, 219, 220–1, 224, 225, 277

Greenwood, Davydd, 86

"guided constructions", 289–90, 304

Hakataya "culture", 225

hand-made pottery, 104–5, 107, 115, 126, 130–1, 165, 203, 245, 253, 344

hands-on training, 15, 16, 145, 197, 240; *see also* learning

Hanen, Marsha, 318

Hargrave, Lyndon L., 60, 301

Harris, Marvin, 281

heliocentrism, 322, 323

Hempel, Carl G., xxii, 12, 272, 275, 281, 300, 307, 316
Hewett, Edgar L., 267
hierarchic ordering, 23, 46–7, 58, 78, 83–5, 167, 202, 214, 257, 287, 344; see also taxonomic ordering
hierarchical ranking, see hierarchic ordering
Hill, James N., 272, 287–9, 298
historical classifications, 80, 178–9, 220–1, 224, 344
historical purposes, 108, 162–3, 344
historicist philosophy, xxii
Hohokam "culture", 225, 267
Holland, Dorothy, 279
Holmes, William H., 267
Holsinger, Kent, 8
horizon styles, 121
house types, 32, 94, 164, 208, 219, 220–1, 224–5, 277
humanities, 308, 309
Huxley, Julian, 70
hypotheses, 288–9, 311, 312, 315; see also hypothesis-testing
hypothesis-testing, 288–9, 300, 311, 312
hypothetico-deductivism, 12, 300

ideal types, 53, 72, 73, 77, 85, 187–8, 299, 344
idealized concepts, 51, 71, 72, 195, 280; see also ideal types
identifiable types, 183–4, 345
identity, 34, 36–8, 146–8, 182–3, 345; and type formulation, 183, 185; and type labels, 43; categorical, 33; establishment of, 147, 168, 182–3, 192, 199; extrinsic features of, 58; mental conceptions of, 34, 42, 43, 58, 59; numerical, 147; of attributes, 174; of classes, 45–6; of computer-generated types, 206; of phenetic types, 208; of words, 44; part of type concept, 30, 33; property of types, 19, 21, 22, 34, 36, 58, 59, 69, 94, 168, 178, 239, 281, 290; social, 34, 82–3; see also criteria of identity, ethnic identification, individual identity, type identity, typological identity
immutability, 34
implicative statements, 307
implicit type definitions, 31, 63, 184, 345; see also type definitions
"imposed" constructions, 289–90, 304

imprintation, 42, 345
incidental purposes, 21, 158–9, 165, 345
independence of types, 80, 81, 83, 345
indeterminacy, 131
index clusters, see ceramic index clusters
index fossils, 163–4, 220, 231–2, 265
individual identity, 34, 36, 345
individual meanings, 19, 35, 37, 301, 346
"induced typologies", 180, 289–90
induction, 60, 67, 281–2, 290, 304, 346
inductive classifications, 182, 346; see also induction
inferential attributes, 22, 176, 179, 191–2, 218, 221, 241
inferential variables, 22, 176, 285, 341, 346
information theory, xxii, 24, 244–61
informative typologies, 244, 346
instantiation, 150–2, 153, 346
instruction, see hands-on training, learning
instrumental purposes, 21, 158–9, 162–5, 283, 347
instrumental relativism, 6, 347; see also instrumentalism
instrumental types, 19, 66, 69, 277
instrumental typologies, 70, 93, 162, 215–17, 226, 242, 277, 346
instrumentalism, 6, 13–15, 69, 145, 147, 309, 347; see also conceptual instrumentalism
interdependence of attributes, 173
interdependent variables, 104
intergradation of types, 68, 71–2, 77–8, 280
internal features, see intrinsic features
internal cohesion, 46, 58, 71–2, 94, 280–1, 287, 347
interpretive purposes, 161–2, 285, 347
intersubjective agreement, 4, 142, 258–9, 347; in language use, 56; in type concepts, 187; in type representation, 56; in typing and sorting, 138, 145, 147, 187, 238, 242
intersubjective communication, 124
intersubjective consistency, see intersubjective agreement
interval scales, 88, 152–3, 174–5, 347
interval variables, 347; see also interval scales
intrasubjective agreement, 56, 187, 242, 347
intrinsic attributes, 22, 69, 102, 162, 178,

180–1, 190, 220–1, 223, 243, 292–3, 334, 348; *see also* intrinsic features
intrinsic classification, 257
intrinsic evidence, 45, 76, 102, 181; *see also* intrinsic features
intrinsic features, 172, 180; and decision-making, 69; and functional types, 224; and taxonomic ordering, 224; and type designation, 102, 193, 194, 202, 223, 224; and type identification, 203; and typological boundaries, 45; description of, 110, 190; of "cultures", 227; of identity, 69, 207
intrinsic purposes, 21, 159–62, 219, 256, 348
intrinsic variables, 22, 162, 174, 178, 224, 348; *see also* intrinsic features
intuition, 40, 66–7, 182, 239, 244
intuitive gestalts, 42, 53–4, 55, 348
intuitive significance, 35, 42, 54, 348
intuitive taxonomies, 206
intuitive types, 19, 53–4, 56, 66–7, 100, 186, 215, 229, 348
invariants, 53, 54, 170, 349
invention of types, *see* type invention
irrelevant types, 349

Jakobson, Roman, 56
Jevons, W. S., 7, 67, 278–9, 281
joints in nature, 67, 86, 280, 300
judgments, xviii, 275, 299; about attributes, 252, 258; aesthetic, 85; and objectivity, 258; in classifying, 72, 77, 192–3, 194, 252, 258, 294, 297, 299; in collecting, 53; in sorting, 194, 197, 199–200, 259, 299; in umpiring, 200–1; of ethnic identity, 219; of similarity, 22, 254–5, 257; variables, 258; *see also* decision-making, type selection

Kant, Immanuel, 13
Kaplan, Abraham, 8, 74
Kelley, Jane H., 318
Klejn, Leo S., 277
Kluckhohn, Clyde, 269–70, 275, 282, 305
Krieger, Alex D., 269–70, 283, 296, 301, 311
Kuhn, Thomas, 317–25; critique of positivism, xxii–xxiii, 12–13, 314, 317–18, 320, 322–3; on macro-

paradigms, 321; on paradigm shifts, 25, 306, 310, 321; on paradigms, 25–6, 268, 306, 319–20, 321, 325; on scientific concepts, 25–6; on scientific progress, 317–18, 321; quoted, 321, 322
Kulubnarti, 106, 129

labeling, 44, 349
labels, *see* type labels
Lakoff, George, 39
language, 50–1, 59, 315–16, 349; and classification, 19, 40, 43–4, 45–6, 240, 313; and concepts, 315–16; classification of, 203, 205; consistency in use of, 56; learning of, 59, 138, 197–8, 309; legitimation of, 87; of formal logic, 245–6; of paradigms, 319; philosophy of, 6, 316; relation to speech, 4, 50–1; structural features of, 76; symbolic dimensions of, 85–7; *see also* formal language, observation languages
law of equivalence, 79
Leach, Edmund, 86, 272
learning, 59–60, 61–2, 144, 146, 197, 198, 259; *see also* hands-on training
legitimation, 86–7
Lévi-Strauss, Claude, 80, 89
Levin, Michael E., 271
lexicon, 44, 76, 349; *see also* language
linear ordering, 207, 349; *see also* seriation
linguistic taxonomies, 122
linguistics, xx, 4, 7, 122, 203, 212, 300
Linnaeus, Carolus, 59
Linnean classification, 58–9, 71, 94, 154, 203, 300
Linton, Ralph, 270
logic, 8, 73–5, 144–5, 245, 281, 316
logical compounds, 245–6
logical empiricism, 316–18, 323, 349
logical independence of variables, 171
lumpers, 280, 304, 349; *see also* lumping
lumping, 249–50, 280–1, 349; in development of taxonomies, 23, 203, 206; in development of type concepts, 61, 92; in development of typologies, 102, 111, 149, 194, 249–50, 260–1; vs. splitting, 25, 265, 280–1, 304; *see also* agglomerative programs, lumpers

Mach, Ernst, 11, 12, 322–3, 325
McGregor, John C., 267

McKern Midwest Taxonomic System, 225, 268
macroparadigms, 321
making of types, *see* type formulation
Margolis, Howard, 57, 286, 294
Marxism, 308
materialism, 269, 309
mathematical probability, 247, 349
mathematical psychology, xxii
mathematical reality, 87
mathematics, 4, 13, 87, 89, 247, 349
Mauss, Marcel, 85
Maxwell, James, 324
Mead, Margaret, 269
meaning, 35–8, 42–5, 145–8, 171–2, 178, 350; and selection of variables, 171–2; and type selection, 185; arbitrary, 288; chronological, 35; conventional, 148; cultural or emic, 269–70, 301, 304, 335, 339; etic, 340–1; historical, 283; inherent or natural, 5, 7, 148, 288, 324; learning, 50, 59–60; of classes, 45; of concepts, 43–4; of gestalts, 42–3; of phenetic types, 218; of sensory images, 42; or words, 16–17, 29, 39, 44, 50, 70, 224, 276, 287, 322–3; property of typehood, 22, 34, 36, 69, 94, 103, 168, 183, 192, 239, 281, 290; related to other types, 93, 94; related to purpose, 7, 19, 36, 93, 94, 145–6, 155, 178, 191, 240, 301; *see also* criteria of meaning, individual meaning, type meaning, typological meaning
meaningfulness, 35–6, 153–4, 350; of attribute clusters, 103, 177–8, 191, 241; of objectivity claims, 4; of scale types, 153–5; of statements, 154–5, 257–8, 294, 319, 321; of type categories, 32; of types, 68, 91, 94, 168, 186, 269; of variables, 172; *see also* individual meaning, meaning, meaningless types, type meaning, typological meaning
meaningless types, 36, 93, 183, 208, 275, 292, 294, 350
measurement, 88–90, 152–4, 174–5, 244, 256–8; and attributes, 172–3, 183, 190; in genetic classifications, 293, 300; in taxonomies, 298; information-theoretic representation, 256–8; physical, 12, 153; relation to classification, 14, 16, 88–90, 143, 152–4, 256, 257; scales, 174–5;

scientific, xxii–xxiii, 3, 152–4, 244, 256–8; theory of, xxii–xxiii
Medieval Nubian Pottery Typology, 20–1, 102–42, 350; classificatory procedures in, 102, 104–6, 107, 122, 209, 221, 222, 229; dating procedures in, 135–9; development of, 20, 60, 99–109, 123–4, 165, 180, 319; emic significance of types in, 293–4; features of, 21, 110–27, 203–4; information-theoretical analysis of, 244–61; invariants in, 170; learning of, 148; naturalness of types in, 279; purposes of, 13–14, 15, 58, 102–3, 159, 163–4, 165, 167, 244, 260, 320; reality of types in, 150; sorting procedures in, 129–35, 238; type attributes in, 176, 178; type boundaries in, 68, 143–4, 279; type definitions in, 144–5, 151, 152, 290; type descriptions in, 144, 372–5; type discovery in, 151; type labels in, 17; type names in, 31–2, 124–7; type relationships in, 206, 215; type variables in, 170, 172; uses, 21, 128–42, 145, 318
Meinarti, 106, 123–4, 129
Meltzer, David J., 318
mental dimensions of typehood, xvi, 30, 33, 39
mental images, 147–8
mental templates, 16, 20, 42, 162, 223, 279, 282–4, 350; *see also* emic categories, emic significance, emic types
mentalism, xx, 269, 309
Mesoamerica, 110
method of pottery construction, 104, 106, 119, 126, 176, 350
microparadigms, 318–19, 321
mnemonic purposes, 126, 165, 203, 218–19, 227, 235
modalities, 71–2; absence of, 111; and type definition, 71, 195, 240; created by nature, 68, 239, 279; of form, 159; relation to type boundaries, 71–2, 195, 239, 279; *see also* bimodal, central tendencies
Mogollon "culture", 164, 225, 267
Mohs' hardness values, 236–7
monothetic classifications, 226, 350
morphological classifications, 58, 80, 93, 159–60; *see also* phenetic classifications
multiple purposes, 14, 58, 165–7, 253–4

Munsell system of color notation, 173, 236–7, 238
mural art classifications, 219
mutability of types, 34, 227, 239, 242, 350
mutual exclusiveness, 351; of attributes, 172–3; of class labels, 196; of classifications, 217; of "cultures", 224; of ordering methods, 209; of purposes, 158, 160; of type norms, 172; of types, 47, 77–8, 80, 81–2, 88, 91–2, 214, 240, 245, 249, 297
mythology, 86–8, 308

Nagel, Ernest, 14
National Science Foundation, 271, 309
natural classifications, 278–9, 351; combined with artificial classification, 88, 279; informativeness, 254; oldest, 71; vs. artificial classification, 67, 217, 265, 278–9, 304; see also natural types, naturalness
natural language, 7, 44–6, 59
natural meanings, 7, 148, 324
natural order, 87–8, 302, 303
natural sciences, 11–13; and explanation, 74–5; and prediction, 74–5; classification in, 267, 278, 293–4; computer methodologies in, 293–4, 300; empiricism in, 11–13; methodologies, 300; progress in, 306, 310; research objectives in, 314; see also biologists, biology, physics, physical sciences
natural selection, 11
natural types, 13–14, 67–8, 351; and boundaries, 71, 279–80, 300; contrasted with artificial types, 15, 20, 24, 66, 67–8, 93, 239, 279; discovery of, 67–8, 217; existence of, 13–14, 86, 93, 231, 272, 279, 304; not object of classification, 13–14; see also natural classification, naturalness
naturalness, 58, 68–9, 71, 87, 198, 215, 253–4, 273, 279, 300; see also natural classification, natural types
Navajo Indians, xx, 6
necessary conditions, 15, 66, 70, 89, 144–5, 147, 177, 179, 191, 197, 226, 292, 319, 324, 351
Nelson, N. C., 265
neutron activation, 236, 237

New Archaeologists, 67, 74, 164, 272–4, 281
New Organon, 314
Newton, Isaac, 12, 315, 317, 321, 324
Newton's Laws of Motion, 12
Newton's Principia, 321
nominal scales, 152–4, 174–5, 351
nominal variables, 351; see also nominal scales
nominalism, 149, 351
nomothetic paradigm, 271–4, 301–2, 311–12, 351
non-genetic classifications, 47, 203, 205–6, 215, 294, 299–300, 352
nonrandomness, 89, 191–2, 291–2, 352
normal science, 317
norms, see type norms
Northeast, see American Northeast
numerical identity, 147
Numerical Taxonomy, 206–7, 251, 273, 275, 277, 293, 300, 352; see also cluster analysis

object attributes, 180–1
object clustering, 285–7, 353; as basis of type concept formulation, 63–4, 182–3, 192, 254–5; representation of, 60; vs. attribute clustering, 25, 52, 60, 285–7, 304
objectivity, 258–60, 347, 359; attainability, 87, 176, 184, 275, 294; component of types, 151; demand for, 236; desirability of, 145, 147, 244; efforts at, 236; goal of classifications, xix, 4, 15, 87; in computerized classifications, 275, 291, 294, 302–3; of judgments, 252; value of, 244, 258–60
observation languages, 316–17, 322, 353
occult types, 36, 353
one-level typologies, see basic typologies
ontological commitment, 150, 353
Open Systems Theory; see General Systems Theory
open typologies, xviii, 15–16, 50, 149, 160, 226–8, 242, 353
ordering of types, 202–13, 241, 292–3, 353, 368
ordinal scales, 174–5, 353
ordinal variables, 354; see also ordinal scales
ordinary sets, 73, 353

overdetermination, 22, 354; defined, 56, 187; reasons for, 144–5, 171, 196, 241, 297

overgeneralization, 303

painted decoration, *see* pottery decoration

paleontologists, 265

paradigm shifts, 24, 25, 166–7, 274, 305–6, 308, 317–19, 354; *see also* paradigms

paradigmatic classification, 67, 95, 280, 287, 304, 354

paradigms, 266–75, 308–12, 314–25, 361; and progress, 314–25; empiricist, 314–16; in anthropology, 308–9; in artifact classification, 266–75, 309–12; methodological, 24; nature of, 12, 15–16, 306, 308; pesudoproblems in, 322–5; sovereignty of, 319–20, 321; succession of, 166–7, 266–75, 308–12; theoretical, 12, 24; theory of, xxii, 314–25; *see also* paradigm shifts

partitioning, 47, 91–2, 354; *see also* segmentation

pattern recognition, 41, 198, 354

Pecos Chronology, 225

Pepper, Stephen, 201

periodic table of the elements, 88

permissible transformations, 154, 354

personality formation processes, 309

Petrie, W. M. Flinders, 163, 208, 232

petrographic analysis, 236

phenetic classifications, 216, 217–19, 222, 355; *see also* morphological classifications

philosophy, 4, 306–8, 316; *see also* philosophy of science, social philosophy

philosophy of language, *see* language

philosophy of science, xv–xvii, 5, 7, 8, 11–16, 21, 142–54, 244–61, 275, 300, 313–25

phylogenetic classifications, *see* genetic classifications

phylogeny, 279

physical anthropology, 205

physical dimensions of typehood, xvi, 30, 32–3

physical sciences, 13, 307, 321; *see also* physics

physical topology, xxii

physics, 12, 153, 300, 315; *see also* physical sciences

pigeonholes, 77, 80, 157, 197, 255, 297

Pike, Kenneth, 282

Pitt Rivers, Lane-Fox, 85

Plato, 13

Plog, Fred T., 272

Poincaré, Henri, 323

political science, 46, 274

polythetic classifications, 69–70, 226, 355; archaeological typologies, 19; artifact typologies, 66, 78, 92, 273; attributes in, 151, 168; criteria of typehood in, 151, 243; nature of, 66, 69–70, 78, 226; vs. monothetic classifications, 226

polythetic types, 273, 277; *see also* polythetic classifications

polytypic classifications, 70; *see also* polythetic classifications

Popper, Karl, xxii, 12, 316

population statistics, 307

positivism, xxii

"positivist" classification, 287–9, 304, 355

potential types, 94, 193, 355

pottery cataloguing, *see* ceramic recording

pottery colors, 104, 107, 119, 140, 176, 355

pottery decoration, 104, 111, 114, 140, 336–7, 355, 373; designs, 111, 355; elements, 111, 336; fields, 111, 336; motifs, 111, 114, 336; programs, 111, 337; relief decoration, 105, 119, 176, 360; painted decoration, 105, 119, 176, 354; styles, 113, 121, 140, 356

pottery fabric, 102, 104, 106, 107, 119, 176, 342, 356

pottery families, 106–8, 110, 124, 356

pottery rim profiles, 237

pottery slip, 126, 356

pottery styles, 104, 111

pottery sub-families, 107, 356

pottery surface treatment, 105, 107, 111, 119, 140, 176, 356

pottery vessel forms, 180, 356; and type formulation, 92, 102, 104, 107, 161, 166, 222; as domain of variability, 176, 188; as significant variables, 180, 251, 252; attributes of, 178, 195; classification of, 53, 104, 110–11, 122, 129, 159, 170, 222; illustration of, 109, 112, 373; in Medieval Nubian Typology, 102, 104, 107, 109, 110–12, 122; recording of, 139–40

pottery ware groups, 105–6, 107–8, 110, 124, 125, 357
Powell, John Wesley, 266–7, 313
practical taxonomies, 281; *see also* practical typologies
practical type descriptions, 187, 357
practical types, 67–8; *see also* practical typologies
practical typologies, 239–43, 357; bases of type inclusion, 69, 93, 292; character-istics of, xviii, 50, 61, 67–8, 94–5, 185, 193, 239–43, 297; defined, 7–8; development of, 19, 23, 55, 60, 66, 73–4, 95, 168, 183, 185–6, 240–1, 286; in daily use, 8; principles of, 24, 239–43; problems in use of, 56, 61, 95; purposes of, 168, 172; role of statistics in, 291–2; type definition in, 64; *see also* practical types, practicality
practical utility, *see* practicality, utility
practicality, 232–8, 260–1, 357; and purpose, 235; in classifying, 235–7; in closed typologies, 227; in open typologies, 227; in sorting, 77, 187, 237–8; of gestalts, 147; overriding consideration in classifications, xx, 4, 5, 8, 23–4, 124; principles of, 241–2; rules of, 233; *see also* feasibility, practical typologies, utility
praxis, 3–4, 17, 357
prediction, 307, 308, 310, 312, 357
prescriptive attributes, 357
prescriptive type concepts, 286, 357
Principia, 321
principles of practical typology, 239–43
probabilism, xxii, 247, 307, 358
probabilistic uncertainty, 247, 358
programmatic statements, xviii, 4, 65, 182, 226, 274, 276, 303; *see also* theoretical literature
progress, xxiii, 13, 25, 314–25
projectile point typologies, 40, 47, 170, 178, 220, 221
properties of types, 34–6; *see also* dimensions of typehood
proportions, 246–9
prototypic classification, 255, 257
provisional type definitions, 102, 184; *see also* provisional types
provisional types, 56, 102, 108, 127, 168, 183, 185, 192, 240, 358

pseudoproblems, xxiii, 322–5, 358
psychology, xxii, 42–3, 46, 54, 79, 274

Qasr Ibrim, 135–9; archaeological conditions at, 135–6, 137; contribution to Medieval Nubian Pottery Typology, 108–9, 110, 135; dating procedures at, 74, 135, 136–9, 140–2, 234–5; pottery recording procedures at, 108, 130–5, 139–40; pottery ware percentages at, 77
qualitative difference of variables, 171
qualitative mathematics, 89
quantification, 298; *see also* measurement
quantitative difference of attributes, 173
quantitative typologies, 88
Quine, Willard, 150
Quinn, Naomi, 279

radical empiricists, 11; *see also* empiricists
radiocarbon dating, 138, 180, 208, 234
Raiffa, Howard, 261
random variables, 245, 359
randomness, 89, 191, 292, 359
ratio scales, 88, 152–3, 175, 174, 359
ratio variables, 359; *see also* ratio scales
rational classification, 66, 359
Read, Dwight, W., 8, 272
"real" types, 54
realism, xxiii, 15, 71, 149–52, 359; *see also* reality
reality, 87–8, 149–52, 258–60; and utility, 258–60; degrees of, 69; of nature, 187, 197; perception of, 242; relation to theory, 3–4; relation to type concepts, 4, 54–5, 68, 149–52, 242, 268, 273, 288; search for, 87–8; *see also* realism
realized types, 94, 193, 360
recognition, *see* type recognition
recording procedures, *see* ceramic recording procedures
reductionism, 308–9
Reisner, George A., 232
relativism, 6, 321
relativity, 323
relevance, *see* type relevance
relevant types, 360
relief decoration, *see* pottery decoration
representational dimensions of typehood, xvi, 30–2, 33; *see also* typehood
representationalists, 148
retrodiction, 310

rock art classifications, 219
Rose, Pamela, 109
Rosenkrantz, Roger, 261
Rouse, Irving, 269–70, 283, 296, 311
Russell, Bertrand, 11–12, 316

Sabloff, Jeremy, 266, 270
Salmon, Merrilee, 312
scale-types, 152–3, 174–5, 360
Schlaifer, Robert, 261
Schlick, Moritz, 316
Schliemann, Heinrich, 163
scientific classifications, 54, 81, 85, 360
scientific languages, 323
scientific paradigms, see paradigms
scientific proof, 12, 306, 317
scientific revolutions, 12–13, 306, 310, 317–18, 319–20
scientific thought, 39–41, 87–8, 148, 271–2, 306–9, 314–25
seams in nature, see joints in nature
secondary purposes, 57, 102, 108, 129, 165, 203, 204, 241, 253
segmentary systems, 77, 80–3, 361
segregation, 47, 240, 361; see also partitioning
selection, see type selection
semiotics, 7
sense empiricism, 11, 315, 361; see also empiricism
sense observation, 314
sensory images, 31, 41, 361
sensory impressions, 35
sensory perceptions, 41, 361; see also sensory images, sensory impressions
sequence dating, 208, 361
seriation, 207–9, 241, 361; chronological, 216, 219, 221, 225; combined with taxonomy, 122, 209; in Medieval Nubian Pottery Typology, 122, 209; of "cultures", 225; of ordinal attributes, 174; of types, 208–9, 241, 292–3; purposes of, 241, 293; relation to classifying, 23; relation to taxonomy, 202; use of statistics and computers in, 212–13, 293; see also frequency seriation, lineal ordering
Service, Elman, xx
set-theory, 89, 362
sexual reproduction, 280
Shannon-Hartley measure, 247

sherd tallying, 108, 131–3, 139–40, 151
shifting criteria of typehood, 65–6, 179, 362
significance of types, 35, 42, 53–4, 362
significant attributes, 362
significant variables, 362
similarity spaces, 256, 362
Simpson, George G., 61, 71, 72, 279, 294
Smith, William, 163
Smoke, K. L., 57
Sneath, P. H. A., 300
social anthropology, 81, 85; see also anthropology
social organization, 81–6, 162, 164, 219–20
social philosophy, 306
social ranking, 83–5, 362
social sciences, 81, 85, 89, 274, 300, 305–8, 310
social systems, see social organization
sociobiologists, 82
sociology, 4, 46, 274; see also social sciences
Sokal, Robert, 300
sorters, 196–201, 362; agreement among, 144–5, 195, 238, 241; aptitude of, 59, 198; decision-making, 22, 71, 200–1, 251–2; experience of, 129, 131, 138, 198, 237, 241; instruction of, 145, 198; reliance on gestalts by, 147, 198, 237, 241; requirements of, 145, 198; see also sorting
sorting, 22–3, 47, 57, 129–35, 194–201, 237–8, 298–9, 362–3; consistency in, 187, 238, 241, 242; decision-making in, 56, 188, 199–201, 240, 299; definition of, 22–3, 47, 157, 197; learning, 59, 138–9, 145, 192, 197; of fragmentary material, 157, 228; of mail, 61, 193; of objects, 52, 54, 60, 64, 89, 186, 194, 214; of sites, 224; operations, 54, 57, 66, 73, 79, 145, 157, 194–201; practicality in, 23, 77, 147, 187, 227, 230, 234, 237–8, 241; problems, 57, 61, 72, 77, 194, 197–8, 299; procedures, 72, 129–35, 138–9, 198–9, 204, 226, 230, 234–5, 237–8; purposes in, 197, 235, 302; relation to classifying, 47, 57, 78, 194, 226, 296, 297, 298–9; requirements in, 66, 80; role in typologies, 19, 21, 47–8; see also sorters
sorting categories, 47, 68, 77, 204, 363
sorting systems, 77, 82, 92–3

Southwest, *see* American Southwest
sovereignty of paradigms, 319–20
spatial classifications, 161, 162, 216, 220, 363
Spaulding, Albert, 8, 269–70, 272–3, 282–3, 291, 311
species, 64–5, 149–54; boundedness of, 71, 77, 93, 280, 300; classification of, 45–6, 71, 79, 84, 153, 204, 205; concept of, 146–54; definition of, 13, 64–5, 70, 152; description of, 186–7; discovery of, 15–16, 150–1; endangered, 79–80; taxonomic ordering of, 45–6, 84, 203–4, 257, 300; *see also* biological classification
splitters, 280, 363; *see also* splitting
splitting, 206–7, 249–50, 280–1; and lumping, 61, 102, 111, 149, 249–50, 260, 265, 280–1; computer programs, 206–7, 281; in taxonomies, 84, 92, 203; subdivision of types, 192, 203; *see also* divisive programs
statistical measures, 81, 89, 153–4, 157, 174; *see also* statistical procedures
statistical procedures, 48, 76, 77, 79, 81, 147, 153–4, 157, 174, 212–13, 274–5, 290–4; in classifying, 212–13, 274–5, 290–2; in cluster analysis, 188, 212–13, 229, 274–5, 291–4; in seriation, 210, 212, 213; in sorting, 73; statistical comparisons, 81, 89, 147, 159, 197, 202, 204, 302; uses of, 23, 25, 212–13, 274–5, 290–4; *see also* statistical measures
statistical significance, 35, 67, 177–8, 191, 212, 241, 292, 363
statistics, 212, 290–3; *see also* statistical measures, statistical procedures
Stegner, Wallace, 313
stepwise differentiation, *see* type differentiation
Steward, Julian, 270
stratification, *see* stratigraphy
stratigraphy, 101, 106, 130, 137, 163, 180, 208, 210, 330, 363
strength of association, 68, 212, 292
structuralism, 42, 85–7, 309
Structure of Scientific Revolutions, 306
structure of typologies, 20, 50, 76–90
styles, *see* pottery styles
stylistic typologies, 111, 216, 219, 363
sub-families, *see* pottery sub-families

subjectivity, xix, 5, 48, 151, 188, 190, 200, 293
Sudan Antiquities Service, 108, 109
sufficient agreement, 259; *see also* inter-subjective agreement
sufficient conditions, 70, 144, 147, 177, 179, 191, 363
surface covering, *see* pottery slips
surface finish, *see* pottery surface treatment
symbolization, 43, 85–8, 364
synthetic definition of typology and type, 20, 91–5
Systematics in Prehistory, 273, 287

tautology, 164, 221, 224, 312
taxa, 88, 203, 221, 224, 364
taxonomic classification, 287
taxonomic clustering, 58, 241, 364; *see also* taxonomic ordering
taxonomic levels, 80, 84, 106, 108, 167, 178, 203, 222, 285, 364
taxonomic ordering, 80, 167, 202–7, 218, 221, 281, 333, 364
taxonomic ranking, 333; *see also* taxonomic ordering
taxonomic splitting, 64, 287, 364
taxonomies, 202–7, 298, 299–300, 364–5; computer-generated, xvii, 55, 92, 206–7, 281; defined, 23, 47, 84, 202; functional, 222, 285; genetic, 202, 205–6, 215, 299–300; historical, 221, 224; making of, 23, 202–4, 212, 218–19, 280, 292–3; non-genetic, 205–6, 215, 299–300; of "cultures", 225; purposes of, 58, 167, 202–4, 206, 212, 218, 241; vs. one-level typologies, 78, 88, 104, 106, 154, 214, 215, 298
Taylor, Walter W., 270, 284, 296, 301, 311
technological classifications, 161
Teller, Paul, xxi
templates, *see* mental templates
Teotihuacán, 137, 223
testability, 144
theoretical literature, xvii–xviii, 4, 265–6, 268–95, 298–9; *see also* programmatic statements
theoretical relativism, 6, 365
theory of knowledge, 244
theory of measurement, xxii
theory of probability, xxii
thing-variables, 245, 258, 365

Tractatus Logico-Philosophicus, 316
tradition, 232, 237
transmitted information, 248, 253, 258,
    260, 261, 365
type attribution, 64, 194, 366; *see also* type
    identification, typing
type definitions, 15, 30–1, 63–6, 78, 143–6,
    184–5, 366; and discovery of types, 149,
    152; and type naming, 124; consistency
    of, 78; defined, 63; dimension of
    typehood, 30–1, 63, 184; impossibility of
    formulating, 63, 64–6, 70, 184–5;
    involving boundaries, 71–2, 299;
    involving modalities, 71–2, 77;
    modification of, 57–9, 65, 184, 206,
    227, 242, 286; purposes of, 186–7, 188;
    role of attributes in, 168, 177, 185, 187,
    194, 218, 237, 252, 286, 289–90;
    shifting criteria of, 179, 243; utility of,
    15, 72, 144–6, 151–2, 324; *see also*
    explicit definitions, provisional type
    definitions
type descriptions, 22, 64–6, 110–11,
    119–20, 186–8, 366–7; and information
    theory, 251–3; components of, 58, 72,
    109, 110–11, 119–20, 128, 171, 175–6,
    178, 186, 188, 237; dimension of
    typehood, 18, 29, 30, 33; formulation of,
    33, 37, 56, 100, 186–8; idealization of,
    195; modification of, 53, 57, 60, 102,
    106, 108; overdetermination in, 56, 144,
    145, 171, 187, 196, 197, 241, 297;
    purposes of, 144–5, 186–8, 241; realism
    in, 150–2; relationship to type
    definitions, 63, 64–6, 144–5, 186, 252;
    role in sorting, 138, 197–8, 227,
    241–2; role of attributes in, 60, 77,
    250; selectivity in, 169; utility of, 22,
    144–5
type designation, 185–6, 191–3, 367;
    decision-making in, 64–5, 102, 188,
    192–3; defined, 22, 186; of emic types,
    223; role of attributes in, 88, 102, 104,
    168, 191, 289; role of purposes in,
    178–9, 191; role of statistics in, 177, 191;
    role of variables in, 92–3, 181, 191; *see
    also* type formulation
type differentiation, 54–5, 92, 367; bases
    of, 241; decision-making in, 192–3;
    defined, 367; in Medieval Nubian
    Pottery Typology, 104; role of centers

and boundaries in, 143; stepwise, 55,
    63–4, 65–6, 70, 162; *see also* type
    formulation
type discovery, 33, 67–8, 149, 182, 239,
    338, 367
type formulation, 19, 22, 49–62, 182–4,
    240–1, 367; decision-making in, 200;
    defined, 19, 367; dialectics of, 19, 59–60;
    modification in, 57; of provisional types,
    185–6, 240, 290; practical considerations
    in, 22; principles of, 240–1; processes in,
    49–62, 73–4, 182–4, 240–1; role of
    attributes in, 177, 182–3, 185, 188, 195,
    199, 241; role of differentiation in, 54–5;
    role of foreknowledge in, 51–2, 184; role
    of gestalts in, 53–4; role of purposes in,
    52, 168, 204, 277; role of quantification
    in, 88–9, 212, 292; role of variables in,
    189–90, 228; *see also* type definition, type
    differentiation
type frequency, 367
type identification, 146, 367; *see also* type
    attribution, typing
type identity, 30, 33, 37, 147, 367; *see also*
    identity
type invention, 33, 67–8, 183, 239, 349,
    367; *see also* type formulation
type labels, 31, 196, 367
type meanings, 35–6, 38, 148, 368; based
    on experience, 148; contrasted with
    individual meanings, 38, 301; defined,
    35–6, 368; determined by distributions,
    276; learning of, 59–60; modification of,
    58–9; part of type concept, 30, 38;
    property of types, 35–6, 168, 192, 239,
    281–2; relation to purposes, 36, 88, 183,
    240; *see also* emic significance, meaning,
    type relevance
type names, 31–2, 124–6, 368
type norms, 71–2, 77–8, 92, 187–8, 193,
    368
type properties, *see* properties of types
type recognition, 43, 360, 368; *see also*
    typing
type relevance, 36, 38, 79, 360; *see also*
    relevance
type representation, 30–1, 33–4, 43–4, 51,
    55–6, 64, 276, 368; *see also* type
    description
type selection, 168, 185–6, 215, 240, 292
typehood, xvi, 27–38, 41–8, 93–4, 179,

292, 312, 369; *see also* dimensions of typehood, elements of typehood
type-variety systems, 110, 203, 205, 303, 368
typing, 22–3, 196, 369; agreement among sorters in, 144–5; decision-making in, 22–3; in open typologies, 227, 228; learning of, 16; probabilities in, 199, 200; problems in, 193–6; procedures in, 22–3, 196, 200; role of type descriptions in, 241; useful attributes for, 187, 236; *see also* type attribution, type identification, type recognition
Typological Debate, 7, 9, 24–5, 64–5, 231, 265–304, 310–12, 369
typological identity, 33, 34, 37, 146, 369
typological meanings, 19, 35, 37, 148, 301, 369
typological spaces, 256, 369

umpire, *see* baseball umpire
uncertainty, 246–50, 258–9
unconditional probability, 369
unconditional proportions, 247
understanding, 307–8, 310–11, 312, 370
undiscovered types, 33
unformulated types, 33
UNESCO, 109
unidentified types, 131
unilinear evolutionism, 309, 370
universality of variables, 170
universe of variability, *see* domains of variability
unrealized types, 33, 152, 370
useful types, 183–6, 370; constituents of, 30–3; equated with emic types, 283–4; for dating purposes, 111, 163–4, 167, 244, 259–60, 279; generation of, 177, 240, 279, 294; properties of, 18–19, 34–6, 61, 183–4, 239, 287; related to purposes, 57, 183–6, 283–4, 292; selection of, 63–4, 68–9; selection of variables for, 172; statistical significance of, 212, 292; *see also* practical types, useful typologies
useful typologies, 370; generation of, 7, 65, 185–6, 286–7; kinds of, 242; of art historians, 161; properties of, 242–3; related to purposes, 4, 165–6, 242, 288,

302; vs. logical typologies, 8, 73–4; *see also* practical typologies, useful types
usefulness, *see* utility
uses of types, 194–201
utility, 232–8, 242–3, 258–61, 370; basis for retention of types, 58–9; defined, 233, 370; of complex type concepts, 188–9; of computer algorithms, 275; of computer-generated types, 23, 33, 206; of emic types, 284; of fuzzy set theory, 73; of gestalts, 147–8; of information, 260–1; of occult types, 36, 94; of type descriptions, 72, 241; of typologies, 165–6, 321; of unformulated types, 33; of variables, 189–90; principles of, 242–3; related to purposes, 6, 99, 162–3, 165, 230, 242, 321; related to theory, 6; *see also* practicality, useful types, useful typologies

vagueness, 144
variable-product, 370
variable selection, 171–2, 189–90, 251–2, 371
variability in archaeological classifications, 23, 214–32
variability of association, 177–8, 191, 241, 370
vernacular classifications, 40–1, 371; *see also* folk classifications
verstehen, 307
von Bertalanffy, Ludwig, 300
Voorrips, A., 302–3
Voss, R. S., 254
Vygotsky, L. S., 79, 286

ware groups, *see* pottery ware groups
ware-space, 371
Whallon, Robert, 8
wheel-made pottery, 104, 107, 126, 130, 371
White, Leslie, 87
Willey, Gordon R., 266, 270
Wittgenstein, Ludwig, 6, 186, 316
words, 43–4, 56, 58, 76, 315–16, 371
Wylie, Alison, xxi

Zadeh, L. A., 73
zoology, 148